10 **The Rebuilding of Greater Russia**
Putin's foreign policy towards the CIS countries
Bertil Nygren

11 **A Russian Factory Enters the Market Economy**
Claudio Morrison

12 **Democracy Building and Civil Society in Post-Soviet Armenia**
Armine Ishkanian

13 **NATO–Russia Relations in the Twenty-first Century**
Aurel Braun

14 **Russian Military Reform**
A failed exercise in defence decision making
Carolina Vendil Pallin

15 **The Multilateral Dimension in Russian Foreign Policy**
Edited by Elana Wilson Rowe and Stina Torjesen

16 **Russian Nationalism and the National Reassertion of Russia**
Edited by Marlène Laruelle

Russian Nationalism and the National Reassertion of Russia

Military action in South Ossetia, growing tensions with the United States and NATO, and Russia's relationship with the European Union demonstrate how the issue of Russian nationalism is increasingly at the heart of the international political agenda. This book considers a wide range of aspects of Russian nationalism, focusing on the Putin period. It discusses development of the phenomenon since the Soviet era, examines how it grows out of – or is related to – ideology, culture, racism, religion, and intellectual thinking, and demonstrates how it affects many aspects of Russian society, politics, and foreign policy. This book examines the different sociopolitical phenomena that are variously defined as "nationalism," "patriotism" and "xenophobia". As Russia reasserts itself in the world, with Russian nationalism as one of the key driving forces in this process, an understanding of it is essential for understanding the dynamics of contemporary international relations.

Marlène Laruelle is a Senior Research Fellow in the Central Asia and Caucasus Institute of the School for Advanced International Studies, The Johns Hopkins University, USA. She has published widely, including most recently *Russian Eurasianism: An Ideology of Empire*.

Routledge contemporary Russia and Eastern Europe series

1 **Liberal Nationalism in Central Europe**
Stefan Auer

2 **Civil–Military Relations in Russia and Eastern Europe**
David J. Betz

3 **The Extreme Nationalist Threat in Russia**
The growing influence of Western Rightist ideas
Thomas Parland

4 **Economic Development in Tatarstan**
Global markets and a Russian region
Leo McCann

5 **Adapting to Russia's New Labour Market**
Gender and employment strategy
Edited by Sarah Ashwin

6 **Building Democracy and Civil Society East of the Elbe**
Essays in honour of Edmund Mokrzycki
Edited by Sven Eliaeson

7 **The Telengits of Southern Siberia**
Landscape, religion and knowledge in motion
Agnieszka Halemba

8 **The Development of Capitalism in Russia**
Simon Clarke

9 **Russian Television Today**
Primetime drama and comedy
David MacFadyen

Russian Nationalism and the National Reassertion of Russia

Edited by Marlène Laruelle

Routledge
Taylor & Francis Group
LONDON AND NEW YORK

First published 2009
by Routledge
2 Park Square, Milton Park, Abingdon, Oxon OX14 4RN

Simultaneously published in the USA and Canada
by Routledge
270 Madison Ave, New York, NY 10016

Routledge is an imprint of the Taylor & Francis Group, an informa business

Typeset in Times by Wearset Ltd, Boldon, Tyne and Wear
Printed and bound in Great Britain by TJI Digital, Padstow, Cornwall

British Library Cataloguing in Publication Data
A catalogue record for this book is available from the British Library

Library of Congress Cataloging in Publication Data
A catalog record for this book has been requested

ISBN10: 0-415-48446-4 (hbk)
ISBN10: 0-203-87972-4 (ebk)

ISBN13: 978-0-415-48446-6 (hbk)
ISBN13: 978-0-203-87972-6 (ebk)

Dedicated to John B. Dunlop – pioneer of the study of contemporary Russian nationalism

Contents

Figures

Tables

Contributors

Beth Admiraal Assistant Professor at King's College Pennsylvania. She is the author of "Russian Orthodoxy and Democracy in Postcommunism," in C. Marsh (ed.), *Burden or Blessing? Russian orthodoxy and the construction of civil society and democracy* (Boston University, 2004, pp. 17–24); and "Orthodox Behavior and Strategic Thinking," *The Birth of Democracy and the Rebirth of Religion* (St Andrew's Press, Moscow, 2001, with Regan Lance Reitsma).

Mikhail A. Alexseev Associate Professor of Political Science at San Diego State University. He is the author of *Immigration Phobia and the Security Dilemma: Russia, Europe, and the United States* (Cambridge University Press, 2005) and *Without Warning: Threat Assessment, Intelligence, and Global Struggle* (St Martin's Press, 1997) and is the editor of *A Federation Imperiled: Center–periphery conflict in post-Soviet Russia* (St Martin's Press, 1999). Alexseev has been the principal investigator of a multi-year international research project on migration and ethno-religious violence in the Russian Federation funded by the National Science Foundation, the John D. and Catherine T. MacArthur Foundation, and the National Council for Eurasian and East European Research (Title VIII, US Department of State). He has published articles in *Political Science Quarterly*, the *Journal of Peace Research*, *Political Behavior*, *Political Communication*, *Europe–Asia Studies*, *Nationalities Papers*, *Post-Soviet Geography and Economics*, *The Fletcher Forum of World Affairs*, and *Pacific Focus*. He is a member of the Carnegie/MacArthur-sponsored Program on New Approaches to Russian Security of the Center for Strategic and International Studies in Washington, DC.

Wayne Allensworth Analyst at the Foreign Broadcast Information Service from 1991 to 2002. He is the author of *The Russian Question* (Rowman & Littlefield, 1998), as well as of numerous articles on Russia. He received an MA in Comparative Politics from the University of Texas in 1990. He lives in Fort Worth, Texas.

Marlène Laruelle Associate Fellow at the Institute of Political Studies (IEP, Paris) and at the French Center for Russian, Caucasian and East European

Studies at the School of Advanced Social Sciences Studies (EHESS, Paris). Fellow at the Woodrow Wilson International Center for Scholars in 2005–2006 and Senior Research Fellow at the Central Asia and Caucasus Institute (SAIS, Johns Hopkins University, Washington, DC) since September 2007. She has published papers in *Nationalities Papers*, *Central Asian Studies*, *Nations and Nationalism*, *Kritika*, *Diogenes*, *The China and Eurasia Forum Quarterly*, *Cahiers du monde russe*, *Revue d'Études comparatives Est–Ouest*, *Osteuropa*, and *Ab Imperio*. She has published three books in French on Russian nationalism, two books on Central Asia co-authored with Sébastien Peyrouse, and, in English, *Russian Eurasianism: An ideology of empire* (Johns Hopkins University Press–Woodrow Wilson Press, 2008).

Anastassia Leonova PhD candidate in Political Systems and Institutional Change at IMT Institute, Lucca, Italy. She holds an MA in Sociology from the University of Manchester, 2005. Her doctoral research deals with social and political protest in contemporary Russia. Broadly, her interests encompass the problems of social change, value and identity transformation. She has written on problems of female representation, radical youth political movements, police violence, xenophobia (both together with L. Gudkov and V. Dubin), adolescent socialization and family relations (together with N. Zorkaya) and on other subjects, as a research fellow of the Levada Center.

Victor Shnirelman Doctor in History, Chief Researcher at the Institute of Ethnology and Anthropology, Russian Academy of Sciences, in Moscow. An author of more than 300 publications, including 20 books, on archaeology, social anthropology, history, and modern ethnopolitics. Among his books are *Who gets the past? Competition for ancestors among non-Russian intellectuals in Russia* (Johns Hopkins University Press–Woodrow Wilson Press, 1996), *Russian Neo-Pagan Myths and Anti-Semitism* (Hebrew University of Jerusalem, 1998), *The Value of the Past: Myths, Identity and Politics in Transcaucasia* (National Museum of Ethnology, Osaka, 2001), *The Myth of the Khazars and Intellectual Antisemitism in Russia, 1970s–1990s* (Hebrew University of Jerusalem, 2002), and *Byt' alanami: intellektualy i politika na Severnom Kavkaze v XX veke* (Moscow: Novoe literaturnoe obozrenie, 2006). He focuses on ethnicity and nationalism in historical perspective, politics of the past, and social memory.

Valerie Sperling Associate Professor in Clark University's Department of Government and International Relations (Worcester, MA). She is the author of *Organizing Women in Contemporary Russia* (Cambridge University Press, 1999) and the editor of *Building the Russian State* (Westview Press, 2000). She has also authored and co-authored several journal articles and book chapters on the Russian women's movement (in *Signs* and *Women and Politics*), as well as an article on militarism and patriotism in Russia (in *Nations and Nationalism*, 2003). She is also a faculty associate at Harvard University's Davis Center for Russian and Eurasian Studies. Her latest book, *Altered*

States: The Globalization of Accountability (Cambridge University Press, 2009), explores the nexus between transnational institutions and state accountability.

Andrei P. Tsygankov Professor at the Departments of Political Science and International Relations at San Francisco State University. A Russian native, he is a graduate of Moscow State University (Candidate of Sciences, 1991) and the University of Southern California (PhD, 2000). He has published *Pathways after Empire: National identity and foreign economic policy in the post-Soviet world* (2001), *Whose World Order? Russia's perception of American ideas after the Cold War* (2004), and *Russia's Foreign Policy: Change and continuity in national identity* (2006), as well as many journal articles. In Russia, his best-known books are *Russian Science of International Relations* (2005, co-edited with Pavel Tsygankov, also published in Germany and China) and *Sociology of International Relations* (2006, co-authored with Pavel Tsygankov, also published in China). Tsygankov's articles have also appeared in Russian academic journals.

Andreas Umland Assistant Professor of Contemporary Russian History at the Catholic University of Eichstaett-Ingolstadt, Bavaria. Former Visiting Fellow at Stanford's Hoover Institution from 1997 to 1999 and Harvard's Weatherhead Center from 2001 2002, and Bosch Visiting Lecturer at Ekaterinburg's Urals State University from 1999 to 2001, and Kyiv's Mohyla Academy from 2003 to 2005. In 2004 he was temporary lecturer in Russian and East European studies at St Antony's College, Oxford. He has published papers in *Problems of Post-communism*, *East European Jewish Affairs*, *Osteuropa*, *Österreichische Zeitschrift für Politikwissenschaft*, *Politicheskie issledovaniya*, *European Political Science*, *Political Studies Review*, *Demokratizatsiia*, the *Journal of Slavic Military Studies*, *Voprosy filosofii*, *Obshchestvennye nauki i sovremennost'*, *Ab Imperio*, and other journals. He is editor of the book series Soviet and Post-Soviet Politics and Society (www.ibidem-verlag.de/spps.html).

Alexander Verkhovsky Born in 1962, Verkhovsky graduated from the Moscow Oil and Gas Institute with a degree in Applied Mathematics in 1984. In 1989 he became editor-in-chief of the *samizdat* independent newspaper *Panorama* in Moscow. From 1991 to 2002 he was vice-president of the *Panorama* Information and Research Center. Since 2002 he has been Director of the SOVA Center for Information and Analysis (http://sova-center.ru). Since 1994 his main area of research has been political extremism, nationalism, and xenophobia in contemporary Russia. He is author or co-author of a number of books on these issues (and also on religion and politics in contemporary Russia), including *Political Extremism in Russia* (1996), *National-Patriotic Organizations in Russia* (1996), *Political Xenophobia* (1999), *The State Policy towards Ultra-nationalist Organizations* (2002), and *Political Orthodoxy: Russian Orthodox nationalists and fundamentalists, 1995–2001* (2003), and many articles.

Veljko Vujačić Associate Professor of Sociology at Oberlin College. Vujačić's fields of specialization include sociological theory, political and comparative-historical sociology, and social movements, with a special focus on communism and nationalism in the former Soviet Union and Yugoslavia. His articles on these themes and topics have appeared in *Theory and Society*, *Post-Soviet Affairs*, the *East European Constitutional Review*, *East European Politics and Societies*, *Comparative Politics*, the *Harriman Review*, *Research in Political Sociology*, the *Encyclopedia of Nationalism*, the *International Encyclopedia of the Social Sciences*, *Revolutions in World History*, and a number of edited volumes. He is currently working on a large comparative-historical study of Russian and Serbian nationalism and the disintegration of the Soviet Union and Yugoslavia.

Foreword

John B. Dunlop

It is a privilege to be asked to write a preface for this fine collection of essays devoted to the subject of Russian nationalism in Vladimir Putin's Russia. The political role and significance of Russian nationalism – the volume's editor, Marlène Laruelle, defines nationalism as a system of thought in which the nation occupies a predominant place – is markedly different today from what it was in the 1970s and 1980s, when I first began to publish my findings on the topic. The subject of Russian nationalism today continues to present a significant challenge to those seeking to understand the complex processes currently taking place in Russia and attempting to grasp where the country might be heading.

I recall that when I first began to publish my research on Russian nationalism in the 1970s, several of my academic colleagues expressed bewilderment that I should choose to squander my time on such an esoteric and unrewarding topic. The Soviet Union and its legitimizing ideology, they insisted, a tad condescendingly, had a long future ahead of it, one that would stretch well into the twenty-first century.

While some specialists evidently lacked the imagination to envision a post-communist Russia that would not be legitimized by Marxism-Leninism, others took seriously what I and other *de facto* "pioneers," such as the late Darrell Hammer of Indiana University, were writing about Russian nationalism. I recall spending a year as an academic visitor at the London School of Economics and Political Science (LSE) during the academic year 1974–1975 and receiving strong encouragement from such specialists as the late Leonard Schapiro, the late Hugh Seton-Watson, Michael Bourdeaux, Martin Dewhirst, and the late Leopold Labedz, to name but a few. Peter Reddaway, then of the LSE, served as my host for the year and has continued for thirty years to be an unflagging source of support. I also received encouragement from an official at the British Foreign Office, who invited me to discuss my findings over lunch, and from the late Abraham Brumberg, then of the Bureau of Intelligence and Research at the US State Department, as well as from Walter Laqueur of the Center for Strategic and International Studies in Washington, DC, and Teresa Rakowska-Harmstone, then of Carleton University in Ottawa. All of these specialists were distinguished by the fact that they were attentive students of the Soviet Union who were prepared to keep an open mind concerning the possible futures of that important country.

Following the collapse of the Soviet Union in 1991, I learned that my published research into Russian nationalism during the 1980s had also been of interest, inter alia, to the USSR's KGB. During a visit to Stanford University a former full member of the Politburo under Gorbachev, Alexander Yakovlev, informed me that he had earlier read my books *The Faces of Contemporary Russian Nationalism* (1983) and *The New Russian Nationalism* (1985) in Russian translations prepared by the Soviet secret police. The same information was subsequently imparted to me by the editor of a Russian nationalist "fat journal." As distinct from a number of Western specialists, the KGB apparently wanted to keep close track of Russian nationalism and of what Western scholars were writing about it.

At the time that the Soviet Union fell apart, in 1991, I found myself in Munich, Germany, in the capacity of a visiting Olin Visiting Senior Fellow at Radio Liberty-Radio Free Europe. The extraordinary material that I was able to collect during 1991–1992 while in residence at the radio stations served as the foundation for my 1993 book *The Rise of Russia and the Fall of the Soviet Union*. In that volume, published during Yeltsin's first term, I took note of the marked lack of appeal, at that time, of Russian nationalist themes to the Russian electorate.

Following the publication of my 1993 book I gradually shifted over to the study of the Russian north Caucasus, which became the subject of my two most recent books, and I also spent two years editing the *Chechnya Weekly*, a publication of the Jamestown Foundation in Washington, DC. My "sojourn" in the north Caucasus stretched out for over a decade, and it was only in 2007 that I began to return to my original focus on Russian nationalism. Important developments occurring in Putin's second term made such a return imperative.

To turn to the excellent collection of chapters contained in the present book, I would second the editor's contention, made in her Introduction, that "Nationalism was not born of the collapse of the communist regime; it existed *underneath* and *in* it, much more than *against* it, and had only to adapt itself to the events of 1991." The various chapters of this book help us to understand how this was possible, reaching back as they do to the Stalin period and forward to Putin's second presidential term.

A number of the chapters discuss the worrisome growth of xenophobic and racist sentiment among the ethnic Russian populace of the Russian Federation. This tendency has been meticulously documented by the Levada Center in Moscow; one of the contributors to the present volume is a representative of that first-rate organization. It should be noted that an increase in ethnic tension and hatred has also been intentionally promoted by elements in the Russian special services. In an interview published in the 17 June 1998 issue of *Izvestiia* the aforementioned former full Politburo member, Alexander Yakovlev, noted that the notorious anti-Semitic organization Pamyat' had been brought to life by the KGB during the Gorbachev period and that its leader, Dmitrii Vasil'ev, had in fact been a KGB asset. The KGB had also, Yakovlev said, intentionally promoted several neo-Nazi organizations.

What was practiced by the special services under Gorbachev was, not surprisingly, repeated and indeed expanded under Vladimir Putin. Alexander Belov-Potkin, the leader of the xenophobic anti-immigrant Movement against Illegal Immigration (DPNI), whose activities are discussed by several of the contributors to this collection, served earlier as one of Dmitrii Vasil'ev's top aides. Another extremist leader, the subject of one of the chapters in this book, the neo-Eurasianist activist Alexander Dugin, has enjoyed support in the Russian presidential administration and in the Russian military general staff, as I sought to demonstrate in an article published in *Harvard Ukrainian Studies* in 2004.

Those Western specialists who were engaged in research into the subject of Russian nationalism during the Brezhnev period were frequently called upon to decipher murky Aesopian language, for example in village prose writer Valentin Rasputin's well-known fictional work *Farewell to Matyora*. Today, too, a healthy imagination is on occasion required to fathom what some committed nationalists are attempting to say. In early 2008, to take a single example, Archimandrite Tikhon Shevkunov, reputed to be Putin's spiritual confessor, aired a film on Russian state television entitled *The Destruction of the Empire: A Byzantine lesson*. The film was shown several more times on state television and enjoyed a considerable *succès de scandale*.

As the magazine *The Economist* observed in its 14 February 2008 issue:

> The film's usage of modern words and imagery is so conspicuous that the moral cannot escape a Russian viewer. Instead of sticking to its traditions, Byzantium tried to reform and modernize, as the West demanded, and it paid the price.... In the absence of any new ideology, [the film] manipulates a story of Byzantium to justify Russia's anti-Westernism and xenophobia in a 1,000-year history. The film also carries an implicit message to Mr. Putin: do not listen to the West, stay in power, close off the country.

General Nikolai Patrushev, the then head of the FSB, *The Economist* reported, served as a powerful supporter of the broadcasting of this film on state television.

Shevkunov's film has been compared to Nina Andreeva's notorious neo-Stalinist letter published in the newspaper *Sovetskaia Rossiia* in March 1988, which sought, somewhat obliquely, to help prepare the ouster of Gorbachev from power. Shevkunov's film appears to have been intended to play a role in thwarting the accession of a perceived neo-Westernizer, Dmitrii Medvedev, to the Russian presidency. Like Andreeva's earlier effort, Shevkunov's film proved unsuccessful in its seeming primary aim.

To sum up, this stimulating and wide-ranging collection of essays, edited by Marlène Laruelle, is a good place to start for those interested in where the advocates and defenders of various strains of Russian nationalism would like to take their country both today and in the coming decades.

1 Introduction

Marlène Laruelle

In the second half of the 1970s there was a significant rise in the number of works published on contemporary Russian nationalism. Authors such as John Dunlop, Alexander Yanov, and William Laqueur worked for many decades to bring attention to bear on a phenomenon that was formerly little known and barely distinguishable from Soviet nationalism.[1] Then, during the 1990s, after the disappearance of the Soviet Union, several works appeared that focused on the rise of the extreme right and on the risk of "fascization," even of "Nazification," of post-Soviet Russia.[2] Today, a new set of works have emerged on the question of Russian nationalism, whose focal point no longer involves analyzing small groupuscules to ascertain how marginal or, on the contrary, how representative they are, but which attempt to account for a social, cultural, and political field that is in fact much more widespread. Indeed, in the Russian Federation today, nationalism comprises the common denominator, the constitutive element of social consensus and of "political correctness." Nationalist issues, expressed under the label *patriotism*, have become defining components of Russia's political language in the sense that all parties speak it. No public figure, regardless of his or her functions, is able to acquire political legitimacy without mentioning his or her attachment to the Russian motherland and without justifying his or her policy choices in terms of the nation's supreme interests.

Although this patriotic rhetoric is common in many countries, it has taken on new meanings and forms for Russia over the past decade. The patriotism instituted by the Kremlin must be analyzed as an ideology of action, as the will to remobilize a Russian society whose daily experience is detached from the state. The authorities indeed expect that their excessive promotion of patriotism will yield precise results, including greater respect for the army and for military service, more paying of taxes, less corruption and flouting of the law, consumption of national products to revive the economy, increased charitable social works, and a more efficient organization of structures for supervising youth. This patriotic refrain now forms the key element in deciding the legitimacy or illegitimacy of policy proposals made to Russian society. The current Russian political regime thus cannot be understood as a "return to the USSR"; it reveals a type of Westernization and modernization that, paradoxically, is now being pursued through authoritarianism and nationalism. To get a fair picture of this

Russian nationalism, it is therefore necessary to look not only at the political but also at the sociological developments of Russian society as a whole.

Methodological orientation

Any reflection on Russian nationalism first requires an attempted definition of the phenomenon under consideration. Continual characterizations of it as "vague," "multiform," or "complex" often do no more than reveal the absence of an appropriate model of analysis. Our guiding postulate in this regard is that a definition is no more than an instrument, and that defining nationalism prematurely and too rigidly would presuppose the existence of an essence of the phenomenon. The obvious advantage of an empirical approach is that it avoids getting bogged down in concepts and enables a subsequent refinement of the theoretical elements being used. So, we will begin with a broad interpretation of nationalism, understood simply as a system of thought in which the nation occupies a predominant position. An important element of discussion is indeed the degree of "predominance," such that "nationalism" is considered to have a more pronounced consciousness of national belonging than that which every individual might share.

Our approach to the phenomenon of Russian nationalism is informed by some key methodological choices, and primarily by the desire to maintain an historical perspective on the phenomenon. This is so for several reasons. The first is to avoid falling into the trap of thinking that nationalism is undergoing a "renaissance" in post-Soviet space. Nationalism was not born of the collapse of the communist regime; it existed *underneath* and *in* it, much more than *against* it, and had only to adapt itself to the events of 1991. The main doctrines in force today, and the personal and ideological divisions existing within the various movements, often have roots in previously conflicting aspects of Soviet traditions. The idea that a renewal of nineteenth-century nationalist thinking is currently under way, then, is an illusion. Despite recurrent references to great authors of that century, and the frequent republication of their works, the themes of contemporary Russian nationalism find their fundamental inspiration in the Soviet twentieth century and, to a lesser degree, in the emigration of the interwar period. Though the tsarist era may attract nostalgia and its thinkers are afforded respect out of principle, the link to both has been broken. The historical lines of thought leading to contemporary nationalism are of more recent date. Russian nationalism ought therefore to be conceived of not as in opposition to the Soviet experience, but as the continuation of a phenomenon that existed within it.

The second reason for focusing attention on history aims at a more cautious use of several doctrinal terms currently in circulation. In this respect, "fascism," as well as "national Bolshevism" or "Eurasianism," will be viewed as doctrines that once had precise historical existences but are now at an end. These terms cannot therefore be applied to contemporary cases unless used in conjunction with the prefix "neo," or else, with parsimony, when the actors themselves make the parallel or when the connection seems convincing. The point here is not simply to propose a correct classification of apparently highly specialized intellectual lineages, but to prevent the development of a vocabulary that is uncertain and systematically discriminating, and that makes analysis impossible. Prospective approaches to the phenomenon of nationalism will likewise be rejected. The aim is not to predict the possibility of the "extremists" taking power, nor to adopt a catastrophist scenario based on supposed parallels between post-Soviet Russia and Weimar Germany, two already standard themes of studies on the radical Russian right.[3]

The second methodological choice concerns the degree of inclusion implied by the term "nationalism." There can be no question here of excluding from "nationalism" so-called imperialist or statist currents, as some authors have repeatedly suggested be done. This is first and foremost because the term "nation" that is contained within the term "nationalism" can refer to a vision of the collective that can be either ethnic or political. Ethnocentrism and nationalism are therefore not synonymous terms, since the first is a possible, but not a necessary, element of the second. Further, though the Russian tradition is often said to be shaped by the German or Central European model of an apolitical cultural nation, it cannot be reduced to it. In Russia there is also a strong statist tradition grounded in a dynastic fidelity to the Romanovs, as well as an ideological one based on the construction of a Soviet state. Despite the well-known, and often exaggerated, conflicts that pit apologists for the state against partisans of an ethnic approach to the nation, the Kremlin has decided to promote both models of the nation in parallel, in the hope that they are not contradictory.

The nationalist phenomenon has always elicited many various readings, which can be schematically divided into two overarching categories, one primordialist, the other constructivist. The present work subscribes to the second perspective: it undermines from the outset the notion that there is a unity to the phenomenon of nationalism, and emphasizes its constructed character. Identity is not immutable; it is not a given but a human construction. It is subject to incessant re-elaboration, creating diverse symbols and constructions that are modifiable over time. We also adopt a constructivist approach to the fact that the Soviet Union institutionalized collective identities and gave to national belonging a role as social marker. The Soviet regime was in fact constructed, with interruptions in the 1930s, through a procedure involving "positive discrimination" toward national minorities, which were assigned, to various degrees defined by the central authorities, identities, territories, and specific administrative and cultural rights.[4] This institutionalization contributed to transforming nationalism into an instrument in the struggle for power, and in part explains the – at first glance – surprising ability of the elite to shift from points of reference that were officially Marxist-Leninist to discourses centred on the defence of national and/or ethnic interests.

This instrumentalist approach makes it possible to avoid the discussion – irresolvable with regard to the question – about whether Soviet and post-Soviet Russian nationalism was born as a response to that of the other peoples of the USSR or of the Russian Federation, or whether, on the contrary, it was the precursor of the latter and inspired them.[5] The question of knowing whether

Russian nationalism is reactionary effectively supposes a form of naturalness in the reaction, and forgets the fact that all the populations of this space were subject to similar political and social processes. All nationalists, Russian and otherwise, claimed that a power with internationalist pretensions had dispossessed them of a part of their rights. The crucial aspect here is therefore not to know "who started it" but to take note that, just like its neighbors, Russian nationalism entertains an ambiguous relation to what many see as being its own state and rule. Like the other nationalisms of the region, Russian nationalism also claims to suffer from "minority syndromes," and it also engages in its own idealization of the people as "victim," regardless of the fact that other nationalisms see it as enjoying all the advantages of a majority.

Nationalism as a modern phenomenon

The phenomenon of borrowing from the West is not new in Russia. As early as the 1820s–1840s the Slavophile movements undertook to import that recently invented product, national sentiment, after removing its German label, and ended up by transforming the term "Enlightenment" into that of "West" and "romanticism" into that of "Russia."[6] Indeed, from the nineteenth century on, Russian nationalism has been built on feelings of European domination and Western intellectual colonization. These feelings produced an "ideology of *ressentiment*"[7] provoked by the sense that, after the reforms of Peter the Great, Russians were no longer the makers of their own civilization. Russian nationalism, then, has always been "imitative of and in competition with"[8] Western nationalism.

This fact is further confirmed by the extent to which Russia today participates, albeit involuntarily, in European life. Its populist politicians, its neo-Nazi groupuscules, its identity conflicts, its nostalgia for a bygone era, and its fears of the changes induced by globalization all place it squarely within Europe and in step with Western countries, whether the Russian nationalists recognize that or not. Far from being archaic, nationalism is an expression of the modernity in which contemporary Russia lives. It is illustrative of the processes of massive social self-devalorization that resulted from the rapid changes of the past two decades, and as such can be read as an attempt to provide a spokesperson for the outcasts of modernization in its post-Soviet version. Nationalism among the elites is instead presented as asserting the needs of identity, of collectivity, and of religious feeling in the contemporary world, and is seen as a political response to the global evolutions of societies.[9]

In Russian, as in English, the word "patriotism" possesses a positive aura, and is presented as a respectable and moral way to defend one's country. In English, "nationalism" designates both national construction and an ideology of national supremacy. In Russian, though, the term is more specific. In the Soviet tradition, "nationalism" was a term that designated aggressive attitudes in which the interests of one ethnic group were placed above those of others, whereas folkloric glorifications of one's "nationality" were, on the contrary, perceived to be positive and harmless. "Nationalism" was therefore seen as the exaggerated form of a supposedly natural phenomenon – being proud of one's nation – and as self-evident by virtue of each individual's belonging to a national collective. However, the introduction of Western European terminology and concepts in the 1990s has added to the definitional complexity, as new definitions have occasionally come to superimpose themselves over the old ones. In point of fact, several Russian nationalist movements today portray "nationalism" as a political necessity for Russia in its desire to become a modern nation like any other. However, there are also, in contrast, academic currents concerned about the new official "patriotism" that saddle with the charge of "racism" every claim assertive of national character.[10]

Is nationalism a political entity just like any other? Does it possess unity despite its extreme partisan divisions? Should it be put forward as basic to any understanding of contemporary societies, or, on the contrary, should it, owing to its pretended marginality, be thought of as having little bearing on them? One of the points of this study is to foreground some marginal aspects of the phenomenon, as well as some that are less so. At the level of established identitarian doctrines and arguments, there can be no doubt that Russian nationalism is widely circulated and innervates much larger and more influential milieus. Functioning in a similar fashion, there exist many cognates to nationalism – definitions of Russia as a Eurasian empire, glorifications of the Slavs' pre-Christian past, nostalgia for great Soviet power, feelings of belonging to a specific Orthodox civilization, etc. – that may be held as much by radical groupuscules as by well-established and more "politically correct" movements in state institutions.

The aim of this volume is to shed light on the imbrication of different sociopolitical phenomena that are often defined in too precipitate a fashion, such as "nationalism," "patriotism," and "xenophobia." In fact, limiting oneself to an interpretation that would see in the "patriotism" put to work by the Kremlin a "fascization" of Russia, and a contemptible rapprochement between the authorities and the extreme right, can be done only at the risk of providing a simplistic analysis of a complex phenomenon, that of constituting a specific post-Soviet social consensus. Current "nationalism" appears to be having a *stabilizing* function on Russian society after it was hit hard by the referential, political, and economic upheavals it has had to weather over the past two decades. After the brutal changes of the 1990s the Putin regime has brought to light Russian society's need for a confident social and political conservatism. These changes include a depreciation of the importance of parliamentarism and of political parties, a heightening of social inequalities due to privatizations, the formation of a class of oligarchs, the humiliation suffered as a result of losing its status as a great power, setbacks following the economic crisis of summer 1998, disappointment with the West over the Yugoslav rifts, and the two wars in Chechnya.

Nationalism and the reasons behind Vladimir Putin's success

As observers had anticipated, the Kremlin orchestrated perfectly its victory in the presidential elections of 2 March 2008. Vladimir Putin's official heir, Dmitri Medvedev, was elected to the presidency of the republic with over 70 percent of the votes. The new president was installed on 7 May, and the following day at the Duma (Russia's parliament) Putin was nominated prime minister, receiving 392 votes for and 56 (mostly the Communists) against. However, beneath this controlled exterior the Russian political system remains in certain respects unstable. For the first time, Russia will have two centers of political power: the president and his officials in the Kremlin, on one hand, and the formerly weak prime minister and the Duma, on the other hand. There is no recent tradition of such diarchy in Russia, and while many analysts have assumed that Putin would ensure a shift of certain (if not most) powers from the presidency to the prime minister's office, such a transfer is by no means guaranteed.

This two-headed system could prove to be a dangerous instrument in the hands of Kremlin elites, who are not inclined to consensus-building. The power relationship between the country's two strongmen remains to be negotiated, and while Medvedev continues to show deference to Putin, it remains unclear when and whether he will attempt to wrest the reins of power from his predecessor. On domestic and foreign policy, Putin continues to position himself as the country's undisputed leader. He has persuaded many of his close associates to leave the presidential administration and has installed them in United Russia or the Duma. The presidential party, for its part, continues to make guarded, not to mention critical, comments on the new president. So, at present Dmitri Medvedev seems to have little room for maneuver. And notwithstanding his repeated assertions that he alone will decide the course of the country, he has no loyal team surrounding him and in fact seems rather isolated. The figure of Medvedev may well end up polarizing the competition between liberal circles and those of the more hawkish *siloviki* (men of the army, militia, and special and secret services). Putin, by contrast, managed to balance their power relations with relative success.

This new diarchic system is also going to have to handle an international situation ripe for major tensions, most especially in Georgia, where Kosovo's independence in spring 2008 has reopened the question of the secessionist regions of Abkhazia and South Ossetia. In this context, both the great military parade of 9 May 2008 – to show off Russia's new missiles and tanks in the Red Square and mark its return as a military power – and the discussions on whether to have Misha – the bear that was the emblem of the 1980 Moscow Olympic games – as the official mascot of the 2014 Sochi Winter Olympics confirm today that references to Soviet-era grandeur can still act as key elements of consensus among Russian political elites. Common explanations of Russian politics that rely on the idea of unchanging Russian traits – that is, the notion that Russians by nature favor authoritarian regimes or that Western-style democracy does not work in the Russian context – do little to explain the events that are unfolding before our eyes.

After eight years as the Russian head of state, Vladimir Putin remains very popular: between 60 percent and 80 percent of Russians polled claim to be satisfied with his performance. This popularity may be explained, in part, by the Kremlin's stranglehold over the media (television and press), which have nearly all been bought up by press groups with direct links either to the largest national companies or to oligarchs close to the president.[11] The whole of the political field is also in the Kremlin's hands: opposition parties have virtually no access to the media, and recalcitrant oligarchs such as Mikhail Khodorkovsky have either been dispossessed of their companies or imprisoned.[12] Political opponents such as former prime minister Mikhail Kasianov and chess champion Garry Kasparov have found their political efforts hindered or derailed at every step. The Duma and the government bureaucracy also carry little power: the former has become a kind of "house of registration" that simply rubber-stamps decisions taken by the president. The second is enfeebled by a parallel presidential administration made up of people close to the president who constitute the real center of decision making.

However, Vladimir Putin's popularity cannot be explained solely by the restrictive and undemocratic conditions of contemporary Russian political life. Rather, the former president's widespread support also springs from his success in personalizing a series of recent changes in Russia – especially economic and political stabilization – for which a great majority of the population had been hoping. Putin has in effect come to embody Russia's "recovery": he has succeeded in putting an end to the country's domestic disintegration, to the state's total inability to have the law respected, and to the country's degraded image on the international stage. As a result, he remains a genuinely popular politician. Though he is not solely responsible for the amelioration of the country's economic situation, which is in large part due to increases in oil and gas prices, he has been able to turn this situation to his advantage in the political realm. At the beginning of 2007, Russia's gross domestic product (GDP) finally returned to the same level as in 1990, the penultimate year of communist power. The country has had six straight years of growth, averaging 6 percent per year. In addition to the oil manna, there has been success in other domains (metallurgy, aluminum, arms, and food processing), as well as a strong increase in domestic household consumption, the – remarkable – complete repayment of public foreign debt, a doubling of spending on education, and a tripling of spending on health over the past five years.

Sociological surveys show that Putin's support base effectively mirrors Russian society: there are among his supporters as many women as men, and as many young as old people. They come from diverse social milieus, have varied levels of education, and are equally likely to have a negative or a positive vision of the Soviet regime. Because of his past in the secret services, Putin can indeed be perceived as a man who has remained true to the modes of management of the Soviet regime. This Soviet continuity is shown in the growing role played in the administration by the *siloviki*, who currently occupy at least a third of top-level positions, especially economic decision-making positions. But Putin can also be viewed as a Western-style modernizer. Indeed, before becoming president he had worked in the liberal administration of the mayor of St Petersburg, Anatoli Sobchak (1937–2000), and none other than the first post-Soviet Russian president, Boris Yeltsin (president from 1991 to 1999), designated him as his heir. In the 2000s he has pursued this modernizing course, albeit it in an authoritative way. As the recently deceased sociologist Yuri Levada subtly noted, Vladimir Putin "is a mirror in which everyone, whether communist or democrat, sees what he wants and hopes to see."[13]

"Nationalism" is not actually a phenomenon confined to the margins of society but an interactive process, the principal function of which is to integrate individuals and to legitimize the policy of elites while guaranteeing social cohesion in a period of significant upheaval. It is therefore likely that the current presidential apparatus perceives "patriotism" as a necessary element for modernizing Russia, and, paradoxical as it might initially seem, for a certain form of Westernization. Indeed, the Kremlin's aim is to restore Russia's status as a world power by modernizing the country's economy, as well as by engendering a "civil society" in which individual acts are motivated by the development of national power. The production of patriotic ideology thus indicates the extent to which globalization, whether lived or imagined, does not necessarily imply a passage to the "post-national."[14] Similar phenomena involving transformations in collective belonging, reformulations of the national bond, developing of "ethnic identities," and exacerbated community tensions are at work the world over, most particularly within the very Europe that imagines it has overcome such questions.

Internal logics of the volume

In this analysis we hope to shed light on the fact that the study of contemporary Russian nationalism can no longer be limited to typological classifications of diverse parties or groupuscules, of their place on the political checkerboard, or their electoral results; this stage, though necessary, must now be completed. The nationalist phenomenon cannot be apprehended in its diversity and importance except by taking into account the way it has permeated numerous adjacent spheres: elite policy-making circles, diffuse intellectual and religious fashions, marginal milieus and youth subcultures, generalized feelings of uneasiness toward the West, etc. Whereas the study of nationalist radical parties occupied a large part of the research that investigated this question for the 1990s, the path that Putin's Russia has taken necessitates a readjustment of perspective on the three matrix elements that will be implicit throughout the current work. The first is the birth of an official patriotic ideology and the reappropriation by Putin-like power of various doctrinal elements of Russian nationalism. The second is the extremely widespread diffusion of xenophobic sentiments in society at large and the increase in violent acts committed against "southerners," which have been exacerbated by tensions in the Caucasus. The third is the diffusion, in intellectual, artistic, and scholarly circles, of nationalist arguments that, no longer perceived as radical or marginal, have become part of a discourse entirely integrated into present-day social norms in Russia.

For this reason, this work is divided into four parts. The first part provides a historical and theoretical approach to Russian nationalism, underscoring certain key elements such as its historical continuity and thematic diversity (Marlène Laruelle), the importance of the Stalinist period as a moment of crystallization of modern Russian nationalism (Veljko Vujačić), and the debates provoked by the importation of the concept of "fascism" into Russia (Andreas Umland). The second part is more specifically focused on the extremist elements and on the New Right in Russia. The radical groupuscules of the 1990s have in part disappeared and reconstructed themselves around different dynamics such as the skinhead movement and the Movement against Illegal Immigration (Alexander Verkhovsky). However, Alexander Dugin's neo-Eurasianist movement is constantly evolving and creating paradoxical links with powerful political circles (Wayne Allensworth).

The third part focuses on the modes by which nationalism is being diffused throughout society. For instance, a culturalist wave is currently submerging the social and human sciences in Russia and has enabled the sanctioning of numerous nationalist slogans (Victor Shnirelman). Within the space of a few years, xenophobia has succeeded in becoming a mass phenomenon affecting all social milieus irrespective of their political preferences (Anastassia Leonova). This xenophobia is above all distinguished by the treatment it reserves for "foreigners." Whether the foreigners in question are Caucasians, Central Asians, or Chinese, all are charged with overwhelming the Russian people (Mikhail Alexseev). Lastly, the fourth and final part concentrates on the birth of official patriotic ideology. This birth can be seen in the field of foreign policy, especially toward Slavic countries, although the most hard-line nationalist groups have not succeeded in infiltrating it (Andrei Tsygankov); in the reclaiming of Orthodoxy by political power (Beth Admiraal); and in the cult of the military and patriotic education (Valerie Sperling). As a result of this analysis, this book hopes to provide some relevant grids through which to interpret and understand better the evolution of contemporary Russia.

Notes

1 Cf. for example J. B. Dunlop, *The Faces of Contemporary Russian Nationalism*, Princeton, NJ: Princeton University Press, 1983; same author, *The New Russian Nationalism*, New York: Praeger, 1985; *The New Russian Revolutionaries*, Belmont, MA: Nordland, 1976; *The Rise and Fall of the Soviet Union*, Princeton, NJ: Princeton University Press, 1993. See also A. Yanov, *The Russian Challenge and the Year 2000*, New York: Basil Blackwell, 1987; same author, *The Russian New Right: Right-Wing Ideologies in the Contemporary USSR*, Berkeley: University of California Press, 1978; as well as W. Laqueur, *Black Hundred: The Rise of the Extreme Right in Russia*, New York: HarperCollins, 1993.

2 Cf. for example S. D. Shenfield, *Russian Fascism: Traditions, Tendencies, Movements*, Armonk, NY: M. E. Sharpe, 2001; S. Reznik, *The Nazification of Russia: Antisemitism in the Post-Soviet Era*, Washington, DC: Challenge Publications, 1996; T. Parland, *The Extreme Nationalist Threat in Russia: The Growing Influence of Western Rightist ideas*, London: RoutledgeCurzon, 2004.

3 On this topic, see the debates that took place in *Post-Soviet Affairs* between Stephen E. Hanson, Jeffrey S. Kopstein, and Stephen Shenfield: S. E. Hanson, J. S. Kopstein, "The Weimar/Russia Comparison," 3, 1997, 252–283; S. Shenfield, "The Weimar/Russia Comparison: Reflections on Hanson and Kopstein," 4, 1998, 355–368; S. E. Hanson and J. S. Kopstein, "Paths to Uncivil Societies and Antiliberal States: A Reply to Shenfield," 4, 1998, 369–375.

4 T. Martin, *The Affirmative Action Empire: Nations and Nationalism in the Soviet Union, 1923–1939*, Ithaca, NY: Cornell University Press, 2001.

5 For a discussion of this interaction, see E. Pain, "Aktivizatsiia etnicheskogo bol'shinstva v post-sovetskoi Rossii: resursy russkogo natsionalizma," *Ab Imperio*, 3, 2003, 305–333.

6 N. V. Riasanovsky, *Russia and the West in the Teaching of the Slavophiles: A Study of Romantic Ideology*, Cambridge, MA: Harvard University Press, 1952; B. Zenkovsky, *Russkie mysliteli i Evropa. Kritika evropeiskoi kul'tury u russkikh myslitelei*, Paris: YMCA Press, n.d.; A. Walicki, *The Slavophile Controversy: History of a Conservative Utopia in Nineteenth-Century Russian Thought*, Notre Dame, IN: University of Notre Dame Press, 1989.

7 M. Angenot, *Les idéologies du ressentiment*, Montreal: XYZ, 1997.

8 The expression is from J. Plamenatz, quoted in C. Jaffrelot, "Les modèles explicatifs de l'origine des nations et du nationalisme. Revue critique," in G. Delannoi and P.-A. Taguieff (eds.), *Les Théories du nationalisme. Nation, nationalité, ethnicité*, Paris: Kimé, 1991, p. 167.

9 P. Perrineau, "L'extrême droite en Europe: des crispations face à la société ouverte," in P. Perrineau (ed.), *Les Croisés de la société fermée. L'Europe des extrêmes droites*, Paris: Éd. de l'Aube, 2001, pp. 5–10.

10 For more details on this last point, see M. Gabowitsch, "Combattre, tolérer ou soutenir? La société russienne face au nationalisme russe," in M. Laruelle (ed.), *Le Rouge et le noir. Extrême droite et nationalisme en Russie*, Paris: CNRS-Éditions, 2007, pp. 67–114.

11 The term "oligarch" is used to define the Russian tycoons who became rich when large Soviet companies were being privatized in the 1990s and who display a manifest desire to become engaged in politics, or at least to influence Russian public life through media control. If some of them were close to Yeltsin, others financed opposition forces. Putin brought them under control during his first mandate (2000–2004). They followed his line or went into exile abroad, or were arrested.

12 Mikhail Khodorkovsky, one of the main Russian oligarchs, was CEO of the oil company Yukos and possessor of the largest Russian fortune. He was arrested in 2003 and sentenced in 2005 to nine years of prison for fiscal evasion. Some months before his arrest, he had stated his intention to dedicate his time to his NGO Open Russia and run in the presidential elections against Putin.

13 *Kommersant*, 17 March 2000: 2.

14 A. Dieckhoff, *La Nation dans tous ses états. Les identités nationales en mouvement*, Paris: Flammarion, 2000; O. Dollfus, *La Mondialisation*, Paris: Presses de Sciences Po, 2001; D. Wolton, *L'Autre Mondialisation*, Paris: Flammarion, 2003.

Part I

Historical and conceptual issues in the study of Russian nationalism

2 Rethinking Russian nationalism

Historical continuity, political diversity, and doctrinal fragmentation

Marlène Laruelle

This aim of this chapter is to rework some of the standard notions pertaining to the issue of nationalism. First of all, it seeks to inscribe contemporary Russian nationalism in a historical continuity by showing how its internal logic and its conflictual relation to the state are rooted in the tsarist and above all the Soviet past. Second, it attempts to show that it is no longer possible to define the various doctrines and currents of nationalism in strictly ideological terms, since their postulates are very widely spread throughout Russian society. In order to obtain a precise vision of their capacity to influence political life, it seems preferable to distinguish them on the basis of their access to power and their social representativeness. So, instead of analyzing Russian nationalism in purely ideological terms, I have divided the political spectrum into four more or less distinct concentric circles in the hope of better understanding its multiplicity and relevance. Finally, I put into question the standard way of classifying the nationalist movement, arguing against the widespread use of "fascism" and "Nazism," not to mention distinctions between left and right, orthodoxy and neo-paganism, and ethnocentrism and imperialism. My objectives here are to show that Russian nationalism presents a far less fragmented picture than that usually painted, and to shed light on the shifting character of its institutional antagonisms and ideological divisions, and the trajectories of its leading figures. What emerges from this is an understanding of how this "nationalist climate" has come to have such success in contemporary Russia.

The question of origins: nineteenth century or Soviet era?

The nineteenth century as matrix of main theories of the nation

The nationalisms of the Slavophiles (1830–1840), of the Pan-Slavists (1850–1870), and, at the turn of the century, of the neo-Slavophiles were influenced by the German philosophical tradition of romanticism. Each of these movements conceived of the nation in a culturalist vein, one that glorified the authenticity of its rural life-world and its millenary fidelity to orthodoxy. In parallel to the currents existing in intellectual milieus, and in contrast to them, a state nationalism also existed that was grounded in its dynastic fidelity to the Romanovs.[1] As the former glorified the people and the latter the state, major contradictions and conflicts arose. These gave rise to an increase in the diversity of sentiments of collective belonging. The first type of nationalism that emerged based itself solely on fidelity to the dynasty and to the Russian imperial tradition (Sergei Uvarov, Konstantin Pobedonostsev); a second type, *à l'allemande*, based itself on the search for the authentic culture of the people (Slavophiles, Pan-Slavists, Populists); and a third type existed that emphasized respect for religious and philosophical values, was often messianic, and viewed modern ethnic nationalism with suspicion (it was made up of the *pochvennichestvo* movement and isolated authors writing at the end of the century, such as Konstantin Leontiev, Vladimir Soloviev, and Nikolai Fiodorov).[2] Some thinkers forged links between the first two types of nationalism (e.g. Mikhail Pogodin and Stepan Shevyriev); and others between the second and the third types (e.g. Fiodor Dostoievsky). Further, all three doctrines maintained differing attitudes toward the state and contradictory relations to one another. The Slavophiles were opposed to the state of Nicholas I, the Pan-Slavists to the Slavophiles, the *pochvenniki* to the Pan-Slavists, the *fin-de-siècle* figures to their predecessors, and so on.

It was necessary to wait for the serious undermining of tsarism in 1905 to see the first "extreme right wing" emerge in Russian politics. In contrast to its French, Italian, and German contemporaries, it never enjoyed any theoretical reinforcement from intellectuals won over to its cause. For conservative Russian thinkers it even constituted a pole of rejection rather than a mirror that reflected, in a radical manner, implicit but accepted ideas. Thus, it remained particularly weak on the theoretical level and was restricted to a mass movement manipulated by a power in crisis. In the hope of creating a large pro-monarchical movement within the masses, the tsar, the army, and certain elite functionaries decided to support the main radical political party that formed toward the end of 1905, namely the Union of the Russian People. Made up of a heterogeneous group of small merchants, nobles, servicemen, and members of the clergy, this party remained integral to a system that in turn gave it financial and political aid. Breaking with the establishment was never on its agenda.[3]

Of the nationalist movements born on the streets in 1905, the only one that survived was the Black Hundreds, the virulent anti-Semitism of which was based on the notorious *Protocols of the Elders of Zion*, which outlines an alleged plot led by the world Israelite Alliance.[4] Throughout its existence, the movement was manipulated by imperial power, and particularly by the Okhrana services, which financed it and prevented police intervention during pogroms. Unlike the Italian Fascists and the Nazis, the Russian movement never attempted to break with its financiers by trying to establish itself as an independent force. Similarly, whereas French "integralist nationalism" was Catholic but in conflict with the hierarchy, the Russian nationalist extreme right never emerged from the shadows of reactionary clergymen, the leading figure of which was John of Kronstadt. Both of the aforementioned movements may be defined as reactionary but not as fascist, since their unconditional fidelity to the tsar and to the Church, and their respect for social hierarchies, put them closer to conservatism.[5]

In the interwar period, Russian émigrés, in both the West and the Far East, were particularly politically active. The movements were diverse and heavily inspired by contemporary Western tendencies. At this time a number of movements emerged: the National Bolsheviks, whose principal theoretician was Nikolai Ustrialov; the Eurasianist movement, which was present in Western and Central Europe and in the Far East, and had many adherents who rallied to the defense of the USSR;[6] and sympathizers of National Socialism among Russian émigrés in Germany. Also worth mentioning is the NTS, the National Union of Workers of the New Generation, who were influenced by solidarism and Italian corporatism, and who collaborated with Nazi Germany. In addition, there were two parties that, for the first time in the history of Russian politics, could qualify as fascist: Konstantin Rodzhaevsky's Pan-Russian Fascist Party, based in Manchuria between 1931 and 1945; and Anastasi Vosniatsky's Pan-Russian Fascist Organization, set up in the United States.[7] Their popular support among émigrés was weak, but today they form a historical point of reference and a theoretical base for those that seek to combine German National Socialism with Russian messianism.

Russian nationalism during the Soviet era: dissidence or officiality?

Contrary to widespread opinion, Russian nationalists did not wait for the *perestroika* (reconstruction) and *glasnost'* (transparency) of the latter half of the 1980s before making a comeback and seeking to attain institutional recognition. Nationalists were actually already present throughout the Soviet era, when they were intimately if somewhat ambiguously connected to the state and Party apparatuses. After Stalin's liquidation of the internationalist Old Bolsheviks, the incoming generation of Soviet state employees, swept to power thanks to the purges at the end of the 1930s, harbored, along with the rest of the population, many ethnic stereotypes regarding Jews, Balts, and Caucasians, not to mention the country's other national minorities.[8] Once mass terror no longer held sway as the normal mode of state functioning, the Party apparatus set out to develop a patriotic Soviet ideology in an attempt to consolidate its power over a society slowly slipping from its grasp. Cementing the regime's political legitimacy, however, required developing a language in common with the population, and within these parameters nationalism presented itself as a basic material, since it was much more popularly supported than the discourse on classes had ever been. Stalin's comments on the *form* and *content* of socialism and nationalism, which were open to dual interpretation, thus led to the forging of new collective representations of national identity whose allegiance was to the socialist state. The greater the regime's uncertainty as to how to respond, or inability to respond, to the social expectations it itself had created became, the more symbolic and economic frustrations expressed in nationalist terms resonated throughout society. Centrifugal tendencies, then, did not affect merely the peripheral regions, but also the central republic, the system's "vertebral column"; the implosion of the Soviet Union emerged from within Russia itself.

After the internationalist policies of the first years of the Bolshevik regime and Lenin's scathing assessment of "Great Russian chauvinism," Stalin, in the mid-1930s, revived Russian nationalism: in 1934 a rereading was carried out of historical arguments to the favor of the tsarist empire; in 1937 the 125th anniversary of the Battle of Borodino was celebrated; and in 1939 Eisenstein made a film paying tribute to Alexander Nevsky. This reversion to a vision of Russia as "big brother" found its empirical correlate in the brutal physical liquidation of national communists who had striven to inculcate socialism in the national minorities. With the country's entry into war in 1941, glorification of patriotism increased tenfold. But even prior to the war it had led to the deportation of millions of persons belonging to the so-called "punished peoples," beginning in 1937 for the Koreans of the Far East, in 1941 for the Germans of the Volga, and lasting from before the war until 1944 for the populations of the Caucasus. If this collective violence toward certain nationalities diminished with the end of World War II (though it was not abolished at the juridical level, since some peoples were not rehabilitated until *perestroika*), Stalinist politics remained stamped by its anti-Semitism. The terror against Jews, which reached its apogee during the famous "Doctors' plot," came to an end only with Stalin's death in 1953. Yet the following decades of official anti-Zionist policies did no more than thinly disguise the recurrent dread the authorities felt toward Jews, and may be regarded as the matrix of contemporary Russian anti-Semitism.[9]

Outside the circles of power, it was not until Stalin's death that Russian national feeling could receive new expression: the end of terror gave new life to a certain public expression, and the releasing of millions of camp prisoners compelled society to reflect upon the regime. In accordance with a nineteenth-century tradition according to which culture replaces politics, discussions on the country's future took place in the major literary journals. Even before the shock of the Twentieth Congress of the Communist Party of the Soviet Union (CPSU), the famous "village prose" had appeared, with its idealization of a peasant way of life on the verge of disappearing, but it was to take on its full magnitude in the 1960s. Nikita Khrushchev's speeches on the birth of the Soviet nation – which came to stand for the demise of the federal structure – as well as the renewal of atheist campaigns raised the alarm among the Russian intellectual milieus concerning the preservation of national cultural patrimony. At the start of the 1960s the first ecological critiques appearing during a mobilization of intellectuals against the installation of a cellulose factory on Lake Baikal.[10] Such ecological concerns were quickly appropriated and monopolized by conservatives like Vladimir Chivilikhin (1928–1984), who in his *Svetloe oko Sibiri* (The Clear Eye of Siberia) sought to discredit Khrushchev's reforms and, more generally, the regime's obsession with industrialization.

The ousting of the First Secretary in 1964 and the Siniavsky–Daniel trial the following year marked the birth of the dissident movement. Leonid Brezhnev's strategy, however, was to seek reconciliation with the intelligentsia: he gave backing to nationalist elements and gradually co-opted the claims for preserving patrimony being voiced by various legal associations such as Rodina, the Society for the Defense of Cultural Patrimony, and the Russian Club. Journals such as *Nash sovremennik* and *Molodaia gvardiia*, which signaled the birth of an official "right" in the USSR, rapidly became the major sites for diffusing nationalist literature.[11] In 1965–1966, *Molodaia gvardiia* published an essay by the painter Ilia Glazunov entitled *Doroga k tebe* (The Road Leading to You), in which the author did not simply limit himself to exalting nature and Russian historical monuments, but overtly tried to redeem Orthodoxy and the pre-revolutionary period. By the decade's end a discrete but clear opposition had been established, divided between a Stalinist movement, represented by the journal *Oktiabr'*, and tsarist nostalgists associated with *Molodaia gvardiia* who unhesitatingly criticized the Soviet experiment and endorsed Slavophilism, although many major personalities shifted between the currents.

Caught off guard by the sudden undermining of the system, the authorities tried to clamp down on literary journals. The 1970s were marked by constant indecision on the part of the Party apparatus and of the state toward the nationalists, who by this time had organized themselves into a self-proclaimed "Russian Party," which was in the process of being institutionalized in the form of various cultural and historical organizations.[12] Some members of the Politburo wanted to ban these organizations from publishing, while others thought they were a good weapon against the liberals, judged to be much more dangerous, and preferred to support them. This latter tendency was the one that prevailed during the period of political détente with the United States and of rising nationalist sentiment in the federated republics, since both phenomena induced Moscow to maintain order in its ranks by promoting confusion between Russian and Soviet nationalisms. Accordingly, between 1971 and 1982, eleven "village prose" writers were awarded the most prestigious Soviet prizes, ensuring that each of their works would have several million copies printed,[13] while journals such as *Nash sovremennik*, *Molodaia gvardiia* and *Moskva* experienced an increase of more than 100 percent in their print run. In 1980 the nationalist painter Ilia Glazunov received the distinguished title of National Artist of the USSR, despite even the KGB's express concerns about the anti-Semitic character of his paintings. However, this alliance between power and Russian nationalist milieus should not conceal the coexistence of numerous conflicts, which also resulted in many of the most recognized artists being censored.

At the turn of the 1970s and 1980s the political authorities no longer seemed able to exert control over the Russian nationalist movement, which had largely become socially and ideologically independent. Issues of *Nash sovremennik* continued to challenge further the Soviet past.[14] In 1982, Yuri Andropov tried to slow down this development and attacked *Volga*, a journal that had published a violently anti-communist essay by Mikhail Lobanov revealingly entitled "Osvobozhdenie" (Liberation). The First Secretary launched a virulent campaign of critique against journals, publishing houses, and censorship bodies that allowed such ideas to be published. But the authorities could not turn back the clock. Between 1983 and 1985, seventeen nationalist writers had had books published with print runs of over a million copies each.[15] Yuri Bondarev was awarded his second USSR prize, and the popularity of authors such as Viktor Astafiev, Vassili Shushkin, and Valentin Rasputin had become impossible to challenge. For their part, the latter began to produce even harsher analyses of the country's situation, denouncing not only censorship and the absence of precautionary ecological and patrimonial measures, but also the failure of agricultural policies in which villages deemed "without prospect" were left in neglect. This occurred in a period of shock following the 1979 census, which registered the high birth rate among Soviet Muslims, the demographic decline of the Slavs, and the explosion in rates of alcoholism and divorce, all factors revealing of the malaise of Russian society.[16]

Notions of world plots against the USSR, with their anti-Semitic corollary, worked to consolidate diverse radical nationalist movements. They also exploited the notion that the Russian people were a victim to the Soviet experiment and during the latter years of *perestroika* all made appeals to have the status of the Russian Federation (RSFSR) aligned with that of the other republics so they could benefit from the institutional structures they were lacking, such as a specifically Russian Communist Party and Academy of Sciences. This damning assessment of the state of the country nevertheless sparked the birth of a new movement within Russian nationalism, hitherto divided between nostalgists for tsarism and hard-line Stalinists. In a noteworthy text entitled "Metafora sovremennosti" (Metaphor of the Present), published in *Literaturnaia gazeta* in 1979, Alexander Prokhanov denounced "village prose's" hidden elitism, which he thought cultivated the vision of a world already long gone; yet, he claimed, it was only by turning toward modernity that the greatness of Soviet power could be maintained. He thus encouraged nationalists to search for another ideology rather than passéism, and promoted an "urbanization" of national feeling in which self-expression would find a means in technological progress.

The* perestroika *years: Russian nationalism finds catharsis

The wealth of debate within the nationalist milieu, which, depending upon the author and sensibility, variously articulated tsarist nostalgia, the cult of Stalin, and "modernism," made it into a hotbed of nationalism in the early years of perestroika and a situation of regained freedom of speech. Between 1985 and 1987, Russian nationalists lent support to Mikhail Gorbachev's modernizing approach, so nationalist circles came to have a certain influence on questions relating to *perestroika*. For example, they helped to persuade the authorities to abandon a project to rechannel Siberian rivers designed to improve the situation of Central Asia, and got them to condemn corruption and develop anti-alcoholism policies.[17] Yet this situation changed dramatically in spring 1988. The increasing influx of references to Western culture, the rehabilitation of communist figures such as Nikolai Bukharin, the reissuing of banned authors, one of whom was Boris Pasternak, and the general feeling of a precipitate power having lost control over a political process it had started, radicalized the nationalist movement. This turn was epitomized in Nina Andreeva's celebrated pro-Stalinist text published by *Sovetskaia Rossiia* in March 1988 entitled "Ne mogu postupit'sia printsipami" (I cannot sacrifice principles), which threw the door wide open for the hardening of the nationalist camp.

During the perestroika years, diverse expressions of Russian nationalism came to crystallize in an association called Pamyat (Memory). In 1980, after the 600th anniversary celebrations of the battle of Kulikovo,[18] which enabled the nationalist camp to express itself in broad daylight, many associations, such as Vitiazi (the Valiant), radical nationalist members of the Society for the Defense of Cultural Patrimony (VOOPIIK), as well as several figures linked to the "Russian Party" within the state apparatus and the Soviet Union Writer's Union, grouped together in association. This assocation chose its name, Pamyat, after the novel of the same name by nationalist writer Vladimir Chivilikhin, who won the USSR State Prize for it in 1982.[19] In the first half of the 1980s, Pamyat for the most part arranged historical, literary and musical evenings. In 1984–1985 the arrival of a new leader, Dmitri Vasiliev, a trained photographer and director whose career began under the influence of Ilia Glazunov, signaled the movement's rapid politicization. This space of meeting, theorization, and collective experience of nationalism soon went from organizing cultural activities to making political claims centered on anti-Zionism and notions of a Judeo-Masonic plot.

A talented orator, Vasiliev traveled the country organizing conferences that were recorded on cassette and widely diffused in milieus of nationalist sensibility. In 1986–1987, many sections of Pamyat were set up in the country's main cities, but shortly thereafter the movement experienced its first schisms: the so-called national communist currents, which stressed the greatness of Stalin's Soviet Union and endorsed religious conceptions inspired by neo-paganism, were rejected by the majority of the association. In fact, under Vasiliev's leadership the association became overtly pro-monarchist and Orthodox, taking as its example the Black Hundreds of the early twentieth century.[20] Further to these ideological divisions, Pamyat also underwent organizational divisions. For some in the movement, membership of the Communist Party was a necessary condition of their existence and hence they desired to inject the CPSU with more nationalist rhetoric. Others, meanwhile, wanted to seize the historical chance presented by the recognition of multipartyism in March 1990 to organize a political party. So, in spring 1990 Pamyat split into two parties: the Orthodox-oriented Republican Party of Nikolai Lysenko and the National Bolshevik-oriented Party of National Revival. As legal successor to the original Pamyat, Vasiliev's National Patriotic Front insisted on rejecting the term "party," which it construed as too Western, though in practice it became a partisan organization too. Thus, paradoxically, many partisans of the nationalist movement consider the golden age of Russian nationalism to have been prior to democratization, a time when it was less divided than it was to become.

Apart from Pamyat, several other movements with a nationalist background also attempted to established organizational structures. The demise of the Soviet Union, the interethnic conflicts that rocked the Caucasus, and Ukraine's and the Baltic States' push for autonomy all sparked concern in military circles and Party officials. Between 1989 and 1991, Soviet conservatives, military officials mindful of the country's stability, and orthodox monarchists at last free to express themselves in the light of day together attempted to form an alliance. In his *Dostatochnaia oborona* (A Sufficient Defense), published in 1989, Alexander Prokhanov launched a call for an alliance between the military and nationalist intellectuals. A year later, in his *Post-perestroíka* (Post-*perestroika*), Sergei Kurginian took on the task of trying to unify communism and orthodoxy by constructing a Soviet "meta-religion." With Prime Minister Nikolai Ryzhkov's backing he came to play an important role as a critic of the program proposed by Grigori Yavlinsky and Stanislav Shatalin to proceed to a market economy in 500 days. Indeed, both Prokhanov's Analytical Center and Kurginian's Experimental-Creative Center – itself associated with the USSR's Council of Ministers – were involved in a desperate attempt to formulate a patriotic Russo-Soviet ideology that would forestall the country's collapse and directly contribute to unifying the diverse nationalist groups.[21]

In fall 1989, thanks to Gorbachev's liberalizing policies, many parliamentary factions formed in the Supreme Soviet to try to preserve the unity of the Soviet structure. This, for example, was the case with the Block of Patriotic Social Organizations of Russia, with the Parliamentary Group of Russia, created on the initiative of Sergei Vasiliev and Nikolai Pavlov, and wih the Russia Club, an umbrella group of the RSFSR's pro-communist deputies active in 1989 and throughout the first half of 1990. The most active and the largest of these organizations internal to the Sovietophile movement was the Union Movement. Unofficially created in 1988 by Russian deputies of the federated republics such as Viktor Alksnis (Latvia), Evgeni Kogan (Estonia), and Yuri Blokhin (Moldavia), the group was home to parliamentarians who held diverse political opinions but all shared a desire to preserve the Soviet federal structure. In February 1990 the movement developed into a parliamentary group and set itself the chief goal of defending the Russian minorities in the republics. Comprising more than 500 deputies, it quickly became one of the major political forces in the Supreme Soviet, advancing a third way by endorsing both Gorbachev's proposal to proceed to a market economy *and* the maintaining of gains acquired in socialism.[22]

In the spring of 1990, official recognition of multipartyism contributed to the nationalist camp's demise and the institutionalization of numerous small political parties. The Viktor Aksiuchits-led Christian Democrat Movement of Russia, the Union of National Revival under Alexander Romanenko, and Mikhail Astafiev's Democratic Constitutional Party, who claimed the legacy of the prerevolutionary Cadets, were among the first to achieve official status. Within the CPSU the most conservative members, led notably by General Albert Makashov, regarded at the time as the leader of the so-called Red patriots, attempted to stem Moscow's loss of influence and power.[23] In summer 1991 the Union movement, which was staring at the imminent defeat of its strategies to preserve a unified Soviet organization, unsuccessfully attempted to transform itself into a political party under Alksnis's leadership.

So, despite numerous attempts to create a unified political organization, the ideological spectrum of opponents to *perestroika* quickly disintegrated into multiple movements. These can be schematically classed into three groups. The first is made up of hard-line Stalinist communists, a group formed around Albert Makashov and Viktor Anpilov. The second comprises former members of the democratic movement such as Aksiuchits and Astafiev, who rallied the opposition to Gorbachev. The third and most nationalistic group is the Slavophile tendency, characterized at the time as "National Patriots." This diversity of doctrinal affiliations continued even after the country's collapse. But conflicts dating from *perestroika* between, on one side, Mikhail Gorbachev and Alexander Yakovlev, and, on the other, Egor Ligachev were transformed when some of Gorbachev's former aides, such as Alexander Rutskoi and Ruslan Khasbulatov, rallied to the nationalist cause, and then led the opposition to Yeltsin in the fall of 1993.

From this historical brief, many conclusions emerge to enable a better comprehension of the doctrines of contemporary nationalism. After the phases of Stalin's massive terror, the Soviet Union had to use nationalism as one of the main social cements. The Communist authorities did so by vaguely reviving a model of nationalism inspired by the holistic romanticism of the previous century. Paul Zawadzki, then, is quite right in noting that "[t]he relations between communism and nationalism were complex, woven of oppositions and elective affinities. Was it instrumentalization of the national-populist languages by agents of power, or capture of communism by the nationalist culture?"[24] No matter which option is chosen, it seems indisputable that Russian nationalism was predominantly official and non-dissident. The major literary journals such as *Nash sovremennik* and *Molodaia gvardiia* vied, sometimes against one another, for the role of recognized conceptual center of a practically state-funded nationalism. Of course, some of the most prestigious movements were, in fact, clandestine. It is hence traditional to consider that the "dissident right" was born with VSKHSON, an underground neo-Slavophile organization led by Igor Ogurtsov and Yevgeni Vagin that emerged in Leningrad in 1964. Its primary objective was to topple the Soviet regime in order to establish a so-called third way combining popular monarchy, strong unionism, and principles of Christian democracy.[25] Many very important intellectuals such as, for example, Alexander Solzhenitsyn and Vladimir Osipov (who from 1971 to 1973 was the editor of the famous journal *Veche*,[26] and then of *Zemlia*, before being sentenced to several years in a camp) also left their mark on the dissident movement through their national engagement. Interestingly, such engagement was not perceived at the time as being in contradiction with the defense of human freedom that was at the heart of the dissident principle.[27]

Regardless of the symbolic prestige accorded to these dissident currents today, it is not within them that current nationalism was elaborated. It was much more influenced, as was its tsarist predecessor, by its difficult and often unacknowledged proximity to a political power that it hoped to win over to its cause. The binary division proposed by numerous scholars between those Russian nationalists who agreed to work within the Soviet system and the others who refused to do so, or were simply not able to, thus does not seem pertinent. Individuals often found themselves in a twofold game in which even official authors were subjected to censure, and sometimes had the publication of their texts refused. Further, the theoretical influences and personal relations between "officials" and "dissidents" were considerable, so much so that after *perestroika* the two movements merged into one another. These findings remain valid for the contemporary period. The principal traits they describe apply to it perfectly, from the difficulties of identifying with an imperial state, to the desire to be recognized as a national ideology by the state while nevertheless refusing to accept the loss of autonomy that all too directive statist pressures imply, and the multiple sites of passage between individuals and institutions. All of this makes it difficult to define an oppositionalist or dissident nationalism by contrast to an official nationalism.

The social niche of nationalism: marginality or mainstream?

The extremely varied field of Russian nationalism may be divided into several concentric circles. The first circle is that of men of power, such as the former president Vladimir Putin, and other important figures, such as the mayor of Moscow, Yuri Luzhkov, the former prime ministers Yevgeni Primakov and Viktor Chernomyrdin, and the "techno-political scientists" of the presidential apparatus and of United Russia responsible for formulating the political precepts of the day, such as Vladislav Surkov. The second circle comprises the principal political parties with representation at the electoral level. The Communist Party and the Liberal Democratic Party of Russia were the only two such parties until the 2003 elections, when a newcomer, the Rodina bloc, joined them. A third circle groups together those extra-parliamentary political parties that have no electoral presence but have been stable for many years, have charismatic leaders, and have both an identifiable discourse and strategy, such as the former Russian National Unity of Alexander Barkashov, and Eduard Limonov's National Bolshevik Party. A fourth and final circle includes a set of even more radical extra-parliamentary factions. These factions are of variable duration, their syncretistic ideologies ambiguous, and their leaders well known for shifting from one partisan experiment to another.

A Russian public space increasingly marked by nationalism

In all post-socialist countries, whether in Central and Eastern Europe or the former Soviet Union, the 1990s radical right was often more ideologically driven and more openly anti-democratic than that in Western countries.[28] Its field of action, however, was limited because the authorities, finding expression in a variety of public domains, had already monopolized nationalist rhetoric. In the 1990s the Russian Federation underwent profound changes that were as much political as cultural and social, and led to its becoming preoccupied with its new national and state identity. This identity has come to be grounded in an often crude vision of how Russian elites imagine a nation-state *à l'occidentale*, and on a set of local, historical, geographical, and cultural specificities that they wish to foreground. The "return to order" championed by Vladimir Putin since

2000 and the will of the authorities to take things in hand have now become increasingly obviously bolstered by rising patriotic sentiment.

Instead, to understand the growth of Russian nationalism it is imperative to look at what occurred in the 1990s in the wake of the Soviet collapse. Putin has certainly benefited politically from the violence, disruptions, and poverty of Yeltsin's political and economic reforms, as well as from the collapse of state institutions in the 1990s. As Russia attempted to restructure itself as an independent state, Russian citizens witnessed their standard of living crumble and poverty levels skyrocket as their country's wealth was carved up by an oligarchy derived from the *nomenklatura* of the previous system. Corruption and crime increased dramatically, life expectancy dropped frighteningly, large numbers of young men lost life and limb fighting an unpopular war in the restive republic of Chechnya, and Russia's international power and reputation disappeared. Life became unpredictable as a result of wild inflation, and the future seemed to hold little promise. The majority of Russians thus lost faith in Yeltsin, and his government's policies were generally considered complete failures.

After the tragic events of autumn 1993 and the bloody crushing of the Parliament, the competing power groups in Russia began to fear more than anything else the country becoming too politically polarized. In an effort to unite it they produced a new political idea that might be called "patriotic centrism." The aim of this idea, from which Putin has benefited greatly and manipulated to his advantage, was to eliminate ideological oppositions and to encourage political reconciliation of different factions through patriotic rhetoric. As early as 1994–1995 the Kremlin tried to revive the patriotic rallying cry of the motherland as a way of promoting national unification. Later, in 1996, a first attempt was made to institutionalize this political patriotism (Boris Yeltsin at the time urged a search for a new national ideology). During the 1996 presidential campaign, Yeltsin's proponents drafted the media into the service of presidential power – a precursor to the Kremlin's current control over the media. This practice enabled Yeltsin to saturate the news with messages designed to scare voters away from his popular Communist opponent Gennadi Ziuganov, on the pretext that Russia might "return to the past." Then, around 1997–1999, this ideological push entered the political stage, championed by such leading political figures as General Alexander Lebed (1950–2002), the former prime minister and Minister of Foreign Affairs Yevgeni Primakov, and the Mayor of Moscow, Yuri Luzhkov, who is famed for architecturally rebuilding Moscow along nationalist Russian lines.

The 1999 legislative elections revealed for the first time the widespread consensus that had come to exist across the political spectrum, including liberals. This consensus was built around the idea that Russia's development should take a particular national path that focused not only on reform but above all on order and stability. All saw the country's situation at the end of Boris Yeltsin's second term in similar terms. On the domestic front, central power, embodied by a sick president, was in decline; the state's authority was practically non-existent; respect for the law was overtly scorned; and the feeling of having sold national wealth cheaply to oligarchs was extremely widespread. Moreover, regional governors instituted veritable feudal fiefdoms that endangered the very unity of the Federation – and certain national republics regularly threatened Moscow's authority, talking often of secession. At the international level the Russian state appeared to shrivel and its geopolitical interests were ill-defined. In addition, the West's handling of the Yugoslav crisis and NATO's bombing of Serbia were perceived as a humiliation for Russia. Even Russian liberals put out calls for solidarity with Serbia in the name of Pan-Slavism or Pan-Orthodoxy. The Kremlin's inability to deal with the Chechen question during the 1990s further exacerbated the feeling among Russians that the Russian state was weak, unable to control its own people and to finance a competent army. For Russia's political elites, Chechnya reinforced the push for political consensus that championed strong state authority and stability, and the more extreme groups, whether liberal or communist, were marginalized.

The traumas of the 1990s – whether Chechnya, the economy, or political "civil wars" – have had a lasting impact on the contemporary situation. They contribute even today to the discrediting of so-called democratic or liberal parties. Indeed, Putin's opposition has little if any popular support. Former liberal parties such as Yabloko or the Union of Right Forces are for the most part discredited because they have not performed a *mea culpa* to apologize for their role in the problems of the 1990s. For public opinion, these groups embody the brutality of the changes of the Yeltsin years, the negative social impact of the 1990s privatizations, the monopolizing of national assets by oligarchs, and the disasters of Chechnya. References to the West as a model are often badly received by the majority of the population, which is above all concerned that the country get back on its feet and stabilize. The Putin government has aimed over the past few years to make Russia into one of the twenty-first century's world leaders, one that embraces the game of globalization and knows how to take advantage of it. It has championed technological modernity, the necessity of being efficient and competitive in a fast-moving international market economy, and the effective utilization of the country's human potential and natural resources. For it, economic success brings not only riches to the political and business elites, but also political power and international authority.

If the 1990s comprise the years of ideological polarization and the birth of a trend toward "patriotic centrism," the years since 2000 should be viewed as a period of political consensus and recentralization around what is *politically possible*, with the presidential party as the core and Russian national triumph as the rhetoric. Official reappropriation of the nationalist idea, considered marginal at the start of the 1990s, was particularly obvious during the parliamentary elections in December 2003 and December 2007. Nationalism in one form or another today dominates the whole of the Russian electoral field, confirmation both of the narrowing of political life in Russia around the presidential party, and of the Kremlin's drive to monopolize the discourse on the nation.

Official patriotism – an element of social mobilization?

To achieve this end, the political power elites in the Kremlin have worked to mobilize the population behind the state enterprise while at the same time restricting the political freedoms of individuals. On the one hand, they have successfully improved the living standards of the Russian people, making it plain to the citizenry that the Putin path will lead to material advantages. Positive changes to the everyday lives of Russians have produced growing grassroots support and enthusiasm for Russia's current trajectory. On the other hand, Putin and most politicians have increasingly turned to patriotic rhetoric in an attempt to enlist the population to rebuild a Great Russia. In return for opting out of politics and leaving such matters in the hands of the current power-brokers, the Russian people will receive material well-being and be able to be full of pride in their country.

Russian political life is no longer structured by the competition between different visions of the world, between different ideologies or approaches to politics (such as the ideological differences between Yeltsin's liberals and the Communists in the 1990s). Instead, Russian politics has become divided between different factions of like-minded thinkers who are all connected to the Kremlin, and whose struggles are often turf wars internal to the bureaucracies. In the absence of any meaningful public debate on what political, social, and economic direction Russian society should take, patriotism has become the ideological *posture* shared by all parties. Words and terms that were confined in the 1990s to the most radical and unappealing nationalist movements, like that of Zhirinovsky, are today fully part of Russian public life and can no longer be viewed as extreme. Public speeches are filled with references to Russia as a "Great Power" (*derzhavnost'* or *velikoderzhavnost'*), to "statehood" (*gosudarstvennost'*), to the preservation of the nation (*sberezhenie natsii*), to empire (*imperiia*), and to the motherland (*rodina*) or the fatherland (*otechestvo*). The country's principal political leaders have thus worked to change their tune to fit in with the general climate, notably by concentrating on those issues which have the most electoral significance: xenophobia toward "Southerners"; demographic anxieties; the desire to re-establish a great Russian power – that is, one that is respected on the international scene and in the near abroad; and concern over ethnic questions, and over the balance between "ethnic Russians" (*russkie*) and "national minorities."

This new patriotism is not as rigid an ideology as Soviet-style Marxism-Leninism and it is mostly devoid of content. Those who refuse to present themselves as "patriots" are delegitimated and ushered off the public stage. But as soon as a politician displays his or her patriotism, they are free to speak from and for a variety of political viewpoints (monarchy or republic, tsarist or Soviet nostalgia, orthodoxy or secularity, ethnic or imperial definition of Russianness, etc.). However, the political patriotism of Putin's government has of late been taking on more concrete forms and agendas. We can see this process in the education sector, for example, with the implementation of so-called patriotic education programs for youths, debates on the introduction of courses on Orthodox culture in schools, the publication of new history textbooks rehabilitating Stalin, the Kremlin's forming of pro-presidential youth movements, etc. The cult of World War II, which has continued on from the Soviet period, is omnipresent in the new patriotic politics as an example of a *winning Russia* to which more wins are to come.

Perhaps most importantly, the newly prominent and politically charged rhetoric about the greatness of the motherland is well received in society. Broad sectors of Russian society support the powers that be in their declarations of nationalism and national pride. Putin's focus on a positive self-image for Russia is intended to smooth the economic upturn and society's "recovery." The stakes of patriotic recovery can thus be likened to a desire for revenge for the upheavals of the 1990s, but equally to a desire on the part of Russian citizens for normality. They want to live in a politically and economically functioning state in which they can imagine a future. This situation has so far meant a narrowing of political life and a hardening of Moscow's relations with Western countries. However, certain gains of the 1990s have not been put into question: freedom of movement, private property, the right to entrepreneurship, the resolute commitment of large Russian companies to the market economy and globalization, for example.

The media seem to play a crucial role in disseminating this nationalism. Indeed, the massive submission of this "fourth power" to the political authorities highlights the media's status as proponents of nationalist discourse in their own right. Whether one speaks of the press and television, which the Kremlin have brought under control, or of the more apparently autonomous sectors such as the internet and the cinema, it is quite apparent that at the present time the media as a totality play an increasingly large role in exacerbating xenophobic tensions within Russian society.[29] This nationalist climate is not solely restricted to political and media circles, but is also to be found in certain sections of cultural and academic life. Thus, in Russia today the notion that the mission of sciences is the justification of the so-called Russian specificity is very widespread in academic milieus, as are approaches defined as "civilizationist." Disciplines such as history, sociology, economics, and literature, as well as the new disciplines of culturology and geopolitics, propagate nationalist and, more generally, ethnicist precepts, with consequences that are as yet little studied.[30]

This new Russian patriotism endorses reformulations, modernized by post-Soviet conditions, both of former Soviet ideology and of traditional Russian nationalism. What is most characteristic of this discourse is the desire for social consensus, and the idea that there is a fundamental historical continuity in the Russian state over and above any political ruptures. Such ruptures are indeed not considered pertinent insofar as the "essence" of Russia is said to lie not in its political regime – imperial, communist, presidential republic, etc. – but instead in the country's greatness, in its place on the international stage, in the existence of a sphere of influence over its neighboring countries, and in its sense of a world mission. This glorification of a nation emptied of any civic objective clearly indicates a desire to "exit from the political." Focusing on the national is supposed to circumvent every challenge against the current political authorities, and indirectly to justify the development of authoritarian practices. This development in part explains the consensual rallying to an elective autocracy by the majority of the Russian population, whose demand for authority and, to a lesser degree, for ethnicity has been remarked upon by Western observers for some years.

The second circle: the CPRF and the LDPR

Up to the parliamentary election in December 2003, the study of nationalism in Russian politics had been traditionally limited to two "historic" parties, the Communist Party of the Russian Federation (CPRF) and the Liberal Democratic Party of Russia (LDPR). Both have had permanent parliamentary representation since the beginning of the 1990s and have shared the same tributary function.

The Communist Party of the Russian Federation is anything but a monolithic entity. Several currents developed within it that all opposed each other, not only on issues concerning the appropriate degree of nationalism to encourage, but also on issues concerning which economic system to adopt.[31] Some were pragmatists, others were more ideologically driven, and still others were nostalgic either for the monarchy or for Stalinism.[32] Since the beginning of the 1990s, "internationalist" communists have been practically non-existent in Russia. Although several small parties (Trotskyists, anarchists, unionists, etc.) continue to refer to communism, they remain outside of the electoral field and of the field of attraction of the CPRF, which they regard as social democratic.[33] Public assertions of so-called communist convictions have thus become almost a sure sign of "nationalism." Throughout the 1990s and the 2000s the Communist Party's strategy has been complex. At the parliamentary level it adopted a centrist politics of co-optation, while at the level of discourse it openly situated itself within the so-called patriotic opposition. However, its function, which consisted in channeling discontent while remaining within the system, weakened when Putin came to power, as he was able to capitalize on a number of the opposition's defining themes.

Zhirinovsky's personality and his party, the LDPR, have caused much ink to be spilled, particularly after their brilliant electoral results in 1993, though one can only bemoan the often imprecise terms that are applied to them, and notably that of fascism.[34] The LDPR has certain discernible doctrinal elements. It is more clearly anti-communist than the CPRF; it is more favorable to economic liberalism and to small entrepreneurship; it advances doctrines that are quite imperialist; and it openly acknowledges its xenophobia. The fundamentally provocative nature of Zhirinovsky himself, who accepts and even owns up to his contradictions, is not helpful when it comes to delineating his party's exact ideas. However, concerning Zhirinovsky one must speak more of a style than of a doctrine. He is the archetypal representative of populism as defined by Pierre-André Taguieff – that is, "political style likely to give form to diverse symbolic materials and to establish oneself in multiple ideological places."[35] The key elements are all there: the issuing of personal calls to the people; denunciations of a-national elites; a charismatic personality; anti-fiscal protests; demands for referendums; and calls to cleanse the country of so-called inassimilable elements, for example in the Russian case the populations of the Caucasus and of Central Asia. Like Western populist parties, the LDPR vacillates between making pleas for a welfare state (a significant electoral issue in Russia) and adherence to neo-liberal principles. In both cases, by assimilating the public servants who have been waiting long months for their salaries, with the emerging middle class able to survive only thanks to "business," Zhirinovsky claims to be speaking in the name of the losers of the Russian version of modernization – that is, of the savage privatizations of the 1990s.

These two parties, the CPRF and the LDPR, share a certain number of features, and above all their conflation of the people-as-*demos* with the people-as-*ethnos*. Despite their statist and imperialist pretensions, their precepts are closer to those of ethno-nationalism. Both parties, albeit to differing degrees, espouse a form of national populism or identity populism that conflates the "wee folk" with the nation, which they claim to be defending from an assortment of enemies made up mostly of oligarchs and foreigners. They also have in common the ambiguous, and heavily demagogic, function of being official parties, even as they present themselves as upholders of social protest which remain outside the system. This is how they work virulently to distinguish themselves from a type of political power whose auxiliaries they have become, unintentionally so in the case of the CPRF, much more consciously so in that of the LDPR. Although their strategies to gain respectability have led their "doctrines [to] collapse under the weight of tactics,"[36] their political choices differ. Whereas the CPRF's theories are more thoroughly worked out, and it is more committed to the national question and to the economic domain, the LDPR seems limited to the promotion of a populist style that is compatible with diverse political points of reference.

The extension of the second circle: Rodina's evolution

In the 2003 parliamentary elections, a new political formation appeared on the Russian scene, Rodina (Motherland). It initially benefited from extensive goodwill from the authorities, but quickly became victim to multiple splits between advocates of closer ties with the Kremlin and those who wish to become opposition leaders. Despite its resurgent schisms, Rodina symbolized a turning point in the political history of the country. Bolstered by around 5.5 million voters, this bloc became the fourth largest political force in Russia, and the most recent one to hurdle the 5 percent threshold needed to sit in the Duma. However, this success was not only a success in electoral terms or within the parliamentary system. Rodina also cast a telling light on the gradual officialization of nationalism on the contemporary Russian scene. As a result of it, parties and nationalist figures from marginal circles could form alliances for the first time, and in the process discourses previously considered radical were transformed into "politically correct" doctrines. The strength of Rodina, which portrayed itself as standing for "leftist nationalism,"[37] lay in its ability to combine nationalist, radical, and moderate forces, to choose which of the latter will work best in the situation at hand, to interlink the various lines of argument, and to extract their essential elements so as to play to the increasing importance of the issue of patriotism in Russia.

Rodina was a conglomerate made up of various nationalist currents, the differing evolutions of which suggest a fourfold division. The first includes lobbies for the defense of the Russian diaspora, which were formerly organized around the Congress of Russian Communities and which today seek to capitalize on the political success of their figurehead, Dmitri Rogozin.[38] The second comprises groups nostalgic for the Soviet Union (in particular, military figures such as General Valentin Varennikov, one of the planners of the August 1991 putsch), as well as "leftist" politicians unable to identify with the CPRF, for example Sergei Glazev, who espouses a Russian-style social democracy. The third unites the partisans of Sergei Baburin, who defends ethnic Russians against the other peoples of the former empire, and makes statements with strong ethnicist connotations. And Rodina's fourth current, which is not one of the lesser ones, is made up of defenders of political orthodoxy, such as the celebrated publicist Natalia Narochnitskaia, the Orthodox journalist Alexander Krutov, and, still more so, Alexander Chuev, vice-president of the Duma Committee for Religious and Social Organizations. All of them support the demands made by the Moscow patriarchate to declare the Russian Federation a specific "Orthodox civilization," one based on the predominance of ethnic Russians within the Federation, and all have attracted attention for their Pan-Slavic remarks in support of Yugoslavia.

Ever since entering the political scene, Rodina has sought to criticize its two main rivals, the CPRF and the LDPR, in their struggle against the presidential party. At the same time, however, it has borrowed from them the elements of their success, which resides in the conjoining of two forms of populism. The first, said to be contestatory, gives primacy to the tributary function and places the people-as-*demos* in opposition to the wealthy; the second, which is identitarian, presses home the ethno-nationalist dimension, depicting a people-as-*ethnos* in a struggle against foreigners. Rogozin and Baburin represented this second identitarian faction, identifiable by its more nationalist objectives, while Glazev embodied the contestatory fraction, which focused on social struggles. The Rodina bloc, despite its numerous schisms and excommunications, and the multiple restructurings it has undergone between 2003 and 2006, has thus been able to unite under one partisan banner the many formerly disparate nationalists who had subscribed neither to the CPRF nor to the LDPR. Many of them had previously had no access to parliamentary activity because they belonged to movements in which nationalism was not the central element. Rodina thus made it possible to structure the hitherto dissociated careers of individuals and of nationalist discourses into the form of a political party and a parliamentary faction. It also succeeded in providing more respectable formulations of nationalist ideas that until then had been considered radical, and it has regularly obtained the support of deputies within the presidential majority.[39]

Thanks to Rodina, a certain national radicalism has gone from being marginal to being "politically correct," and has succeeded in its entryist policy of infiltrating the structures of political representation. However, Rodina's Kremlin-led marginalization, and then its *transformation* in 2006 in Fair Russia, reveals that United Russia is concerned by this "leftist" nationalist competition. The recent rapprochement between specific figures from Rodina, such as its deputy, Andrei Saveliev, and the leader of the well-known Movement against Illegal Immigration (DPNI), Alexander Belov, is evidence that Rodina's most radical section intends to continue its fight against United Russia by other means and with other allies.

The third circle: the radical right without parliamentary representation

The third circle of classification groups together political parties that have no parliamentary presence but that have maintained a stable existence for over a decade. Although they connote radicalism and loudly proclaim their refusal to play the classic political game, they nonetheless provide a store of ideas and slogans from which political parties can borrow, and give young politicians the opportunity to try their hand at radical nationalism before embarking on more official careers in state structures. Within the kaleidoscope of these nationalist currents, two main parties left a major influence on the 1990s as much because of the relative sophistication of their doctrines as because of the number of their members, Alexander Barkashov's Russian National Unity (RNU) and Eduard Limonov's National Bolshevik Party (NBP). They embodied two major ideological orientations of the nationalist camp: the first combines allusions to Italian Fascism and German Nazism, espouses racist ideas and has a conservative vision of society; the second is inspired by National Bolshevism, bases itself on references that are as nationalist as socialist, and wants to be seen as overtly revolutionary.[40]

Alexander Barkashov's Russian National Unity (RNU) borrowed a number of symbolic aspects from Nazism: the swastika; the Hitlerian salute; a paramilitary uniform for members; and multiple references to the program of the Nationalsozialistische Deutsche Arbeiterpartei (NSDAP), including to a mixed economy and to eugenic theories. Barkashov contended that the USSR had implemented a radical program of miscegenation of Slavs with non-Aryan peoples in order to make the former disappear.[41] The RNU can thus be distinguished from many of its rivals by its clearly racial definition of the Russian nation. It considers religious and linguistic elements to be of little relevance, believes that the nation's interests are superior to those of the state, which it thinks should be transformed into an ethnic entity in the service of an eponymous people, and wants to prohibit mixed marriages. The party also believes that there is a global cosmopolitan plot against the Russians and cultivates neopagan assumptions, yet at the same time it refuses to condemn Christianity and seeks to demonstrate Christ's Aryan line of descent.[42]

The success of the movement and its visibility on the public stage, in particular during the first half of the 1990s, were due in large part to its presence alongside insurgents during the conflict between Yeltsin and the White House in

October 1993. In fact, Barkashov, who was arrested after the events and then given an amnesty in spring 1994, left prison as a national hero. This was the time when the RNU enjoyed its golden age. The party had a considerably developed territorial network and was particularly influential in the Stavropol and Krasnodar regions; its internal structure was very centralized and hierarchical, with membership to the movement involving several levels. It offered members (a number of whom, incidentally, worked in the security organs) a paramilitary training and the opportunity to participate in voluntary surveillance militias, which were often involved in mafia dealings. It has provoked several racist incidents toward immigrants. The movement also appears to have been infiltrated by the secret services, and has unsuccessfully engaged in an entryist strategy into union milieus and the Orthodox Church.[43] In September 2000 an internal coup resulted in the exclusion of Barkashov. Today the future of the movement, which broke up into multiple factions, remains uncertain.

Created in 1993–1994, Eduard Limonov's National Bolshevik Party is one of the most stable and most ideologically established nationalist movements. It differs from that of Barkashov in terms of its ideological reference points, but also in terms of its more educated social base, intellectualist character, and near absence of anti-Semitic remarks.[44] The formulation of National Bolshevism owes much to the presence within the party of the doctrinaire Alexander Dugin, who was a member from 1994 to 1998. The party's doctrine, a so-called general theory of uprising,[45] is grounded in the idea of forming an alliance between revolutionary radicalism on the right and on the left (references to anarchism are numerous), and in a glorified romantic vision of action. It calls for a dictatorial regime and believes that the country's problems could be resolved by renewing the tradition of Great Russian imperialism.

The movement's aggressive and coarse style, verging on obscenity, is plainly visible in the party's paper, *Limonka*, which glorifies violence against state structures.[46] By dint of the provocative style that its leader seeks to give it, its references to anarchism and to terrorism, and its violent street actions, the NBP can be regarded as more of an attitude produced from youth counterculture than as a political party, especially since Dugin's departure. In the 2000s the NBP has become the principal party of the extra-parliamentarian movement in terms both of number of activists (about 20,000) and of public visibility, despite the authorities having invalidated its registration and rendered it illegal as of June 2005. Since this date, Limonov's supporters, called the *Limonovtsy*, who were already separate from the rest of the so-called radical nationalist movement, have continued to forge for themselves a unique political path, joining a new camp, the "anti-Putin" camp spearheaded by former chess champion Garry Kasparov.

The fourth circle: the marginal factions

Russian ultra-nationalism today is made up of multitudes of associations, of newspapers, and of journals of negligible circulation and uneven regularity. Its doctrines are often poorly worked through conceptually and vary according to a particular leader's prospects for advancement. Its social bases are difficult to determine and it frequently borders on the clandestine. However, it has been possible within the space of its fifteen or so years of existence to watch the most stable movements and their charismatic leaders come to light. Despite the diversity of activities, the parties' personnel are often interchangeable: the same figures meet up, and appear to constitute a fairly unified social milieu. In analyzing this fourth circle, some essential preparatory groundwork must be carried out to avoid falling back onto totalizing and reductive terminology, though the difficulty of the exercise should be kept in mind, since these parties often hold flexible discourses, which, depending on the interlocutor, might advance either a more elitist and refined, or a "catchier," version of their doctrine.

This radical current includes numerous small parties that have attempted to maintain a legal existence. Several of them are worth mentioning: in the 1990s, Alexander Ivanov-Sukharevsky's Popular National Party, Nikolai Lysenko's National Republican Party of Russia, and Aleksei Vdovin and Konstantin Kassimovsky's Russian National Union; in the 2000s, Yuri Belaev's Party of Freedom, and Alexander Sevastianov and Stanislav Terekhov's National Great Power Party. All these movements, which rarely have more than a thousand members, are difficult to differentiate from one another. Never confronted with the realities of being in power, they have neither strategy nor any defined doctrines that enable them to be distinguished from their rivals. All have experienced legal problems, either for inciting racial hatred, for fiscal fraud, or for the illegal storing of arms. They are also often close to mafia networks, organize lucrative commercial activities (particularly related to private security services), and target urban and youth milieus, which themselves often border on delinquency. With their cult of violence, the authoritarian character of their leaders, their belief in a general plot against them uniting enemies of all kinds, their dreams of exalting paramilitary actions, their at once reactionary and revolutionary doctrines, and, finally, their refusal to make any concessions to public opinion, they can be defined as neo-fascist.

The neo-Nazi phenomenon has caused much ink to be spilled in Russia, as it has in the West. At the beginning of the 2000s the Russian skinhead movement was catapulted into public visibility, effectively enabling these extra-parliamentary parties to reject critiques passing them off as mere unrepresentative groupuscules and to affirm the existence of a numerically significant social base that sympathizes with their convictions. On the ideological level the skinhead movement attempts to revive the racist and even exterminatory theories of historical Nazism, and is inspired by American White Power ideology.[47] Largely independent of each other, these groups cultivate their radicalism and provoke shock by exhibiting swastikas and portraits of Hitler. They have been responsible for violent xenophobic actions, particularly against Caucasians and Central Asians, and have attracted attention for their anti-Semitism.[48] The Russian skinhead movement is founded on the Western model and combines a racial ideology of defending whites with provocative lifestyles and fashions, as well as street actions that often seem to be instrumentalized for political gain by the authorities.[49] It is very often linked to the informal movements which emerged from the *underground* culture that has developed in Russia's large cities since the 1980s, for example, a rock nationalist movement. Its degree of radicalism varies, but the movement is particularly significant.

In this last circle, it is important to include the associations that constituted the avant-garde of nationalism at the time of *perestroika*: the spiritual heirs of Pamyat, Alexander Shtilmark's Black Hundreds, two ultra-Orthodox monarchist parties, the Pan-Russian Party of the Monarchic Center, and the Union of the Russian People. These associations claim a century-long ideological continuity by trying to inscribe themselves in a lineage with emigration and dissidence, and by declaring themselves to be the direct descendants of their predecessors of the early 1900s. Today, however, they find themselves marginalized by currents that are much more consensual in their vision of the Soviet experience, and less nostalgic toward tsarism. Monarchists indeed comprise a "minority within a minority," and have nearly lost their place on the spectrum of radical politics, which today is largely dominated by republican convictions.

Questioning the relevance of the ideological "watersheds"

Trying to provide this nationalist kaleidoscope with the internal logic it seems to lack, many works on the extreme right in Russia attempt to base their classifications on doctrinal differences in a bid to separate out and order the particular political categories that make it up. However, it turns out that choosing doctrinal elements to define "radical" nationalism in its totality and to differentiate it from "non-radical" nationalism is not germane: these elements differ according to movement, its leadership figures, their doctrinal influences, and the emphasis placed on specific issues, and often are limited to a "snapshot" of these groups at a given date, thus preventing any account of possible evolutions between *perestroika* and the Putin years. Moreover, all the conceptual combinations are in theory possible: neither the choice of political regime (monarchism or republicanism), the conception of nationhood (culturalist or racialist), nor the special focus or otherwise on the Jewish question or on religious beliefs (orthodox, neo-pagan, or indifferent) makes any meaningful classification possible. It is therefore necessary to question the standard "watersheds" of the nationalist movement, to demonstrate the lack of reality of any left–right binary, the dangers of an immoderate usage of terms such as fascism and Nazism, the false centrality accorded to anti-Semitism in neglect of xenophobia, or the arbitrary nature of the line between an "ethno-nationalist" and an "imperialist" movement.

Russian nationalism in the political spectrum: on the "right" or on the "left"?

It is difficult to attempt to situate nationalism on the right–left spectrum for Russia, as it is more generally. In his typology of right-wing phenomena, René Rémond advances two postulates: first, the plurality of right wings; and, second, their continuity from generation to generation. He does not attempt to explain the right–left division sociologically but rather by means of values such as the relation to the nation, to progress, to revolution, to decentralization, and to freedom. But while this makes sense for precise historical moments, it is inadequate over the long duration, since the right and the left have both appealed to these same values at various points in their history. Right and left, then, are not essentialist notions but relative ones, defined more by their complementarity than by their specific content.[50] These ambiguities, which irrespective of country or epoch are constitutive for defining so-called left-wing and right-wing values, subtend arguments that are both economic and political, and that can be combined in various ways.

During Soviet times, to be accused of following a "rightist path" meant being – or accused of being – compromised to various degrees by the Western political or economic model. In the 1960s a type of Russian nationalism was institutionalized that, as conservative and pro-Stalinist, defined itself as right-wing in a political though not in an economic sense, since it obviously did not wish to foster privatization. Then, during *perestroika*, things were inverted. The right became conservative, which is to say it wanted to maintain the Soviet Union and its economic system; whereas it was the left that militated for movement, change, and therefore for the adoption of market principles. This division of the political spectrum underwent another reversal around 1995–1996, when the introduction of liberal reforms set the right wing once more in favor of "liberalism" and the left in favour of "socialism."[51] The Soviet experience, then, radically complicates any attempt to situate nationalism on either side of a binary divide on the political spectrum, and it demands that the right wing in the economic sense (the right to free enterprise and minimal state intervention) be dissociated from the right wing in the political sense of defending conservative values.

Historically, economic liberalism has had a very weak tradition in Russia: the so-called pro-Western Russian thinkers of the nineteenth century in reality took the West as a model only on the political level. They called for a democratization of the autocracy, and desired a republican, or at least a parliamentary, system. But the majority of them were of socialist sensibility, and few supported economic liberalism.[52] In addition, the material difficulties resulting from the collapse of the USSR, and the radical reforms undertaken under Boris Yeltsin's leadership, have not worked to paint a positive picture of free-market economics. With some exception, contemporary Russian nationalism is above all nostalgic for the Soviet welfare state, and for its social and economic omnipresence. Hence, in Russia the radical right is not anti-communist. Instead, it valorizes the Soviet economic experience: The more extreme it is, the more it glorifies the Stalinist years and the first five-year plans. If instead of focusing on expected economic values one focuses on the political values defended, it is evident that the Russian Communist Party is very clearly "right-wing," and that the "left" (definable in this case by a belief in economic and social progress and the parliamentary system, and by a desire to liberalize mores) is practically non-existent on the electoral scene in Russia.

The vast majority of today's nationalist currents are thus marked by Soviet nostalgia, which presumes a valorization of so-called leftist economic arguments (for example, the presence of state regulators in economic management, and the maintaining of strong nationalized sectors). The issue of land privatization is the most sensitive. Cultural arguments in support of the collective possession of land regarded as being uniquely Russian, coupled with a cult of the Earth Mother, have intensified the resolve of nationalists to reject land privatization, although the privatizing of industry provokes fewer reactions. Conjunction of political liberalism and economic liberalism, then, is rare in the current Russian political field. What we are dealing with here are liberal parties in the political sense – that is, parties oriented toward the Western model that combine parliamentary democracy with a market economy, and that condemn nationalism: the Union of the Right Forces of the former (vice-) prime ministers Boris Nemtsov and Sergei Kirienko, and Grigori Yavlinsky's Yabloko Party. But their electoral results show how weakly this conjunction is represented: neither party succeeded in either 2003 or 2007 in surmounting the 5 percent, then 7 percent, hurdle, and today both are without parliamentary representation.

The "right," however, means much more even on the economic level than simply the market economy. It includes under its banner various demands, for example those for lower taxes, for the protection of artisans and trade, for a reduced number of state employees, and so on. These arguments are mostly used by Vladimir Zhirinovsky's movement, skinhead groups, and the Movement against Illegal Immigration. In the style of Poujadism or of the French Front National, they defend the idea of a kind of neo-liberalism that is favorable to "business" but also concerned about the disappearance of the welfare state. The conjunction of political conservatism and populist economic liberalism, which in the 1990s seemed confined to Zhirinovsky's party, has actually become more extensive in the 2000s. More and more nationalist movements seek to portray themselves as pro the small businesspeople, traders, and artisans who gained from the economic changes resulting from Russia's move toward the private sector. The gradual waning of the idea of state regulation is slowly being replaced by doctrines on the necessary *laissez-faire* required for a market economy. The right–left division thus proves to be quite unhelpful for the study of contemporary Russia and the place occupied in it by nationalism, even on the political checkerboard.

The importation of "Nazism" and "fascism" into Russia

The terms (neo-) Nazism and (neo-) fascism are all too often employed to refer to some sort of dehistoricized reality that dispenses with the need for analysis, in a gesture that is simply content to identify, in an accusatory manner, a phenomenon that, by using the famous *reductio ad Hitlerum* principle, one seeks to discredit. A consistent use of these terms hence presupposes a refusal of their polemical overuse, and a mindfulness of the intellectual and political affiliations they presume. Hence, neo-Nazism is to be understood as referring to currents that openly lay claim to National Socialism in its Hitlerian version, and neo-fascism as referring to those whose with characteristics that can be specifically defined as fascist, whether they acknowledge their debt to Western movements that are by the same token fascist, or whether they reject them while borrowing their ideology. Prior to the end of the USSR, Russian nationalists, even when dissident, had few connections with their Western colleagues, and references to Western nationalist experiences were extremely rare. Theoretical borrowings started to occur, however, in the 1980s, and especially in the 1990s, though they often went unacknowledged.

Russian–Soviet nationalism largely developed around the myth of a people victorious against "fascism," and of the price paid by the Russians during World War II. Still today, school textbooks persist in presenting it as a "patriotic war" of defense of Soviet territory against the German invader. The term "fascism" is systematically used to define German Nazism, which is not distinguished from the Italian case. Nazism is very rarely mentioned, the Nazi regime's racial doctrines are ignored, and the Holocaust is largely minimized. This specifically Soviet culture explains to a great extent why Russian nationalists can positively invoke Nazism only with great difficulty. And it explains why Barkashov's National Unity has had throughout the years to cloak the ideas it has borrowed from Nazism in nuance, and had to expunge its originally positive evaluation of Hitler, for fear of losing its potential appeal. While some radical groups prefer to make references to "National Socialism," a wider term than "Nazism" insofar as it revalorizes the leftist movements of the 1920s liquidated by Hitler, the even more marginal "neo-Nazis" focus uniquely on rehabilitating the institutionalized violence of the 1930s–1940s regime.

There are certain other currents that, while condemning the Western interwar experience and declaring themselves incapable of drawing from its ideological arsenal, use arguments that can be defined as fascist. By this is meant not those references to fascism as a regime, which comprise a significant and non-exclusive use of the term "fascism,"[53] but references to the political and intellectual currents (which emerged at the end of the nineteenth century) that sought to combine a non-Marxist socialism with populist and elitist nationalism, and revolutionary predictions of a new order.[54] Many currents, bolstered by such amalgams, refer in practice to National Bolshevism, since this enables them to make reference to Russian nationalist experiences without having to mention all that they actually owe to the Italian, German, and French experiences. However, there is one case that stands out in relation to this largely disavowed mimicry of the Russian neo-fascist currents, that of Alexander Dugin. He can be considered as one of the rare "Westerners" in the sense that he acknowledges having intentionally imported into Russia political and philosophical theories that were originally formulated in the West.[55]

The spectrum of Russian nationalism is wide, and not all of it can be simply designated "fascist," less still "neo-Nazi." The three main parties with electoral presence, the Communist Party, the LDPR, and Rodina/Fair Russia, are better understood as populist rather than fascist. Their political projects are authoritarian but not totalitarian; they promote a limitation of democracy, not a suppression of its principle; and they call neither for a militarization of society nor for mass indoctrination. Like Western populist parties, the CPRF, the LDPR, and Rodina/Fair Russia do not invoke the fascist practices of the interwar years, and are much more conservative than revolutionary. The currents that can in fact be considered as "neo-fascist" do not have any place in the Russian electoral field and remain on the margins of official political life, while the "neo-Nazis" inhabit only the extreme periphery of these currents. As is the case for all the radical currents, however, these parties are particularly active in the media, especially on the internet, and enjoy a visibility greatly superior to their real sociological representation.

If we want to avoid visions of a large reified set grouped under the term "fascist threat," it is necessary to take into account both terminological differentiations and the interest attached to particular doctrines. In Russia, "fascist threat" is an expression that only goes to serve the objectives of the authorities, and that makes impossible any assessment of the diverse underlying intellectual traditions. For example, the National Bolshevik Party's totally unforeseen political career since 2006 and its move away from other movements of the radical spectrum are partly explicable by its anchorage in a doctrine that extols the virtues of revolutionary action over glorification of the nation.

The place of anti-Semitism in Russian nationalism

The place of anti-Semitism in Russian nationalist theories is complex. Up until the last decades of the nineteenth century the main intellectual currents of nationalism, such as Slavophilism and Pan-Slavism, were not really concerned with the "Jewish question," even if the official policies of the tsarist empire were clearly discriminatory against its Jewish minority. Radically anti-Semitic groups, modeled on Western movements, appeared only at the beginning of the twentieth century. During Soviet times, Stalin's decades-long reign saw an unprecedented targeting of the Jewish enemy, construed in terms of cosmopolitanism. After Khrushchev's eviction, official Soviet anti-Semitism took on a new metaphor in the so-called discipline of Zionology, and was accompanied by a militant foreign policy. The Soviet delegation to the United Nations, for example, was the principal instigator of the 1975 resolution denouncing Zionism as "a form of racism and of racial discrimination."[56] Then, during the 1970s and 1980s, many highly respected intellectual figures started diffusing anti-Semitism, for example the academician Igor Shafarevich (1923) in his pamphlet *Russophobia*,[57] the ethnologist Lev Gumilev (1912–1992) in his works on the Jewish Khazaria of the eighth and ninth centuries,[58] or still more so Vadim Kozhinov (1930–2000) in his *History of Russia and of Russian Literature.*

Perestroika allowed expressions of anti-Semitism to emerge into broad daylight. Recourse to the Zionist metaphor was no longer needed, and several well-known "Zionologists" from Soviet times, such as Valeri Skurlatov, Valeri Emelianov, Evgeni Evseev, and Vladimir Begun, became members of the Pamyat movement.[59] Today every nationalist movement exploits the "Jewish question" in its own way. Some grant it only limited importance, especially so-called statist movements (Kurginian, for example, denounces the myth of the Jewish plot that animates the ethno-nationalists[60]). However, others turn it into the matrix of their conspiratorial discourse, in the form of either traditional anti-Judaism or racial anti-Semitism. Vadim Rossman has classified anti-Semitic currents into five categories depending on their specific conception of the nation, variously defined in terms of geopolitics (the neo-Eurasianists), of religion (the Orthodox nationalists), of the social (the neo-Bolshevik Nationalists), of the cultural (the neo-Slavophiles), or of the racial (the neo-Nazi factions).[61] The most ambiguous current of Russian nationalism in its relation to Jews remains Eurasianism. The neo-Eurasists, in particular Alexander Dugin, are much more anti-Semitic than the founding fathers of the movement, and consider the opposition between Jews and Russians as fundamental. Nevertheless, Dugin has developed a complex system of thought in which he also declares that Israel is the only country to have successfully put into practice many of the principles of conservative revolution for which he calls.[62]

Within the National Bolshevik movements, anti-Semitism is present but does not occupy an important place, since here the Jews are only a symbol of capitalism and liberalism, and it is the two latter that stand accused of being responsible for the economic collapse of post-Soviet Russia. This movement is strictly opposed to the neo-Slavophiles, for whom communism, on the contrary, is a foreign ideology that was imposed on Russia by Jews. In neo-Slavophile discourse one can find all the classic themes of the Judeo-Bolshevik conspiracy. The great political figures of the USSR, alleged to have been "all Jews," are said to have been on a mission to bring about Russia's demise. Close to the neo-Slavophiles, the nationalist Orthodoxy movement insists on the notion that the Jewish conspiracy is not basically economic but religious, its aim being to destroy the only remaining Christian people, the Russians. Inspired in part by the works of Metropolitan John of St. Petersburg (1927–1995), this tendency plays the card of a deicide, regicide, and infanticide people, and appears to enjoy the more or less explicit support of the patriarchate.[63] In neo-Nazi factions, which constitute the most marginal current of contemporary nationalism, the opposition between Russians and Jews is construed in racial terms similar to that between Aryans and Semites, where the latter stand accused of "corrupting" the genetic pool of the Slavs.[64]

The so-called Jewish question is therefore not a matter of indifference to any of the Russian nationalist movements. All of them propagate one style or other of anti-Semitism, covering the entire spectrum of positions, which range from religious accusations that the Jews are a deicide people, to references to race, or simply economics, or pro- or anti-communism. At the end of the 1990s, more than 200 low-circulation newspapers were regarded as anti-Semitic,[65] but this considerable discursive presence rarely led to violent acts against Jews (graffiti, desecration of cemeteries, or vandalism). In practice, the main targets of radical xenophobic factions were the more easily "identifiable" immigrant populations. Nevertheless, in recent years violent acts against synagogues seem to have multiplied. More, the socially accepted nature of public references to some people's

Jewishness is perturbing. Within the public arena, for example, it is common, and totally acceptable, to point to the "Jewish origins" of some oligarchs. Similarly, in politically engaged milieus the term "Russophone" (*russkoiazychnyi*) is endowed with strong connotations and is used as a euphemism to designate those whose maternal language is Russian but who are not "ethnically" Russian, which is to say Jews. According to numerous opinions polls, more than 60 percent of the Russian population would oppose a president of the republic of an Israelite confession,[66] revealing the old and deeply rooted nature of this problem in Russian society. So, even if anti-Semitic acts remain infrequent, the current intellectual background has made possible the emergence of a "climate of opinion" that is quite considerably anti-Semitic.

In the political field, the more respectable a party wants to be, the more its anti-Semitism has to be kept to a minimum or veiled – that is, dressed up as an accusation of Zionism or cosmopolitism. Xenophobia, however, can be openly expressed without adversely affecting electoral success. It might also be noted that conspiracy theories may focus more on the West than on the Jews, even if a link between the two is made. Feelings of Russia's defeat seem to warrant blaming the "West" for its woes, which thereby takes the heat off the symbolically classic enemy, the Jews. One of the reasons for this differentiation between, on the one hand, anti-Semitism and, on the other, xenophobia and anti-Westernism relates to the political tactics of the authorities themselves. The authorities are hardly likely to engage in anti-Semitic rhetoric, but, for obvious political reasons linked to the Caucasus, they greatly instrumentalize popular resentment against "foreigners," and seem to consider criticizing the West a "politically correct" thing to do.

Orthodoxy or neo-paganism?

The issue of religion has always produced splits within the nationalist movement. Indeed, the universal character of Christianity (and also of Islam) poses problems for those who are unable to accept religion's transnational character, and who claim a collective specificity that also extends to the religious level. In addition, Christianity's historical and theological links with Judaism do not find favor with these movements, which, albeit to differing degrees, are quasi-systematically driven by anti-Semitism. Hence, the search for a pre-Christian national religion has become one of the characteristic elements of some nationalist, and often radical, movements, which stand opposed to all those who content themselves with invoking Christianity and glorifying a presumed medieval or modern national past in which it is alleged to have played a dominant cultural role.

In Russia the revalorization of ancient Slavic paganism has also sparked much debate. However, if its rehabilitation is difficult to date, it should be noted that during tsarist times not one nationalist current, not even the Aryanists, sought to reject Orthodoxy in favor of paganism. All were content to combine the myth of the Aryan origin of the Slavs with a traditional Orthodox sensibility.[67] Instead, the neo-pagan phenomenon emerged during Soviet times, and probably from out of the Stalinist nationalist circles that aimed to rehabilitate Slavic identity. The movement became institutionalized during *perestroika* with the foundation, in 1988, of the Society of the Magi, and then, in 1990, of the Union of the Veneds, the very group which, within a particularly fertile amorphous series of groupings, continues today to be one of the chief neo-pagan associations.[68] The cultural references made by neo-pagan associations are of two types. Some are inspired by Western movements and are close to the international journal *Hyperborée*, while others trace a specifically Russian line of descent from a paganism based on the false manuscript of the Book of Vles. Some associations are not particularly politicized but instead highly intellectualized. This is the case for Thesaurus, which is close to Russian theosophist and anthroposophical groups, but not for the Union of the Veneds and Ilia Lazarenko's Church of Nav, which are quite clearly partisan and incline more toward public demonstrations. Few, however, have institutionalized specific forms of religious ritual or worship, the majority of them being content to advocate paganism more as a national philosophy rather than as a religious practice.[69]

What seems to distinguish Russian neo-paganism from its Western counterparts is its resolve to make itself compatible with Orthodoxy. There are some systematically and violently anti-Christian currents, but they are rather in the minority on the neo-pagan spectrum. In the 1970s this syncretic rhetoric was capitalized on by the great figures of Russian nationalism. Thus, not only Glazunov and Rasputin but also Shafarevich repeatedly declared that Orthodoxy had always maintained close links to ancient paganism, and that this "double faith"[70] clearly distinguished it from other Christian confessions. The Orthodox cross is thus supposed to represent the Slavic version of the swastika, a symbol of the intimate connection between these two religions, and of the fundamentally national and non-universal character of Orthodoxy. If the neo-paganists have not launched calls for the converted to gather together in the religious sense, it is nonetheless the case that neo-paganism thoroughly innervates Russian society, in which it has disseminated nationalist historical themes that are fully compatible with Orthodox sentiment. Its success as a national, rather than religious, doctrine can be in part explained by the legacy of Soviet atheism itself. Even nationalists on the search for a strictly national faith have a hard time identifying with the message of Christianity. They find it much easier to adhere to a so-called religion that requires neither regular ritual practice nor theological background, but only a glorification of the nation and of the earth.

If this conjunction between neo-paganism and Orthodoxy has been made possible, it is also because Orthodoxy has major nationalist currents within it. In fact, the patriarchate is divided into numerous tendencies, some of which are openly involved in political life and are represented by highly ranked individuals within the ecclesiastic hierarchy.[71] Patriarch Alexei II himself would prefer to see Orthodoxy given a privileged institutional status and was critical of secularism and secularization. Although in these respects he did not belong to the most radical currents, he has preferred to support these latter rather than to give expression to moderates and reformers, whom he had blocked from attaining important institutional positions. Notable among the most radical movements are the Orthodox Brotherhood, the Gonfalon-carriers, the "Christian Rebirth" association of the former dissident of *Veche*, Vladimir Osipov (who holds more liberal views than do his members and deputies), and the more recent movement that is opposed to the introduction of individual computer codes. All these groupings are recognizable by their nostalgia, which is more monarchist than Soviet, and by their conservative or reactionary political aspirations.[72]

Outside the patriarchate there are also numerous associations that lay claim to an Orthodox heritage, and variously exploit the question of faith.[73] However, it is impossible not to be struck by the low level of religious practice in Russia. The results of sociological surveys reveal that the number of people who frequent places of worship is similar to that in Western European countries, hence very low. Nevertheless, the space devoted to Orthodoxy in the public realm in Russia, both as institution and as a point of moral reference, is quite considerable. And it actually seems to be becoming even more pronounced, as the political authorities lend it more support. The Church quite naturally tends to capitalize on this "clericalization" of society by making increasingly specific demands. In 2003, for example, it went so far as to demand the introduction of courses on Orthodox culture in primary schools. Moreover, the current trend within the nationalist movements of calling for the canonization of the great political figures of the monarchy is particularly revealing of the high degree to which religious issues are currently conflated with national historical symbols. The contemporary situation is thus revealing of the extent to which religion is instrumentalized as a political referent, and of its particularly developed identitarian role.[74]

Imperial expansion or ethnic withdrawal?

Many researchers, albeit using differing terminology, have divided Russian nationalism into two camps: one that gives priority to the state; and one that is centered solely on the ethnicity of the Russian people.[75] This division is pertinent insofar as it constitutes the fault line at the heart of Russian nationalism – that is, the relation to the state and the empire. Indeed, Russia has never had a state without an empire. By the twelfth and thirteenth centuries the principality of Novgorod already extended as far as the Urals. With the founding of Moscow in the same epoch, the Russian state, although barely in existence at the level of institutions or central power, was already an empire in full territorial expansion, to the detriment of the Finno-Ugric populations of Russia's north. After the fall of Kazan and Astrakhan in 1552 and 1556 respectively, Russia began to extend its domination over the entirety of Siberia, capturing lands that had been part of the Mongol Empire. In the nineteenth century it was at its most extensive, occupying the Far East and Central Asia, and found itself directly confronting not only China and Japan but also Great Britain. Moreover, the place that could be considered in territorial terms to be its "original core," the Principality of Kiev, is today situated in Ukraine. How, then, can this rupture between state and nation be overcome by the emergence of a national feeling that is no longer solely founded on dynastic fidelity rather but on the glorification of the people, considered as the primary source of political legitimacy?

Russian nationalism of tsarist times, like that of Soviet and post-Soviet times, has as its chief internal rupture and "Gordian knot" the relation to this state that one would like to be one's own but which is not wholly so. This impossibility of identifying oneself with the state or empire is not unilateral since, for its part, the state entity does not necessarily recognize itself in Russian nationalism. Indeed, it has always tried to oppose nationalism so as to maintain the internal balance of the empire, and yet, when and as needed, has instrumentalized various ethnic elements. The disappearance of the USSR has only accentuated the problem, just as the creation of a federal Soviet structure and the loss of Western territories (Finland, Poland) did not help to resolve the matter after the fall of the monarchy. Still today, Russia is a federal state in which national minorities have recognized rights: in no official text is it stated that "ethnic" Russians (*russkie*) constitute an eponymous nation. The state instead promotes a *Rossian* civic identity (*rossiiskii*), which is not recognized as pertaining to any specific ethnic group. The vast spread of the Russian language, the Federation's territorial expanse, not to mention the even vaster expanse of the tsarist empire, or that of the Soviet Union, cover an area larger than anything that could be defined as being "ethnically" Russian. This relation is complicated by a converse phenomenon that has come about only recently, namely the presence of approximately 20 million people who claim to be Russian but live outside Russia in the near abroad. Thus, the addition of the phenomenon of Russians living outside Russia to the older one of non-Russian peoples living in Russia has only worked to compound the issue.

During Soviet times the nationalist spectrum was generally divided between, on the one hand, those who upheld notions of cultural and religious primacy, of national rebirth, of the Slavophile heritage, and of the tsarist past and, on the other, those for whom what essentially mattered was the strength of the state and who saw in Stalinism the crowning moment of Russia's development. The former more often found themselves in difficult positions with the authorities and circulated predominantly in dissident milieus, whereas the latter more regularly enjoyed the support of the state apparatus and the Party, since their nationalist sentiment was fully compatible with Soviet patriotism. This binary division should nonetheless be qualified: it cannot have complete explanatory value or be thought of along essentialist lines. Though it defines two ideal types, it does not enable the devising of a definitive classificatory typology that would leave no political current without the right of appeal, since not all of them fit unilaterally into one of the schemas, and many combine both. Several great nationalist figures have switched from one side to the other, particularly after the fall of the USSR, a time when nationalists who had been very critical of the Soviet experiment suddenly became nostalgic for it. This bipolarity also recalls that which exists between the so-called French and German conceptions of the nation, which in reality are antagonistic only in polemical works resolved to oppose them and are much less so in the opinions of nationalists themselves.

Finally, this division should not be taken to imply that the statist movement is not itself also part of nationalism. Some scholars do seem to imply this, but they unintentionally repeat the accusations the "ethno-nationalists" direct at the "statists." Numerous debates between these two movements have taken place concerning this topic. The neo-Eurasianists, who are the most radical in their insistence on empire, have been criticized for almost two decades by the "ethno-nationalists," who accuse them of aspiring to destroy the unity of the Russian people by expending it demographically in service of the other peoples of the empire.[76] Among the ethno-nationalist movements, one nonetheless ought to differentiate between those who bear a racialist conception, and who are in the minority, and those who limit themselves to an ethnicized definition of the nation, even if both conceptions are not always sufficiently distinct in the minds of those who propagate them. Throughout the existence of the Soviet Union the study of racial issues was considered inappropriate. The notion was widespread that not even tsarist Russia ever knew such types of determinist questioning. Today, breaking this taboo remains difficult, even as ethnicist conceptions of peoples are being widely disseminated throughout intellectual and political discourses in post-Soviet republics. The function of racism has thus in large part been replaced with ethnicism, which, for its part, is very firmly rooted in Russo-Soviet traditions, such as those of differentialism and ethno-pluralism. So, although racial conceptions of inferior–superior hierarchical relations between peoples are uncommon, essentialist definitions of the national collectivity are particularly widespread.

However, rarely do ethno-nationalist currents follow their argument to its logical conclusion by resolving for the constitution of an ethnically pure Russian state, or their adherents declaring themselves ready to abandon territories and advocate isolationism. Separatist sentiments do exist among Russians, and many radical groups have repeatedly called either for the official recognition of "ethnic" Russians as the eponymous people of Russia or for the constitution of new administrative subjects that would grant ethnic Russians specific rights, as if they were only a minority among others. However, in reality the majority of ethno-nationalists want the existing borders of the Federation to be preserved, or even to see former republics return to Russia's fold, on the condition that the native peoples do not enjoy any autonomy and are forced to recognize that they inhabit a state belonging to Russians, which would involve according linguistic primacy to Russian, religious supremacy to Orthodoxy, abolition of the federal status of the country, and so on.

On the other hand, the statists themselves combine ethno-nationalist traits with their imperialist designs. Even if figures such as Zhirinovsky or Dugin advocate rebuilding the Russian Empire, neither of them desire equality of rights for the various so-called Eurasian peoples, instead wanting Russians, in the ethnic sense of the term, to enjoy political supremacy. Both also play the card of glorifying religious and cultural national specificity, and make ethnicist, or even racialist, remarks concerning the Russian people. In addition, the "statists" (*gosudarstvenniki* or *derzhavniki*) are divided among themselves on the issue of which state borders should be preserved or restored. Some hold an imperialist vision of Russia, which they think has a vocation to take back control of the former Soviet space, while others adhere to the notion that Russia should be a great power but one limited to the present territorial borders of the Federation. The former believe in a state that would achieve a "horizontal" or extensive expression, whereas the latter are staunch supporters of Putin's much-vaunted reinforcing of the vertical axis of power, and opt for an "intensive" state that occupies a more restricted space.

As the 1990s progressed, ethno-nationalist and statist lines of argument were to a large extent conflated. Though each side continued to maintain a preference for one of the approaches, they both propagated notions expressing the supposed continuity of the Russian state, irrespective of the regime, discounted the notion of sharp ruptures in identity, and demanded that Russia be less federal and more ethnically uniform. Since 1992 there have been many attempts at fusing ideologies, assumed to be the task of trying to unify the nationalist currents around essentially emotional and present-day values. The Soviet experiment, partly in spite of itself, played into the hands of Russian nationalism: the disappearance of the regime as well as of its opponents enabled the USSR to be reintegrated *post mortem* into the Russian nationalist imaginary.[77] The attempt to classify radical nationalist movements according to doctrine thus appears doomed to failure: although each movement can be presented in its specificity, through its combination of specific ideological elements and its political career over the past twenty years, it continues to be difficult, or indeed impossible, to classify these movements systematically by placing them with respect to global criteria such as a right–left spectrum or an ethno-nationalism–imperialism binomial. Moreover, the development of new forms of radicality that are less ideological but have a more developed social base has caused these classifications little by little to lose their interest, signaling a new phase in the evolution of nationalist thought and policy in Russia.

The problems thrown up by the often difficult relations between Russian nationalism and the state, which were especially acute in Soviet times, and also in the Yeltsin era, during which many nationalist movements argued that the liberal state was foreign to Russia, today appear to be undergoing a complete recasting. Vladimir Putin's success has resided precisely in his ability to monopolize certain themes that hitherto had been the sole province of nationalists. Now finding themselves dispossessed of their discourse, the nationalists have lost one of their main social functions. All the same, Putin's intention seemed to be to privilege a statist understanding of the Russian nation, albeit one that is not free of ethnicist themes. This instrumentalization of nationalism by the political authorities is thus continuous with the ever-ambiguous relationship that, since the nineteenth century, the Russian authorities have entertained with the idea of Russian nationalism.

Notes

1 E. C. Thaden, *Conservative Nationalism in Nineteenth Century Russia*, Seattle: University of Washington Press, 1964.

2 In Western languages, readers may consult W. Dowler, *Dostoïevski, Grigoriev and Native Soil Conservatism*, Toronto: University of Toronto Press, 1982; D. Stremooukhoff, *Soloviev et son œuvre messianique*, Lausanne: L'Âge d'homme, 1975; L. Gerstein, *Nikolaï Strakhov: Philosopher, Man of Letters, Social Critic*, Cambridge, MA: Harvard University Press, 1971; S. Lukashevich, *Konstantin Leontev: A Study in Russian "Heroic Vitalism"*, New York: Pageant Press, 1967; S. Lukashevich, *N. F. Fedorov: A Study in Russian Eupsychian and Utopian Thought*, Newark: University of Delaware Press, 1977.

3 H. Rogger and E. Weber (eds.), *The European Right: A Historical Profile*, Berkeley: University of California Press, 1965; C. Rawson, *Russian Rightists and the Revolution of 1905*, Cambridge: Cambridge University Press, 1995.

4 For a history of the *Protocols*, see P.-A. Taguieff, *Les Protocoles des Sages de Sion. Faux et usages d'un faux*, Paris: Berg International–Fayard, 2004. On the place occupied by the Jewish question on the Russian right wing, see H. Rogger, *Jewish Policies and Right-Wing Politics in Imperial Russia*, London: Macmillan, 1986.

5 Not all share this viewpoint, and many scholars believe that already at the beginning of the twenthieth century, Russia had all the traits necessary for the emergence of fascist trends. H. Rogger, "Was there a Russian Fascism? The Union of Russian People," *Journal of Modern History*, 4, 1964, 398–415.

6 M. Laruelle, *L'Idéologie eurasiste russe ou comment penser l'empire*, Paris: L'Harmattan, 1999.

7 E. Oberlander, "The All-Russian Fascist Party," *Journal of Contemporary History*, 1, 1966, 158–73; J. Stephan, *Russkie fashisty. Tragediia i farsh v emigratsii, 1925–1945*, Moscow: Slovo, 1992.

8 N. Mitrokhin, "La mythologie ethno-nationaliste au sein de l'appareil du Parti et de l'État en Union soviétique," in M. Laruelle and C. Servant (eds.), *D'une édification l'autre. Socialisme et nation dans l'espace (post-)communiste*, Paris: Petra, 2008, pp. 23–42.

9 L. Rapoport, *Stalin's War Against the Jews: The Doctors' Plot and the Soviet Solution*, New York: Free Press, 1990; G. V. Kostyrchenko, *Out of the Red Shadows: Anti-Semitism in Stalin's Russia*, New York: Prometheus Books, 1995.

10 Y. M. Brudny, *Reinventing Russia: Russian Nationalism and the Soviet State, 1953–1991*, Cambridge, MA: Harvard University Press, 2000, p. 46.

11 V. S.-E. Zawilski, "Saving Russia: The Development of Nationalist Thought among the Russian Intelligentsia, 1965–1985," thesis, University of Toronto, 1996.

12 N. Mitrokhin, *"Russkaia partiia": dvizhenie russkikh natsionalistov v SSSR 1953–1985 gg*, Moscow: NLO, 2003.

13 Brudny, *Reinventing Russia*, p. 103.

14 On the ambiguous relations of power to nationalist literary movements in the Brezhnev years, and later in those of Andropov and of Chernenko, see J. B. Dunlop, *The New Russian Nationalism*, New York: Praeger, 1985.

15 Brudny, *Reinventing Russia*, p. 127.

16 K. Parthé, *Russian Village Prose: The Radiant Past*, Princeton, NJ: Princeton University Press, 1992.

17 K. O'Connor, *Intellectuals and Apparatchiks: Russian Nationalism and the Gorbachev Revolution*, Lanham, MD: Rowan & Littlefield, 2006.

18 The Battle of Kulikovo (1380) marks one of the first Russian victories over the Mongol Empire. Prince Dmitri Donskoi succeeded in inflicting a major blow to the troops of the Golden Horde led by Khan Mamay and by this means affirmed Moscow's domination over the other Russian principalities, thereby signalling the start of a process to "unify Russian lands."

19 V. Pribylovski, "Le mouvement Pamiat, 'école des cadres' du nationalisme russe durant la perestroika," in M. Laruelle (ed.), *Le Rouge et le noir. Extrême droite et nationalisme en Russie*, Paris: CNRS-Éditions, 2007, pp. 99–114.

20 W. Korey, *Russian Antisemitism, Pamyat and the Demonology of Zionism*, Chur: Harwood Academic Publishers for the Vidal Sassoon International Center for the Study of Antisemitism, Hebrew University of Jerusalem, 1995, pp. 115–146.
21 J. B. Dunlop, *The Rise of Russia and the Fall of the Soviet Empire*, Princeton, NJ: Princeton University Press, pp. 165–169.
22 W. Laqueur, *Histoire des droites en Russie. Des centuries noires aux nouveaux extrémistes*, Paris: Michalon, 1996, pp. 271–273.
23 S. Lebedev, *Russkie idei i russkoe delo. Natsional'no-patrioticheskoe dvizhenie v Rossii v proshlom i nastoiashchem*, St. Petersburg: Aleteiia, 2007, p. 350.
24 P. Zawadzki, "Les populismes en Pologne," in P.-A. Taguieff (ed.), *Le Retour du populisme. Un défi pour les démocraties européennes*, Paris: Universalis, 2004, p. 69.
25 J. B. Dunlop, *The New Russian Revolutionaries*, Belmont, MA: Nordland, 1976.
26 D. Hammer, "Vladimir Osipov and the Vetche Group (1971–1974): A Page from the History of Political Dissent," *Russian Review*, 4, 1984, 355–375; P. Duncan, "The Fate of Russian Nationalism: The Samizdat Journal Vetche Revisited," *Religion in Communist Lands*, 16, 1, 1988, 36–53.
27 For a general history of the dissident movement, see C. Vaissié, *Pour votre liberté et pour la nôtre*, Paris: Robert Laffont, 1999.
28 S. P. Ramet, *The Radical Right in Central and Eastern Europe since 1989*, University Park: Pennsylvania State University, 1999.
29 M. Laruelle (ed.), *Sovremennye interpretatsii russkogo natsionalizma*, Stuttgart, ibidem-Verlag, 2007; same editor, *Russkii natsionalizm. Sotsial'nyi i kul'turnyi kontekst*, Moscow: NLO, 2008.
30 M. Laruelle, "The Discipline of Culturology: A New 'Ready-Made Thought' for Russia?" *Diogenes*, 204, 2004, 21–36.
31 G. Flikke, "Patriotic Left-Centrism: The Zigzags of the Communist Party of the Russian Federation," *Europe–Asia Studies*, 51, 2, 1999, 277. On the CPRF, see L. March, *The Communist Party in Post-Soviet Russia*, Manchester: Manchester University Press, 2002.
32 On the birth of leftist extremism in contemporary Russia, see A. Verkhovsky, A. Papp, and V. Pribylovsky, *Politicheskii ekstremizm v Rossii*, Moscow: Panorama, 1996, pp. 76–81.
33 For more details, consult A. Verkhovsky (ed.), *Levye v Rossii. Ot umerennykh do ekstremistov*, Moscow: Institut eksperimental'noi sotsiologii, 1997.
34 See, for example, G. Frazer and G. Lancelle, *Absolute Zhirinovsky: A Transparent View of the Distinguished Russian Statesman*, New York: Penguin, 1994; E. Klepikova and V. Solov'ev, *Zhirinovsky: Russian Fascism and the Making of a Dictator*, Reading, MA: Addison-Wesley, 1995, etc. For a more detailed analysis of the literature, see A. Umland, "The Post-Soviet Russian Extreme Right," *Problems of Post-communism*, 44, 4, 1997, 53–61.
35 P.-A. Taguieff, *L'Illusion populiste. De l'archaïque au médiatique*, Paris: Berg International, 2002, p. 80.
36 P. Milza, *L'Europe en chemise noire. Les extrêmes droites en Europe de 1945 à aujourd'hui*, Paris: Flammarion, 2002, p. 316.
37 A. Titkov, *Party No. 4. Rodina: Whence and Why?* Moscow: Panorama, 2006.
38 M. Laruelle, "La question des Russes du proche-étranger en Russie (1991–2006)," *Étude du CERI*, 126, 2006, 38 pp.
39 For more details, see M. Laruelle, "*Rodina*: les mouvances nationalistes russes, du loyalisme à l'opposition," *Kiosque du CERI*, May 2006, 17 pp., www.ceri-sciencespo.com/archive/mai06/artml.pdf (accessed 2 July 2008).
40 T. Parland, "Russia in the 1990s: Manifestations of a Conservative Backlash Philosophy," in C. J. Chulos and T. Piirainen (eds.), *The Fall of an Empire, the Birth of a Nation: National Identities in Russia*, Aldershot, UK: Ashgate, 2000, pp. 116–140.
41 V. Likhachev, *Natsizm v Rossii*, Moscow: Panorama, 2002, p. 13.

42 J. B. Dunlop, "Alexander Barkashov and the Rise of National Socialism in Russia," *Demokratizatsiia*, 4, 1996, 519–530; S. G. Simonsen, "Alexandr Barkashov and Russian National Unity: Blackshirt Friends of the Nation," *Nationalities Papers*, 4, 1996, 625–639.
43 On legal questions, see A. Verkhovsky, E. Mikhailovskaia, and V. Pribylovsky, *Politicheskaia ksenofobiia. Radikal'nye gruppy, Predstavlenie liderov, Rol' tserkvi*, Moscow: Panorama, 1999, pp. 50–59.
44 For a biography, see A. Rogachevski, *A Biographical and Critical Study of Russian Writer Eduard Limonov*, Studies in Slavic Language and Literature 20, Lewiston, NY: Edwin Mellen Press, 2003.
45 Likhachev, *Natsizm v Rossii*, p. 66.
46 S. D. Shenfield, *Russian Fascism: Traditions, Tendencies, Movements*, New York: M. E. Sharpe, 2001, p. 207.
47 V. Shnirel'man, *"Chistil'shchiki moskovskikh ulits." Skinkhedy, SMI i obshchestvennoe mnenie*, Moscow: Academia, 2007.
48 Likhachev, *Natsizm v Rossii*, pp. 108–136.
49 For example, with the support of Major Yuri Luzhkov, skinhead groups in Moscow have served to make immigrants flee. N. Mitrokhin, "Ot Pamiati k skinkhedam Luzhkova. Ideologiia russkogo natsionalizma v 1987–2003 gg.," *Neprikosnovennyi zapas*, 31, 2003, 37–43.
50 R. Rémond, *Les Droites en France*, Paris: Aubier, 1982.
51 G. Evans and S. Whitefield, "The Evolution of Left and Right in Post-Soviet Russia," *Europe–Asia Studies*, 50, 6, 1998, 1023–1042.
52 F. Venturi, *Les Intellectuels, le peuple et la révolution. Histoire du populisme russe au XIX*[e] siècle, Paris: Gallimard, 1972.
53 P. Milza, *Les Fascismes*, Paris: Seuil, 1991.
54 Z. Sternhell, *Les Droites révolutionnaires en France, 1885–1914*, Paris: Seuil, 1997.
55 M. Laruelle, *Eurasianism in Russia: The Ideology of Empire*, Washington, DC: Johns Hopkins University Press–Woodrow Wilson Press, 2008, pp. 107–144.
56 A. Umland, "Soviet Anti-Semitism after Stalin," *East European Jewish Affairs*, 29, 1–2, 1999, 159–168 at p. 165.
57 J. B. Dunlop, "The 'Sad Case' of Igor Shafarevitch," *Soviet Jewish Affairs*, 1, 1994, 19–30; A. A. Znamenski, "In Search of the Russian Idea: Igor Shafarevitch's Traditional Orthodoxy," *European Studies Journal*, 1, 1996, 33–48.
58 V. Shnirelman, *The Myth of the Khazars and Intellectual Antisemitism in Russia, 1970–1990s*, Jerusalem: Vidal Sassoon International Center for the Study of Antisemitism, Hebrew University of Jerusalem, 2002.
59 Korey, *Russian Antisemitism, Pamyat and the Demonology of Zionism*.
60 S. Kurginian, "Natsional'naia doktrina," *Rossiia*, 2, 1993, 21–24.
61 V. Rossman, *Russian Intellectual Antisemitism in the Post-communist Era*, Vidal Sassoon International Center for the Study of Antisemitism, Hebrew University of Jerusalem, Lincoln: University of Nebraska Press, 2002.
62 Laruelle, *Eurasianism in Russia*, pp. 107–144.
63 V. Likhachev, *Politicheskii antisemitizm v sovremennoi Rossii*, Moscow: Academia, 2003, pp. 136–155.
64 V. Shnirel'man, "Tsepnoi pes rasy": divannaia rasologiia kak zashchitnitsa "belogo cheloveka," Moscow: SOVA, 2007, http://xeno.sova-center.ru/29481C8/9EB7A7E (accessed 17 July 2008).
65 Rossman, *Russian Intellectual Antisemitism in the Post-communist Era*, p. 4.
66 Ibid., p. 8.
67 M. Laruelle, *Mythe aryen et rêve impérial dans la Russie du XIX*[e] siècle, Paris: CNRS-Éditions, 2005.
68 E. Moroz, *Istoriia "Mertvoi vody" – ot strashnoi skazki k bol'shoi politike. Politicheskoe neoiazychestvo v postsovetskoi Rossii*, Stuttgart: ibidem-Verlag, 2005.

69 M. Laruelle, "Alternative Identity, Alternative Religion? Neo-paganism and the Aryan Myth in Contemporary Russia," *Nations and Nationalism*, 14, 2, 2008, 283–301.

70 The "double faith" phenomenon is well attested by numerous historical and ethnological sources that demonstrate the persistence of pagan rituals and concepts that existed within Orthodoxy, and parallel to it in the Russian peasant world right up until the upheavals the latter underwent in the twentieth century. Cf. P. Pascal, *La Religion du peuple russe*, Lausanne: L'Âge d'homme, 1973.

71 A. Verkhovsky, V. Pribylovsky, and E. Mikhailovskaia, *Natsionalizm i ksenofobiia v rossiiskom obshchestve*, Moscow: Panorama, 1998, pp. 168–189.

72 A. Verkhovsky, *Politicheskoe pravoslavie. Russkie pravoslavnye natsionalisty i fundamentalisty, 1995–2001*, Moscow: SOVA, 2003.

73 K. Rousselet, "L'Église orthodoxe russe entre patriotisme et individualisme," *XX*[e] siècle. Revue d'histoire, April–June 2000, pp. 13–24.

74 M. Gauchet, *La Religion dans la démocratie. Parcours de la laïcité*, Paris: Gallimard, 1998.

75 Some authors divide these two tendencies into multiple configurations. For example, Vera Tolz gives five possible definitions of the Russian nation: an imperial or Eurasian unifying vision, a nation of the Eastern Slavic peoples, a community of Russophones, a racial definition, and a civic identity. See V. Tolz, "Forging the Nation: National Identity and Nation Building in Post-communist Russia," *Europe–Asia Studies*, 50, 6, 1998, 993–1022.

76 A good example of such polemics is that which opposed the ethno-nationalist Ksenia Mialo to the neo-Eurasianists in the 1990s. Such oppositions already existed in the Soviet era, where, for example, the Eurasianist historian Lev Gumilev was subjected to critiques by ethno-nationalists like Apollon Kuzmin, who accused him of wanting to make Russian people disappear in the service of Turkic populations.

77 Thus, on 15 March 1996 the Duma withdrew its recognition of the Minsk Agreement of 8 December 1991, which was voted in by its predecessor the Supreme Soviet, and instead decided to recognize the legality of the referendum of 17 March 1991, in which 70 percent of the population voted in favor of maintaining the USSR.

3 Stalinism and Russian nationalism

A reconceptualization

Veljko Vujačić

In a recent article in *Foreign Affairs*, Sarah Mendelson and Theodore Gerber and have demonstrated the highly ambivalent attitude of young and adult Russians towards Stalin. Using three surveys of several thousand Russians carried out between 2003 and 2005, these two researchers have come up with some astonishing results. Thus, fewer than one-half of all respondents in one of the surveys categorically rejected the idea that they would vote for Stalin if he were alive, while some 13 percent of respondents under the age of 30 stated that they would definitely vote for him. In another survey a full 51 percent of respondents regarded Stalin as a "wise leader" (39 percent disagreed), 43 percent thought that Stalin's role in the repressions was exaggerated (47 percent disagreed), and only a minority (28 percent) thought that Stalin should not be credited with victory in World War II. These results seem all the more surprising in view of the fact that most Russians (70 percent) are fully aware that Stalin executed millions of people.

Mendelson and Gerber also found that less educated and adult Russians over 30 are more likely to be "supportive of Stalin," but are rightly disturbed by the fact that younger Russians show considerable ignorance of the tragic Stalinist past, a finding confirmed in their focus-group interviews. Although Mendelson and Gerber are cautious not to conflate these ambivalent and contradictory attitudes toward Stalin with support for "Stalinism," and partially attribute the "confusion of youth" to the officially approved change in Russian textbooks, which no longer contain extensive discussions of Stalin's repressions (unlike those of the 1990s), their findings suggest that a considerable change of attitudes is under way in Russia. Putin's well-known statement that the collapse of the Soviet Union was the greatest geopolitical catastrophe of the twentieth century, pronounced on the eve of the sixtieth anniversary of victory in World War II (April 2005), the reintroduction of the melody of the Soviet anthem, albeit with a new "Russian" text ("Soviet in form, Russian in content," in a symbolic reversal of Stalin's well-known "socialist in content, national in form" nationality policy), and the Russian president's unwillingness to condemn the 1939 Molotov–Ribbentrop pact are integral elements of this selective rehabilitation of the Soviet past.[1]

This new symbolic reality stands in sharp contrast not only to the heyday of Russian democracy in the early 1990s but also to earlier epochs of Soviet history, from Khrushchev's thaw to Gorbachev's *perestroika* and *glasnost'* when "the end to silence" and the lifting of censorship led to unprecedented revelations about the crimes of the Stalin era. In both of these periods the process of de-Stalinization was not only an integral element of the reform process but also a code for the opening of the Soviet system to cultural Westernization. Indeed, as Stephen Cohen argued long ago, attitudes toward the Stalin legacy were an important symbolic marker dividing the "friends and foes of change" in the Soviet system.[2] Not accidentally, both Khrushchev's thaw and Gorbachev's *perestroika* marked an informal if not always official symbolic break with the cult of state power that was integral to the Russian imperial-autocratic tradition. By contrast, Stalin's symbolic revival of elements of that tradition through the cult of Ivan the Terrible and Peter the Great was central to his state-building project, even if carried out under the auspices of a communist regime and with different ideological goals in mind.[3]

When viewed from the point of view of the *longue durée* of Russian and Soviet history, therefore, it is logical that Putin's emphasis on the state (*gosudarstvennost'*) would be accompanied by a partial restoration if not full rehabilitation of the Soviet-Russian past, and especially the one historical experience that even the most anti-Soviet Russians view with a degree of national pride – namely, victory in World War II. In contrast to the late-tsarist period, which is not within collective memory, and the numerous ideological elaborations of different versions of the Russian idea that have more influence on nationalist elites than on the "the masses," the experience of World War II is part of the informal collective memory of ordinary Russians, including many young adults who have been brought up by their grandparents. As a result, this element of the Soviet experience, which culminated in the rise of Soviet Russia as a great power (*velikaia derzhava*), constitutes a "usable past" that can serve as a more real foundation for the "invention of tradition" than earlier historical precedents or more abstract versions of the Russian idea. The failure of Russia's democratic movement to capitalize on its victory over the Soviet system in the early 1990s and integrate such symbolic elements into a new nation-founding myth, the ceding of the field of national(ist) discourse to the right wing and the Communists, and Yeltsin's partial reversal to a "neo-patrimonial" style of leadership during his second term of office (1996–2000) are all processes that paved the way for Putin's symbolic rehabilitation of the statist current in Soviet-Russian history.

When to all this is added the largely unanticipated "withering away" of the post-Soviet Russian state's most elementary functions, from tax collection to the *de facto* loss of monopoly on the means of legitimate violence to the mafia and various protection agencies, the privatization of state functions by the oligarchs and regional barons, the chaotic state and moral decline of the Russian army (aptly demonstrated not only in Chechnya but in the everyday brutality of the army service experience), and the deadly attacks of Chechen rebels in Moscow, Beslan, and elsewhere, it becomes understandable that a considerable segment of the Russian population expresses support for Putin's state-building efforts. What is, of course, much more problematic, as Mendelson and Gerber's research points out, is that the "restoration of order" (*poriadok*) is associated with an ambivalent, contradictory, and often quite positive attitude toward the kinds of autocratic practices that seemed to have been relegated to "the dustbin of history" in the wake of the collapse of communism and the dissolution of the Soviet state in 1991. Instead, select elements of the autocratic past have made a comeback into official state ideology, with disturbing effects on Russian public opinion.

It is the argument of the present chapter that while the above-mentioned contextual factors indeed played a role in this partial symbolic revival of the Soviet past, the problem goes much deeper than that. Indeed, however much the ambivalent contemporary attitudes towards Stalin are rooted in the ignorance of a new generation of Russian youth about the Stalinist past or the disillusionment of adult Russians with democracy in the 1990s, there is little point in denying that the Soviet experience, however contradictory and ambivalent, is the main historical storehouse from which a usable Russian past can be constructed, for the simple reason that it is the only one within living collective memory. As Putin himself stated, defending his decision to adopt the old Soviet anthem:

> If we agree that that the symbols of the preceding epochs, including the Soviet epoch, must not be used at all, we will have to admit then that our mothers' and fathers' lives were useless and meaningless, that their lives were in vain. Neither in my head nor in my heart can I agree with this.[4]

All these considerations raise the question of the role of the Soviet experience, and in particular of the Stalinist epoch, in the forging of Russian national identity. The theme is obviously too large to be addressed in a single chapter. Therefore, in what follows I will concentrate on reconceptualizing Stalin's distinct "contribution" to the forging of a new Soviet-Russian identity. I will also try to demonstrate why the Stalinist epoch is fraught with such ambivalence in the Russian national mind and why its full-scale rehabilitation is unlikely if not outright impossible. In concluding, I will speculate on the implications of Putin's symbolic revival of *gosudarstvennost'* for state and nation building in contemporary Russia.

Soviet nationality policy and the Russian question in the 1920s

The Stalinist "solution" to the problem of Russian national identity in the 1930s should be placed, even if briefly, in the broader context of Soviet nationality policy of the 1920s. As is well known, Lenin's attack on Great Russian chauvinism represented an extension of his theory of imperialism to the sphere of nationality relations *within the Soviet Union*, with the dominant and "advanced" nation found historically guilty of imperial exploitation of the lesser and "more backward" nations. The logical consequence drawn from this was that the nationalism of the dominant nation was suspicious on account of its intrinsic chauvinist nature, whereas the nationalism of the oppressed and backward nations was deserving of support as long as it did not infringe upon the still higher interests of the international proletariat. In the excellent summary statement of Yuri Slezkine:

> Under imperialism ("as the highest and final stage of capitalism") colonial peoples had become the global equivalents of the western working class. Under the dictatorship of the (Russian) proletariat, they were entitled to special treatment until the economic and psychological wounds of colonialism had been cured. Meanwhile, nations equaled classes.[5]

The form that this special treatment for oppressed "proletarian" nations took was the pervasive territorialization and institutionalization of ethnicity in the 1920s and early 1930s. The creation of union republics and autonomous republics as territorially defined units of and for members of the titular nationality, who were accorded preferential treatment in the allocation of bureaucratic positions, cemented the association between ethnicity, administration, and territory. By the late 1920s this policy of "indigenization" resulted in a more ethnically diverse Communist Party leadership and the creation of national republican elites with an interest in advancing the cause of local constituencies, even if within the ideological boundaries set by the Party. The proliferation and codification of local languages, seen as the "national form" through which the universal proletarian message ("socialist content") could be conveyed to ethnic groups, led to the flourishing of national cultures as the first "dialectical step" toward their ultimate fusion in a universal Soviet proletarian culture of the future. The creation of native educational institutions as the vehicle of proletarian literacy campaigns and a means of overcoming peripheral "backwardness" bolstered the ranks of republican intelligentsia groups as the classic carriers of national culture. Finally, the treatment of ethnicity as an ascriptive category in the newly introduced internal passports (1932) and bureaucratic personnel forms cemented ethnic identity on the individual level. In short, through its pervasive instutionalization and codification of ethnicity on both the group and the individual levels, early Soviet nationality policy contributed to the long-term solidification of national particularism, turning the Soviet Union into an "incubator of new nations" instead of their "melting pot."[6]

The way in which this policy affected ethnic Russians as the "oppressor nation," however, is not as readily apparent. In the 1920s the officially defined role of ethnic Russians was to serve as the main collective medium for the transmission of proletarian internationalist consciousness ("socialist content") while simultaneously helping the oppressed nations to overcome their "backwardness" and build their own "national forms."[7] Since the attacks on the Orthodox Church as a repository of reactionary ideological traditions and imperial Russian history as a catalogue of chauvinist crimes against the smaller nationalities reduced the legitimate Russian national past to the revolutionary antecedents of the Great October, the Russian national form was emptied of all but the most proletarian content.[8] Institutionally, the Russian Republic (RSFSR) was a residual rather than real Russian national homeland, the territory left over when all the other "national homelands" (republics, autonomous provinces, national districts) had been carved out of imperial *Rossiia*. Accordingly, on the individual level, ethnic Russians living in the RSFSR could enjoy preferential treatment only as proletarians – that is, on the basis of class, not ethnic origin. Finally, the USSR as the territorial (if not historical or institutional) reincarnation of the old empire was not treated as a potential nation either, and the subsequently developed notion of the Soviet people (*sovetskii narod*) was devoid of ethnic content, even if it did acquire some emotional connotations over time.[9]

In spite of these institutional and ideological disadvantages, ethnic Russians were in fact *the dominant nation* in the Soviet Union. The absence of a separate Communist Party organization of the RSFSR and the overlap between Russian and Union institutions was a clear recognition of the fact that Russia was the center of the new Soviet Union in more than a geographical sense. The disproportionate size of the RSFSR and its Communist Party organization, and the fact that the republican parties were seen not as national but as territorial organizations subordinated to a highly centralized Union party, were other aspects of the same phenomenon. The special role of the Russian proletarian vanguard in helping the peripheral nationalities overcome their "backwardness" and the use of Russian as the unofficial lingua franca of internationalist communication were testimony to the fact that Russians were the main ethnic glue of the new Soviet state, even if only as carriers of the universal communist message.

Not accidentally, many Russian communists, the best-known Bolshevik leaders included, used "Russia" as a synonym for "Soviet Union" long after the reincorporation of the former borderlands and the change in the Party's name from Russian to Soviet (1925). The sheer pride derived from the fact that Soviet Russia was the first land of socialism sometimes led Bolshevik leaders to formulate the proletarian nation's "world-historical tasks" in terms strikingly reminiscent of Slavophile or Pan-Slavic messianism.[10] Finally, as far as the struggle against Great Russian chauvinism was concerned, it was limited by the higher interests of the industrial proletariat, disproportionately concentrated in the Russian heartland of the Soviet Union. As Stalin explained to the Twelfth Congress of the RCP(B) in April 1923:

> We are told we must not offend the non-Russian nationalities. That is perfectly true; I agree that we must not offend them. But to evolve out of this a new theory to the effect that the Great Russian proletariat must be placed in a position of inequality in relation to the formerly oppressed nations is absurd. What was merely a figure of speech in Comrade Lenin's well-known article, Bukharin has converted into a regular slogan. Nevertheless, it is clear that the political basis of the dictatorship of the proletariat is primarily and chiefly in the central, industrial regions, and not the border regions which are peasant countries. If we exaggerate the importance of peasant countries to the detriment of the proletarian districts, it may result in a crack in the proletarian dictatorship. That is dangerous, comrades.[11]

By arguing that the struggle against Great Russian chauvinism must not result in a new form of inequality, Stalin clearly departed from Lenin, whose advocacy of "inequality for the former oppressor nation" was certainly not "merely a figure of speech." But equally clearly, Stalin had remained faithful to Lenin in that he too argued that "the interests of the Great Russians' national pride (understood not in the slavish sense) coincide with the *socialist* interests of the Great Russian (and all other) proletarians."[12] Moreover, if the accomplishments the Great Russian proletariat constituted a legitimate source of national pride in the "non-slavish sense," this did not mean that Russian proletarians would play the role of vanguard forever. Theoretically, at least, the special role of the Russian proletariat would last only until the last vestiges of peripheral backwardness were removed, entitling the proletarians of all nationalities to be proud "in the socialist sense." On the other hand, were the proletarians of the peripheral nations to fill their "national forms" with too much national content and begin to feel too proud in the more conventional patriotic sense, they were found objectively guilty of the sin of "local" and, at a later date, of "bourgeois" nationalism.[13]

Proletarian against peasant: socialism in one country and the birth of Soviet-Russian identity

Stalin's line of reasoning, however, had implications not only for the relations between Russians and non-Russians, but also for the relationship between the Soviet vanguard and the Russian nation. If the Russians were entitled to feel proud only as proletarians, what to do about the obvious fact that the vast majority of Russians were still non-proletarian? And if the failure of revolution in the West objectively turned the Soviet Union ("Russia") into *the country of socialism* and the Russian proletariat into its backbone, what to do about the discrepancy between the well-developed Soviet political superstructure and its still meager industrial-proletarian base?[14] Finally, under the NEP alliance (*smychka*) of workers and peasants, how was the Russian proletariat to advance without treading upon a peasantry whose "petty-bourgeois" property instincts were given a new lease of life during NEP, revealing the objectively backward ways of this "ally" of the Russian working class?

When viewed from the correct proletarian point of view, therefore, the Russian question appeared in a more complex light than that of the non-Russian nationalities. Whereas the oppressed nationalities could overcome their backwardness and become Soviet through the medium of their particular national cultures, the Russian peasant could not.[15] Since the culture of the "Holy Russia of icons and roaches," as Trotsky had explained, presented the main obstacle to the elevation of the Russian people (*narod*) to a higher, Soviet, and "truly national" level of existence, Russian peasant culture was objectively unredeemable.[16] The dogged persistence with which the sundry peasant poets of the 1920s sang praises to rural Russia, equating its backward values with those of progressive, urban-proletarian, Soviet Russia, only added offense to injury. Bukharin's angry attack against the celebration of peasant values in literature, and on Yesenin in particular (1927), was a clear signal that the NEP *smychka* was no license for ideological backslides into "peasant socialism" or "quasi-popular nationalism," but rather a transitory station on the road to the final triumph of urban-proletarian Soviet Russia.[17]

But the dehumanization of the peasantry and, together with it, of everything that "old Russia" represented reached its apogee in the writings of Maxim Gorky, who took on the ungrateful task of helping the regime forge a new Soviet man.[18] In one of his essays written for the broader public in 1929, Gorky felt compelled to respond to the queries of those of his readers who, "as a result of a limited understanding of culture" and "irritation" at the imperfections of Soviet existence, longed for "the certainty of a good life."[19] Reminding these "culturally limited" readers that the party of Lenin was engaged in a "task of unparalleled, of colossal difficulty," one of "building a socialist society of people who are really equal," Gorky spelled out the exact nature of the difficulty in some detail:

> Human material, talented by nature, but poorly educated or quite illiterate, profoundly uncultured, profoundly anarchized by the Romanov autocracy and Russian capitalism, which was monstrously uncivilized;
>
> a peasantry – eighty-five per cent of the population – inured for centuries to thresh rye for bread with an axe's head, to eat their stew with a wooden shoe, crushed by poverty-stricken existence and hard labor, superstitious, intemperate, completely ruined first by an imperialist, and then by a civil war, a peasantry which even now after ten years under the revolutionary influence of the town, still retains, in the majority, the psychology of the small proprietor, the psychology of the blind mole;
>
> a long-winded, weak-kneed intelligentsia, which for a hundred years had been solving questions of "social etiquette," which met the October Revolution with passive sabotage or with active, armed resistance, and which often continues to struggle "in word and deed" against Soviet rule, even up to the present day, committing conscious and unconscious sabotage;
>
> the small townsfolk of a host of provincial towns, an army of abject slaves to capital, an army of marauders whose thievish custom it was to fleece the workers and peasants;
>
> mills and factories, wretchedly equipped, and half-wrecked in the bargain; a complete lack of factories for the production of heavy machinery;
>
> dependence on foreign capital, though with an untold abundance of raw material, which the capitalists in their anxiety to make quick millions, had not learned to manufacture, preferring to plunder and squander the people's estate;
>
> a vast country with a negligible number of railways, with wrecked bridges, shattered rolling stock, a country with no highroads to connect it;
>
> and over and above this, the active, unabating and blackguardly hatred of the world bourgeoisie –
>
> Such is the tally, and by no means a complete one, of the heavy heritage which fell to the working class and its Party.[20]

Leaving aside questions of "infrastructure," circumstantial factors (civil war, etc.), and the plots of foreign capitalists, Gorky's attack on old Russia – occurring as it did at the most critical moment for the Soviet regime (the "grain procurement crisis" and the looming kulak question) – was a clear justification for Stalin's class war against the bourgeois specialists and the peasantry. But Gorky's almost hysterical hatred for traditional Russia went far beyond the "objective needs of the moment," revealing a deeper social-psychological motivation. In his desire to eliminate all vestiges of Russian backwardness and create a new Soviet man superior to the idiotic peasant, the cowardly intellectual, the provincial philistine, the petty-bourgeois thief, and the Western capitalist, Gorky was motivated by an all too obvious *ressentiment.*[21]

Stalin – the destroyer of old Russia in the name of the new Soviet Russia – was no stranger to *ressentiment.* One does not have to agree fully with Robert Tucker's contention that Stalin came to Bolshevism through his psychological identification with Russian nationalism in order to appreciate that he was indeed an "eastern Bolshevik" rather than a "western Menshevik."[22] In this respect, Stalin stood out even among his Bolshevik comrades, most of whom were significantly more Western in cultural and social-psychological terms.[23]

Stalin's doctrine of "socialism in one country" was related to (if not necessarily exclusively the product of) his anti-Westernism. Indicative in this respect is the fact that, virtually alone among the Bolshevik leaders, Stalin had raised the possibility that Soviet Russia could become the country "that will lay the road to socialism" *even before October 1917.*[24] In a series of speeches delivered over the next few years, Stalin emerged as the key spokesman for the view that "the October revolution, by establishing a tie between the peoples of the backward East and of the advanced West, is ranging them in a common camp of struggle against imperialism."[25] But, in a curious twist, Stalin argued that the ultimate triumph of communism depended more on the mobilization of the oppressed workers and peasants of the East than on revolution in the developed West. This was because revolution in the East would deprive world imperialism of its "most reliable" and "inexhaustible" reserve, so that "the definite triumph of socialism" was "unthinkable" without a revolution in the East.[26] By contrast, Stalin explained, "the West, with its imperialist cannibals, has become a breeding ground of destruction and slavery. The task is to destroy this breeding ground, to the joy and comfort of working people of all countries."[27] By 1920, when foreign intervention in the protracted Civil War and the Russo-Polish war had resulted in a further upsurge in "Red patriotism," the future *vozhd'* of the Soviet-Russian and world proletariat put it in openly messianic terms:

> Paraphrasing the well-known words of Luther, Russia might say: "Here I stand on the border line between the old, capitalist world and the new socialist world. Here, on this border line, I unite the efforts of the proletarians of the West and of the peasants of the East in order to shatter the old world. May the god of history be my aid!"[28]

In Stalin's vision of "revolution through war," the USSR played the role of a socialist fortress whose military security was the first precondition for overcoming "capitalist encirclement" and replacing it with "socialist encirclement." In this

Manichean world divided into two camps – the camp of "Anglo-American imperialists" and the socialist camp embodied in (not merely represented or led by) the USSR as the first country of socialism – the revolution was identified with the foreign policy interests and territorial expansion of the Soviet state.[29] As the cause of the international working class and the Soviet Union fused into one, *the Russian proletariat* was accorded a vanguard role in the vanguard state of the world revolution. As Stalin explained in his letter to the poet Demyan Bedny, whom he chastised for his satirical attacks on Russia's heritage of "backwardness:"

> The whole world now admits that the center of the revolutionary movement has shifted from Western Europe to the USSR as the center of the liberation struggle of the working people throughout the world. The revolutionaries of all countries look with hope to the USSR as the center of the liberation struggle of the working people throughout the world and recognize it as their only Motherland. In all countries the revolutionary workers unanimously applaud the Soviet working class, and first and foremost the *Russian* working class, the vanguard of the Soviet workers, as their recognized leader that is carrying out the most revolutionary and active policy ever dreamed of by the proletarians of other countries. The leaders of the revolutionary workers of all countries are eagerly studying the highly instructive history of Russia's working class, its past and the past of Russia, knowing that besides reactionary Russia there existed also revolutionary Russia, the Russia of the Radishchevs and Chernyshevskys, the Zhelyabovs and Ulyanovs, the Khalturins, and Alexeyevs. All this fills (cannot but fill!) the hearts of the Russian workers with a feeling of revolutionary national pride that can move mountains and perform miracles."[30]

In assigning a special world-historical role to the Russian proletariat and viewing the history of Russia (not only of proletarian Russia) as "most instructive," Stalin clearly departed from Lenin, whose formulations on revolutionary national pride he quoted by way of justification. Similarly, Stalin's view of Leninism as "the highest achievement of Russian culture" would have astonished the leader of the October Revolution.[31]

It would be far too simple to conclude from this, however, that Stalin was a "Russian nationalist" or even a "National Bolshevik," for the meaning of these terms is by no means transparent. Stalin's letter to Bedny, let us remember, was written in the midst of the "cultural revolution" and the collectivization drive – the whole-scale attack on all traditional Russian values and their main social embodiments: the bourgeois specialist and kulak "class enemies."[32] Only a few months later, in his speech to the leaders of Soviet industry, Stalin revealed the main lesson he had derived from "the most instructive history of Russia":

> One feature of the history of old Russia was the continual beatings she suffered for falling behind, for her backwardness. She was beaten by the Mongol khans. She was beaten by the Turkish beys. She was beaten by the

> Swedish feudal lords. She was beaten by the Polish and Lithuanian gentry. She was beaten by the British and French capitalists. She was beaten by the Japanese barons. All beat her – for her backwardness: for military backwardness, for cultural backwardness, for political backwardness, for industrial backwardness, for agricultural backwardness.... Such is the law of the exploiters – to beat the backward and the weak. It is the jungle law of capitalism.... That is why we must no longer lag behind. In the past we had no fatherland, nor could we have had one. But now that we have overthrown capitalism and power is in the hands of the working class, we have a fatherland and we will uphold its independence.... We are fifty or a hundred years behind the advanced countries. We must make good this distance in ten years. Either we do it, or we shall go under."[33]

Stalin's speech represented much more than a justification of his relentless industrialization drive to a group of Soviet managers. It was also more than an expression of the simple (but important) idea that the transformation of the Soviet Union into "a country of metal" offered the only hope for overcoming Russia's status of a perennially backward and exploited "proletarian nation" vis-à-vis the advanced Western countries. Finally, Stalin's speech was not just an appeal to "Russian nationalism." What Stalin was suggesting to his audience, in fact, was nothing less than the possibility of creating and assuming a *new Soviet-Russian national identity.*

Gregory Freidin appears right in arguing that the Bolshevik alternative to Russian peasant identity was not a "proletarian internationalist" but rather " 'a socialist in one country' – a Great Russian who defines himself as someone both superior (more progressive) and in opposition (class antagonism) to his compatriots in the countryside."[34] So does Robert Tucker when he states that Stalin was offering his audience "Soviet Russian nationhood as a collective identity to be proud of, and presenting the socialist-building enterprise as a Russian mission in world history." In doing so, argues Tucker, Stalin was responding to an "identity need present in many of the new state's citizens."[35] But just how many of the new state's citizens felt the need for a *Soviet*-Russian identity? If Gorky is to be believed, 85 percent of the population consisting of the peasantry – those "blind moles" buried in their private plots – felt no such need. The "bourgeois specialists," many of whom might have felt such a need, were hidden if not open *smenovekhovtsy*, desiring a Russia "Soviet in form, national in content."[36] Neither group was ready to be assimilated to *Soviet* Russian nationhood *voluntarily*.

This is why the creation of Stalin's *Sovetskaia Rossiia* presupposed the destruction of old and even NEP Russia, the transformation of "Russians" (i.e. peasants) into proletarians, and the subordination of Russian to a new Soviet-Russian identity. This is also why collectivization took on the character of a military-patriotic campaign in which the working-class vanguard was mobilized on the basis of Soviet patriotism, and not only class hatred for the "backward" peasantry. Not accidentally, the 25,000ers – the industrial workers recruited for the first collectivization drive – were hailed as "the best sons of the Fatherland" and subsequently glorified "in Soviet textbooks and historical works in an adulatory style generally reserved for current leaders and veterans of the Great War of the Fatherland (the Second World War)."[37] Undoubtedly, this was because through their heroic conduct these proletarians were giving meaning to, indeed *were creating, a Soviet-Russian identity*. Simultaneously, by taking part in the "elimination of the kulaks as a class" these proletarians were removing the greatest obstacle to the triumph of this still fragile Soviet-Russian identity and, together with it, to the consolidation of Stalin's political elite in the making. The persecution of the bourgeois specialists and their replacement by a new generation of Soviet specialists was the milder, urban middle-class counterpart of this process.[38]

When seen from the national point of view, therefore, the true significance of collectivization lies in the fact that it made Soviet identity the only legitimate content of Russian national identity. Thus, what transpired in 1934 when the word *rodina* (motherland) made its seemingly dramatic reappearance was no "Great Retreat" in the sense of a return to old Russian values.[39] Rather, the resurrection of the Russian "national form" – complete with Pushkin, army ranks, school uniforms, and traditional family values – was a sign that the last socially and culturally significant and thus politically threatening (dangerous "from the proletarian point of view") vestiges of old *Rus'* had been destroyed. Once rendered politically harmless, select Russian symbols and traditions could be assimilated to a new Soviet-Russian identity. As Ken Jowitt has argued, Leninist regimes "are interested in the selective reintegration of tradition only *after* the political relevance of tradition has been decisively altered," and Stalin's Russia in the aftermath of collectivization was the first example of this dynamic.[40]

But why selectively reintegrate elements of a tradition that has been decisively defeated? One clue was given by Stalin himself in 1934 when he criticized Soviet history textbooks for substituting "sociology for history," and reducing it to a succession of epochs (feudal, capitalist) in which there were "no facts, no events, no people, no concrete information, not a name, not a title, and not even any content itself."[41] In other words, class struggle alone could not fill the content of the Russian national form even to a minimally satisfactory degree because it could not inspire anyone but the most class-conscious proletarians to action. Patriotism, on the other hand, could have mass appeal precisely because there was a need for it, especially in such critical institutions as the Red Army.[42] The symbolic inclusion into "socialist patriotism" of those politically harmless remnants of tradition that would strengthen identification with the Soviet homeland by evoking a non-existent continuity with old Russia carried the advantage of making the regime more acceptable to the unconverted and facilitating the mobilization and co-optation of key political and social constituencies.

A second function of the revived Russian national form in the 1930s was to help cement the role of Russians as the "ethnic glue" of the Soviet state. The vanguard role of the Russian industrial proletariat in helping the peripheral nations ("peasant countries") overcome their backwardness that Stalin had stressed early on, became a social reality with rapid industrialization. Thus, between 1926 and 1939 the absolute number of ethnic Russians outside of the

RSFSR increased from 5.1 to 9.3 million, while their relative proportion in the total Soviet population outside the RSFSR grew from 8.6 percent to 14.9 percent. Russian migration to Kazakhstan and the other Central Asian republics was especially large, totaling 1.7 million people. As a result, the proportion of ethnic Russian dramatically increased in many union republics as well as in the autonomous republics within the Russian federation.[43] Since most of the migrants were leading cadres, university graduates, technical specialists, or skilled workers, they typically enjoyed high status in the host societies and were well represented in Party and government structures. Moreover, the migrants brought in their train Russian elementary and vocational schools, reinforcing the role of Russian as the language of "internationalist" communication.

After 1938, when Russian became a mandatory subject in all non-Russian elementary schools, as well as the only language of communication in the Red Army, this role of Russian as the main medium for the transmission of the proletarian message from the center to the periphery was officially recognized. As a result, linguistic Russification became an important factor in internal state cohesion. The increasing number of references to the "great" Russian people (*velikii russkii narod*, not just Lenin's *velikorussy* or Great Russians), and its special role in the "gathering" of the Soviet nations in the propaganda and history textbooks of the late 1930s, were the ideological correlate of this linguistic reality.[44]

It would be wrong, however, to think of Russification as a process separate from Sovietization. Rather, in line with Stalin's famous dictum, Russian remained the form, Soviet the content. The inextricable connection between the two was made explicit in Ushakov's 1939 dictionary, in which the term "Russian" (*russkii*) was illustrated both by Turgenev's phrase on the "mighty, truthful and free Russian language" and by Stalin's definition of "the Russian revolutionary sweep" as a "life-giving force which awakens thought, propels one forward, crushes the past, opens up the future."[45] It is hardly necessary to point out whose illustration, Turgenev's or Stalin's, carried more weight at this particular historical juncture.

Indeed, it is striking that even those ethnic Russians who acted as the agents of Soviet power in newly occupied territories (after 1939) thought of themselves as subjects of Soviet power rather than as the political vanguard of a Sovietized (and therefore "progressive") "Russian imperialism." According to Jan T. Gross, the Soviets "behaved no differently in occupied Poland than they did in their own country." The Soviet personnel and their families arriving in western Ukraine and western Belorussia had experienced the same hardships (and were likely to experience them at any time) to which the population of the newly liberated territories was subjected. "'You'll get used to it, or else you'll croak,' they used to say, not maliciously, but merely summing up the wisdom life had taught them." Needless to add, this was hardly the attitude of Russian *Übermenschen*.[46]

When all this is kept in mind, the ethnically uneven effects of collectivization that hit the "peasant countries" harder than the Russian industrial heartland do not appear particularly advantageous to "the Russians." In fact, once collectivization began in earnest, all (not only Russian) peasants were seen as specimen of a backward class condemned to extinction by the laws of history. Thus, there was no special genocide of the *Ukrainian* (as opposed to Kazakh, Russian, or other) peasantry, just a disproportionate number of Ukrainian *peasant* victims.

As far as the peripheral (Ukrainian and other) "bourgeois nationalists" were concerned, they were indeed persecuted as nationalists, namely for trying to fill their national forms with too much local-patriotic, anti-Soviet, and, therefore, also anti-Russian content. As Stalin explained to some Ukrainian comrades early on, their sin consisted in allowing non-communist intellectuals to abuse the policy of "indigenization" in order to "alienate Ukrainian culture and public life from general Soviet culture and public life," and turn it into a "struggle against 'Moscow' in general, against Russians in general, against Russian culture and its highest achievement – Leninism."[47]

Thus, the peripheral nationalists justifiably considered their nations victims of the "Moscow center." As Moscow was also the geographic and historic center of traditional Russia, they also saw their nations as victims of "Russian imperialism" and/or "the Russians." However, if the first view is correct, the second one confuses ethnic with political reality. Stalin's "Moscow center" coincided with the traditional center of old Russia geographically and historically, but not politically or symbolically. In the Stalinist *Weltanschauung*, the "Moscow center" played the same role for the Soviet Union as the USSR (as the first country of socialism) played for communists abroad: it was the incarnation of the October Revolution and of socialism and, as such, the locus of the sacred in the charismatic communist "hierophony."[48] This, and not Russian imperialism, explains why the "Moscow center" found the violations of the peripheral nation-builders (and all other "deviationists") so offensive. In Stalin's own language the political and symbolic content of the "Moscow center" was not the historic Kremlin, but "Leninism as the highest achievement of Russian culture."[49]

Not accidentally, fifty years after Stalin's great purges, when Gorbachev announced his policy of *glasnost'*, "the imperial center" came under attack not only from the newly formed Popular Fronts in the non-Russian republics but also from Russian intellectuals who saw in its political demise and transformation the main precondition of Russia's rebirth. The "imperial center" in their minds had come to signify Stalinism. This why the redemption of "old Moscow" logically led to an alliance between democratic Russian politicians and intellectuals, and the peripheral nationalist elites joined in a common struggle against the "imperial center" – in complete defiance of the "normal" nation-state logic in which the center is traditionally pitted against the various peripheries.

To the moderately attentive observer, the difference between Stalin's Soviet-Russian party-state and a Russian nation-state must have been obvious even in the 1930s. Nothing illustrates this difference better than the fate of the Russian counterparts of the peripheral "bourgeois nationalists." These were the sundry bourgeois specialist "wreckers" of Soviet industry, the still maladapted *smenovekhovtsy*, and all those who mistook serving the land of the Soviets for serving Russia. A typical representative of this vanishing breed was Nikolai Ustrialov. Initially suspicious of open collaboration with the Soviet authorities, Ustrialov grew both more extreme in his nationalism and more confused over time. In 1935, Ustrialov returned to teach economic geography in Moscow and even wrote an article praising Stalin's 1936 constitution.[50] Even worse than such reckless behavior was Ustrialov's unforgivable forgetfulness. As early as 1925, the year in which the Russian Communist Party had changed its name to the Communist Party of the Soviet Union, Stalin had warned him personally:

> He [Ustrialov] is in the transport service. It is said that he is serving well. I think that if he is serving well, let him go on dreaming about the degeneration of our Party. Dreaming is not prohibited in our country. Let him dream to his heart's content. But let him know that while dreaming about our degeneration, he must, at the same time, bring grist to our Bolshevik mill. Otherwise, it will go badly with him. (*Applause*).[51]

Not surprisingly, it did go badly with him. Questioned about his true views by his faculty chairman in Moscow, Ustrialov intimately confessed that, having misunderstood the true depth of the Party's decisions on collectivization, he had at one time defended the interests of the "non-proletarian working classes" (i.e. peasants), and thus "had spoken against the interests of the Russian people." Naturally, such an unforgivable sin could not go unpunished. No longer of any use to his Soviet homeland, this traitor to the Russian people was executed on 15 September 1937.[52] This was the same year in which the terror peaked and in which the *velikii russkii narod* made its glorious appearance in official propaganda and history textbooks.

It might appear that this state of affairs changed dramatically as a result of World War II. Indeed, with the onset of the war, Stalin sought to present himself as a Russian national leader and to partially live up to the image of a "good tsar" who truly cared for his people. Indicative in this respect was the fact that in his first speech after the Nazi invasion, Stalin addressed his people as "brothers and sisters" and "my dear friends," thus evoking powerful metaphors of family and kinship, and infusing, for the first time, his officially cultivated prewar image of "Stalin, our father" (*nash rodnoi Stalin, otets Stalin*) with some meaning.[53] But Stalin was well aware that in this Time of Troubles it was imperative for the "good tsar" to appeal to his people's patriotism, offer them a greater scope for individual initiative, and place his own personality, even if temporarily, into the background.

Stalin's speech to the soldiers gathered on Red Square, delivered on the occasion of the anniversary of the October Revolution (7 November 1941) and, more importantly, on the eve of the dramatic battle for Moscow, was conspicuous for the absence of any references to Soviet values:

> Comrades, Red Army and Red Navy men, officers and political workers, men and women partisans! The whole world is looking upon you as the power capable of destroying the German invader robber hordes! The enslaved peoples of Europe are looking upon you as their liberators. A great

> liberating mission stands before you. Be worthy of this great mission! The war you are waging is a war of liberation, a just war. May you be inspired in this war by the courageous figures of our great ancestors, Alexander Nevsky, Dmitri Donskoi, Kuzma Minin and Dmitri Pozharsky, Alexander Suvorov, Mikhail Kutuzov![54]

Similar in intent, but more articulate and individualistic, was the kind of patriotism observable during the first two years of the Great Patriotic War against Hitler (1941–1945). As Stalinist ideology with its stereotyped collective heroes gave way to the heroic feats of individuals, the patriotism of "citizens with an active sense of themselves and their wishes" increasingly took the place of an official nationalism defined by "loyalty to the leader and the administrative organs."[55] A powerful expression to these awakened civic feelings was given by the best-known voice of Russian wartime journalism – the surviving *smenovekhovets* Ilia Ehrenburg – in the critical days of October 1941:

> The Germans hoped to provoke a civil war in Russia. But all distinctions between Bolsheviks and non-Party people, between believers and Marxists, have been obliterated: some defend time, others space, but time and space – this is the Motherland, this is the earth, this is such-and-such a height, such-and-such line, such-and-such inhabited place. They pray for the Red Army in old churches, the domes of which have been darkened so that they would not attract German pilots. Muftis and rabbis pray for the Red Army.... Millions of people have just started to be alive. These days of trial were their first books, their first theater, their first happiness.... They will give up everything if only not to be German slaves.[56]

Ehrenburg's nationalism, which made no distinctions between Bolsheviks and non-Bolsheviks, Orthodox priests, muftis, and rabbis, was clearly different both from the official Soviet-Russian kind and the ethnic Pan-Slavic variety. Its main ethos was that of a civic appeal to solidarity in service to the motherland, to the "earth," to the idea of "Mother Russia" – words that so conspicuously replaced Comrade Stalin as the main locus of loyalty during the first two years of the war.[57] However, in addition to these civic patriotic chords, it is impossible not to detect, in Ehrenburg's reference to the fact that "millions of people have just started to be alive," something like a sigh of relief. The meaning of relief was made transparent by one of the characters in Boris Pasternak's *Doctor Zhivago*, who explained that "when the war broke out, its real horrors, its real dangers, its menace of real death were a blessing compared with the inhuman power of the lie, a relief because it broke the spell of the dead letter."[58] Not only journalists, poets, and composers, but many ordinary Russians remembered the first two years of the war as a time of relative freedom, collective solidarity, civic participation, and "spontaneous de-Stalinization."[59]

It is not too difficult to see why this kind of patriotism was distrusted by Stalin and his associates. Nothing conveys this distrust better than Stalin's Order no. 270 (16 August 1941), which treated all those who surrendered in the impossible conditions of 1941 as "deserters" to be shot at the first opportunity, and deprived their families, found guilty by association, of state support.[60] An even more drastic expression of the same attitude was Order no. 227 (28 July 1942), which provided for the formation of special detachments with the right to execute retreating "panic-mongers" in "unreliable units," and to transfer officers whose units suffered defeat or disintegration to penal battalions used for suicide missions.[61] If Stalin's "Not a Step Back" command of July 1942 inscribed itself in patriotic memory as a dramatic instance of the leader's wartime determination in the critical days of the Battle of Stalingrad, it also set the stage for the incarceration and deportation of hundreds of thousands of Soviet prisoners of war in the postwar period.[62]

As of 1943, when the prospect of victory appeared increasingly certain, the limited freedoms enjoyed by the patriotic citizenry during the early stages of the war were gradually withdrawn. Together with the revived cult of Stalin as the infallible wartime leader, which reached unprecedented proportions, a conscious effort was made to subordinate the awakened Russian patriotism to the Stalinist party-state.[63] A characteristic symbolic expression of this effort was the new Soviet national anthem (1943), which squarely placed Great Russians at the head of the Soviet family of nations ("The unbreakable union of free republics was welded forever by Great Rus' "), while simultaneously celebrating "the great path of Lenin," and hailing Stalin as the leader who "taught us to be faithful to the people" and "inspired us to labor and valorous deeds."[64]

Tragically, from the standpoint of civic Russian patriotism, the incredibly costly victory in the Great Patriotic War gave emotional resonance to the notion of *the Soviet motherland*, tying the fate of the Russian people to the cause of the Soviet state and its undisputed leader, as exemplified in the famous war cry "*za Stalina – za rodinu*!" (for Stalin, for the motherland!). Subsequently, Soviet-Russian nationalism acquired the character of a full-blown official state ideology, helping legitimize and consolidate Stalin's postwar political order.[65] The celebration of the Russian "national form" reached new heights as Comrade Stalin himself gave the green light by referring to the Russian people as "the guiding people" of the Soviet Union, and thanked it for its patience in the critical days of 1941–1942 when "some other people could have said to its government: you have not justified our expectations, go away, we will choose another government that will make peace with Germany and guarantee us a peaceful existence." Instead, Stalin admitted, the Russian people's trust in the Soviet government was "a decisive factor in the historical victory against the enemy of mankind, fascism."[66]

But it would be a profound mistake to read into Stalin's words any real concessions to Russian "national content." Characteristically, public references to Stalin's speech were forbidden, and its self-critical overtones were understood "as a serious warning to those who might contemplate initiating an investigation into the reasons for, and circumstances surrounding, the tragedy that the Soviet people had endured," namely Stalin's "mistakes" on the eve of the war.[67] Even

Victory Day (9 May) was abolished as an official state holiday on Stalin's personal initiative, to be reinstated only in 1965 when Leonid Brezhnev turned the memory of the Great Patriotic War into an official cult with the purpose of finding a new source of legitimacy in the aftermath of Khrushchev's thaw.[68]

More telling than the official glorification of the Russian people as "the guiding people of the Soviet Union," therefore, was Stalin's short speech to participants in the Victory Parade, delivered on 25 June 1945. In this "most simple, ordinary toast" to the victors, Stalin proposed to drink to the health of those simple people "who are regarded as 'cogs' in our great state mechanism, and without whom all of us – Marshals and commanders of the fronts and armies – to put it a bit crudely – are not worth a damn." It was thanks to the effort of "tens of millions of such modest people," people "without ranks and titles," said Stalin, that "our great state mechanism in all branches of science, the economy, and military art" is functioning on a daily basis.[69] Few words could have revealed the character of Stalin's Soviet-Russian nationalism better than this reference to tens of millions of people as "cogs in our great state mechanism."

The legacy of Stalinism in the post-Stalin era

Stalinism, wrote the Soviet dissident Alexander Zinoviev in a moving autobiographical memoir, was "the youth of real communism," its formative epoch, when the all major ideological and institutional foundations of the Soviet social order were laid.[70] This statement is as true of the relationship between the Soviet state and the Russian nation as of any other element in the Soviet system. This is not to deny the significance of post-Stalinist developments, and especially of Khrushchev's thaw, when the theme of Russia's victimization by Stalin's *Sovetskaia Rossiia* made its way into a number of important literary works, leaving a lasting cultural and political impact. Nor is it to deny the importance of the efforts of the Brezhnev leadership to co-opt unofficial Russian nationalism for the cause of the Soviet state at the price of giving more scope to both its openly chauvinist and non-Soviet (but not anti-Soviet) manifestations.[71] However, it is to argue that the basic pattern of the relationship between the Soviet state and the Russian nation was set in Stalin's time, and that later developments were variations, if far from unimportant, on a basic motif.

That basic motif was the continued suppression of Russian society by a powerful Soviet-Russian party-state whose ideological core was and remained Marxism-Leninism. Consequently, the state persecuted all authentic forms of Russian nationalism, whether civic or ethnic, while selectively co-opting various elements of nationalist ideology into its official worldview. Such elements included repeated references to the special mission of the Soviet Russian working class in the world socialist movement, to the Russian people as "the elder brother" in the Soviet family of nations, or to the heroic role of ethnic Russians in leading the fraternal nations to victory in the Great Patriotic War. In addition, great scientific-technological breakthroughs (the hydrogen bomb; the conquest of space) were presented as triumphs not only of Soviet socialism but also, as everyone understood, of the Great Russian people as well. Finally, the very might of the Soviet state, the largest state in the world – as postwar propaganda never tired of repeating – could fill (and, as Stalin would have it, could not but fill!) the hearts of all Soviet-Russian proletarians with strong feelings of "revolutionary national pride." Occasionally, even the missing ethnic content of the Russian national form could be filled by promoting a siege mentality in which the enemies of the socialist fatherland appeared under the familiar guise of the "traditional enemies of the Russian people."

A good example of this tactic was Stalin's anti-cosmopolitan campaign that made use of Black Hundred-style anti-Semitism in order to create an artificial identification between the external Western enemy and an internal "cosmopolitan" fifth column bent on subverting the socialist fatherland from within. By providing the socialist citizenry with an identifiable ethnic enemy and keeping its patriotic vigilance at the level of combat readiness, Stalin's solution to the state–society dilemma promised to strengthen loyalty to the organs of state security as the main guarantor of the sovereignty of a "socialist fatherland in danger," while offering a safety valve in the form of compensatory feelings of ethnic (status) superiority. So functionally advantageous was the precedent set by the anti-cosmopolitan campaign that Brezhnev found himself compelled to institutionalize it in the somewhat milder form of official anti-Zionism.[72] As late as 1988 an authoritative dictionary of the Russian language defined "cosmopolitanism" as a "reactionary bourgeois ideological current which, under the guise of slogans in favor of a 'world-wide state' and 'world citizenship,' denies the nation the right to an independent state existence, national traditions, national culture and patriotism."[73] Undoubtedly, by that time it was both politically embarrassing and unnecessary to explain to the Soviet-Russian citizen that cosmopolitanism is also "the ideology of American imperialism striving for world domination," or that "bourgeois cosmopolitanism is the reverse of proletarian internationalism and hostile to it."[74]

None of this meant, however, that Soviet Russia belonged to the Russians as an "ethnically chosen people" of state. Nor was there a halt on institutional nation building in the republics, although in especially important cases such as Ukraine, appropriate preventive measures were taken in order to ensure the continued prevalence of Soviet-Russian "socialist content."[75] As late as 1982, one of the main CPSU ideologists, Richard Kosolapov, reaffirmed the principles of Leninist nationality policy when he argued that although "social classes will largely disappear while we are still in the period of developed socialism," socialist nations would not. This was because nations were "more stable social and ethnic entities" than classes (!). This being the case, the prospect of the "merger of nations" had to be approached "realistically," and from the "Leninist point of view" – that is, postponed to an indefinite future.[76]

Nor was the RSFSR as the prospective national homeland of the Russian people filled with too much additional national content after Stalin's death. The emergence of select government institutions for the RSFSR (the Supreme Soviet, the Council of Ministers), newspapers (*Sovetskaia Rossiia*), and cultural institutions (the RSFSR Union of Writers) was not backed by the creation of a separate RSFSR Party organization (just an RSFSR Party Bureau within the CPSU Central Committee, which was abolished in 1966), an RSFSR Academy of Sciences, or the introduction of preferential educational quotas for ethnic Russians on RSFSR territory. Whereas the overlap between critical Soviet and Russian institutions underscored the continued role of Russians as the "guiding people" in the Soviet Union, it also deprived Russian cultural particularism of territorially defined institutional venues of expression.[77] In short, the continued dominance of ethnic Russians in the USSR was purchased at the price of dissolving the Russian nation into the Soviet state.[78]

But the main weakness of Stalin's coercive imposition of Soviet-Russian identity lay in its discriminatory attitude to the Russian national cultural heritage and its persistent refusal to give Russian society some room for genuine participation. The hopes of Russian cultural elites that the Soviet state would make concessions on both fronts, cultural and social, were cruelly disappointed after World War II, when the main reward for the tremendous sacrifices made by ethnic Russians on behalf of the Soviet state was the reimposition of totalitarian controls. By the early 1950s, Robert Tucker concluded, "the 'great state machine' had become, in the minds of millions of ordinary Russians, a great alien 'It,' which commanded their fear or even their awe but did not inspire any affection or sense of identification."[79] Nevertheless, the flame of civic patriotism lit in the first days of the Great Patriotic War was never quite extinguished. As Boris Pasternak wrote, "Although the enlightenment and liberation which had been expected to come after the war had not come with victory, a presage of freedom was in the air throughout these post-war years, and it was their only historical meaning."[80]

Conclusion

It is possible to view the relationship between the Stalinism and Russian national identity in an altogether different light. Thus, in his study of National Bolshevism David Brandenberger has made a strong case for the view that Stalin's "Russocentric etatism," though primarily envisaged as an instrumental tool for mobilizing mass support for an unpopular regime and its industrialization effort, in effect served as "the catalyst for the formation a mass sense of national identity within Russian-speaking society between the late 1930s and early 1950s, during the most cruel and difficult years of the Soviet period." This was for the simple reason that mass education and propaganda reached unprecedented numbers of newly literate and socially mobilized ethnic Russians in a way that was either not the case or was ideologically inconceivable during the late tsarist and early Bolshevik periods. As a result, contemporary Russian-speakers were "able to articulate what it meant to be members of a Russian national community" in a way that did not hold true for the majority of Russians in the late tsarist and early Bolshevik periods. Thus, the seeds of the new Russia were planted, however unintentionally, by the Stalinist regime.[81]

If the interpretation offered in this chapter is correct, however, the relationship between Stalinism and Russian nationalism is considerably more problematic than Brandenberger's framework seems to imply. To put it simply, to treat the Stalinist incorporation of "Russocentric" motifs into official ideology as an instrumental tool of nation building (even if a partially unintentional one) means to overlook the most distinctive feature of the Stalinist period: the mass terror unleashed against the majority of the Russian population, and especially the forcible collectivization of the Russian peasantry as the main symbol of the Russian nation in traditional Slavophile imagery. The point might seem too obvious to be mentioned, but its consequences for the relationship between the Soviet regime and Russian nationalism were long-lasting. Indeed, without understanding these consequences we would be hard-pressed to offer an interpretively adequate account of the collapse of the Soviet Union and the crucial role of "Russia" (i.e. the RSFSR) and ethnic Russians in that process. This is because the mass terror of the Stalinist period and the collectivization of the Russian peasantry opened an unbridgeable chasm between the Soviet state and the Russian nation, a chasm that came into the open as early as Khrushchev's thaw but assumed an absolutely critical symbolic importance during Gorbachev's *perestroika*. As a result, the very idea of even a modest degree of voluntary identification between the Soviet state and the Russian nation was rejected by a critical segment of Russia's political and intellectual elite. However – and this is a strong implication of Brandenberger's analysis that he himself did not spell out – Stalin's forcible creation of a new *Soviet-Russian identity* that was cemented in the crucible of World War II has presented an important obstacle to Russia's search for a national identity independent of the Soviet past. This, indeed, is the deeper reason for the ambivalence of many Russians toward the Soviet (and even the Stalinist) experience.

What about the 1990s and Putin's new Russia? Here it can be safely said that the early 1990s represented, as Yeltsin himself explained in his presidential inauguration speech in 1991, the first time in Russian (i.e. not only Soviet) history that "a new voluntary interdependence" was "born between the authorities and the people. State authority becomes answerable to the people who elected it, and the people become answerable to the state, which they have placed above themselves."[82] As is readily apparent, and for reasons that cannot fully be explored here, this voluntary interdependence between the state and the people has failed to materialize. Most importantly, from the point of view of the theme of the present chapter, during the 1990s Russia's liberal elite failed to cash in on its considerable "symbolic capital," whether by lustrating the communists, transforming the meaning of existing official holidays like Victory Day by dissociating them from the Stalinist past, or turning transformative historical events (the successful resistance to the August 1991 coup) into founding myths of the new republic. Yeltsin's feeble attempt to develop a new "idea for Russia" ran aground on account of both its overly abstract ideological character and the Russian liberals' disdain for nationalism as an inherently "illiberal phenomenon." As a result, the field of symbolic contest over nationhood was largely left to the communists and nationalists, with the consequence that the likes of Felix Dzerzhinsky were once more placed on the pedestal of "state-building" heroes.[83]

This is not meant to suggest that the creation of new founding national myths and collective memories would have been an easy task, especially given the historical merger of Soviet and Russian identity analyzed in this chapter. Nor would it be correct to assert that we are witnessing a return to Stalinist values, regardless of the partial rehabilitation of the Soviet past under Putin. What can safely be said, however, is that under Putin the state once more has been placed squarely "above the people," who are given little more than the right to plebiscitary acclamation in well-orchestrated elections. As a result, there are few institutional channels through which the Russian *vox populi* can have an impact on state policy. The lack of such institutional channels is not only a problem for liberals and civic nationalists, but also a disappointment to extreme Russian nationalists, who are allowed no real leverage in the state, even as select elements of their worldview are instrumentally used by state officialdom. The fact that the most active Russian opposition groups unite the liberal former world chess champion Garry Kasparov and an extreme nationalist like the writer Eduard Limonov indicates that neither genuine civic patriots nor authentic extreme nationalists see the state as representative "of the people."

More tellingly still, such feelings of alienation from the state are reappearing among ordinary Russians, no matter how much they may cherish the relative stability and "order" of the Putin era. As one former Russian physicist turned underwear salesman bitterly remarked in response to the tyrannical and corrupt ways of the state's newly "efficient" tax collectors, whom he warded off with a combination of threats and small bribes, "For fifteen hundred years the government has been blaming us for just living in Russia."[84] Though merely an "anecdotal" illustration, the very presence of such sentiments speaks volumes about the character of Putin's state-building project. As Lilia Shevtsova has written, "Putin's Russia followed the path toward bureaucratic order – through reliance on the administrative apparat, administrative methods, subordination, loyalty, and instructions from above," as opposed to restoring legal order by fostering citizen participation and institution building. From the point of view of the *longue durée* of Russian history, this strategy amounted to a reversal to the historical modernization methods pioneered by Peter the Great, reflecting an absence of understanding in the elite that "bureaucratic modernization" cannot meet the needs of an articulate and educated population inhabiting a significantly modernized society.[85]

Thus, the problem of state–nation–society relations is likely to return in the post-Putin period, and no amount of newly acquired oil wealth, international posturing, military buildup, or state propaganda will be able to take it off the agenda. As far as patriotism is concerned, on the other hand, the selective rehabilitation of the Soviet past and the incorporation of some of its elements into state symbolism can represent little more than a new variation on imperial and Soviet Russia's long-standing tradition of official nationalism. As long as this is the case, Russian nation building – whether understood in a civic or an ethnic sense – will be thwarted, and the symbolic Russification of the Soviet form will do little to bridge the chasm between the state and the nation.

Notes

* Reprinted with permission from *Post-Soviet Affairs*, vol. 23, no. 2, 2007, pp. 156–183.

1 S. E. Mendelson and T. P. Gerber, "Failing the Stalin Test," *Foreign Affairs*, 85, 1, January–February 2006, 2–8.

2 S. F. Cohen (ed.), *An End to Silence: Uncensored Opinion in the Soviet Union*, New York: W. W. Norton, 1982; same author, "The Friends and Foes of Change: Reformism and Conservatism in the Soviet Union," in S. F. Cohen, A. Rabinowitch, and R. Sharlet (eds.), *The Soviet Union since Stalin*, Bloomington: Indiana University Press, 1980, pp. 11–32. For the connection between cultural Westernization and reform, see R. D. English, *Russia and the Idea of the West: Gorbachev, Intellectuals, and the End of the Cold War*, New York: Columbia University Press, 2000.

3 For the connection between the autocratic tsarist tradition and Stalin's Soviet-Russian state-building project, see R. Tucker, *Stalin in Power: The Revolution from Above, 1928–1941*, New York: W. W. Norton, 1992.

4 Quoted in K. E. Smith, *Mythmaking in the New Russia: Politics and Memory during the Yeltsin Era*, Ithaca, NY: Cornell University Press, 2002, p. 182.

5 Yu. Slezkine, "The USSR as a Communal Apartment, or How a Socialist State Promoted Ethnic Particularism," *Slavic Review*, 53, 2, summer 1994, 414–452 at p. 421.

6 The authoritative work on Soviet nationality policy in this period is T. Martin, *The Affirmative Action Empire*, Ithaca, NY: Cornell University Press, 2001.

7 "The October Revolution and the National Policy of the Russian Communists" (6–7 November 1921), in J. V. Stalin, *Works*, Moscow: Foreign Languages Publishing House, 1953, vol. 5, pp. 115–118.

8 L. Tillett, *The Great Friendship: Soviet Historians on Non-Russian Nationalities*, Chapel Hill: University of North Carolina Press, 1969, pp. 3–34.

9 Slezkine, "The USSR as a Communal Apartment," 434–435, 443.

10 M. Agursky, *The Third Rome: National Bolshevism in the USSR*, Boulder, CO: Westview Press, 1987.

11 "Reply to the Discussion on the Report on National Factors in Party and State Affairs" (25 April 1923), Stalin, *Works*, vol. 5, pp. 269–281.

12 "On the National Pride of the Great Russians" (12 December 1914), in V. I. Lenin, *Selected Works in Three Volumes*, Moscow: Progress Publishers, 1975, vol. 1, pp. 625–628.

13 For Stalin's views on local nationalism at this time, see his "Report on National Factors in Party and State Affairs," Twelfth Congress of the R.C.P.(B.) (23 April 1923), Stalin, *Works*, vol. 5, pp. 241–268. It should be pointed out that as late as 1930 the Sixteenth Party Congress proclaimed Great Russian chauvinism the main danger on the nationality front, although in practice local nationalism would soon become the main target. L. Schapiro, *The Communist Party of the Soviet Union*, New York: Random House, 1971, pp. 480–481.

14 For this ironic inversion of the Marxist base–superstructure model in the Soviet Union of the 1920s, see M. Lewin, *The Making of the Soviet System: Essays on the Social History of Interwar Russia*, New York: Pantheon Books, 1985, pp. 258–285.

15 Slezkine, "The USSR as a Communal Apartment," 424–425.

16 L. Trotsky, *Literature and Revolution*, Ann Arbor: University of Michigan Press, 1960, p. 94.

17 For an excellent analysis of Bukharin's "Angry Remarks" (*Zlye zametki*, 1927) as a prelude to the attack on popular peasant Russia, see G. Freidin, "Romans into Italians: Russian National Identity in Transition," *Stanford Slavic Studies*, 7, 1993, 241–275. See also Agursky, *The Third Rome*, pp. 330–331.

18 Freidin, "Romans into Italians," pp. 263–268, discusses Gorky's role in some detail; Agursky, *The Third Rome*, pp. 278–281, gives a vivid overview of Gorky's attitude toward the peasantry.
19 "On the Good Life" (1929), in M. Gorky, *Culture and People*, New York: International Publishers, 1939, pp. 69–89.
20 Ibid., pp. 82–83.
21 For *ressentiment* as a motivating force in nationalism, see L. Greenfeld, *Nationalism: Five Roads to Modernity*, Cambridge, MA: Harvard University Press, 1992.
22 R. Tucker, *Stalin as Revolutionary, 1879–1929: A Study in History and Personality*, New York: W. W. Norton, 1973, pp. 137–145.
23 E. H. Carr, *Socialism in One Country*, Hardmondsworth, UK: Penguin Books, 1970, vol. 1, pp. 151–203; I. Deutscher, *Stalin: A Political Biography*, New York: Oxford University Press, 1967, pp. 206–210.
24 "Speeches at the Sixth Congress of the R.S.D.L.P. (Bolsheviks)" (26 July – 3 August 1917), in Stalin, *Works*, vol. 3, pp. 166–201. For this point, see Stalin's response to Preobrazhensky, pp. 199–200.
25 "The October Revolution and the National Question" (6 and 19 November 1918), Stalin, *Works*, vol. 4, pp. 158–170 at p. 168.
26 "Don't Forget the East" (24 November 1918), Stalin, *Works*, vol. 4, pp. 174–176.
27 "Light from the East" (1 December 1918), Stalin, *Works*, vol. 4, pp. 181–186.
28 "Three Years of Proletarian Dictatorship" (6 November 1920), Stalin, *Works*, vol. 4, pp. 395–406.
29 Tucker, *Stalin in Power*, pp. 45–50.
30 "To Comrade Demyan Bedny" (12 December 1930), Stalin, *Works*, vol. 13, pp. 24–29. Stalin's letter remained unpublished for the next twenty years but that does not diminish its significance. For the broader context, see Tucker, *Stalin in Power*, pp. 42–43.
31 Ibid., pp. 41–42.
32 For the classic statements on these two aspects of the Stalin revolution, see S. Fitzpatrick (ed.), *Cultural Revolution in Russia, 1928–1931*, Bloomington: Indiana University Press, 1978; M. Lewin, *Russian Peasants and Soviet Power: A Study of Collectivization*, New York: W. W. Norton, 1975.
33 "The Tasks of Business Executives" (4 February 1931), Stalin, *Works*, vol. 13, pp. 31–44.
34 Freidin, "Romans into Italians," pp. 260–261.
35 Tucker, *Stalin in Power*, p. 41.
36 The most detailed treatment of the origins of the "Change of Landmarks" (*smenovekhovstvo*) school of nationalist thought can be found in Agursky, *The Third Rome*. For a good discussion of its intellectual leader, Nikolai Ustrialov, see J. Burbank, *Intelligentsia and Revolution: Russian Views of Bolshevism, 1917–1922*, New York: Oxford University Press, 1986, pp. 222–238; P. J. S. Duncan, "Changing Landmarks? Anti-Westernism in National Bolshevik and Russian Revolutionary Thought," in G. Hosking and R. Service (eds.), *Russian Nationalism Past and Present*, Basingstoke, UK: Macmillan; New York: St. Martin's Press, 1998, pp. 55–77, places *Smena vekh* in the broader context of Russian intellectual history. The integral text of the original *Smena vekh* almanac (Prague, 1921) has been reprinted in I. A. Isaaev (ed.), *V poiskakh puti. Russkaia intelligentsia i sud'by Rossii*, Moscow: Russkaia kniga, 1992, pp. 207–372.
37 L. Viola, *The Best Sons of the Fatherland: Workers in the Vanguard of Soviet Collectivization*, New York: Oxford University Press, 1987, pp. 4, 60–68. Viola, however, concentrates more on the workers than on the fatherland and thus fails to spell out the implications of her research for nationalism and national identity.
38 Fitzpatrick, *Cultural Revolution in Russia*, pp. 8–41, convincingly documents the extent of this transformation in education and the professions, but does not relate it to the question of Soviet-Russian national identity.

39 N. Timasheff, *The Great Retreat: The Growth and Decline of Communism in Russia*, New York: E. P. Dutton, 1946.

40 K. Jowitt, *Revolutionary Breakthroughs and National Development. The Case of Romania*, Berkeley and Los Angeles: University of California Press, 1971, p. 115.

41 D. L. Brandenberger and A. M. Dubrovsky, "'The People Need a Tsar': The Emergence of National Bolshevism as Stalinist Ideology, 1931–1941," *Europe–Asia Studies*, 50, 5, 1998, 873–892 at p. 875.

42 See ibid., p. 881 for Mekhlis's observation made in the context of the Russo-Finnish war to the effect that "Red Army soldiers were not finding existing rhetoric compelling and called for a de-emphasizing of internationalist slogans in favor of a more defensive nation-state orientation."

43 G. Simon, *Nationalism and Policy toward the Nationalities in the Soviet Union: From Totalitarian Dictatorship to Post-Stalinist Society*, Boulder, CO: Westview Press, 1991, pp. 119–120, 376–387.

44 Ibid., pp. 148–150. For history books, see Tillett, *The Great Friendship*, pp. 35–57, and Brandenberger and Dubrovsky, "'The People Need a Tsar'."

45 Freidin, "Romans into Italians," pp. 248–249.

46 J. T. Gross, *Revolution from Abroad: The Soviet Conquest of Poland's Western Ukraine and Western Belorussia*, Princeton, NJ: Princeton University Press, 1988, p. 230.

47 "To Comrade Kaganovich and the Other Members of the Political Bureau of the Central Committee, Ukrainian C.P.(B.)" (26 April 1926), Stalin, *Works*, vol. 8, pp. 157–163.

48 See the inspiring discussion in K. Jowitt, *The New World Disorder*, Berkeley and Los Angeles: University of California Press, 1992, pp. 159–220, which, however, concentrates mostly on the international dimensions of "the Moscow center."

49 If one searches for the geographic-symbolic center of the "Moscow center," the Old Square (*Staraia ploshchad'*), where the Central Committee was located, and the Lubianka Square, with its NKVD/KGB headquarters, seem to be better choices than the Kremlin, despite the fact that the latter remained the main residence of Stalin and his successors.

50 Tucker, *Stalin in Power*, p. 504.

51 "The Fourteenth Congress of the C.P.S.U.(B.)" (18–31 December 1925), Stalin, *Works*, vol. 7, pp. 265–362. Ustrialov was serving in Harbin, on the Manchurian part of the Trans-Siberian Railway.

52 Ustrialov's story is recounted briefly by S. V. Kuleshov in the afterword to *Zvezda i svastika. Bol'shevizm i russkii fashizm*, Moscow: Terra, 1994, pp. 271–315. For Ustrialov's case, see p. 286.

53 "Vystuplenie po radio" (3 July 1941), in I. V. Stalin, *Sochineniia*, Stanford: Hoover Institution, Stanford University, 1967, 2 [XV], 1941–1945, pp. 1–10. The great emotional resonance of this speech is captured well in A. Werth, *Russia at War, 1941–1945*, New York: Avon Books, 1965, pp. 167–174. For the image of *rodnoi* Stalin in the 1930s, see V. Bonnell, *Iconography of Power: Soviet Political Posters under Lenin and Stalin*, Berkeley and Los Angeles: University of California Press, 1997, pp. 164–165.

54 "*Rech' na Krasnoi ploshchadi*" (7 November 1941), Stalin, *Sochineniia*, vol. 2 [XV], pp. 32–35.

55 J. Brooks, "*Pravda* Goes to War," in R. Stites (ed.), *Culture and Entertainment in Wartime Russia*, Bloomington and Indianapolis: Indiana University Press, 1995, pp. 9–28 at p. 14.

56 I. Ehrenburg, "October 4, 1941," in I. Ehrenburg and K. Simonov, *In One Newspaper: A Chronicle of Unforgettable Years*, trans. A. Kagan, New York: Sphinx Press, 1985, pp. 67–71 at pp. 70–71.

57 Bonnell, *Iconography of Power*, p. 256, notes the strong association between the concept of *rodina* and female images in visual propaganda during the first years of the war. Stalin, by contrast, made a more conspicuous appearance only after the decisive

Stalingrad victory, and especially after 1943. This, of course, does not mean that Stalin was absent from official propaganda altogether. See J. Barber, "The Image of Stalin in Soviet Propaganda and Public Opinion during World War 2," in J. Garrard and C. Garrard (eds.), *World War Two and the Soviet People*, New York: St. Martin's Press, 1993, pp. 38–50; J. Barber and M. Harrison, *The Soviet Home Front, 1941–1945: A Social and Economic History of the USSR in World War II*, London: Longman, 1991, pp. 68–73.

58 B. Pasternak, *Doctor Zhivago*, translated by Max Hayward, London: Collins & Harvill, 1958, p. 453.

59 The phrase belongs to the historian Mikhail Gefter. See N. Tumarkin, *The Living and the Dead: The Rise and Fall of the Cult of World War Two in Russia*, New York: HarperCollins, 1994, pp. 63–65. See also L. Lazarev, "Russian Literature on the War and Historical Truth," and G. Gibian, "World War 2 in Russian National Consciousness: Pristavkin (1981–7) and Kondratyev (1990)," in Garrard and Garrard, *World War Two and the Soviet People*, pp. 28–37, 147–161. For the journalists and composers, see L. McReynolds, "Dateline Stalingrad: Newspaper Correspondents at the Front," and H. Robinson, "Composing for Victory: Classical Music," in Stites, *Culture and Entertainment in Wartime Russia*, pp. 28–44, 62–77.

60 D. Volkogonov, *Stalin: Triumph and Tragedy*, London: Weidenfeld & Nicolson, 1991, pp. 427–428. Another measure of the state's distrust of society was the fantastic size of Stalin's NKVD (People's Commissariat of Internal Affairs): at 366,000 full-time employees in 1939, it was twenty times larger than Hitler's Gestapo (7,000) per capita of population. See J. Brooks, *Thank You, Comrade Stalin! Soviet Public Culture from Revolution to Cold War*, Princeton, NJ: Princeton University Press, 2000, p. 10.

61 Volkogonov, *Stalin*, pp. 459–460.

62 Tumarkin, *The Living and the Dead*, pp. 70–73.

63 Brooks, "*Pravda* Goes to War," pp. 21–24; Werth, *Russia at War*, pp. 539–552, 678, 854–857; Deutscher, *Stalin*, p. 552.

64 For the full text, see J. von Geldern and R. Stites (eds.), *Mass Culture in Soviet Russia, 1917–1953*, Bloomington and Indianapolis: Indiana University Press, 1995, pp. 406–407.

65 F. C. Barghoorn, *Soviet Russian Nationalism*, New York: Oxford University Press, 1956.

66 "Vystuplenie na prieme v Kremle v chest' komanduiushchikh voiskami krasnoi armii" (24 May 1945), Stalin, *Sochineniia*, vol. 2 [XV], pp. 203–204.

67 Lazarev, "Russian Literature on the War and Historical Truth," p. 30.

68 Tumarkin, *The Living and the Dead*, pp. 133–136.

69 "Vystuplenie na prieme v Kremle v chest' uchastnikov parada pobedy," Stalin, *Sochineniia* vol. 2 [XV], p. 206.

70 A. Zinoviev, *Nashei iunosti polet*, Lausanne: L'Âge d'homme, 1983.

71 A. Yanov, *The Russian New Right*, Berkeley, CA: Institute of International Studies, 1978; Y. Brudny, *Reinventing Russia: Russian Nationalism and the Soviet State, 1953–1991*, Cambridge, MA: Harvard University Press, 1998.

72 A very interesting contribution on the instrumental uses of anti-Semitism is S. L. Burg, "The Calculus of Soviet Antisemitism," in J. Azrael (ed.), *Soviet Nationality Policies and Practices*, New York: Praeger, 1978, pp. 189–223.

73 S. I. Ozhegov, *Slovar' russkogo iazyka*, Moskva: Russkii iazyk, 1988.

74 The first formulation comes from the 1953 edition of the same dictionary, the second from a 1983 Soviet political dictionary. See M. Heller, *Cogs in the Wheel: The Formation of Soviet Man*, New York: Alfred A. Knopf, 1988, pp. 272–273, fn. 44.

75 R. Szporluk, "The Ukraine and Russia," in R. Conquest (ed.), *The Last Empire: Nationality and the Soviet Future*, Stanford, CA: Hoover Institution Press, 1986, pp. 151–183.

76 Quoted in G. Wartshofsky Lapidus, "Ethnonationalism and Political Stability: The Soviet Case," *World Politics*, 36, 4, July 1984, 355–380.
77 See E. Alworth (ed.), *Ethnic Russia in the USSR: The Dilemma of Dominance*, New York: Pergamon Press, 1980, and in particular the contributions of Alworth (pp. 17–41), Michael Rywkin, Vadim Medish, and Seweryn Bialer (pp. 177–202) to the debate on the position of the RSFSR in the USSR.
78 R. Szporluk, "The Imperial Legacy," in L. Hajda and M. Beissinger (eds.), *The Nationalities Factor in Soviet Politics and Society*, Boulder, CO: Westview Press, 1990, pp. 1–24.
79 R. Tucker, *The Soviet Political Mind*, New York: W. W. Norton, p. 136.
80 Pasternak, *Doctor Zhivago*, p. 463.
81 D. Brandenberger, *National Bolshevism: Stalinist Mass Culture and the Formation of Modern Russian National Identity, 1931–1956*, Cambridge, MA: Harvard University Press, 2002, pp. 2, 247.
82 Quoted in L. Aron, *Yeltsin: A Revolutionary Life*, New York: St. Martin's Press, 2000, pp. 434–435.
83 Smith, *Mythmaking in the New Russia*, pp. 158–184.
84 P. Baker and S. Glasser, *Kremlin Rising: Vladimir Putin's Russia and the End of Revolution*, New York: Scribner, 2005, p. 349.
85 L. Shevtsova, *Putin's Russia*, Washington, DC: Carnegie Endowment for International Peace, 2005, pp. 257–258, 350–351.

4 Concepts of fascism in contemporary Russia and the West*

Andreas Umland

The 1990s have seen remarkable changes in both the Western and the Russian study of fascism, understood as a generic concept. On the one side, Western comparative fascist studies went through a process of consolidation: A number of tendencies in the study of interwar Europe have been synthesized into a relatively unambiguous conceptualization of fascism that has become more or less widely accepted in the English-writing scholarly community.[1] In Russia, on the other side, the notorious standard orthodox Marxist definition of fascism has been abandoned.[2] Subsequently, the post-Soviet Russian interpretation of fascism has suffered from fragmentation, and the usage of the term "fascism" in public discourse from what might be called "hyper-inflation."[3] In what follows I shall shortly juxtapose recent Western and Russian developments, and identify some points where the two trends meet.

The emergence of a nascent consensus in the Western study of fascism

Though non-Marxist scholarly comparative fascist studies emerged as long ago as the early 1960s,[4] they were, over more than two decades, hampered by the absence of a commonly accepted, lucid definition of what exactly is to be studied. A number of eminent scholars, including Juan Linz, George Mosse, and Stanley Payne, to be sure, had a shared understanding of which phenomena are to be labeled "fascist" and which not; and they proposed more or less compatible definitions of the concept.[5] Yet their and others' lists of characteristics of fascism were too cumbersome for an uncomplicated application in empirical research and effective integration in the comparative study of ideologies. Other Western scholars departed from this informal consensus by, for instance, rejecting the idea of a generic fascism altogether.[6] A third group proposed idiosyncratic conceptualizations which, for instance, explicitly excluded Nazism from the class of fascisms,[7] or stretched the concept so as to include a number of non-European inter- and postwar developmental dictatorships.[8] For many years the large German industry of Nazism studies ignored, with only few exceptions,[9] the growing body of non-Marxist comparative research into international fascism (though some German scholars did contribute to this literature).[10]

The publication of Roger Griffin's monograph *The Nature of Fascism* in 1991, and its reprint in 1993, arguably represented a turning point in recent Western comparative studies of fascism.[11] Following a certain pause in Anglo-Saxon comparative theorizing about generic fascism in the 1980s, Griffin presented, after more than a decade, the first comprehensive theory in the English language, which was widely hailed in the 1990s. He also managed to provide a succinct definition of fascism as "palingenetic [expressing the idea of rebirth] ultranationalism." This formula has proven to be useful, and has been applied by a number of scholars engaged in the empirical study of local manifestations of right-wing extremism.[12]

Griffin, moreover, has built around his concept a comprehensive theory of fascism's emergence and rise that combines findings of many scholars. His interpretation focuses on the spread of a feeling that contemporary society is in a process of rapid cultural decline. Paradoxically, such acuity of decadence leads, in the fascist mindset, not to "cultural pessimism" but to a manically optimistic belief that society's current downfall will eventually lead to glorious national rebirth. The nation, in fascist thinking, is at a turning point, and about to rise phoenix-like from the ashes of recent degeneration. Though being radically right-wing in envisaging a society that is structured and cleansed according to ascribed differences between human beings, fascism is neither conservative nor reactionary. It does not aim to preserve or recreate the past. Instead, it wants to build a radically new society and form a "new man."

Griffin thus provided a comprehensive hermeneutic theory of fascist ideology's sources and implications supplanted, in 1995, with an impressive reader of primary texts supporting his interpretation.[13] At about the same time, Stanley G. Payne contributed the third "great" book on fascism of the 1990s, *A History of Fascism*.[14] Payne's magisterial study is a comprehensive comparison of the varieties of all relevant interwar putatively fascist movements and regimes, and in many ways is in accord with Griffin's conceptualization (which, in turn, had been heavily informed by Payne's previous research on generic and Spanish fascism). The third author to join this emerging community was Roger Eatwell, who contributed a number of important theoretical investigations into the concept of generic fascism[15] as well as an excellent survey of inter- and postwar fascism in Germany, France, Italy, and Great Britain.[16]

Last but not least, a number of new volumes of collected papers are now providing comprehensive documentation of the development of comparative fascist studies over the past six decades.[17] In particular, Griffin's and Matthew Feldman's 2004 contribution *Fascism* to Routledge's Critical Concepts in Political Science series constitutes a pioneering project, collecting, in five volumes, 100 scholarly papers, journalistic articles, and political statements under the headings "The Nature of Fascism," "The Social Dynamics of Fascism," "Fascism and Culture," "The 'Fascist Epoch,'" and "Post-war Fascisms."[18]

While retaining some significant distinctions in their approaches to the extreme right, the writings by Payne, Griffin, and Eatwell, as well as some other authors,[19] today form the core of an increasing agreement about how fascism is to be understood, defined and studied. To be sure, a number of students of fascism, among them some leading scholars, have ignored this development or rejected Griffin's idea of an emerging consensus as false or undesirable or both.[20] Paradoxically, however, some of these critics use conceptualizations of fascism that appear broadly compatible with Griffin's, Payne's, and Eatwell's.[21]

Concepts of fascism in post-Soviet Russia

Whereas Western scholarship seems to be gradually converging on a more or less uniform conceptualization of fascism, the Russian interpretation has been going in the opposite direction since the introduction of *glasnost'*, and been witnessing a multiplication of the meanings of "fascism." Among the most bizarre expressions of the rapid disintegration of this concept in Russia in the mid-1990s have been the announcements of the creation of "anti-fascist centers" by such organizations as the Rossiiskii Obshchenarodnyi Soiuz (Russian All-People's Union) led by Sergei Baburin, as well as by the Pravo-radikal'naia partiia Rossii (Right-Radical Party of Russia), led by Sergei Zharikov and Andrei Arkhipov. While it is debatable whether Baburin's steady radicalization from a moderate to an increasingly radical nationalist during the 1990s led him to become fully fascist,[22] Zharikov and Arkhipov have, from the start of their involvement in politics as Zhirinovsky's assistants in the early 1990s, been full-blown fascists who did not bother to camouflage their affinity to the German "conservative revolution," and their keen interest in Nazism.[23]

Russian scholarly research into, and para-scholarly writing on, fascism witnessed at least four distinct trends in the post-Soviet period.[24] First, there are some publicists who still uphold more or less modified versions of the Soviet standard definition of fascism. Surprisingly, for instance, as late as 1995 a two-volume Soviet pamphlet on fascism of 1985 was reprinted.[25] It reproduces the three major deficiencies of mainstream Soviet research: it had been informed by a misleading, if not absurd, notion of fascism; it was often empirically slender; and it used, paradoxically, the Italian-derived term *fashizm* to denote, above all, German Nazism.[26] The latter was in contrast to the above-mentioned Western trend that hesitated to put Nazism, without reservations, under the heading of generic fascism (Linz), or rejected altogether Nazism's membership in the class of fascisms (Sternhell, Gregor). The conspirological standard Soviet interpretations of fascism as "dictatorship of financial capital" have, moreover, sometimes been linked to anti-Semitic trends in Russian publicism, above all to theories that presented – and sometimes still portray – Zionism as an ideology of Jewish world domination and a form of "fascism."[27]

Also frequently tied to the above approach has been a second school comprising those authors who conceptualize fascism as a fundamentally Western form of extremism which is, by definition, non-Russian. These observers either prefer to ignore putatively fascist trends,[28] or explicitly exclude even their possibility in Russian society. Thus, for instance, the historian A. Iu. Zudin voiced an opinion held by many Russian analysts of the post-Soviet political scene when claiming that right-wing radicalism and fascism are "products of Western civilization," and that those fascist trends that are nevertheless observable in Russia are, simply, "imported goods."[29]

Third, there are a number of publicists who use the term liberally, and who call "fascist" a broad variety of authoritarian and nationalist tendencies, even those in the Russian liberal movement.[30] Some of these authors, to be sure, follow a trend that has also been present in the Western study of fascism and seems, in view of recent research, to have gained legitimacy: They extend the concept of fascism in a way as to include in this class also the ideologies of some officially "communist" totalitarian regimes such as Stalin's.[31] Insofar as there have recently appeared a number of important studies that highlight the relevance of nationalist and anti-Semitic trends during high Stalinism and after, such an approach seems not entirely unjustified.[32] It has gained additional relevance in connection with the growth of manifestly nationalist tendencies in the post-Soviet Russian communist movement.[33] However, the usefulness of this approach is lost when, for instance, Samoilov, in his three-volume comparative analysis of Hitler, Mussolini, Stalin, Mao, etc., defines fascism as "hunger for power," or "evil" expressed in political terms. Samoilov goes on to call Boris Yeltsin and other liberal politicians with authoritarian tendencies "pro-" or "half-fascist."[34]

A fourth tendency seems to draw on earlier Soviet research on Western concepts of fascism under the heading of "critique of bourgeois theorizing."[35] It continues some relatively enlightened approaches in late Soviet-Russian research on fascism.[36] These trends are also represented by a number of researchers outside Moscow and St. Petersburg, such as, for instance, at the Faculties of History and International Relations of the Urals State University of Yekaterinburg, including Valeri Mikhailenko[37] and the late Valentin Bukhanov.[38] This emerging school is partly in accordance with recent trends in Western fascist theorizing, as it used to pay only lip service to the orthodox Soviet definition of fascism; does not use "fascism" as a synonym for either German Nazism, Western right-wing political forces in general, or all totalitarian regimes; and does not misuse the term "fascist" to label all sorts of historic or contemporary Russian, Jewish, or Western politicians who have, or are suspected to have, done some damage to Russian imperial interests.

Sometimes this tendency still departs from Western interpretations of fascism when it, for instance, includes Franco's regime in the class of fascist dictatorships.[39] However, in general, this fourth trend in Russian theorizing about fascism is informed about major Western research on fascism, and either implicitly or explicitly reflects upon its main findings.[40]

It is, moreover, intriguing that, in 1995, the foremost Russian representative of this trend and doyen of Russian fascist studies, Alexander Abramovich Galkin (b. 1922) did for Russia a job somewhat similar to the one Griffin had done for Western fascist studies a couple of years before. Without yet having learned of Griffins formula of "palingenetic ultranationalism," Galkin condensed his previous conceptualizations of fascism into the notion of "right-wing conservative revolutionarism." Galkin clarified that fascism "tries to overcome real contradictions in society, and to destroy everything that appears to it as hindrances for the preservation and rebirth of the peculiarly understood eternal fundamentals of being."[41] Though, arguably, less lucid than Griffin's concept (and, partly, oxymoronic), Galkin's approach resembles Griffin's project in both its intent and its substance. It too provides a succinct definition of what is to be studied by researchers of fascism, focuses on the ideological core rather than political style or institutional manifestations of fascism, and sees fascism as a combination of extremely right-wing and palingenetic ideas.

This fourth school, finally, is also largely in agreement with Western comparative research into neo-fascism in acknowledging the presence of some striking resemblances between the interwar and post-Soviet situations, and of a potential fascist threat in Russia.[42]

Western and Russian approaches to Russian fascism

The latter illustrates a major reason why the above developments are relevant. While it might be an overstatement to speak of a "Weimar Russia,"[43] the emerging post-Soviet political scene – including parliamentary and extra-parliamentary parties as well as a growing "uncivil society" – does pose the question of how to adequately conceptualize its various Russian right-wing extremist trends, and whether "fascism" might or might not be a useful concept here.[44]

In recent studies of the issue, one can observe two contradictory trends. On the one side, there is a tendency among many – if not a majority of the – observers both in the West and Russia to use the term "fascism" primarily or even only with regard to those ideologies that are *mimetically* fascist – that is, that imitate interwar varieties of fascism, above all German Nazism.[45] Often, therefore, strong attention is paid to Alexander Barkashov's neo-Nazi Russkoe Natsional'noe Edinstvo (RNE; Russian National Unity). The RNE is, for instance, the organization that Stephen Shenfield has, in his well-informed research into Russian fascism, focused on most heavily (though, one should add, he dealt extensively with other trends too).[46] Other observers seem to identify "fascism" with the swastika, the Roman salute, biological racism, etc. Some even seem to be prepared to allow the term's application only if the putative fascist in question explicitly pays tribute to Hitler, Mussolini, Codreanu, and their likes.[47]

Such an approach is paradoxical in two ways. First, the German Nazis themselves rejected the label "fascism." They – in some regards, rightly so – pointed out the differences between their ideology and Italian Fascism. The same logic that allowed comparativists to nevertheless classify Nazism as "fascist" should apply to post-Soviet Russian nationalist ideologies too. If one uses "fascism" in the generic sense, its application should depend on the respective ideology's structural proximity to the ideal-type formulated in a definition of generic fascism, and not on the absence or presence of some external trappings of a particular kind of historical fascism. This is even more true insofar as the specific permutation of fascism referred to here – Nazism – did not give generic fascism its name, but represented its perhaps most extreme manifestation.

A limitation of "fascism's" application to only those Russian groupings that imitate German Nazism and their ultra-nationalist allies in World War II is misleading in a second way too. Naturally, the more serious representatives of Russian ultra-nationalism avoid being associated with a regime that murdered, deported, enslaved, etc. millions of Eastern Slavs.[48] What else would one expect from an authentic Russian ultra-nationalist than to be genuinely outraged about his (or, less probably, her) equation with a movement that was as radically anti-Russian as the Nazis'? Being a genuine Russian nationalist and a neo-Nazi at the same time seems, after World War II, to be at least in some ways an obvious contradiction. One could thus argue that Barkashov is right in claiming that the RNE is not a form of Russian fascism – insofar as it is not really Russian.

One the other hand, there have been some cases when observers have used the term "Nazism" rather than "fascism" for classifying a whole range of different varieties of late- or post-Soviet Russian ultra-nationalism. For instance, Semyon Reznik and Viacheslav Likhachev have used *natsizm* in the titles of their broad surveys of large sections of the Russian extreme right.[49] As I have argued elsewhere, such a terminological solution is unfortunate.[50] By utilizing the term "Nazism" for all sorts of fascist (and perhaps even non-fascist nationalist) ideologies, we lose our ability to identify "real" Nazis. If we use "Nazism" as a label for those who reject any affinity to Hitler's ideology (even though their basic ideas might be structurally similar), how should we then refer to those who do indeed manifestly copy the ideas and style of the Nationalsozialistische Deutsche Arbeiterpartei (NSDAP), and perhaps do not even try to deny their ideological debt to the Third Reich?[51]

Conclusions

There is a certain discrepancy in international right-wing studies today. While Western comparative theorizing about fascism and right-wing extremism in general has made significant advances during the past decade, the attention paid by Western comparativists to recent Russian developments has remained limited. Only a few of the leading scholars in the field have started to integrate post-Soviet developments in their surveys of international fascism.[52] This is regrettable insofar as the post-Soviet extreme right-wing political scene provides a rather multifarious picture. Potentially, the varieties of Russian putatively fascist groupings would seem to be politically more relevant than the thoroughly researched but mostly marginal extreme right-wing trends in contemporary Western Europe – a subject over-researched in hundreds of articles and books.

The Russian community of researchers of fascism, on the other hand, is still struggling to free itself from various abuses of the concept, and to catch up with recent Western research. Not least because of the dire financial situation of many Russian libraries, universities, and research institutes, the majority of Russian specialists will for the foreseeable future remain outside the main debates in the West. They will have limited access to Western scholarly literature and be unable to attend relevant conferences outside Russia. In view of these circumstances, it would be beneficial for both international fascist studies and the study of current Russian anti-democratic trends if Western comparativists paid more attention to the wide variety of putatively fascist phenomena in post-Soviet Russia and tried to integrate Russian and Western findings on them into their research.

Notes

* Originally published in *Political Studies Review*, 3, 1, 2005, 34–49. Reprinted with kind permission from © Blackwell Publishing. An earlier Russian version appeared as "Sovremennye poniatiia fashizma v Rossii i na Zapade," *Neprikosnovennyi zapas*, 5, 31, 2003, 116–122.

1 R. D. Griffin, "The Primacy of Culture: The Current Growth (or Manufacture) of Consensus within Fascist Studies," *Journal of Contemporary History*, 37, 1, 2002, 21–43. For recent reviews of the latest developments in fascist studies, see S. Reichardt, "Was mit dem Faschismus passiert ist: Ein Literaturbericht zur internationalen Faschismusforschung seit 1990. Teil 1," *Neue politische Literatur* 49, 2004, 385–405; A. Costa Pinto, "Back to European Fascism," *Contemporary European History* 15, 1, 2006, 103–15; A. Bauernkämper, "A New Consensus? Recent Research on Fascism in Europe, 1918–1945," *History Compass*, 4, 3, 2006, 536–66; A. Umland, "Fashizm i neofashizma v sravnenii: novye zapadnye publikatsii 2004–2006 gg.," *Forum noveìshei vostochnoevropeiskoi istorii i kul'tury*, 4, 1, 2007, www1.ku-eichstaett.de/zimos/forum/docs/8umlandrezension.pdf (last accessed 20 December 2008).

2 W. Wippermann, *Zur Analyse des Faschismus: Die sozialistischen und kommunistischen Faschismustheorien 1921–1945*, Frankfurt am Main: Diesterweg, 1981; L. Luks, *Entstehung der kommunistischen Faschismustheorie: Die Auseinandersetzung der Komintern mit Faschismus und Nationalsozialismus 1921–1935*, Studien zur Zeitgeschichte, Stuttgart: DVA, 1984; S. G. Payne, "Soviet Anti-fascism: Theory and Practice, 1921–45," *Totalitarian Movements and Political Religions*, 4, 3, 2004, 1–62.

3 In using this metaphor I am alluding here to the frequent complaint in Western studies of generic fascism that the concept is suffering from "inflation" – for example, G. Allardyce, "What Fascism Is Not: Thoughts on the Deflation of a Concept," *American Historical Review*, 84, 2, 1979, 367–388.

4 E. Nolte, *Der Faschismus in seiner Epoche: Action française, italienischer Faschismus, Nationalsozialismus*, Munich: R. Piper, 1963; E. Weber, *Varieties of Fascism: Doctrines of Revolution in the Twentieth Century*, Princeton, NJ: Van Nostrand Reinhold, 1964.

5 J. J. Linz, "Some Notes toward a Comparative Study of Fascism in Sociological Historical Perspective," in W. Laqueur (ed.), *Fascism: A Reader's Guide*, Harmondsworth, UK: Penguin, 1979, pp. 13–78; G. L. Mosse, "Toward a General Theory of Fascism," in W. Laqueur (ed.), *International Fascism: New Thoughts and New Approaches*, London: Sage, 1979, pp. 1–45; S. G. Payne, *Fascism: Comparison and Definition*, Madison: University of Wisconsin Press, 1980.

6 Allardyce, "What Fascism Is Not"; W. Pfeiler, "Der Begriff Faschismus als politisches Instrument und als wissenschaftliche Kategorie," in H. Timmermann and W. D. Gruner (eds.), *Demokratie und Diktatur in Europa: Geschichte und Wechsel der politischen Systeme des 20. Jahrhundert*, Berlin: Duncker & Humblot, 2001, pp. 97–106.

7 Z. Sternhell, *Neither Right nor Left: Fascist Ideology in France*, Princeton, NJ: Princeton University Press, 1996; Z. Sternhell, M. Sznajder, and M. Asheri, *The Birth of Fascist Ideology: From Cultural Rebellion to Political Revolution*, Princeton, NJ: Princeton University Press, 1994.

8 A. James Gregor, *Contemporary Radical Ideologies: Totalitarian Thought in the*

Twentieth Century, New York: Random House, 1968; same author, *The Ideology of Fascism: The Rationale for Totalitarianism*, New York: Free Press, 1969; *The Fascist Persuasion in Radical Politics*, Princeton, NJ: Princeton University Press, 1974; *Italian Fascism and Developmental Dictatorship*, Princeton, NJ: Princeton University Press, 1979.

9 W. Wippermann, *Europäischer Faschismus im Vergleich 1922–1982*, Frankfurt am Main: Suhrkamp, 1983; same author, *Faschismustheorien: Die Entwicklung der Diskussion von den Anfängen bis heute*, 7th edn., Darmstadt: Primus, 1997; W. Wippermann and W. Loh (eds.), *"Faschismus" – kontrovers*, Stuttgart: Lucius & Lucius, 2002; H. Woller, *Rom, 28. Oktober 1922: Die faschistische Herausforderung*, Munich: Deutscher Taschenbuch Verlag, 1999.

10 E.g. G. Allardyce (ed.), *The Place of Fascism in European History*, Upper Saddle River, NJ: Prentice Hall, 1971; P. Hayes, *Fascism*, New York: Free Press, 1973; Laqueur, *Fascism*; S. Ugelvik Larsen, J. P. Myklebust, and B. Hagtvet (eds.), *Who Were the Fascists? Social Roots of European Fascism*, Oslo: Universitetsforlaget, 1980.

11 R. D. Griffin, *The Nature of Fascism*, London: Pinter, 1991 and Routledge 1993; A. Umland, "Staryi vopros zadannyi zanovo: chto takoe fashizm?" *Politicheskie issledovaniia*, 1, 31, 1996, 175–176.

12 In Germany, for instance, Griffin's concept has been used by M. Minkenberg, *Die neue radikale Rechte im Vergleich: USA, Frankreich, Deutschland*, Wiesbaden: Westdeutscher Verlag, 1998; S. Reichardt, *Faschistische Kampfbünde: Gewalt und Gemeinschaft im italienischen Squadrismus und in der deutschen SA*, Cologne: Böhlau, 2002; and A. Umland, "Neue ideologische Fusionen im postsowjetischen russischen Antidemokratismus: Westliche Konzepte, antiwestliche Doktrinen und das postsowjetische politische Spektrum," in E. Jesse and U. Backes (eds.), *Gefährdungen der Freiheit: Extremistische Ideologien im Vergleich*, Schriften des Hannah-Arendt-Instituts 29, Göttingen: Vandenhoeck & Ruprecht, 2006, pp. 371–406.

13 R. D. Griffin (ed.), *Fascism*, Oxford: Oxford University Press, 1995.

14 S. G. Payne, *A History of Fascism, 1914–1945*, Madison: University of Wisconsin Press, 1995.

15 E.g. R. Eatwell, "Toward a New Model of Generic Fascism," *Journal of Theoretical Politics*, 4, 2, 1992, 161–194; same author, "Fascism," in A. Wright and R. Eatwell (eds.), *Contemporary Political Ideologies*, London: Pinter, 1993, pp. 169–192; R. Eatwell, "On Defining the 'Fascist Minimum': The Centrality of Ideology," *Journal of Political Ideologies*, 1, 3, 1996, 303–319; same author, "Zur Natur des 'generischen Faschismus': Das 'faschistische Minimum' und die 'faschistische Matrix,'" in U. Backes (ed.), *Rechtsextreme Ideologien in Geschichte und Gegenwart*, Cologne: Böhlau, 2003, pp. 93–122.

16 R. Eatwell, *Fascism: A History*, London: Chatto & Windus 1995 and Penguin, 1997.

17 E.g. R. D. Griffin (ed.), *International Fascism: Theories, Causes and the New Consensus*, London: Arnold, 1998; A. Kallis (ed.), *The Fascism Reader*, London: Routledge, 2003; A. Fenner and E. D. Weitz (eds.), *Fascism and Neofascism: Critical Writings on the Radical Right in Europe*, Studies in European Culture and History, Basingstoke, UK: Palgrave Macmillan, 2004; A. Nolzen and S. Reichardt (eds.), *Faschismus in Deutschland und Italien: Studien zu Transfer und Vergleich*, Göttingen: Wallstein, 2005; R. Griffin (ed.), *Fascism, Totalitarianism and Political Religion*, London: Routledge, 2006; R. Griffin, W. Loh, and A. Umland (eds.), *Fascism Past and Present, West and East: An International Debate on Concepts and Cases in the Comparative Study of the Extreme Right*, Soviet and Post-Soviet Politics and Society 35, Stuttgart: ibidem-Verlag, 2006; C. Blamires (ed.), *World Fascism: A Historical Encyclopedia*, 2 vols., Santa Barbara, CA: ABC-CLIO, 2006.

18 R. D. Griffin with M. Feldman (eds.), *Critical Concepts in Political Science: Fascism*, 5 vols., London: Routledge, 2004.

19 E.g. N. Copsey, "Fascism: The Ideology of the British National Party," *Politics*,

14, 3, 1994, 101–108; D. Prowe, "'Classic' Fascism and the New Radical Right in Western Europe: Comparisons and Contrasts," *Contemporary European History*, 3, 3, 1994, 289–313; D. Baker, *Ideology of Obsession: A. K. Chesterton and British Fascism*, London: I. B. Tauris, 1996; A. Kallis, "'Fascism,' 'Para-fascism' and 'Fascistization': On the Similarities of Three Conceptual Categories," *European History Quarterly*, 33, 2, 2004, 219–249; same author, "Studying Inter-war Fascism in Epochal and Diachronic Terms: Ideological Production, Political Experience and the Quest for 'Consensus,'" *European History Quarterly*, 34, 1, 2004, 9–42.

20 E.g. D. Renton, *Fascism: Theory and Practice*, London: Pluto, 1999; M. Knox, *Common Destiny: Dictatorship, Foreign Policy, and War in Fascist Italy and Nazi Germany*, Cambridge: Cambridge University Press, 2000; A. James Gregor, *Phoenix: Fascism in Our Time*, New Brunswick, NJ: Transaction, 1999; S. Breuer, *Nationalismus und Faschismus: Frankreich, Italien und Deutschland im Vergleich*, Darmstadt: Wissenschaftliche Buchgesellschaft, 2005.

21 E.g. W. Laqueur, *Fascism: Past, Present, Future*, New York: Oxford University Press, 1996; M. Blinkhorn, *Fascism and the Right in Europe, 1919–1945*, Harlow: Pearson Education, 2000; R. O. Paxton, "The Five Stages of Fascism," *Journal of Modern History*, 70, 1998, 1–23; same author, *The Anatomy of Fascism*, New York: Alfred A. Knopf, 2004.

22 S. Gunnar Simonsen, *Politics and Personalities: Key Actors in the Russian Opposition*, PRIO Report 2, Oslo: Peace Research Institute, 1996, pp. 18–27; L. Belin, "Sergey Baburin: Leftist Looking for a Home," RFE/RL news, www.rferl.org/specials/russianelection/bio/baburin.asp.

23 *Sokol Zhirinovskogo*, 1–4, 1992; W. Sloane, "Who's Afraid of Vladimir Wolf?" *Moscow-Magazine*, April–May, 1992, 40–7; *Segodnia*, 22 December 1993; E. Limonov, *Limonov protiv Zhirinovskogo*, Moscow: Konets veka, 1994; E. Al'bats, *Evreiskii vopros*, Moscow: PIK, 1994; D. Crouch, "The Crisis in Russia and the Rise of the Right," *International Socialism*, 66, 1995, http://pubs.socialistreviewindex.org.uk/isj66/crouch.htm; www.letov.ru/DK/ktoporu.html; www.letov.ru/DK/ataka.html.

24 See also the discussions in V. Tolstych, A. Galkin, V. Loginov, and A. Buzgalin, "Der russische Faschismus im Widerstreit," *Utopie kreativ: Diskussion sozialistischer Alternativen*, 52, 1995, 65–72; Iu. Galaktionov, *Germanskii fashizm kak fenomen pervoi poloviny XX veka: Otechestvennaia istoriografiia 1945–90-kh godov*, Kemerovo: Kemerovskii gosudarstvennyi universitet, 1999; and H. Schützler, "Faschismus – ein Thema in der russischen Historiographie der 90er Jahre?" in M. Weibbecker, R. Kühnl, and E. Schwarz (eds.), *Rassismus, Faschismus, Antifaschismus: Forschungen und Betrachtungen gewidmet Kurt Pätzold zum 70. Geburtstag*, Cologne: PapyRossa, 2000, pp. 231–242.

25 B. N. Bessonov, *Fashizm: ideologiia, politika*, 2 vols., Moscow: Luch, 1995.

26 D. M. Proektor, *Fashizm: put' aggressii i gibeli*, Moscow: Nauka, 1985.

27 V. Obukhov, "Sionizm kak mezhdunarodnyi fashizm," *Molodaia gvardiia*, 8, 1994, 196–209.

28 E.g., implicitly, A. I. Riabov, "Neofashizm segodnia," *Nauchnyi kommunizm*, 3, 1990, 75–83.

29 A. Iu. Zudin, "Fashizm v Rossii: obrazy i real'nosti novoi opasnosti," *Politicheskie issledovaniia*, 2, 26, 1995, 41–43; also quoted in Schützler, "Faschismus," 236.

30 E.g. G. Pavlovsky, "Progulki s antifashistami," *Vek XX i mir*, 5–6, 1994, 92–101.

31 The major Western representative of this approach is the doyen of US fascist studies, A. James Gregor, *Contemporary Radical Ideologies: Totalitarian Thought in the Twentieth Century*, New York: Random House, 1968; same author, *The Ideology of Fascism: The Rationale for Totalitarianism*, New York: Free Press, 1969; *The Fascist Persuasion in Radical Politics*, Princeton, NJ: Princeton University Press, 1974; *Italian Fascism and Developmental Dictatorship*, Princeton, NJ: Princeton University

Press, 1979. See also his recent studies *Phoenix: Fascism in Our Time*, with an introduction by Allesandro Campi, New Brunswick, NJ: Transaction Publishers, 1999, and *The Faces of Janus: Fascism and Marxism in the Twentieth Century*, New Haven, CT: Yale University Press, 2000.

32 A. M. Nekrich, *Pariahs, Partners, Predators: German–Soviet Relations, 1922–1941*, New York: Columbia University Press, 1997; L. Luks (ed.), *Der Spätstalinismus und die "jüdische Frage": Zur antisemitischen Wendung des Kommunismus*, Cologne: Böhlau, 1998; A. Lustiger, *Rotbuch: Stalin und die Juden. Die tragische Geschichte des Jüdischen Antifaschistischen Komitees und der sowjetischen Juden*, Berlin: Aufbau-Verlag, 1998; D. L. Brandenberger, *National Bolshevism: Stalinist Mass Culture and the Formation of Modern Russian National Identity, 1931–1956*, Russian Research Center Studies 93, Cambridge, MA: Harvard University Press, 2002; E. van Ree, *The Political Thought of Joseph Stalin: A Study in Twentieth-Century Revolutionary Patriotism*, London: RoutledgeCurzon, 2002; G. V. Kostyrchenko, *Tainaia politika Stalin: vlast' i antisemitizm*, Moscow: Mezhdunarodnye otnosheniia, 2003; N. Mitrokhin, *"Russkaia partiia": Dvizhenie russkikh natsionalistov v SSSR, 1953–1985 gg.*, Moscow: NLO, 2003.

33 V. Bugera, "Sotsial-fashizm," *Marksist: nauchno-politicheskii zhurnal*, 2, 1994, 27–54; V. Vujačić, "Gennadiy Zyuganov and the 'Third Road,'" *Post-Soviet Affairs*, 12, 2, 1994, 118–154; A. James Gregor, "Fascism and the New Russian Nationalism," *Communist and Post-Communist Studies*, 31, 1, 1998, 1–15.

34 E. V. Samoilov, *Fiurery: obshchaia teoriia fashizma*. 3 vols., Obninsk: SELS, 1993. For a critique, see V. I. Zamkovoi, *Totalitarizm: sushchnost' i kontseptsii*, Moscow: IMPE, 1994, p. 4.

35 E.g. P. Iu. Rakhshmir, "Sovremennye tendentsii burzhuaznoi istoriografii fashizma," *Novaia i noveishaia istoriia*, 6, 1971; L. I. Gintsberg, "Fashizm i istoriia noveishego vremeni," *Novaia i noveishaia istoriia*, 4, 1971, 33–48; K. Gossweiler, "Krizis burzhuaznoi istoriografii fashizma," in *Ezhegodnik germanskoi istorii 1974*, Moscow: Nauka, 1975, pp. 316–337; P. Iu. Rakhshmir, "'Gitlerovskaia volna' v burzhuaznoi istoriografii Zapada," in *Ezhegodnik germanskoi istorii 1975*, Moscow: Nauka, 1976, pp. 266–271; same author, *Proiskhozhdenie fashizma: istoriia i sovremennost'*, Moscow: Nauka, 1981.

36 A. Galkin, "Capitalist Society and Fascism," *Social Sciences: USSR Academy of Sciences*, 2, 1970, 80–85; A. A. Galkin, *Sotsiologiia neofashizma*, Moscow: Nauka, 1971.

37 V. I. Mikhailenko, *Ital'ianskii fashizm: Osnovnye voprosy istoriografii*, Sverdlovsk: Izdatel'stvo Ural'skogo universiteta, 1987.

38 V. A. Bukhanov, *Evropeiskaia strategiia germanskogo fashizma*, Sverdlovsk: Izdatel'stvo Ural'skogo universiteta, 1991; same author, *Gitlerovskii "novyi poriadok" v Evrope i ego krakh 1939–1945*, Ekaterinburg: Izdatel'stvo Ural'skogo universiteta, 1994; *Evropeiskaia strategiia germanskogo natsional-sotsializma i ee krakh. Ideino-politicheskie problemy*, Ekaterinburg: Izdatel'stvo Ural'skogo universiteta, 1998.

39 I. Mazurov, "Fashizm kak forma totalitarizma," *Obshchestvennye nauki i sovremennost'*, 5, 1993, 39–51.

40 A. Galkin, "O fashizme – vser'ez," *Svobodnaia mysl'*, 5, 1992, 13–23; P. Iu. Rakhshmir, "Fashizm: vchera, segodnia, zavtra," *Mirovaia ekonomika i mezhdunarodnye otnosheniia*, 10, 1996, 153–157.

41 A. A. Galkin, "Fashizm: korni, priznaki, formy proiavleniia," *Politicheskie issledovaniia*, 2, 26, 1995, 6–15 at p. 10; also quoted in Schützler, "Faschismus," 235.

42 A. A. Galkin, "Rossiiskii fashizm?" *Sotsiologicheskii zhurnal*, 2, 1994, 17–27; A. Galkin and Yu. Krasin, "Russische Wahlen in den Ruinen sowjetischer Modernisierung: Informationen zum Nachdenken," *Das Argument*, 36, 2 (204), 1994, 199–209; A. Galkin and Iu. Krasin, "O pravom radikalizme v rossiiskom obshchestve," *Obozrevatel'*, 12, 1995, 52–58.

43 A. Ianov, *Posle El'tsina: "Veimarskaia" Rossiia*, Moscow: KRUK, 1995.
44 A. Umland, "Russischer Rechtsextremismus im Lichte der jüngeren empirischen und theoretischen Faschismusforschung," *Osteuropa*, 52, 2, 2002, 901–913.
45 L. J. Ivanov, *Rußland nach Gorbatschow. Wurzeln-Hintergründe-Trends der sich formierenden Gruppierungen – Perspektiven für die Zukunft*, Passau: Wissenschaftsverlag Rothe, 1996.
46 S. D. Shenfield, "The Weimar/Russia Comparison: Reflections on Hanson and Kopstein," *Post-Soviet Affairs*, 14, 4, 1998, 355–368; same author, *Russian Fascism: Traditions, Tendencies, Movements*, Armonk, NY: M. E. Sharpe, 2001.
47 Further on this issue, see A. Umland, "Alexander Dugin, die Faschismusfrage und der russische politische Diskurs," *Russlandanalysen*, 105, 2006, 2–5, www.russlandanalysen.de/content/media/Russlandanalysen105.pdf (accessed 20 September 2006); same author, "Neue ideologische Fusionen im russischen Antidemokratismus" and "Kontseptual'nye i kontekstual'nye problemy interpretatsii sovremennogo russkogo ul'tranatsionalizma," *Voprosy filosofii*, 12, 2006, 64–81.
48 See on this issue J. W. Borejsza, *Antyslawizm Adolfa Hitlera*, Warsaw: Czytelnik, 1988; M. Burleigh, *Germany Turns Eastward: A Study of* Ostforschung *in the Third Reich*, Cambridge: Cambridge University Press, 1988; J. Connelly, "Nazis and Slavs: From Racial Theory to Racist Practice," *Central European History*, 32, 1, 1999, 1–33; A. Dallin, *German Rule in Russia, 1941–1945: A Study in Occupation Policies*, Boulder, CO: Westview Press, 1981; H. Schaller, *Der Nationalsozialismus und die slawische Welt*, Regensburg: Friedrich Pustet, 2002; H.-E. Volkmann (ed.), *Das Russlandbild im Dritten Reich*, Cologne: Böhlau, 1994; W. Wippermann, "Antislavismus," in U. Puschner (ed.), *Handbuch zur "Völkischen Bewegung" 1871–1918*, Munich: Saur, 1996, pp. 512–524.
49 S. Reznik, *Krasnoe i korichnevoe: Kniga o sovetskom natsizme*, Washington, DC: Vyzov, 1991; same author, *The Nazification of Russia: Antisemitism in the Post-Soviet Era*, Washington, DC: Challenge Publications, 1996; V. Likhachev, *Natsizm v Rossii*, Moscow: Panorama, 2003.
50 A. Umland, "Pravyi ekstremizm v postsovetskoi Rossii," *Obshchestvennye nauki i sovremennost'*, 4, 2001, 71–84.
51 Of course, a somewhat similar problem exists when using the term "fascism," as originally it was the name of a particular Italian ideology. Here, however, it has become customary in international comparative fascist studies to distinguish explicitly between generic fascism and Italian Fascism. This has been done, in English, by the capitalization of "Fascism" when the Italian variety is meant, and, in German, by the introduction of the term *Italofaschismus* (as distinct from *allgemeiner Faschismus*).
52 Gregor, *Phoenix*, pp. 145–170; same author, *The Faces of Janus*, pp. 107–127; W. Laqueur, *Fascism: Past, Present, Future*, New York: Oxford Univerisity Press, 1997, pp. 178–196.

Part II

The "far right" and "New Right"

Ideological recompositions

5 Future prospects of contemporary Russian nationalism

Alexander Verkhovsky

Nationalism as a movement driven by the idea of building a nation, be it civic or ethnic, has potential for success in two cases: either when it is associated with ideas of social modernization – as was the case with the "modernizing nationalism" of the French Revolution – or when it is used for institutionalizing the state, as has recently been the case in many post-socialist countries. Today's Russian nationalism is neither; all of its versions are directed against modernization. From this perspective it is neither necessary for the country's development nor does it have any strategic potential.[1] Russia is fully institutionalized as a state, and any remaining doubts about this soon disappeared during the first half of the 1990s (at this very time there was a noticeable decline in the kind of Russian nationalism that had emerged in the late 1980s and at the beginning of the 1990s during the USSR's crisis and collapse).

The old dilemma of ethnic versus imperial nationalism[2] is gradually falling into disuse. The Russian Empire is no longer a compelling goal, but neither is the idea of Russia as a civic nation. Neither civic nor even imperial, today's Russian nationalism is instead almost exclusively ethnic.[3] The ethnic nature of Russian nationalism, and the popularity of ethnic sentiments among the ethnic majority of a large, independent country, is just further proof that this Russian nationalism is without strategic prospects. However, this lack of strategic potential does not mean that it has no prospects at all. While Russian nationalism[4] is of no benefit to the country's future, other ideological trends, though they may offer more constructive ideas, also lack such potential. On the other hand, the future is inescapable, and modern nationalism can play a noticeable role in its emergence. However, the agents of this nationalism may appear different from what they were in the 1990s.

Preliminary outcomes for nationalist movements

In examining the various branches and trends of the nationalist movement,[5] it is impossible not to notice the serious crisis that a significant part, if not the whole, of the nationalist sector faces. Further research is admittedly necessary, but for the purposes of this chapter it is possible to make some observations. In particular, we will focus on the activities organized by Russian nationalists on 4 November 2006 and 2007, because the intrigues and conflicts surrounding the Russian Marches in 2006 and 2007[6] planned for that date were key events for the nationalist scene in 2006–2007, alongside the violence in Kondopoga in early September 2006.[7]

As of 2002 the role of Vladimir Zhirinovsky's Liberal Democratic Party (LDPR) as a nationalist party had gained considerable importance. This became especially evident in many of the regional elections, as it did in the federal elections. Locally, the LDPR is closely linked to other nationalist groups, sometimes to the point of sharing many of the same members (this was the case in Kondopoga, for example). Some LDPR members are ultra-nationalists, but few of the party leadership are. In fact, there was only one, Nikolai Kurianovich, who was a patron of skinheads. On 31 October 2006, apparently in connection with his involvement in preparing the Russian March, he was ousted from the parliamentary party faction and from the broader LDPR. On 4 November 2006 (National Unity Day) the LDPR held a separate meeting, unrelated to the Russian March. On the same day in 2007, the LDPR was not active at all. Vladimir Zhirinovsky has consistently maintained that the LDPR is what one calls LDPR Ltd.[8] – that is, engaged in mimicking nationalism and the opposition, in collaborating with various businesses and in unconditionally supporting the Kremlin on all substantial issues. The mere presence of LDPR Ltd. in the Duma, and therefore on the public scene, has placed significant restraint on the nationalist movement.

The current activities of the key nationalist players formed back in the 1990s vary. Some of them, such as fragments of Russian National Unity (RNE; all abbreviations are from the Russian) have traditionally avoided publicity; others, like Sergei Baburin, often get involved in visible, dynamic projects. However, the overall visibility of such figures and organizations is low. This is partly due to the degree of fatigue among people and structures, but more importantly because they are still unable to offer the public anything attractive and have not had the originality necessary to mobilize the community, in contrast to the so-called "Orthodox public" or skinheads.

With the exception of some isolated elements, this part of the nationalist sector is simply dying off. As the most visible such group, Baburin's Popular Will Party has been trying to act independently, but later was transformed into the National Union Party, which included several other smaller groups. Baburin's response to the 2006 Russian March was cautious. He sought to maintain his links with the radicals, while being careful not to provoke the authorities. He allowed the Russian March participants to join his officially permitted rally, which enabled the march's main organizers, the Movement against Illegal Immigration (DPNI), to claim afterwards that the march had actually taken place between the metro station and the venue of Baburin's rally. In Moscow the People's Will meeting, where the march ended, attracted fewer than 1,000 participants, while a few hundred others had allegedly been stopped by police and so were not able to attend the meeting. However, Baburin refused to give the floor to DPNI leader Alexander Belov during the rally.[9] The next year Baburin organized a separate march, which was much smaller than the main one, with not more than 400 participants, even including some small allies.

On the issue of religious diversity it is noticeable that the neo-pagans, who formerly had a dramatic presence, today have little impact, and active anti-Christians like Alexander Aratov have become marginalized. The more visible figures such as Vladimir Avdeev are indeed no longer so focused on opposing Christianity, and are primarily perceived as racists rather than as pagans.[10] Yet a certain amount of religious confusion is to be expected among nationalists – and in the public at large, for that matter.[11] One can always expect to find certain elements of neo-paganism in society. Nazi traditions are important to skinheads, and neo-Nazism is closely linked to neo-pagan symbols and rhetoric in contemporary Russian nationalism. This is what prevents Orthodox activists from identifying with skinheads.

Igor Artiomov's Russian All-National Union (RONS) demonstrated some potential for such cooperation in May 2006 when it jointly organized, along with a number of Orthodox and neo-Nazi activists, a rather aggressive homophobic campaign. But this campaign was not followed up, nor was any other joint action organized. In summer 2006 a small group of neo-Nazis led by MP Nikolai Kurianovich joined the Union of Orthodox Gonfalon-Carriers, but the Gonfalon-Carriers are a small group of specific nature and identity. At the time of the Russian March in 2006, Orthodox activists chose to organize a separate meeting to emphasize their legality and to distance themselves from the neo-pagans and neo-Nazis sitting on the main organizing committee. However, many nationalists attended both meetings, Kurianovich[12] and Baburin included. Later, RONS was involved in Baburin's new party, the National Union. It is interesting that while Baburin himself is rather moderate, the National Union's youth organization includes mostly radical ethno-nationalists, many of them skinheads.

Since 2002, various groups of Orthodox Christian political activists have gradually been joining forces. They have all not entirely agreed on the Church's internal issues, but the only ones who remain isolated are those who have opted for marginalization, such as Konstantin Dushenov and his circle, or the so-called *oprichniks*, a reclusive group living mostly in the woods.[13] With these exceptions, the entire spectrum, extending from radical orthodox brotherhoods to high-ranking patriarchate officials, have been engaging in fairly productive cooperation. In November 2005, Christian Orthodox monarchists (modeled on the Black Hundreds in the literal sense) made their sincerest attempt at consolidation since the early 1990s by reviving the Union of Russian People (SRN). Since then, however, the SRN has been torn apart by internal conflicts and has lost any hopes of playing a significant role on the nationalist scene. On 4 November 2007 the radical wing of the SRN organized a sacred procession instead of a political march.

In fact, Orthodox nationalists prefer to act jointly with the Russian Orthodox Church leadership, finding it much more effective than cooperation with other political organizations. Direct political actions, such as the Orthodox meeting on 4 November 2006, mentioned earlier, have not had a great impact. A total of about 200 people were involved in the meeting organized by the Gonfalon-Carriers, the Union of Orthodox Citizens, Vladimir Khomiakov's Popular Council (Narodnyi Sobor; later this organization was headed by the RNE veteran Oleg Kassin), and a number of smaller groups. The general potential of Orthodox activists to influence Russian society appears weak. It is true that Christian Orthodoxy today is an almost inescapable element of nationalist ideology. But even if the nationalist movement needs Orthodox activists, the latter will not necessarily be given high-profile roles.[14]

After a period of some confusion, Dugin's branch of National Bolshevism assumed a clearly nationalist image. The key point came in spring 2005 when it set up the Eurasian Youth Union (ESM), which became known for its role in organizing the Right March on 4 November 2005. Moreover, ESM members have frequently committed violent acts. The Eurasia Movement and Dugin himself officially remain in the political arena, and this fact alone speaks volumes about the official trend.

The establishment of the National Bolshevik Front (NBF) in August 2006 produced a militant, radical nationalist force, one that is at the same time entirely loyal to the authorities (for long-term tactical, if not strategic, reasons). It was made up of discontented nationalist members who had left Eduard Limonov's National Bolshevik Party (NBP) and a subsequent association between the ESM and NBF (in fact, this faction of the National Bolsheviks rejoined Dugin, who used to be the NBP's chief ideologist before 1998). Despite the fact that the NBF and ESM may collaborate with other parts of the nationalist movement, their basic principle of direct cooperation with government creates a certain distance between them and other nationalists. On 4 November 2006 the ESM decided to mark National Unity Day in other newly independent states (NIS) but not in Russia.

It is still hard to predict the future outcome of this strange phenomenon. But it may appear not so bad, given that the present government is increasingly tending towards nationalism. Yet the prospects for neo-Eurasianist ideology are extremely poor. A popular "sort of Eurasian" rhetoric (for example, vague assumptions concerning the Orthodox Christian/Muslim, Slavic/Turkic, or Western/Eastern nature of "Russian civilization") is common in society at large, but this sort of Eurasian ideology is fuzzy and therefore does not need genuine ideologists like Dugin and his followers. All current ideological teachings in Russia – including, among others, the Russian Orthodox Church and half of the muftis – denounce "neo-Eurasianist" rhetoric, and especially Dugin's version of it. Indeed, by contrast to the role he used to play,[15] Dugin's intellectual role today consists simply in marking a certain ideological reference point, nothing more.

The Nazis or skinheads are the largest and most dynamic segment of the Russian nationalists.[16] This movement is fundamentally neo-Nazi, but it accepts cooperation with nationalists of all sorts, and with those who do not know and/or do not care to know the difference between nationalist groups. The skinhead movement, being a subculture rather than a political movement,[17] is not inclined to consolidation. Secrecy is another important consideration. It is easier to maintain confidentiality with fewer vertical links and less transparent structures. Admittedly, certain ultra-nationalist groups such as the Popular National Party and the Freedom Party did successfully "domesticate" a small section of the skinheads, but now these parties are in decline and the majority of sustainable skinhead gangs remain independent.

Even in Moscow there have been serious disagreements between consistent neo-Nazis and more "omnivorous" groups. For example, Dmitri Diomushkin's neo-Nazi Slav Union was involved in the organizing committee of the 2006 Russian March jointly with the DPNI and with Alexander Sevastianov and Stanislav Terekhov's National Great Power Party (NDPR). Formally speaking, the latter two organizations are not skinhead groups. However, Dmitri Rumiantsev's National Socialist Society (NSO), Maxim "Tesak" ("Hatchet") Martsinkevich's Format-18, and similar groups did not participate in the organizing committee. Their members attended the march but displayed hardly any symbols. One reason for these disagreements may have been a desire to keep the ranks of the neo-Nazis pure, but it is also probable that the NSO and similar groups are more involved in real, systematic physical violence, so for their current opponents participation seemed risky. Again on 4 November 2006 they attempted to make a statement by attacking an anti-fascist meeting, but were stopped by police. In St. Petersburg, on the other hand, the neo-Nazis were unified, and with too few police to prevent them they formed a joint column that marched throughout the city center, clashing physically with radical anti-fascists.

The next year the NSO and Slav Union took part in the main Russian March organized by the DPNI. Those in neo-Nazi columns numbered about 1,500 among the total of 2,500 participants of that march. The NSO column and some other neo-Nazis left the march before the final meeting because Rumiantsev was not allowed to give a speech there. Yuri Beliaev's Freedom Party, whose headquarters is located in St. Petersburg, rarely cooperates with Moscow-based organizations.[18] Strong regional differences continue to divide the skinhead movement, and hence concerted actions involving more than one region are rare. Attempts to organize marches similar to that held in Moscow (which 2,500–3,000 people attended) failed in virtually all other cities in 2005. No one came to Kondopoga despite the DPNI's appeals for them to do so. But on 4 November 2006, regional "Russian Marches" were much more noticeable. Marches were also organized in Vladivostok, Stavropol, Chita, and some other cities (though not St. Petersburg), but on a smaller scale than in Moscow. And in 2007 a Russian March took place in at least twenty-two regions as compared to about fifteen regions in 2006.

Viewed from the ideological perspective, however, if the Nazi–skinhead groups do have any chance of success at all, this is because the majority of the Russian public categorically reject neo-Nazism in its straightforward form. Many people perceive neo-Nazism as an unreasonably radical version of the majority's "reasonable xenophobia." So, the skinhead movement as such does not appear to have any serious prospects, despite its dynamic growth in numbers and its major "achievements" in terms of violence and racist propaganda.

To sum up this brief overview of Russian nationalists, we have observed either the total irrelevance of their respective slogans and ideas to the public at large (e.g. the neo-Nazis, Orthodox monarchists and Dugin's followers), or a counterproductive method of building their organization (e.g. the LDPR or the remaining parts of the RNE), or just the fact that they have totally exhausted their mobilization potential. The main example of the latter is Gennadi Ziuganov's Communist Party (CPRF). It was seen by many observers as one of the main nationalist forces, even taking into account the party's pluralistic nature. Its nationalist manifestations were very evident until the beginning of the new century, but then the Kremlin and new nationalist populists occupied traditional CPRF nationalistic positions. It was very visible after Kondopoga, when Ziuganov wanted to establish a new kind of CPRF "Russian project," but the ideological initiatives of the Kremlin and national populists were much more successful, and the CPRF had to give up.

What this means is that the nationalist movement has come to a dead end, even though some of its branches may show some dynamism. The most dynamic among them are associated with the neo-Nazis, but this in itself is no indication of potential future success for a real neo-Nazi party. However, it should be readily admitted that the nationalists, especially their radical sections, have managed to do quite a lot. The skinhead movement has created a tremendous amount of human potential, which is much more active than the thousands of "RNE veterans," though neither should the latter be disregarded. Discussions in the mass media on the topic of "nationalities," and the findings of public opinion polls, reveal that nationalism has many unorganized but open and vocal supporters. Active participants of the movement, including the skinheads, are aware of this potential. The overall intellectual level of the skinheads has improved, partly because of the increased median age of participants; moreover, the fact that they now rarely leave the movement as they age further indicates internal changes.

On the other hand, ethnic xenophobia cannot but generate political nationalism, particularly in a community where xenophobia affects around 52–55 percent of the population. According to the Levada Center (formerly the VTsIOM), a stable ethno-xenophobic majority formed in Russia sometime around 1999–2000, when xenophobic sentiments rose with the onset of the Kosovo crisis and the new war in Chechnya.[19] Of no less importance is the fact that not only social scientists but a large part of the Russian public with at least some sort of awareness now understand that this phenomenon extends far beyond the marginal splinter groups of "Russian fascists" and has reached a point where it signals a qualitative shift in public consciousness. These observations are widely reflected in the mass media and are being transmitted to the majority of the public, including those who were hitherto not aware of this development. What is not yet formed in the majority opinion, or in any sort of significant minority opinion for that matter, is any idea concerning the political manifestation that the emerging ethno-xenophobic sentiments may produce. However, there is no doubt that most people feel there should be some sort of political manifestation, and expect it to emerge in the future.

New populist nationalism

It is important to recall that in the early 1990s, populist nationalism had more success in mobilizing people than any other movement: the National Salvation

Front in 1992–1993, the CPRF in the mid-1990s. This populist nationalism was rather inaccurately labeled the "Red and Brown" movement. The first decade of the new century has infused fresh blood into the populist nationalist movement.

Initially, only the party-building, organizational aspects of the movement were at issue. Establishing the Rodina (Motherland) bloc, for example, allowed for the more effective promotion of populist nationalism than the CPRF was capable of at that time. Nonetheless, it should be noted that the Rodina bloc never once in its brief life achieved the degree of consistency that the CPRF achieved long ago and has never lost, despite all its schisms and internal dissent. By mid-2006 it had become clear that all the main "Red and Brown" projects had failed, because they had lost either their influence or their synthetic essence or, as in most cases, both. This happened to the NBP, the CPRF, and Rodina (bloc and party). With both the CPRF and the NBP the rhetoric of moderate nationalism was simply and effectively adopted by the government; thus, for the CPRF, nationalist slogans lost their mobilizing potential, and for the NBP they became unacceptable.[20]

Trying to foster populist nationalism by combining elements of social populism with elements of ethnic xenophobia – successfully done by the CPRF for many years, and then by Rodina with some initial success – may not be the best recipe after all. It does not produce an ideological foundation that is consistent or easy to understand, but instead leads to the organization of ideological and other types of conflict that are actively fueled by the Kremlin's "political technologists." But one might ask whether it is really necessary to have a consistent ideology in order to create an effective political movement. Neither the "ruling party" nor the government has a consistent ideology, but this fact does not bother either them or their voters. We believe that this version of "death of an ideology" is just a sign of the degradation faced by public policy in its traditional forms.

We can see the success of slogans against "migrants," also a hybrid based on social and (predominantly) ethnic xenophobia. The examples of Rodina, and especially the Movement against Illegal Immigration (DPNI), demonstrate how quickly it is possible to become popular by using the "fight against migrants," and especially against "illegal migrants," for popular appeal. A vast majority in all segments of society believe that "migrants" – rather than "migration" – are the problem. This notion, then, is interpreted in accordance with the ethnocentric sentiments prevalent in Russia today.[21] As a result, migrant-phobia (*migrantofobiia*) enjoys widespread support throughout Russian society, including among bureaucrats, the law enforcement authorities, and in the mass media. As a result of this broad consensus, combined with the verbal manners of the "fighters against migration," who usually desist from making brutally racist statements, their arguments are commonly quoted by mainstream media,[22] imposing them on the public in the same way as the "fighters" impose them on media figures.

At the same time, the DPNI does not seek to promote any particular ideology; the movement simply does not need ideologists. Migrant-phobia is not only a euphemism for racism, one that blurs the difference between "unwelcome foreigners" and equally "unwelcome" compatriots. It is also a natural – in the sense of not having been imposed by ideologists – fusion of ethno-xenophobia and social xenophobia, both of which target “newcomers,” and which have been around since Soviet times. Two factors make this fusion so successful. First, more than 50 percent of Russians consistently share ethno-xenophobic sentiments. Second, there is a growing cultural gap between local residents and new immigrants. Since the mid-1990s there have been fewer ethnic Russians, and fewer people in general who speak fluent Russian and were educated in Soviet schools, living among migrants from the north Caucasus and Central Asia.

Migrant-phobia is obviously connected with the Chechen wars and with Islamophobia caused by terrorist attacks. In this sense we can say that migrant-phobic ideas in Russia have increasingly been “modernized” and appear similar to present-day West European xenophobia. The Russian mass media reiterate and exaggerate this similarity as a sign of its “relevance,” thereby legitimizing migrant-phobia as a sentiment and, consequently, Russian nationalism, which is focused almost entirely on this theme.

Nationalism today is much more tolerant than before of internal ideological differences, a point very clearly revealed in Dmitri Rogozin’s sector of the Rodina bloc. In this relation, what should be underscored is the important role the “conflict of civilizations” theory has in its Russian (e.g. both anti-Western and Islamophobic) version.[23] Even classic anti-Semitism is still relevant, as was demonstrated by the “letter of 500.”[24] The debates surrounding this letter within the nationalist camp clearly showed that anti-Semitism, although apparently irrelevant to the general public, retains a certain mobilizing potential for the circle of “sympathizers.” That between 10,000 and 20,000 people signed the letter to the prosecutor general is a significant achievement for present-day Russia.

Following Rodina’s breakup, the DPNI gained a virtual monopoly over nationalist populism/migrant-phobia discourse. The events in Kondopoga massively increased the movement’s popularity. For the first time ever, a pogrom campaign resulted in visible success (the Chechens left the city and did not come back for a long time), and this fact was widely broadcasted by the mass media. If the DPNI found a winning formula, it was precisely because it focused on rousing sentiments that are shared by virtually all social groups from the masses to the elites, while avoiding excessive ideological constructions.

What prevents the DPNI from gaining the leadership of the nationalist movement? The simple answer is a lack of organization. We may assume that this lack of organization was not simply a deficit but was a conscious choice by the DPNI’s leader Alexander Belov (Potkin). From the pragmatic perspective the choice made good sense. In a virtually already established soft authoritarian regime, the absence of organizational structure, and of political ambitions in a narrow sense (ambitions to seize power), means that the movement does not become a direct target of government pressure, with some exceptions. The authorities’ fairly balanced response to the 2006 and 2007 Russian Marches demonstrates the point.

In Russia today it is impossible to become a formal and open leader of an organized and evolving movement without clashing with the government. Thus, the DPNI was not taking any risks. Instead, it attempted to strengthen its support by appealing to those who are fearful of conflicts with government, or consider such conflicts inappropriate. Besides, the absence of organization partially protected the DPNI from the schisms that are common to this type of Russian nationalism. Indeed, many high-profile and older nationalist leaders voiced direct support for the last of the Russian Marches, which were predominantly associated with the DPNI. This small group has gradually become the symbol of an extremely informal but broad movement.

We should also bear in mind that the DPNI is in fact based on Nazi–skinhead groups. This means that today the most radical forms of nationalism are no longer entirely marginalized, although openly neo-Nazi manifestations remain somewhat risky. The growth of skinhead violence (since at least 2003, dozens of people have been killed, and hundreds injured, in racist attacks each year[25]) shows that the nature of the movement is changing: from mere propaganda and campaigning, it has moved toward engaging in "direct action." Granted, it cannot yet be called a terrorist movement, but a number of events have shown that political terrorism from radical nationalists is no longer just a threat.

The maneuvers of Dmitri Rogozin, who convened the 2006 Russian March headquarters in his office and later, in December, revived the Congress of Russian Communities, assisted by the same figures of Belov and Kurianovich, show that Rogozin was attempting to take over Belov's initiatives and methods. Given the obvious fact that Rogozin, even though in a limited way, has been taking orders from certain officials in the Kremlin (remember his "voluntary" resignation from the Rodina Party leadership), it can be assumed that some of those within the ruling circles were increasingly interested in populist nationalism. The same suspicions arise in connection with Belov's unusually harsh statements against Moscow's mayor, Yuri Luzhkov, in early November 2006; few people would dare to make such statements without sufficient protection.

But the parliamentary electoral campaign in fall 2007 changed the situation. It was obvious that Belov, Rogozin, and other people within that circle had some grounds for hope for support from above, from certain high-level bureaucrats. That could be the only reason why such experienced politicians tried to organize a nationalistic party – the Great Russia Party – and to take part in the election. But these hopes were destroyed: the new party, headed by Andrei Saveliev, a man very close to Rogozin, was not registered and could not participate in the election. Baburin's National Union could not register for the election because of the many false signatures submitted in its support. Saveliev and some others took part in an informal coalition with the Patriots of Russia party (a small but registered party with practically no ideology), but this party gained only about 1 percent of the votes.[26]

The December parliamentary elections attracted significantly less activity in nationalistic circles than the Russian March, however. Perhaps the reason was that everybody understood that everything would be decided not by the voters but by the Kremlin. The latter sent a clear signal to nationalists: on the one hand, their parties were not allowed to participate and, on the other hand, Dmitri Rogozin was invited in November 2007 to be the Russian representative to

NATO. Kremlin was ready to tolerate nationalists but did not want them taking part in elections and in "big politics" in general. And the nationalists understood that they had no possibility of insisting on taking part. Following the Russian March, the DPNI started campaigning in favor of an electoral boycott. Gradually other nationalist groups gave their support to the boycott. As the end of the electoral campaign drew near, even Andrei Saveliev began supporting an electoral boycott. Starting from that moment, the DPNI has become more and more radical in its opposition to the Kremlin. At the end of May 2008 the DPNI and Saveliev supporters declared that they do not recognize the official authorities as legitimate. At the same time, Belov has been trying to reconfigure the DPNI from a network of different groups to a party-like organization, which has a very negative impact on the mobilization abilities of the DPNI. This way may be seen as a retreat from previous achievements: a party-like organization is more effective in a democratic political system, but in today's Russia it has proven ineffective. This transformation means that the new organizational approach suggested by the DPNI failed (maybe temporarily).

A new two-party system

I shall now set out some assumptions in order to make predictions about the future of national populism. In particular, I take as my starting point the widely held view that the Russian political class reflects the ideas generated by the masses, and that politicians are not leaders but followers. Further, I assume that politicians reproduce, with a couple of years' delay, the sentiments of most citizens (the delay is necessary to capture the development and make sure it is sustainable). It is possible to date the formation of a sustainable ethno-xenophobic majority to around 2000; then, in 2002–2003, xenophobia became a widely exploited feature of the election campaigns (mainly by the LDPR), and it contributed to Rodina's success in parliamentary elections.

Today, not only are xenophobic sentiments still in the majority,[27] but the "nationalist shift" among politicians has come to stay. Moreover, the need to compete for the attention of the new majority has resulted in this shift being increasingly visible, a fact that is borne out in individual political histories as a gradual relaxing of moral standards, and of the boundaries of political rhetoric. There are virtually no other issues that can compete effectively with ethno-religious xenophobia for public attention. Attempts at opposing the Kremlin are too weak to arouse interest. Public campaigns orchestrated by the government do not attract significant public attention either (except that Operation "Successor," the public campaign to promote Medvedev as a natural successor to Putin, may do). Social protest (for example, the isolated, short-lived protests against "monetization of benefits") is an eternal issue, but it has not triggered any public movement. Pure social populism lacks active agents – that is, except for the failing CPRF and other, extremely weak, left-wing movements. Most importantly, social populism is not even up for debate, since few people oppose it in terms of rhetoric, and the government willingly supports it with allocations from oil revenues.

There is a social populist majority in Russian society, but it is not an active majority. There is no social populist competition among politicians, or, more exactly, such competition (for example, that between the United Russia and Fair Russia parties) is perceived not as being part of public and political life, but rather as being a form of relationship between different parts of the bureaucracy and the "population." The social populist majority remains unable to structure public perceptions. The government-sponsored "one-and-a-half party system" impacts the public even less than the age-old populist competition between federal, regional, and local authorities. By contrast, the ethno-xenophobic majority has already started to restructure political sphere in a certain way. This majority is opposed by the anti-nationalist minority; however, anti-nationalism is weak in Russia. For example, the CPRF, while seeming to denounce nationalism, remains a moderately nationalist party. The few democratically oriented parties and organizations that exist are very weak, even as a combined force. The majority of the population tend to perceive them as a target of baiting rather than as an independent political force. More, even these parties sometimes hold nationalist views. The democrats' intolerance of nationalism underwent a major crisis as they began a massive collaboration with Rodina in 2005. The debates that have taken place in the "democratic camp" in the wake of the 2006 Russian March about the degree to which nationalism may be tolerated demonstrated that the tolerance toward it is fairly high.

The radical democratic opposition associated with the Another Russia project was open to collaboration with nationalists from the very beginning; the idea of Garry Kasparov is to unite all forces that are in opposition to the Kremlin. The presence of nationalists in Kasparov-related projects is becoming more and more visible. After the Kondopoga events, some of Kasparov's United Civic Front activists referred to pogroms as legitimate civil protests. In May 2008 the National Assembly established by Kasparov and his allies even included some Stalinists, Islamists, and activists of the ultra-nationalist Great Russia party. On the other hand, the moderate nationalist movement The People (Narod), headed by Alexei Navalnyi, a member of Yabloko (who was excluded from the party, but not until much later), and Sergei Guliaev, the leader of the Petersburg March of Dissenters (not a big organization, but including various oppositional activists), was not influential inside Another Russia. And from 8 June 2008 The People has been in coalition with the DPNI and the Great Russia party.

Yet the government has restrained radical nationalists. The reason for that is that any government, and particularly an authoritarian one, will always make an effort to restrain radicals of all types. There is thus a significant part of the ethno-xenophobic majority that, siding with the government, refuses to condone radicalism. However, though the government has restrained radical nationalists, it is itself also ethno-nationalist, albeit moderately so. This had seemed believable before on the basis of a number of signs: the official government propaganda adopted imperialist rhetoric;[28] the official patronage of nationalist groups, such as Dugin's ESM, was rather visible; and reaction to ultra-nationalism, even in its more blatant forms such as "the letter of 500" or the LDPR's propaganda, was very moderate. The anti-Georgian campaign in 2006, which was openly racist, received endorsement from top government officials, clearly showing that the government's imperial nationalism is not limited to latent or in-built manifestations – such as pervasive, unpunished discriminatory practices – but is also capable of being expressed in openly ethno-nationalist policies.

However strong an authoritarian government may be, it cannot completely ignore public pressure. And today, real, tangible pressure comes not from the failing liberals or the Communists, but from radical nationalists. Their power has been built by their gradual, palpable gaining of public attention. Two entirely informal "dominant parties" have emerged from this dynamic: the moderate nationalism of the government and the radical nationalism of the populists. The establishment and style of celebration of the new national holiday on 4 November, called People's Unity Day, has served dramatically to illustrate how this "new two-party system" works. People's Unity Day was conceived as a commemoration of the 1612 expulsion of Polish invaders, a holiday designed to demonstrate ethnically neutral civic unity. However, it immediately assumed clerical and anti-Western features because the date falls on an Orthodox Christian holiday celebrating the same victory, whereas the wars with the Catholic Rzeczpospolita, alongside the legendary Ice Battle, are treated in Russian historical mythology as pillars of Russia's anti-Western identity. Not surprisingly, radical nationalists immediately picked this holiday as the date on which to hold their marches.

The authoritarian system has promptly suppressed classical political parties, and there is no question of allowing a genuine two-party system. The government will not allow it precisely because the moderates always run the risk of losing to the radicals at the peak of any social movement. Rodina's electoral success in December 2003 was followed by the victories of extreme radicals of the likes of Vladimir Kvachkov and Vladimir Popov in Moscow in December 2005. Kvachkov, known for his attempt on Anatoly Chubais' life, won almost 29 percent of the votes, while the formerly unknown ultra-nationalist activist Vladimir Popov won 4 percent, as opposed to the 1 percent that such candidates usually receive. In this regard the latter's victory is at least as impressive as that of the former. This has meant that the ruling regime from now on will aim to prevent nationalists from running for elections, and the over-controlled 2007 parliamentary elections were a good example.

Conclusion

At the moment it certainly appears as if the government will be able to postpone institutionalizing this "new two-party arrangement," but that depends upon its maintaining its power. In the near future we can expect both radical and moderate nationalists to try to strengthen their ideological, if not organizational, positions. As to organizational perspectives of the new national populism, the latter again needs new forms. In spring 2008 the DPNI leadership found their organization's forms too loose and tried to reorganize the organization on more hierarchical, party-like lines and make it a core of the nationalist "Coalition of 8 June." No doubt it means that nationalists will find soon that they have to become more open and inclusive again, and less oppositional, but today's leadership related to the "Coalition of 8 June" have exhausted their potentialities to a great extent.

In case of serious destabilization, which cannot be ruled out, since there are serious doubts concerning the performance of the current chain of command, the so-called *vertical power*, further questions will arise, for example how the nationalists will deploy their combat potential. But we have no grounds to expect such radical developments. A national populist movement needs time to reorganize in a more effective way. It means that in the near future the Kremlin will keep control of the situation, including partial control over the nationalist movement. In any case, there is nothing to indicate that the "new two-party arrangement" will soon be replaced by anything similarly relevant to the social and political dynamics. In any other situation we still have grounds to apprehend that the balance of forces between, on the one hand, moderate (pro-government) nationalists and, on the other, radical (independent or relatively independent) nationalists would, however slowly, shift towards the latter.

Translated by Irina Savelieva

Notes

1 L. Gudkov and B. Dubin, "Svoeobrazie russkogo natsionalizma," *Pro et Contra*, 2, 2005, 6–24. See also the author's interview with the same researchers: "Est' li perspektiva u russkogo natsionalizma?" in *Russkii natsionalizm. Ideologiia i nastroenie*, Moscow: SOVA, 2006, pp. 263–298.

2 A comparative analysis of views held by different groups is followed by their brief classification in A. Verkhovsky and V. Pribylovsky, *Natsional-patrioticheskie organizatsii v Rossii. Istoriia, ideologiia, ekstremistskie tendentsii*, Moscow: Institute of Experimental Sociology, 1996, pp. 93–94. (Note: the term "nationalism" is understood as *ethnic nationalism* in that book.) It is problematic to differentiate between ethnic and imperial nationalisms in post-imperial societies. See A. Miller, *Imperiia Romanovyh i natsionalizm*, Moscow: NLO, 2006, pp. 148–156.

3 V. Solovey and T. Solovey, "Apologiia russkogo natsionalizma," *Political Class*, 3, 2006.

4 Hereinafter used to mean *Russian ethnic nationalism*. Other ethnic nationalisms have become much weaker in Russia since the 1990s. See E. Pain, *Etnopoliticheskii maiatnik. Dinamika i mekhanizmy etnopoliticheskikh protsessov v postsovetskoi Rossii*, Moscow: RAS Institute of Sociology, 2004, pp. 178–247.

5 The discussion that follows is based on the monitoring carried out by the SOVA Center; its details can be found in the Nationalism and Xenophobia section of SOVA's website at http://xeno.sova-center.ru (accessed 15 June 2008).

6 See SOVA's website for brief reports of the events of 4 November 2006: http://xeno.sova-center.ru/45A29F2/8360E0F; http://xeno.sova-center.ru/29481C8/835BCAD; http://xeno.sova-center.ru/45A29F2/A16C273; http://xeno.sova-center.ru/45A29F2/A17EA0B (accessed 15 June 2008).

7 See SOVA's website for brief reports of the events.

8 V. Pribylovsky, "The Attitude of National-Patriots towards Vladimir Putin in the Aftermath of 26 March," in *National-Patriots, Church, and Putin*, Moscow: Panorama Center, 2001, p. 65.

9 Belov took the floor anyway.

10 V. Shnirelman, "'Tsepnoj pes rasy': divannaia rasologiia kak zashchitnitsa 'belogo cheloveka,'" in *Verkhi i nizy russkogo natsionalizma*, Moscow: SOVA, 2007, pp. 188–208.

11 Many researchers view the faith of Russian citizens as a sort of "religious broth": A. Schipkov, *Vo chto verit Rossiia*, St. Petersburg: Russian Christian Humanitarian Institute Publishing, 1998, pp. 174–175; S. Filatov, "Religiia v postsovetskoi Rossii," in *Religiia i obshchestvo. Ocherki religioznoi zhizni sovremennoi Rossii*, Moscow and St. Petersburg: Letnii sad, 2002, pp. 475–477.

12 As Kurianovich was excluded from LDPR he was not elected to the Duma in December 2007. But his personal capacity in the absence of deputy status was not enough for him to continue to play a political role.

13 B. Knorre, "Oprichnyi mistitsizm v religioznykh praktikakh 'tsarebozhnichestva,'" in *Religioznye praktiki v sovremennoi Rossii*, Moscow: Novoye Publishers, 2006, pp. 384–397.

14 See details in my paper: A. Verkhovsky, "Pravoslavnye natsionalisty: strategii deistviia v Cerkvi i v politike," in *Tsena nenavisti. Natsionalizm v Rossii i protivodeistvie rasistskim prestupleniiam*, Moscow: SOVA, 2005, pp. 175–195.

15 M. Laruelle, "Aleksandr Dugin, ideologicheskij posrednik," in *Tsena nenavisti*, pp. 226–253.

16 Official estimates of the number are difficult to obtain; they vary from 20,000 to 70,000 depending on the source. I would say that the politically active core of Nazis/skinheads numbers about 20,000.

17 V. Likhachev, *Natsizm v Rossii*, Moscow: Panorama Center, 2002, pp. 112–115.

18 Beliaev was arrested in May 2008 and released in November.

19 L. Gudkov, "'Rossiia dlia russkikh': ksenofobiia i antimigrantskie nastroeniia v Rossii," in *Nuzhny li immigranty rossiiskomu obshchestvu?* (Does Russian Society Need Immigrants?), Moscow: Liberal Mission Foundation, 2006, pp. 31–78.

20 M. Sokolov, "Natsional-bol'shevistskaia partiia: ideologicheskaia evoliutsiia i politicheskii stil'," in *Russkii natsionalizm. Ideologiia i nastroenie*, pp. 139–164.

21 V. Shnirelman, "'Nesovmestimost' kul'tur': ot nauchnykh kontseptsii i shkol'nogo obrazovaniia do real'noi politiki," in *Russkii natsionalizm: ideologiia i nastroenie*, pp. 183–222.

22 Ethno-religious intolerance in the media has often been the subject of research. The SOVA Center has also researched this theme. The specifics of anti-migrant hate speech are clearly seen in the findings of our media monitoring. See SOVA's website section for details of this project: http://xeno.sova-center.ru/213716E (accessed 15 June 2008).

23 "Civilizational" discussions have been a dominant intellectual trend in Russia for several years now. See V. Shnirelman, "Civilizatsionnyi podkhod, uchebniki istorii i 'novyi rasizm,'" in *Rasizm v iazyke sotsial'nykh nauk*, St. Petersburg: Aleteia, 2002, pp. 131–145.

24 The letter, addressed to the General Prosecutor, requested that he recognize *Kitsur Shulkhan Arukh* as an extremist book and ban all Jewish organizations – secular and religious alike – since their activities are supposedly based on the ideas of *Kitsur Shulkhan Arukh*. By the beginning of January 2005, this letter, overflowing with references to famous anti-Semitic myths and seasoned with an overtly Judeophobic tone, had already been signed by 500 people, including nineteen members of the State Duma. Later, up to 18,000 signatures were collected.

25 For details, see G. Kozhevnikova, "Radikal'nyi natsionalizm i protivodeistvie emu v 2004 godu i v pervoi polovine 2005 goda," in *Cena nenavisti*, pp. 11–74; same author, "Radikal'nyi natsionalizm v Rossii i protivodeistvie emu v 2005 i pervoi polovine 2006," in *Russkii natsionalizm. Ideologiia i nastroenie*, pp. 8–93; "Radical Nationalism and Efforts to Counteract it in 2007," in *Xenophobia, Freedom of Conscience and Anti-extremism in Russia in 2007*, Moscow: SOVA, 2008, pp. 5–44.

26 This is a poor result, but it is very close to the results of the two main liberal parties. And there is evidence to suggest that there were electoral falsifications against all three of these parties.

27 The past eight years have shown certain variations in ethno-xenophobic sentiments, but the situation has not yet changed substantially. See recent findings of Levada Center surveys: "Mezhetnicheskaya Napryazhennost" (Inter-Ethnic Tension), Levada Center website, 18 November 2008, www.levada.ru/press/2006082500.html (accessed 15 December 2008).

28 See, for example, F. Fossato, "Virtual'naia politika i rossiiskoe TV," *Pro et Contra*, 4, 2006, 13–28.

6 Dugin and the Eurasian controversy

Is Eurasianism "patriotic"?

Wayne Allensworth

The right march and "pogrom nationalism"

The Kremlin had advertised 4 November 2005 as the "Day of National Unity," a day to commemorate the liberation of Moscow from Polish-Lithuanian occupation in 1612,[1] but the chief media story of the day was a 3,000-strong "right march," a demonstration by "patriotic" forces in the capital.[2] The "patriotic" march was organized by the Eurasian Youth Movement (ESM), created by Russia's chief proponent of neo-Eurasianism, Alexander Dugin, but ESM members were accompanied by marchers from the Movement against Illegal Immigration (DPNI)[3] and the National Great Power Party, as well as other hard right groups, including neo-Nazi skinheads and members of the Gorbachev-era ultra-nationalist organization Pamyat dressed as White Guard counter-revolutionaries.[4]

Tensions between the ESM and the other "right marchers" were soon evident. The ESM's Valery Korvin claimed before the march, for instance, that there would be "no skinheads, no swastikas, and no 'Sieg heil!'" at the event. But, as *Moskovskii Komsomolets* noted, it did not turn out that way: ESM organizers predicted 500 participants, but the demonstration's numbers were swelled by the very people Korvin had distanced himself from beforehand.[5] At a rally that followed a march through Moscow, ESM speakers focused on slamming Ukrainian "Orange" revolutionary leaders, as well as the "rose revolution" in Georgia and what the ESM claimed were Russian proponents of a pro-Western "color revolution."[6] While ESM marchers stressed resistance to "Orange" forces and remained fixated on the Eurasian theme of re-establishing the empire, the DNPI's Alexander Belov hammered away at the dangers of open borders with former Soviet states, claiming that Afghan heroin was flowing into Russia via Tajikistan. Belov reportedly told the assembled demonstrators that "[t]hey've opened the border with Tajikistan – the source of the narcotics flooding Russia! They say it is in our geo-political interests!"[7] Another version of Belov's comments had the DPNI leader saying that he "spit" on the ESM's "geo-politics."[8]

Belov's remarks indicate outright hostility between the ESM and the DPNI, or at least their leaders. According to some reports, the ESM leaders were wary of the DNPI and did not want their participation in the demonstration.[9] In subsequent articles posted on the APN website, supporters of Dugin's ESM attempted to distance the Eurasianists from the other participants (the author Yuri Tiurin called their program "pogrom nationalism"[10]) and even claimed that the Moscow authorities favored the "pogrom nationalists" as a means of discrediting the "right march."[11] According to Tiurin, the "pogrom nationalists" had tried to rename the demonstration a "Russian (*russkii*) march," thus playing into the hands of Russia's enemies. Eurasianism was an ideology that could make Russia strong again by reunifying the empire, while "pogrom nationalism" was divisive, alienating the other nationalities of the Russian Federation and the former Soviet Union. This, according to Tiurin, is exactly what Russia's enemies wanted. The target of Belov's verbal attacks, the non-Russians, especially Asian nationalities, were cast by Tiurin as Russia's natural allies in the geopolitical struggle with Washington and the "Atlanticist" forces.

The clashes over the right/*russkii* demonstration brought to light issues that had divided the "patriotic" movement – a loose coalition of far right groups – dating from the early 1990s. Alexander Dugin, the most influential of the "patriotic" publicists, and his neo-Eurasianist ideology have played a central role in those controversies, which have revolved around the aims of the "patriotic" movement, as well the means of re-establishing a "Great Russia."

Dugin's influence

Dugin has influenced the post-Soviet "patriotic" movement ideologically to a greater degree than any other nationalist publicist, especially through his association with Alexander Prokhanov, the editor and publisher of *Zavtra* (previously *Den'*). Dugin's Eurasianist writings in *Den'/Zavtra* gave the "patriotic" opposition the outline of an ideology that became the basis for Prokhanov's efforts to unite "Reds" (mainly grouped in the Russian Communist Party) and "Whites" (the nationalists) around Russia's historical Eurasianist mission. Dugin's vocabulary ("Atlanticism," "Eurasianism," "mondialism") permeated the discourse of the "patriotic" movement: Prokhanov, for instance, once summed up the editorial line of his newspaper as the promotion of Eurasianism, which he defined as the union of Slavs and Turks, Muslims and Orthodox.[12]

In the 1990s, Dugin published articles in the military press and appeared in a series of television broadcasts on the state-run Ostankino network. More recently, as Dugin's star rose in the Russian political firmament, his writings have appeared on the pages of influential, elite-oriented newspapers, and he is a frequent participant in round-table political discussions in the Russian media.

The appearance of Dugin's writings in the military press in the 1990s suggested ties to the military that most likely developed from his family connections (his father, grandfather, and great-grandfather were all military officers; for more on Dugin's writing in military publications, see p. 108).[13] He may have established additional connections with the military when he attended the Moscow Aviation Institute, from which his mentor Prokhanov graduated in 1960. Like Prokhanov – who during the 1980s was a favorite of the General Staff for his literary and journalistic efforts to support the Soviet action in Afghanistan – Dugin may have benefited from such ties. His early post-Soviet efforts to push "Eurasianism," for example, indicated his contacts with high-ranking military officers. In the first issue of Dugin's journal *Elementy* (July 1992), for example, no fewer than three generals, at the time department heads at the General Staff Academy, participated in a round-table discussion with Dugin on post-Soviet Russian strategy. In addition, the relative ease with which Dugin turned his *Arktogeia* publishing arm into a prolific producer of Eurasianist books and journals suggests that he had a patron financing the operation.[14]

Dugin subsequently was an advisor to the former Duma chairman Gennadi Seleznev. He announced his affiliation with the Kremlin and the Russian government in 2000. In a long *Zavtra* article on geopolitics, Dugin maintained that his Center for Geopolitical Expertise was "working with" the presidential administration, the government, the Federation Council, and the Duma, and "could become the analytical instrument" for developing a "National Idea."[15] Later that year a regional newspaper, *Cheliabinskii Rabochii*, also claimed an official capacity for Dugin – as an advisor to the Security Council – in a report on a Dugin visit to the Urals.[16] Apart from these claims of an official post, other reports and circumstantial evidence suggested that Dugin had ties to Kremlin "strategist" and presidential administration advisor Gleb Pavlovsky. Indeed, *Izvestiia*'s Andrei Kolesnikov wrote that Dugin and Pavlovsky would cooperate in formulating an ideology for the Kremlin. According to Kolesnikov, the Kremlin needed a new "state ideology" that would "speculate" on "great power attitudes" and Russian "national pride" to deflect criticism of Putin's statist policies.[17]

Dugin commentaries and interviews subsequently appeared on Pavlovsky-connected websites, suggesting an association between the Kremlin "political technologist" and Dugin. There have also been media claims that Dugin wrote analytical briefs for the presidential administration and contributed to developing Russia's national security doctrine.[18] More recently, Dugin himself noted that Pavlovsky, particularly in the wake of Ukraine's "Orange revolution," was borrowing his Eurasianist terminology. Dugin has also influenced television commentator Mikhail Leontiev.[19] Since the time of his association with the "patriotic" coalition in the 1990s, Dugin has not only grown in influence but toned down the more aggressive and esoteric side of his neo-Eurasianist ideology, playing down his former preoccupation with the occult, his conspiratorial worldview, and the influence of fascist ideology on his thinking. His ties to the Kremlin appeared to be still active under Putin, with Dugin even asserting that his Eurasian Youth Movement could act as a counter-revolutionary force, protecting the Kremlin from the forces of US-backed "color revolutions" in the former Soviet Union – if the Kremlin adhered to a Eurasianist political line.[20]

Eurasia as constitutive myth

What does Dugin believe regarding Russia and its Eurasian mission and why has his version of that historical mission been so influential? To understand what Dugin is getting at – and to understand its appeal – a digression is necessary:

Dugin is attempting to fulfill a role once carried out by the storytellers and priests of the pre-modern world, a role he seems quite conscious of. Dugin's neo-Eurasianism is nothing less than a constitutive myth (as well as a geopolitical strategy), one similar in many respects to other stories told over millennia of human history.[21]

In the pre-modern era the priest and storyteller formulated and promulgated the "high" (or "dynastic") and "low" (or "communal") traditions of a people, sometimes combining them to facilitate the cohesion of the tribal-based groups that would form the nation. The nation's myth–symbol complex, or *mythometeur*, is a peculiar blend of myths, memories, and symbols that was the working material of the priest and storyteller. The myth–symbol complex makes claims about the nation's origins, thus providing "the focus of a community's identity" and "constitutive political myth."[22] Often enough, the *mythometeur* "centers around the image of a sacred people with a special relationship to the deity." "Typically, this *mythometeur* posits an ideal past in which that relationship was harmonious and natural, when the community of the faithful lived out God's dispensation in true faith and understanding." The people may have gone astray or been conquered by foreigners, but it is the duty and destiny of the nation "to return to the ideal epoch of their history and become once again God's chosen emissaries on earth."[23]

The Russians inherited their sense of mission from Byzantium. The fusion of "dynastic" and "communal" elements to form the myth–symbol complex of "Holy Russia" – the tsar as defender of the faith and protector of the community of the faithful – originated with the Byzantine Greeks.[24] After Peter the Great's reforms, however, a deep tension developed in the national myth–symbol complex, a tension evident in the Slavophile–Westernizer controversy.[25] The new post-Petrine *mythometeur* of the Westernizers competed with that of the Slavophiles and their epigones. Russia still had a mission, but it was a secularized Hegelian mission, the sacral qualities of that mission originating in "History" as the will of the "Absolute." The controversy highlighted the rise of the new class, the intelligentsia, created by the Petrine reforms, who in the quasi-modernized post-Petrine Russia of the nineteenth century assumed the role of arbiter of the national patrimony that the priests and storytellers had fulfilled in the past.

Pre-Revolutionary Russia never fully entered the modern world as a nation-state, or settled the inevitable questions related to national identity, confused by the rise of Russian nationalism within the empire. What is Russia? Who is Russian? And, finally, what is to be done? Which, of course, depends on what the answers to the first two questions are and what one interprets as Russia's historic mission, if there is one. Soviet repression subsequently subsumed those questions within the communist *mythometeur*, and they were left unresolved, only to resurface in the wake of the Soviet collapse.

Several competing programs are available for inspiring a nationalist/right-wing movement. One stresses the continuities between the Russian Empire and the USSR; another stresses Russia's redemptive and civilizing imperial mission ("Holy Russia"); and a third is the "pogrom nationalism" of the neo-Nazis, which stresses not only the well-being of the Russkii *ethnos* but often its forceful dominance of other nationalities as well. But each of the more popular variations of the Russian myth–symbol complex carries within itself elements that contradict some of the most important propositions of other variants of the "Russian Idea." This competition on the right has become particularly important to those among whom the restoration of "empire" is the overriding concern; less so the form that such a restoration might take. The "Russian" state (usually meaning the territory of the former Soviet Union) must be restored in order for Russia to fulfill its historic mission, regaining a lost state of spiritual and political grace. To that end, the various shades and hues evident in the "patriotic" coalition – Red, Brown, and White – must reconcile themselves to solidarity with the others. Such statist ideologues have searched for a myth–symbol complex that would justify such a solidarity. Many think that they have found it in Dugin's neo-Eurasianism, but, as was noted earlier, the promotion of the Eurasian-Russian Idea has worked to divide the "patriotic" coalition as much as to unite it.

Dugin's neo-Eurasianism

The fundamentals of Dugin's neo-Eurasianist ideology were distilled in articles that appeared in two leading official armed forces journals, *Orientir* and the Defense Ministry newspaper *Krasnaia Zvezda* in 1997. The first was an interview entitled "For Russia Eurasia Is a Fate, Not a Choice"[26]; the second was an article entitled "Why There Will Be No End to the Cold War."[27] A more detailed account of the geopolitics of his version of Eurasianism is put forth in Dugin's "textbook," entitled *Principles of Geopolitics*.[28] The book was reportedly being circulated among the deputies of the State Duma at the time.[29]

Dugin espouses a geopolitical determinism that sees the character of nations and states as formed by the "elements" of geography and climate. The traits of those "great powers" which form the foundations of broad civilizations are, in his view, determined by these "elements" and remain constant, despite changes in regimes and official ideologies. He sees a dichotomy and inevitable conflict between "continental" powers (or "the land") and the "sea" powers (or "the island"). In his *Orientir* interview, Dugin claimed that "certain principles" characterizing the relationship of the nation are "preserved unchanged" in spite of changes in the "external" and "formal ideology" of a particular regime. This puts Dugin squarely in the "single stream" tradition that sees continuities from the tsarist to the Soviet period as being more important than any manifest differences.

Dugin sees the "land" as "traditionalist," integrationist, spiritual, anti-materialist, and views its values as tending toward collectivism and stability. The nations of the "continent" have tended toward state-directed economies, integrating diverse peoples under what Dugin sees as the benevolent leadership of a messianic great power in non-exploitative empires. In Dugin's view the foremost land power in history is Russia, which has inherited the "Eurasianist" mantle from ancient Rome. In contrast, he sees the "sea" as anti-traditionalist, individualist, materialistic, and therefore exploitative. The nations of the "sea/island," according to Dugin, have attempted to dominate other peoples in exploitive mercantile, capitalist "colonial empires," using their military might to sap the natural resources of others, undermining "traditional" nations, and spreading their influence into the rightful sphere of influence of the "land" by encroaching on the "periphery" (or "Rimland") that separates the two great forms of civilization. The "sea" is embodied in recent history by the United States, which has taken on leadership of the "Atlanticist" bloc from Great Britain.

Dugin asserts that the clash of these two civilizations is inevitable. In his view the "island" must expand its influence or die, since its appetite for resources to feed its consumer economy is unending. Russia's historic mission is to rally the nations of the "land" (Eurasia) by forming a broad alliance with continental Europe (minus the sea power Great Britain) led by Germany, plus India, Japan, and the Muslim fundamentalist states led by Iran. This would create a mighty "New Empire," integrated economically and strategically, with Moscow as the natural center. This Eurasianist bloc would oppose the Atlanticists, led by the United States, which attempts to encircle the Eurasian "heartland."

Russia's identity and physical survival are tied to the nation's historic imperial mission, according to Dugin, because only the "Eurasian empire" can guarantee Russian security by uniting the resources and manpower of the Slavic–Muslim heartland with the economic and technological know-how of Europe and Japan (and perhaps China).[30] If the Atlanticists were to succeed in cutting Russia off from potential allies by their encirclement, Russia would not be able to marshal enough resources to oppose the technologically superior Atlanticist juggernaut. If this happened, the Russian nation would disappear, absorbed by a new "continental" integrator, or be gradually diminished demographically under pressure from a hostile Atlanticist bloc that would sap the country's resources.[31]

The ideology of Eurasianism was first promulgated by Russian émigrés in the 1920s. Dugin outlines the fundamentals of the original version of Eurasianism in his book *Principles of Geopolitics*. The original Eurasianists drew on traditional Russian nationalist motifs, especially the idea that Russia was a unique civilization belonging exclusively to neither East nor West. Some, however, saw Russia as much closer to the spiritual East than to the materialistic West. Like Dugin, many Eurasianists were drawn to the notions of "geopolitics" as pronounced by a series of European "geo-strategists," who first posed political, economic, and social clashes in terms of "political geography," and who detected a geographic determinism in the battles of the great powers. Many were supportive of the Bolshevik regime after it became apparent that the "Reds" would reintegrate the fallen Russian Empire.

Dugin's neo-Eurasianist ideology is apparently both imperialist and nationalist – nationalist not in the sense that Russia must have a nation-state; that is, a state that is exclusively (or nearly so) for the Russian nation (*russkii narod*) – but in the sense that the nation can only be itself, can only realize its potential, as a unifying force in an empire. Unlike many other national imperialists, however, Dugin is a philosophical traditionalist who does not see Russia's role as exploitative or repressive, but as unifying in a way that allows for the flourishing of the many nations and religions of the Eurasian heartland. Like Prokhanov, Dugin views Islam as the natural ally of the "continent" in its war with the "island," a view many nationalists are loath to embrace, particularly in view of the ongoing counterinsurgency against Islamic and separatist radicals in the north Caucasus.[32] Dugin is a man of the right who reportedly has a working knowledge of nine European languages. His philosophical commitment to preserve tradition – all traditions – in Eurasia and his emphasis on empire have caused many Russian nationalists to question whether Dugin belongs with them at all or is only promulgating yet another ideology (like Soviet communism) that would neglect the interests of the Russians.

Apart from the original Eurasianists, Dugin's worldview is also the product of his study of the European "conservative revolutionaries" of the interwar period and of his interest in mysticism, paganism, and the occult.[33] Like them – and many others on both the right and the left – Dugin is interested in geopolitics not only as statecraft but, with Eurasianism as idealism, as part of a means of seeking out an "authentic" and purposeful life. His ideology allows at least the theoretical possibility of some other nation acting as continental integrator. If the Russians fail in their historic mission, failing to embrace an "authentic" and purposeful existence, one could envision a Dugin who might embrace that new power and another tradition (perhaps radical Islam?).

The occult in Dugin's ideology

Dugin believes that the history of the world is the history of the clash of the unseen, mystical forces of "chaos," embodied in Atlanticism, and those of "order," represented in Eurasianism – a struggle that has cosmic significance and that often takes the form of conspiracy and counter-conspiracy.[34] In Dugin's ideology a secret "Order of Atlanticists" has clashed with the "Order of Eurasianists" throughout human history. According to Dugin, the Atlanticists have dominated those secret societies (the Masons, for example) devoted to the creation of a global government ("mondialism"; more recently, Dugin has adopted the English term "globalism"). According to Dugin, the Atlanticists have worked to plant their "agents of influence" within the "heartland," efforts that thwarted, for example, Hitler's and Stalin's joint efforts (in the Molotov–Ribbentrop pact) to create the "New Empire."

According to Dugin, agents of both camps operated within the Bolshevik movement, with the army and military intelligence, Stalin, and other Eurasianists opposing the machinations of Trotsky, the NKVD/KGB, Beria, and other Atlanticists. The Atlanticists brought about the collapse of the USSR and dominated the Yeltsin regime. The task of the Eurasianists is to build the "New Empire" and prepare for an eschatological showdown between the forces of "order" and the forces of "chaos," the final act in what Dugin refers to as the "cosmic drama."

Dugin, Russia, and Germany

A review of Dugin's writings dating from the 1990s to the present shows that the Russian neo-Eurasianists have appropriated the ideas of the Belgian geopolitical theorist Jean Thiriart. Thiriart, a pro-fascist in the 1940s, eventually recognized the Russified Soviet Union as the final bastion of civilization in a Europe overrun by rootless American-style consumerism. He called for a new "Holy Alliance" of the USSR and Europe – the "Euro-Soviet empire," one that would expand further to the south, since it would require a port in the Indian Ocean – against the cosmopolitans.[35] Dugin has also borrowed ideas from the French "conspirologist" Jean Parvulesco[36] and the European geopolitical theorists of the first quarter of the twentieth century, especially Karl Haushofer.

Dugin and *Den'/Zavtra*'s Prokhanov attempted to forge an alliance with the French-led European New Right (*nouvelle droite*) in 1992. The *nouvelle droite* articulated a neo-pagan spirituality, an anti-capitalist critique of America and mass culture, and proposed a "third way" economic program for a united Europe without Euro-bureaucracy. New Right intellectuals, through their doctrine of "ethnopluralism," hoped to preserve the cultural autonomy of all nations in the new Europe. The *nouvelle droite* movement amounted to an intellectual attempt to resurrect the loose social relations of the pre-modern polity that most European conservatives identify with Christendom. Like others on the ideological right, the New Right was thereby intellectually struggling to stave off the homogenizing, standardizing, and alienating effects of globalism.[37] The attempted alliance appeared to have fizzled out, but the *nouvelle droite* and the Russian Eurasianists, particularly Dugin himself, both borrowed a great deal from the European, especially German, right-wing thinkers of the 1920s and 30s. Dugin's pro-Germanism is just one more instance of the long-standing ideological flirtation of Russia and Germany.[38]

Industrialization had come late to Germany, in the second half of the nineteenth century (Britain and France having already modernized themselves), disturbing the peace of the pastoral German states united by Bismarck. Germany, like Russia under Peter the Great, was dragged into the modern order abruptly, and the resulting trauma raised the inevitable "German questions," as the "Russian questions" had arisen in Russia. For German nationalists of the period stretching from the mid-nineteenth century to the 1930s, Germany was the land in the middle, between the "West," corrupted by materialist capitalism, and a backward "East." German nationalists, however, were divided over Russia: Was Russia simply the latest incarnation of barbarian hordes threatening European civilization, or were the Russians, like the Germans, a spiritual people, a nation untainted by "Western" materialism? Some Germans thought Russia a potential ally in the struggle against capitalism and rootless cosmopolitanism. As anti-Semitism gained ground in Germany prior to the Great War, many nationalists saw Russia, with its Black Hundreds and pogroms, as the natural ally of Germany, and the anti-Semitic right in Germany was bolstered considerably by the European publication of *The Protocols of the Elders of Zion* in the interwar period.[39]

For some time, German nationalists had intellectually groped about for a "third way" between capitalism, with its disruption of the traditional social order, and the proletarian internationalism of an equally materialist socialism. Some dreamed of a disciplined "Prussian socialism" that would reconcile industrialism with the needs of the nation. They believed that the key to reconciling socialism with nationalism was the notion of "the primacy of politics," the importance of the state (as the embodiment of the national spirit) directing and regulating the economy so as to develop society in accordance with its own interests and not those of the capitalists. Concrete "production" must therefore be disconnected from the abstract sphere of "circulation" and finance in order to accomplish the successful incorporation of modern technology with *Gemeinschaft*. Thus, Hitler did not originate the notion of "national socialism" in Germany. As the "Prussian socialists" saw it (and indeed all thinkers on the right before and since have shared this view), the purpose of the economic sphere is to support and nurture the community. Economic growth must not become a goal in itself, with the community objectified as a unit in capitalism's production–consumption cycle.

Within Germany a new intellectual movement, "the conservative revolution," united more traditional-minded conservatives and reactionaries of *volkisch* agrarian views with modernist right-wing thinkers in a romantic struggle against what they viewed as a corrupt Weimar state. The Weimar government, according to the "conservative revolutionaries," had sold out German interests by accepting the Treaty of Versailles. Weimar's mass democracy was manipulating a disoriented people and promoting individualism. The new movement opposed both the capitalist-liberal model and the threat of socialist revolution, which was constantly on the right's collective mind after the "Red" uprising of 1919.[40]

The "conservative revolutionaries" juxtaposed *Kultur* and *Zivilisation*, the one a reflection of organic *Gemeinschaft*, the other that of an artificial *Gesellschaft*, in their polemics. The "conservative revolution" set the "symbolism and language of *Kultur* – community, blood, will, self, form, productivity, and in some cases race – against the symbolism and language of alien *Zivilisation* – reason, intellect, internationalism, materialism, and finance."[41] *Kultur* was form, which filled the community with direction and purpose. The atomized mass found in *Zivilisation*, by way of contrast, was thought to be formless and uprooted. Community offered a framework for proper ethics, the mass only individual satisfaction of base appetites. The self was fully realized within the *Gemeinschaft*, the organic community that provided the boundaries of the realizable world for mankind.

The community/*Volk*/nation was a specific type, an organic outgrowth of its native soil. The *Kultur* self was alive and creative, expressing the essence of the particular *Volk* in the aesthetic forms of architecture, art, and handicrafts. The *Kultur* life was thus "authentic," an expression conveying the connectedness of the self through the community to the national spirit and thus to the life of the cosmos. Life was a spiritual and aesthetic experience, impossible to express authentically in the life-negating embrace of cold reason, individualism (and its ill-begotten twin, internationalism), and utilitarianism. Authentic production, in the sense of aesthetic creativity, was impossible under the sway of *Zivilisation*, where financial calculations and profit outweighed the will to create.

The conservative revolution was itself divided over the question of technology. Did the machine cut off the self from nature and thus the wellsprings of

Kultur, or was it possible to find a means of producing authentically with industrial technology? Perhaps technology and the machine themselves were but expressions of the *Volk* spirit, the highest materialization yet seen of what Spengler called "Faustian man's" impulse to control nature. Perhaps technics were "organic" in the sense that the machine was the will to power materialized in an instrumental sense, the drill press or turbine an extension of the *Volk* spirit and the machinist himself. If that were so, then under the right conditions the machine could produce authentically through an act of will; it could express the *Volk* spirit of *Kultur* and be put to the service of *Gemeinschaft*. In this way, Jeffrey Herf's "reactionary modernists" embraced technology and diverted the German right, as the Fascists through "futurism" had done in Italy, away from the backwardness of the agrarians and Christian moralists.[42]

The reactionary modernists tended to eschew Nazi "scientific racism," preferring the Spengleresque morphological-idealistic explanation of the *Volk*, but some did embrace the cult of the will to power and exalted in war, the highest aesthetic achievement of modern humankind. Many of them had served in World War I, and this "front generation" saw in the camaraderie and sense of community of the trenches the model for a new, specifically German, socialism. Their path to "authenticity" was the embrace of the new world, of the fusion of romanticism with technology, and of the ecstasy of the combat experience.[43]

The key to understanding early Nazi mobilization was the psychology of the so-called front generation. The phenomenon of the alienated veteran, the warrior who has experienced the heightened sensory awareness of the battlefield and is faced with the prospect of aimless boredom in civilian life, is common enough in the annals of warfare. For many of the philosophically inclined members of the front generation, the war had been a welcome relief from the "inauthentic" and life-negating boredom of modern bourgeois existence. Following Nietzsche, they thought of life as a fundamentally aesthetic experience. The war itself had been a huge canvas on which the technology of modern warfare had splashed the blazing colors of exploding artillery shells, the dark hues of the clouds of gray and black pillars of smoke rising from the ruins of smashed buildings and the craters of a transformed landscape, one made strangely vital by the cacophony of the machinery of death. The embrace of violence and death was the hallmark of a philosophy that found expression outside Germany in Italian Fascism and Fascist-derived movements elsewhere. The longing of some in the front generation for the community of the trenches, as well as for revenge against the Weimar government, which had betrayed the nation and the army, and the narcotic vitalism of combat, found an outlet for expression in the street warfare of the Brownshirts against the Reds, the sense of belonging in the Nazi movement, and the promise of a new, heroic future under a man who was one of them, Adolf Hitler.

Like most political movements, the Nazis were, especially early on, a coalition of "national revolutionaries" who represented strands of "German socialist" ideology. Within the Nazi Party, "left" and "right" wings developed, the Nazi "left" having been anticipated by two members of the "conservative revolution," Arthur Moeller van den Bruck and Ernst Niekisch.[44] Van den Bruck claimed that

"German socialism" could fulfill the socialist task of a misguided Marxism. He contrasted the "young peoples" of the East – Germany and Russia – with the decadent "West." Niekisch and his followers called themselves "National Bolsheviks" and advocated a German–Russian alliance against the "West." In Stalin's Soviet Union, many German nationalists saw the logical fulfillment of the war against "Jewish capitalism" in the nationalization of the means of production and the central planning of social development. Goebbels and the Strasser brothers (Otto and Gregor) were associated with the Nazi "left" for a time. Goebbels advocated cooperation with the "Reds," who could eventually be fully converted into National Socialists, and voiced pro-Russian sentiments in his novel *Mikhail*.[45] Göring and Hitler tilted toward the Nazi "right," which favored a system more akin to Fascist "corporatism."

Convergence with Russia could not be a real prospect for Adolf Hitler. He agreed with the characterization of Soviet communism as "Jewish Bolshevism"; communism in whatever form would always bear the burden of its Jewish origins, as would capitalism, liberalism, rationalism, and bourgeois softness and decadence. The Führer had declared the Slavs *Untermenschen*, and had foreseen the expansion of the Reich's *lebensraum* as the culmination of his plans for a *Drang nacht Osten*. The East was judged to be Germany's natural directional path of expansion, an expansion that would be facilitated by the eventual destruction of the Soviet Union and the Slavs themselves.[46]

The influence of the German "conservative revolutionaries" – especially the "reactionary modernist" wing of that movement – and other thinkers of the European right of the 1920s and 1930s, particularly the pro-Fascist intellectual Julius Evola, is acknowledged by Dugin frequently in his writings. A revolution of the right in Europe, especially in geopolitically strategic Germany, is a necessity in Dugin's ideology. How else can the new "Holy Alliance," and the "Third Rome" stretching from Dublin to Vladivostok, be fully secured? Dugin's mystical geopolitical speculations, tinged with Gnostic overtones, his touting of a "third way" between cosmopolitan and materialistic capitalism and the equally cosmopolitan and materialistic ideology of communism, were common themes among the "conservative revolutionaries," and the pro-Russian bias of the "National Bolsheviks" naturally has attracted an ideologist who is attempting to create a new synthesis, "non-conformist" in nature, while preserving the special place of the Russians in the cosmic struggle.

Dugin's "New Right" of the 1990s embraced technology and geopolitics while celebrating romantic nationalism and spiritualism, expressing a Russian version of the "steely romanticism" the Nazis borrowed from the reactionary modernists of interwar Germany. Moreover, Dugin has glorified the warrior and the vitality of the struggle. He has even gone so far as to declare the eternal struggle between the Atlanticists and Eurasianists beyond good and evil. The approaching Armageddon-like struggle for the world is expressed in eschatological, but not moral, terms by Dugin. The struggle is an end in itself, life an aesthetic experience, a "cosmic drama" in which individuals are merely players. Russia's role in history may have no meaning beyond itself. Indeed, the only way to overcome the boredom of modernity is to fully engage oneself in the struggle, to celebrate conflict and warfare, the dynamics of radicalism against the stunning complacency of "the system," the globalist-bourgeois-liberal-materialist-internationalist prison that threatens to end history by homogenizing the key players – the nations of the "island" and the "continent" – and make an "authentic" life impossible.[47]

The Eurasian debate

Dugin has borrowed heavily from the ideological arsenal of the European right in an effort to renew the Russian Idea, but has not repudiated those Russian thinkers of the past who are considered the precursors of his ideological synthesis. Dugin's ruminations on the nation forming aspects of geography may be Spengleresque, and he borrows heavily from the language of the "conservative revolution," but Nikolai Danilevsky and Konstantin Leontiev, as well as the Eurasianists of the 1920s and 1930s, are given their due.

Dugin's patriotic tone has not, however, prevented clashes over the nature of his neo-Eurasianism and its relationship to Russia's future. To many on the Russian right it appears that the concrete interests of the Russian people themselves will once more be forgotten if "Eurasianism" is embraced as the "national patriots'" ideology. The Russians would bear the burdens of empire but would be required to sublimate their Russianness, to defer to Muslims and Europeans in the interest of unity, to repeat the Soviet experience, when the explicit expression of Russian nationalism was virtually outlawed, watered down into the thin gruel of "Soviet patriotism" (this time as "Eurasian" patriotism), which barely provided enough spiritual nourishment for the nation to survive, much less revitalize itself.[48] Others have attacked Eurasianism as merely another form of homogenizing globalism, a mirror image of the New World Order, in which all the peoples of the "imperial" alliance would be subjected to a form of cultural standardization reminiscent of Sovietism, all in the name of "tradition"![49]

In the past, Dugin has defended his Eurasian variant of the Russian Idea by arguing that the revitalization of the empire is impossible without the revitalization of Russian national consciousness and the strengthening of Russian statehood within the Russian Federation itself. Dugin has maintained that "only those who share the basic tenets of [this] traditional Russian political self-consciousness can be Russian nationalists."[50] Putting Russia first means putting the historic imperial mission first. To be Russian is to be, in part, an imperialist.

More recently, however, Dugin has moved further away from the nationalists, echoing the criticisms and arguments made by his Eurasian Youth Movement of the "pogrom nationalists" who took part in the "right march" in November 2005. "Nationalism," wrote Dugin in March 2006,[51] "was the most important factor" in the "collapse of the Soviet Union," something most "patriots" lament. Dugin identified the "nationalist mood" in the former Soviet republics, accompanied by "Russophobia," as the explosive mixture that detonated and brought down the USSR. Dugin acknowledged that these various phenomena could be identified as "nationalist," and that nationalism of one sort or another was "part of our existence," arguing for a "political nationalism" rather than a "biological" one – that is, for all citizens of the state to be recognized as members of the nation. In Dugin's ideology, in which states, nations, and indeed continents are the vessels for the expression of ideas, "biological nationalism" makes little sense.

In the piece cited above, Dugin warned that "biological nationalism" threatened the unity of the state (he mentioned Chechen separatism as an example). He insisted that the Russian Empire and the Soviet Union had acted to create and perpetuate a political nation "belonging to a common civilization" based on the "unification of various peoples around the Russian [*russkii*] nation [*narod*]." Dugin further warned that "it cannot be ruled out" that "certain political forces" – probably the proponents of "orange revolution" that Dugin's ESM has warned about – would "take advantage" of clashing "ethnic nationalisms" within the Russian Federation during the "complex" period of power transition in 2008. Dugin called for "*rossiiskii natsionalism*" (as opposed to "*russkii natsionalism*") based on "civil society." This would be better than "ethnic nationalism" and "no national identity at all," but worse than the "optimal variant," something Dugin called "Eurasian nationalism," that could unite the "new empire," while allowing for "the development of Russian [*russkii*] identity." And every other *ethnos* would have that same right. Dugin, as a traditionalist, stressed that Russian identity would develop in "its own Orthodox context."

With Dugin again defending his ideology, and his youth organization clashing with nationalists, critics on the right have renewed their assault on Eurasianism and Dugin's general – not particular – traditionalism. Sergei Stroiev, for instance, in May 2006[52] took Dugin to task for the contradictions in his professed Orthodoxy (Dugin is an Old Believer) and his philosophical traditionalism that in part embraces Islam as the ally of Orthodox Russia. If one is Orthodox, then one believes Orthodoxy to be the Truth. How can Dugin reconcile that with his practically universalist views? In Dugin's philosophy, Orthodoxy is "only one of many possible paths to the realization of Tradition." How can fundamentalists of all stripes unite, except in the "traditionalism of traditional religions?" That is to say nothing of Dugin's fascination with the occult (including Satanism) and the postmodern quality of Dugin's eclectic philosophy, including European geopolitics and strategy, Gnostic mysticism, occultism, "traditionalism," and his advocacy of "leftist fascism and rightist communism." What is primary and what is secondary in Dugin's thought? Then there is Dugin's association with ultra-Orthodox Jews, radical Zionists who are, of course, "traditionalists" and thus worthy of being tagged as Eurasian. How, wrote Stroiev, can any Russian (*russkii*) national patriot unite with militant Zionists, or Orthodox believers be the allies of Satanists? The Eurasian Idea (in the geopolitical sense) could have been a useful framework for the patriotic coalition, but Dugin's provocative writings prevent that. According to Stroiev, Dugin has helped discredit the idea of a nationalist–communist alliance; the Eurasian Idea has been compromised in the eyes of nationalists. By serving the present regime ("servile to globalist structures"), Dugin has betrayed the principles he professes.

Dugin disillusioned with Putin? And Russia?

As noted earlier, Dugin was a strong supporter of the Putin regime and has maintained ties with the Kremlin. By 2005, however, it became evident that he had grown disenchanted with the Putin Kremlin. He still apparently had hopes of influence, but, perhaps at closer inspection, was severely disappointed both by Putin himself and by members of the "power structure" entourage. Thus, Dugin no longer spoke of Putin as a "man of destiny" (essentially a Eurasianist); he saw members of the Kremlin administration as no better than the hated "oligarchs"; and he was rather pessimistic about Russia's future. In January and February of 2005, for instance, Dugin wrote of Putin as a man faced with a historic decision: he must choose "patriotism" (read: "Eurasianism") over liberalism or lose his legitimacy. Dugin still viewed him as at heart a "Eurasian man," but wrote of Putin as perhaps being naïve, since his entourage still included Atlanticist elements left over from the Yeltsin era. If liberalism was the choice, Russia would collapse.[53]

By late February and March, Dugin had clearly changed his attitude, both about Putin as a man and about the "power structure" entourage. Earlier, Dugin had spoken of Putin holding Russia's fate in his hands.[54] No longer. In forming his Eurasian Youth Union, Dugin described its members as present-day *oprichniki*. But this "sacred order" was not pledged to support the Kremlin or Putin personally, but to support the "sacred task" of working for what Dugin called "Russia-3," the "Eurasian project" for Russia's future. "Russia-1" was Putin's Russia, bent on preserving the status quo, a mixture of irreconcilable "patriotic" and "liberal" elements. "Russia-2" was the "Orange revolution" project for Russia, which meant certain destruction. But "Russia-1" and "Russia-2" were not fundamental opposites. "Russia-3" would favor the Kremlin only insofar as it followed a line compatible with the Eurasian project. Dugin's *oprichniki* would act as a counter-revolutionary force so long as that served Eurasianist ends. But if the Kremlin were deemed to be working against those ends, then the youth movement could become a revolutionary force itself.[55]

Dugin saw no worthy people in power. The state monopolies being formed in the wake of the Yukos affair were no different from the "oligarch monopolies." He had had hopes for Putin, but Putin had failed to fulfill those hopes. The Kremlin was concerned not so much with the "continuity of power" in 2008, but rather with the "continuity of the ruling clans." Putin had taken not a single step in the direction desired by Dugin.[56] "Patriots" felt "deceived" by Putin.[57] *Vlast'*, the governing authority, was totally corrupt. With the next presidential elections approaching in 2008, Dugin wrote that to preserve "continuity," patriots may have no other choice than to keep Putin in power.[58]

Whither Dugin?

There is nothing bad, nothing inherently wrong with or undesirable about, Russians grappling with the question of national identity and purpose. But the "national question" is like many other phenomena in human society: it can be manifested in positive or negative ways. Historian John Lukacs once tried to distinguish between the positive and the negative sides of the national identity question. A positive identity "grows from a sense of belonging to a particular country," wrote Lukacs. This type of identity is "confident ... [and] essentially defensive." Lukacs saw another type of identity, however, as "self-conscious rather than confident; it is aggressive" rather than defensive in nature. This type of identity is ideological and substitutes for religion. It is suspicious of those who do not agree with nationalist ideology. An aggressive, self-conscious ideology, Lukacs continued, "may fill the emotional needs of insufficiently rooted people" and depends on hatred and suspicion.[59]

Lukacs had in mind the kind of negative phenomenon many would identify as "nationalism," and not the patriotism he sees as normal and healthy, but Dugin's ideology is not so different. It is more abstract than concrete, less concerned with people than with ideas. Perhaps it is a sign of Dugin's ideological bent that he has spent far less time pondering the consequences of Russia's demographic collapse than others on the right have. After all, his ideology does seem to say, "If not the Russians, then someone else." His Islamic allies once posed the Eurasian mission in a Turkic/Islamic form – "*Velikii Turan*" – with a capital in Central Asia. Some of Hitler's followers dabbled in occultism, saw Japanese Shinto and the cult of the samurai as appealing, even "Aryan," while Himmler considered converting to Islam.[60] One can be on the right and be neither patriotic nor a nationalist.

Dugin's search for authenticity in occultism and expansive imperialism, his fascination with revolution and war, paganism, and fundamentalist Islam (at least of the Iranian variety) is a road traveled by many on both the right and the left; if one's time and place disappoints, then alternatives can be found. Patriots love their country warts and all; their people are like an extended family, for better or worse. But what if the "national patriot" of Dugin's sort grows disappointed in his country? Would he, like Hitler in his bunker, declare the Russians unworthy of their historic mission?

Dugin may be a man of the right, but his quest for authenticity and purposeful existence is not one confined to that side of the political spectrum, as witnessed by the bizarre tale of a leftist California teenager named John Walker Linhd and his affiliation with the Taliban.[61] I do not claim that Dugin has reached that point, only that the kind of ideology he has formulated can lead in that direction. But that makes him little different in that regard than the "patriots" who want to cleanse the Russian gene pool, or dream of great power status restored, of Russia being feared as much as respected, and who worship a Georgian who took the name "Stalin" and killed millions of Russians in building his hateful empire. They have much more in common than they know.

Notes

1 www.rferl.org/featuresarticle/2005/11/08650cc8–51a2–493c-b772-f163705cd201.html (Yasmann, 4 November 2005). The new holiday was established by a bill introduced in the Duma in 2004. The bill's sponsors were the Kremlin-backed United Russia and

the nationalist Rodina and Liberal Democratic parties. The holiday replaces the Soviet-era Day of the Great October Socialist Revolution.

2 Estimates vary as to the number of marchers. The Radio Liberty article cited above, for instance, claimed that there were "at least 2,000" participants.

3 The DPNI has not limited itself to the single-issue message of curbing immigration from the former Soviet republics to Russia, as well as non-Russian migration within the Russian Federation. The DNPI is headed by Alexander Potkin, who uses the pseudonym "Belov." Potkin was once press secretary for the Pamyat National Patriotic Front and, according to the SOVA Center's Galina Kozhenikova, has become the most sought-after public speaker among the hard-line nationalists: http://xeno.sova-center.ru/6BA2468/6BB4208/6E811ED?print=on 25 February 2006 (accessed 15 June 2008).

4 www.mk.ru/numbers/1898/article64155.htm (Moshkin, 5 November 2005).

5 Ibid.

6 http://evrazia.org/modules.php?name–ews&file=article&sid=2735. evrazia.org is one of Dugin's websites (Yefrimov, 4 November 2005).

7 www.mk.ru/numbers/1898/article64155.htm (Moshkin, 5 November 2005).

8 The reference is to an unsigned APN report of 4 November 2005. No URL is available. The article turned up via a search engine query.

9 See the above reference.

10 www.apn.ru/opinions/article9480.htm (Tyurin, 7 November 2005).

11 www.apn.ru/publications/article1673.htm (Tyurin, 29 November 2005).

12 See my 11 June 1997 Foreign Broadcast Information Service Media Analysis, "Dugin Advocates 'Geopolitics' in Military Publications" for more on Dugin and Prokhanov. See also my book *The Russian Question: Nationalism, Modernization, and Post-Communist Russia*, Lanham, MD: Rowman & Littlefield, 1998, especially chapter 8, "The Nationalist Intelligentsia, Eurasia, and the Problem of Technology."

13 His father may have been a high-ranking officer in military intelligence, the GRU. See www.rferl.org/specials/russianelection/bio/dugin.asp (Yasmann, no date given); see also www.stringer-news.ru/Publication.mhtml?PubID=2019&Part=39 (Kaledin, 1 May 2003).

14 Dugin has named the military as the institution that has most supported his ideas. Remarks at a Washington, DC meeting, October 2005.

15 "Evraziiskaia platforma" (A Eurasian Platform), *Zavtra*, 21 January 2000.

16 On 26 October 2000.

17 *Izvestiia*, 29 August 2000.

18 See my unpublished paper "Eurasianists and Skinheads: The Role of the Far Right in Putin's Russia," delivered at a 2003 conference in Tyson's Corner, Virginia.

19 Leontiev was a founding member of Dugin's Eurasia movement. He was made a member of the movement's Political Council (RIA, 21 April 2000; sobor.ru, *Nezavisimaia gazeta*, 24 April 2000). The website polit.ru once called Dugin and Leontyev Putin's "mouthpieces": www.polit.ru/analytics/2004/12/29/ecomdan_print.html (29 December 2004).

20 For more on Dugin's ties to the Russian authorities, see my paper "The Eurasian Project: Russia-3, Dugin and Putin's Kremlin," which was delivered at the November 2005 meeting of the American Association for the Advancement of Slavic Studies in Salt Lake City, Utah.

21 The following discussion is largely derived from *The Russian Question*, chapter 8.

22 A. D. Smith, *The Ethnic Origins of Nations*, Oxford: Basil Blackwell, 1986, pp. 57–58.

23 Ibid., p. 63.

24 Ibid., p. 66.

25 In classical Slavophile discourse the "communal" element had overtaken the "dynastic" since the monarchy under Peter the Great had disrupted the historical continuity of the traditional Russian "concert" of tsar, Church, and people, each with their own sphere of activity but nevertheless an organic whole. See *The Russian Question*, Chapter 2.

26 *Orientir*, 3, March 1997.

27 *Krasnaia Zvezda*, 25 April 1997. Dugin's ideology has been influential not only because it had value for those seeking to unite "Reds," "Whites," and "Browns" in a "national patriotic" front, but because the geopolitical aspect of his ideology probably was attractive to many in the military and the military-industrial complex. Military backers likely saw a justification for rearmament and a revival of the army in Dugin's vision of an inevitable clash with the West. Dugin's ties to the military were the subject of my 6 November 1997 Foreign Broadcast Information Service (FBIS) Media Analysis article "Dugin Advocates 'Geo-politics' in Military Publications."

28 Moscow: Arktogeia, 1997.

29 This description of Dugin's ideology is based on chapter 8 of *The Russian Question*.

30 Dugin has more frequently seen China as susceptible to Atlanticist influences and has favored, oddly enough, the island nation of Japan as a Russian ally. During Putin's presidency, Dugin became more ambivalent about China, sometimes seeing a possible Russian–Chinese alliance developing. For Dugin's more recent views on China, see *Vedomosti*, 31 July 2002; www.izvestia.ru/politic/article35641 (Dugin, 2 July 2003); and, finally, a 15 August 2005 comment by Dugin (RIA Novosti):

> There is a growing clash between two futures: The American vision of a world empire led by the one superpower, the U.S., and the concepts of the countries and nations which reject the uni-polar structure in favor of a multi-polar one. Moscow and Beijing have been pushed towards earnest geopolitical partnership by "the events of the past year, when 'color revolutions' gathered momentum in the post-Soviet states," Dugin said. "The American connection in the events in Georgia, Ukraine, Kyrgyzstan and Uzbekistan clearly showed that the U.S. was resolved to reform the post-Soviet space to suit its strategic interests. This decision was directed against Russia and China, whose positions were growing more vulnerable."

31 In his book on geopolitics, Dugin seemed to be claiming that any attempt to integrate the Eurasian "heartland" without Russia would fail, meaning, perhaps, that a Eurasia without a Russia state would not be viable. Geographically, of course, Russia takes up much of the heartland, but Dugin was perhaps thinking only in terms of statehood, meaning that another continental integrator – the Islamic states of Central Asia, for example – could make such an attempt without a Russian state as part of the continental empire. The point is that Eurasia could at least theoretically be integrated by another great power – even China, if Dugin's attitude has indeed changed regarding Beijing and its ties to the Atlanticist bloc.

32 For more on Russian cooperation with the "Muslim world," especially the Turkic peoples of Central Asia, see, for example, *Den'*, 20, 1992, "Islam and the 'Right'"; for a time, *Den'* carried a page devoted to promoting cooperation between Islam and the Russians under the rubric "Slav–Islamic Academy." The *Den'/Zavtra* contributor Geidar Dzhemal once claimed that Islam articulated a "metaphysical" anti-Americanism, which the "New Right" (the self-styled "spiritual opposition") claims for itself. *Den'*, 38, 1992. *Den'*, 12, 1992 carried an article on Islamic revolution by Ayatollah Khomeini. Dugin's Eurasianism has also been influenced by the work of Lev Gumilev. Gumilev was the son of the famous poet Anna Akhmatova. He spent time in the Stalinist gulag, where he developed his theories of "ethnogenesis," which bear a striking resemblance to Spengler's and Danilevsky's ideas on nations and cultures as unique types, as well as to Herder's celebration of the diversity of national cultures, though it seems unlikely that he had read any of these. Gumilev also agreed with the Eurasianists of the 1920s and 1930s on the closeness of Russia and the East, and even maintained that the Russian ethnos had experienced an infusion of "Eastern" blood during the years of the "Tatar yoke," an idea that some "Eurasianists" shared, but one that has been contested by certain quarters of the Russian right. *Den'/Zavtra* has published many articles by and about Gumilev. See, for example, *Den'*, 52, 1992. Gumilev died in June 1992.

33 Viktor Yasmann, citing an article in *Stringer* (1 May 2003), has written that Dugin became interested in the European right when his father secured a job for him at one of the Russian intelligence agencies in the 1970s. According to this account, Dugin worked with classified files on theoreticians of Italian and German fascism. The papers had been seized by Soviet troops during and after World War II. Dugin also reportedly had access to files on the Russian émigré Eurasianists of the 1920s. It was at this time that he developed an interest in mysticism, paganism, and fascism. The Yasmann article is available at www.rferl.org/specials/russianelection/bio/dugin.asp (no date given).

34 Dugin refers to the conspiritological aspect of his thinking in his *Orientir* interview. A fuller exposition of this side of his "geopolitics" can be found in his "Velikaia voina kontinentov" (The Great War of the Continents), which was serialized in the newspaper *Den'* in 1992 (nos. 4–7, 9, 11, 13, and 15). This section is based partly on chapter 8 of *The Russian Question* and partly on the FBIS Media Analysis already referred to.

35 In the past, Dugin frequently examined the ideas of Thiriart in his journalism. Articles by Thiriart, for example, were published in the first issue of Dugin's *Elementy* (1, 1992) and in *Den'* (34, 1992).

36 Dugin took part in the presentation of a Russian translation of Parvulesko's book *Putin and the Eurasian Empire* in St. Petersburg on 27 March 2006, which confirms the continuing influence of the European geopolitical theorists on Dugin's ideology. See the report at www.pravaya.ru/news/7163 (27 March 2006). See also a Rosbalt news agency report of 27 March 2006.

37 For a time, *Den'* carried a regular column entitled *Den'-Kontinent* on the activities of various anti-globalist forces in Europe and Asia. The paper also carried interviews with the leading figures of the *nouvelle droite*, and an occasional reprint of one of Alain de Benoist's (de Benoist being the most prominent intellectual associated with the European New Right) articles. See, for example, *Den'*, 22, 1992.

38 See W. Laqueur's *Russia and Germany: A Century of Conflict*, Boston: Little, Brown, 1965 for more on the German–Russian relationship. Most of this section is based on chapter 8 of *The Russian Question.*

39 Laqueur examined the importance of *The Protocols* to Nazism in *Russia and Germany*, pp. 79–104.

40 See J. Herf's *Reactionary Modernism: Technology, Culture, and Politics in Weimar and the Third Reich*, Cambridge: Cambridge University Press, 1984. Dugin summarized the basic tenets of the conservative revolution in *Elementy* (1, 1992).

41 Herf, *Reactionary Modernism*, p. 16.

42 Michael E. Zimmerman pursued Herf's lead regarding the "reactionary modernists" and technology in his examination of Martin Heidegger's philosophy of being and its relation to the reactionary modernists and the philosopher's associations with the Nazis. See his *Heidegger's Confrontation with Modernity: Technology, Politics, Art*, Indianapolis: Indiana University Press, 1990.

43 Ernst Junger was a proponent of such ideas. For a discussion of Junger, see Herf, *Reactionary Modernismi*, pp. 70–108.

44 For more on van den Bruck and Niekisch, see *Elementy*, 1, 1992, 51–54.

45 Excerpts from *Mikhail* were published in the newspaper of the National Bolshevik Party: *Limonka*, 31, 1996. For more on the internal Nazi struggle between "left" and "right" factions and the conversion of Goebbels to Hitler's ideas on state and economy, see F. L. Carsten, *The Rise of Fascism*, Berkeley: University of California Press, 1967, pp. 124–129.

46 For more on the conflict between pro-Russian and anti-Russian factions in the Nazi movement, as well as Hitler's attitude toward Stalin, see Laqueur, *Russia and Germany*, pp. 126–159.

47 See especially the final installment of Dugin's *The Great War of the Continents*, in *Den'*, 15, 1992, for his opinions on eschatology and the notion of the "cosmic

drama." Dugin's hatred of the "system" has in the past led him to embrace radicals of all shades who are anti-"system," especially the French student radicals of the 1960s who mounted a violent assault on what radical ideologist Guy Debord called "the society of spectacle." For Dugin on "the society of spectacle" and his embrace of violent radicals from the 1960s, see *Limonka*, no. 14, 1995.

48 See, for example, comments by K. Mialo, T. Glushkova, V. Rasputin, and I. Shafarevich in their exchange with the Eurasianist V. Kozhinov, "What Condition Is the Russian Nation In?" *Nash Sovremennik*, 3, 1993. Myalo ponders the absurdity of "Rossiia bez russkikh?" *Moskva*, 6, 1994.

49 See Geidar Dzhemal's article "Europe to Vladivostok, or Asia to Dublin?" *Den'*, 38, 1992.

50 Dugin's views on "Eurasianism" as a form of Russian nationalism were set out in "Apologia natsionalizma," *Den'*, 38, 1993.

51 "Nationalism: russkii ili rossiiskii?" *Vremia novostei*, 15 March 2006.

52 www.forum.msk.ru/material/politic/7368.html (Stroyev, 5 February 2006).

53 See www.nigru.ru/docs/class/509.html (Dugin, 8 February 2005) and www.opec.ru/comment_doc.asp?d_no=54467 (Dugin, 13 January 2005).

54 www.nigru.ru/docs/class/509.html (Dugin, 8 February 2005).

55 See especially Dugin's "Metaphysics of the Oprichnina": http://arcto.ru/modules.php?name–ews&file=article&sid=1252 (Dugin, 26 February 2005); see also www.evrazia.org/modules.php?name–ews&file=article&sid=2266 (Dugin, 3 March 2005).

56 http://evrazia.org/modules.php?name–ews&filc=article&sid=2397 (Dugin, 26 March 2005).

57 http://evrazia.org/modules.php?name–ews&file=article&sid=2314 (Dugin, 22 March 2005).

58 www.pravaya.ru/news/9526?print=1 (Dugin, 27 October, 2006). Early on in Medvedev's administration (June 2008), Dugin was happy about Medvedev's visit to Germany, saying it was a sign of the Kremlin's "Eurasian geopolitical orientation." See http://life.ru:80/news/16055/ (Bakurina, 26 June 2008).

59 J. Lukacs, "The Patriotic Impulse," *Chronicles*, July 1992, 19.

60 See, for instance, www.frontpagemag.com/articles/ReadArticle.asp?ID=4934 (Trifkovic, 5 December 2002).

61 See http://en.wikipedia.org/wiki/John_Walker_Lindh.

Part III

Intellectual and sociological niches of contemporary Russian nationalism

7 New racism, "clash of civilizations," and Russia[1]

Victor Shnirelman

"New racism" on the eve of the twenty-first century

Today racism is once again becoming a plague threatening humanity. It is no accident that the beginning of the twenty-first century was marked by the World Conference against Racism, Racial Discrimination, Xenophobia and Related Intolerance (31 August – 7 September 2001) held in Durban, South Africa, as the result of a UNO initiative. Controversial attitudes at the conference and its contradictory results were also no accident.

One of the most visible marks of the postmodern epoch is a collapse of the universal ideological constructions and a dominance of relativism. This shift accompanies the emergence of numerous new states as well as a remarkable growth in the political activities of ethnic and racial minorities. They bring their own flavor to world politics. On the one hand they interpret the political environment both in the international domain and within their own countries and establish relationships with the neighbors in their own way, develop their own views concerning further development, and also articulate their goals in their own way. On the other, in order to shape their ideas they usually exploit Western terms and concepts, albeit filling them with their own content. Hence, there is a conflation of terms and concepts, which despite their similarity carry messages completely different from the original ones.

In particular, this concerns the terms "race" and "racism." Specialists have been complaining for almost twenty years about the ambiguity of their contemporary meanings. Indeed, a few decades ago many scholars believed that human races really existed as distinct, well-bounded biological categories. At that time they interpreted racism as an aspiration to prove that races differed in their mental powers, which doomed them to social and political inequality. Ultimately, this ideology was aimed at the establishment of a permanent hegemony for the white race.

Nowadays only a few obscurantists who are behind the times share this ideology. Now race is commonly interpreted as a social construction that is used to confirm any kind of social inequality or discrimination with reference to either the biological or the cultural distinction of a group the construction is aimed at. Any manifestation of this sort of ideology, be it in rhetoric, behavior, legislation, or state policy, is considered racist. A pure biological racism is highly unpopular today, and certain national legislations have introduced severe criminal codes that punish those who stir up racial hatred. Therefore, contemporary racists articulate and disseminate their ideas in a covert form. For about thirty years now, scholars have not failed to emphasize that the concept of "race" is blurred or is being replaced entirely by "culture" and "ethnicity." This causes confusion because these latter concepts are intensively used not only by racists but also by ethnic and racial minorities. For those minorities, these concepts serve as very important political resources that help them, first, to retain their distinct positive identity, and second, to claim desired privileges as a result of affirmative action policies. Therefore, they advocate multiculturalism and the "right to be different." It is at this point that leftists support them. Meanwhile, over the past three decades or so a slogan about "the right to be different" has been adopted by the New Right.[2]

The New Right and the "right to be different"

To understand the message of the New Right's calls, one has to examine how they interpret "the right to be different." Indeed, leftists and rightists view this slogan in different ways.[3] For leftists it focuses on the rescue of the cultures and languages of the numerically small indigenous peoples and ethnic minorities that are threatened today with total disappearance from the face of the earth. At the same time, rightists slightly modify the slogan, applying it to all cultures, including those of the dominant majorities. Thus, the message changes drastically. Indeed, in the latter case it is the dominant culture that has to be rescued from the alleged danger of corruption by mass immigration. The New Rightists argue that "immigration [is not] beneficial for the host population receiving the immigrants, who are confronted, against their will, with sometimes-brutal modifications in their human and urban environments."[4] Immigration is treated by the New Rightists as a force for evil par excellence, and they maintain that people have to stay within their own cultural milieu for the whole of their life. To put it another way, the New Rightists seem to promote a cultural segregation while encroaching upon one of the most valuable traits of democracy, freedom of movement.

This slogan is dangerous for the old diasporas such as the Jewish, Armenian, and Gypsy ones, which became established in Europe long before many European nations had come into existence. It also provides no place in Europe for such new diasporas as, for example, the Meskhetian Turks or Kurds, who are unable to return to their homelands because of the inhospitable political environment there. This stance deprives many refugees of asylum and any hope of rescue. Thus, in fact, the New Rightists' slogan "the right to be different" is a manifestation of chauvinism aimed against both immigrants (whatever reservations are made) and affirmative actions toward ethnic minorities. One goal of all this propaganda is to secure the current demographic balance, which provides both the dominant majority with a privileged position in the society, and the Rightists with positive results at elections for representative political bodies (it is well known that immigrants are inclined to vote for leftist parties).

Russia: from a Marxist to a civilizational approach

In Western and Southern Europe the "New Racism" is aimed mostly at immigrants and has come into being as a response to the recent flow of newcomers from the Third World. Over the past fifteen to twenty years, racism has taken hold in Russia as well, but it has developed there on a different basis. Before I delve deeper into that issue, I should like to discuss the most influential racial ideologies in Russia, which are closely linked to identity. In this chapter I shall focus on the so-called civilizational approach to the past and present. This approach represents Russia as a distinct unique civilization and in fact restores the former imperial view, albeit in a new, fashionable form. A civilizational approach is aimed at the integration of the whole of Russia's multiethnic population into a cohesive nation and seeks to establish clear cultural borders that might distinguish Russia as a cultural body from all other, similar entities.

Yet the cultural distinctions of Russia are still to be defined. One of its most important peculiarities is to be found in its unique history. Another is its geographical setting. Indeed, as the Eurasians argued in the 1920s, the Russian territory spread over vast plains and was naturally limited by high mountain ranges and seas. This argument is less valid for the contemporary Russian Federation; yet the neo-Eurasians refer to what they call a sacred geography. They define Russia as a Midgard – that is, the sacred center of the world situated close to the North Pole. A civilizational approach provides Russia with a special status flattering for those who feel nostalgia for its former status as a world power. Indeed, Russia is represented not as a common state but as a civilization, a "Eurasian continent," and is compared to Europe or "Atlantic civilization" rather than to such states as the United Kingdom, France, or Germany.

Today a civilizational approach not only is used extensively by many Russian scholars but also has been introduced into the school curriculum. The collapse of the communist ideology in the USSR in the late 1980s made many historians and political scientists give up the former Marxist socioeconomic approach to history and replace it with the cultural civilizational approach as a new, promising paradigm. The main partisans of the civilizational approach, such as Oswald Spengler and Arnold Toynbee, let alone their unoriginal followers, have neither produced any sophisticated classification of distinct civilizations nor suggested any well-founded definition of a local civilization, nor proved that various civilizations differ from each other by certain innate intellectual characteristics that predetermine their unique historical development. All these faults have already been discussed by critics who have demonstrated the poor analytical basis of the civilizational approach, whose admirers rely more on intuition than on a well-developed theory.

Yet the civilizational approach was welcomed in post-Soviet Russia, where it was generously discussed at many conferences, round-tables, and various meetings up to the level of the State Duma (the Russian parliament). Although there was no unanimity among the scholars, the Ministry of Education of the Russian Federation introduced the civilizational approach to the school history curriculum.

An irony is that, on the one hand, radical democrats and anti-communists promoted the civilizational approach and made all the efforts to cleanse Soviet Marxist ideology from the intellectual milieu. But on the other hand, former instructors both in Communist Party history and in Marxist philosophy, who aspired to get rid of their own questionable past in a radical fashion, also adopted the approach.

It is in this confusing environment that the civilizational approach carved its way into the Russian school system. It first appeared as a school textbook produced by L. I. Semennikova in 1994.[5] In the Soviet days, Semennikova studied the revolution of 1917 and never occupied herself with cultural studies or any general historical problems. Yet her textbook, based on the civilizational approach, seemed to shed a new light on human history and in 1994 even received a grant from the Moscow "Cultural Initiative" Foundation, established by George Soros. The Ministry of Education of the Russian Federation approved the textbook. After that, Semennikova's concept was picked up and reproduced in dozens of similar textbooks issued by various universities, both in the federal center and in the provincial cities.

In brief, her concept was as follows. In her view, three typcs of relatively isolated civilizations or cultural-historical entities coexisted on earth. One of them was the Western, or progressive civilization ("civilizations of continuous development"); another was the Oriental ("cyclical civilizations"); and the third was ahistorical ("non-progressive civilizations"). The Western type was highly dynamic and demonstrated an unlimited capacity for technical advances. The Oriental type (China and India were taken as examples) was more conservative; despite making sporadic technical progress, these civilizations were unable to dispense with Oriental despotism. Finally, ahistorical civilizations (like those of the Australian Aboriginals, the Native Americans, or the Bushmen of Southern Africa) were resistant to any evolution, and they were doomed to live in poverty and backwardness. Thus, Semennikova's schema, while imposing restrictions upon evolutionary perspectives on certain distinct civilizations, provided them with inborn, everlasting attributes that people were unable to overcome. Contacts between civilizations could not help much, as they brought about only destruction of the unique civilizations. Thus, the cultural differences of local civilizations are innate, and for that reason, distinct civilizations resemble biological organisms. Needless to say, this concept provides those possessing racist attitudes with pseudo-academic arguments.

It is interesting how Russia into fits this schema. Surprisingly, although its importance to any Russian author is obvious, this issue was hardly discussed by Semennikova. She treated Russia as a distinct space situated between West and East, but avoided elaboration on its specific characteristics. As a result, readers were still unaware of what the distinct features of the Russian civilization were, beyond its intermediate geographical position, which made Russia a region where achievements of different civilizations mixed and blended. Semennikova failed to discuss Russia's multiethnic composition; the country is by no means populated by ethnic Russians alone. Yet some ethnic minorities (northern, numerically small peoples) are typologically similar to people belonging to "ahistorical civilizations," and others, for example Turkic-speaking and Mongol-speaking peoples, are similar to those who inhabit "Oriental civilizations." It is unclear how they fit into "Russian civilization" if, according to their allegedly "inborn" traits, they constitute integral parts of other civilizations. Otherwise, if they were to develop progressively together with other peoples of Russia, this would undermine Semennikova's belief in insurmountable cultural boundaries between civilizations.[6]

Lev Gumilev's ethno-genetic theory

The civilizational approach is obviously rooted in Eurasianism, brought back into Russian scholarship by the marginal Soviet historian Lev N. Gumilev; it is no accident that certain post-Soviet school textbooks refer to his name.[7] Therefore, we need to discuss his concept, if only in brief.[8] Gumilev based his beliefs on the Eurasian ideas developed by Russian émigré scholars in the 1920s and 1930s. At these ideas' core is a belief in the uniqueness and closeness of well-bounded distinct ethno-cultural entities based on their religious-psychological characteristics. Gumilev argued that the more different local cultures were, the more harmful and disastrous were the results of their mutual contacts. To put it another way, a merger of subethnic groups gave birth to viable communities; interethnic contacts were more difficult; and relationships between groups belonging to different super-ethnoi invariably had fatal results. Gumilev called communities formed at the junction of two super-ethnoi "chimeras," and viewed them as not only fragile but highly "harmful" in their effect.[9] For this reason he opposed mixed marriages, although he rejected any accusations of racism. At the same time, with respect to the issue of an ethnos's origin he demonstrated a biological rather than a cultural bias. In his view, a crucial catalyst of ethnic formation was "passionarity," or the human ability for creative activity, which he treated as an inherited biological trait.[10] He believed that "ethnic groups emerged as natural phenomena as a result of passionary mutations."[11]

Although Gumilev at one time developed Eurasian ideas, he failed to appreciate the warnings of Eurasian scholars against the danger of biological interpretations of the Eurasian theory of culture. He believed that psychological traits might be inherited and did not fail to refer to the anti-Semitic arguments of some European authors of the late nineteenth and early twentieth centuries. In particular, following the influential German economist Werner Sombart, he sought to explain the origin of capitalism, which he disliked very much, with reference to racial mixing.[12] This demonstrates a highly reductionist approach based on biological determinism.

Gumilev viewed a civilization as a period of a decline of an ethnic system accompanied by destructive processes, in particular a degradation of the environment. He associated civilizations' failures with "unnatural migrations" and an emergence of artificial landscapes, such as cities, arguing that unskilled, heterogeneous, urbanized newcomers devastated the natural environment.[13] The idea that immigrants play an indiscriminately harmful role, first put forward by the same

Werner Sombart, makes up the core of all the concepts of contemporary "New Racism." For us, the particular case that Gumilev has chosen to prove his idea of the devastating role played by immigrants is telling. He aimed his arguments at the Jews, who, he said, "lacked a homeland at all."[14]

Gumilev developed his concept in the following way. Super-ethnoi were closely bound to the local natural environment, and ethnic and subethnic groups developed within their own ecological niches. Thus, they did not compete with each other in a struggle for survival and were inclined to cooperate rather than to fight. By contrast, a recently arrived alien ethnic group would be unable to find an appropriate natural niche and would choose to exploit local residents instead. It is this group that Gumilev called a "chimera" and identified with a parasite or a cancerous tumor living at the expense of a biological organism.[15] In Gumilev's view, the Jews, urbanized merchants who developed a highly profitable trade along the caravan routes between Europe and China, played this role in the early-medieval Khazaria. Gumilev did not fail to emphasize that the Jews were aliens there and could not bring about anything but harm. All this reasoning perfectly fitted contemporary "cultural racism."

The civilizational approach of the Russian nationalists, and a school education

Gumilev advocated the integrity of the Russian state and dreamed of cleansing it of unwelcome, non-Russian mixtures ("chimerae"). This idea was highly appreciated and developed further by some contemporary Russian nationalist ideologists, advocates of the "Russian civilization" project.[16] The Association for the Interdisciplinary Study of the Russian Nation (AISRN), founded by the philosopher Yevgeni S. Troitsky in 1988, had been developing and advocating this project for twenty years. Troitsky encouraged various Russian nationalists to collaborate with him, including the Russian Orthodox mathematician and nationalist Igor Shafarevich, the late neo-Eurasian writer Dmitri Balashov, and such proponents of racist ideas as the neo-pagans Pavel V. Tulaev and Vladimir B. Avdeev.

In the 1990s the AISRN was provided space in the Duma of the Russian Federation and closely collaborated with the Department of the Russian People (e.g. ethnic Russians) at the Ministry of Nationalities and Federal Relations of the Russian Federation. In the late 1990s this department was developing a state program of a revival and maintenance of the ethnic Russian people. This project constituted the basis for a draft of the federal law "On the Russian People," which was discussed in the Duma in May 2001. Like other documents, this draft treated all of Russia as a "historical homeland" of the ethnic Russians.[17] Thus, it makes sense to assume that at least some high-level bureaucrats in Russia share the AISRN's ideology. This is not to say that it serves as an official state ideology, but it is evident that high-level bureaucrats cannot but consider it in their political activity. The parliamentary sections of the Communist Party of the Russian Federation (CPRF) and the Liberal Democratic Party of Russia (LDPR) (and Rodina, until recently), which play an active role in the Duma, share similar ideas.

What is this ideology about? In one of his major articles, Troitsky calls on the Russian state to develop its policy with respect to the interests of the mainly "Russian people" and "the Russian nation." He treats the Russian people (nation) in ethnic terms and links it to Russian Orthodox Christianity: "Russian Orthodox Christianity is the main spiritual interest of the nation."[18] He calls for the establishment of a Russian Administrative (state) Council to "supervise the maintenance of the legitimate interests of the Russian people." He was fascinated by a statement of the former State Duma Committee for Geopolitics titled "On the [ethnic] Russian people's right to self-government, sovereignty over all the territory of Russia and their unification within one and the same state" made on 5 December 1996.[19] The Russian people alone is not sufficient for him, and he writes of the "Russian (Orthodox Christian Slavic) civilization," which has to embrace all the Orthodox Christian Slavic peoples.[20] This rhetoric is obviously inconsistent with statements like "a multinational Russia is our mutual legacy." He calls on all the other ethnic groups to defend the interests of Russia, but if one figures out whose interests these are, one realizes that they are only those of ethnic Russians.[21] Troitsky demonstrates his admiration of the civilizational approach, but in fact his "Russian civilization" is simply an ethnic Russian entity.[22]

In the 1990s some other radical Russian nationalists, who demanded the abolition of all ethno-national republics, advocated a similar ideology.[23] The most radical concepts were based on the racial approach; they constructed some imagined "Russian race" and sought to rescue it from the non-Russians.[24] This ideology refers to a "historical" precedent. To achieve their goal, its advocates forge and disseminate a myth of the glorious Russian ancestors, the Slavic Aryans, as though the latter already owned the Eurasian steppe belt in prehistory. This idea legitimates and promotes the idea of a Russian Empire run by ethnic Russians alone or, at the very least, by a Slavic–Turkic combination. Contemporary Russian nationalists, including neo-Eurasians, neo-pagans, and occultists, extensively disseminate this myth.[25]

Thus, in fact, the civilizational approach in question engenders new Russian chauvinism. Yet this does not embarrass the authors of the history textbooks. Despite all the obvious contradictions and reductionism of Semennikova's schema, and its poverty and racial flavor, it was enthusiastically picked up and disseminated throughout Russia in school textbooks. By 2000 the civilizational approach was seized on by many educationalists from the Ministry of Education and included in a draft of the official state concept of historical education.[26] It was also supported by the participants of a discussion arranged by the Moscow Association of the History Teachers in March 2000.[27] In the early 2000s the civilizational approach became fashionable and has been integrated into the national standard for historical education adopted in 2004.[28] Even before the Ministry of Education approved the civilizational approach, the latter began to carve its way to the Russian school system as a result of its introduction into new history textbooks. It was introduced into universities and educational institutes, as well as high schools, in the late 1990s. By the end of the decade it had become popular in Moscow and St. Petersburg and began to make its way to the Russian provinces. In Moscow it was inserted into the instructions intended for teachers of history.[29]

What made the civilizational approach so attractive to the textbook authors? Unlike the Marxist approach, which downplayed the role of national or ethnic factors in history, the civilizational approach emphasized the authenticity and value of any local civilization. Therefore, it seemed to perfectly fit patriotic ideas and to contribute to the shaping of national or ethnic identity. In this way it helped to erase an earlier antagonism embedded into an opposition of "culture" and "civilization,"[30] and turned a civilization into an incarnation of a distinct culture. Hence, this image of a civilization has a nativist and populist flavor. Under an identity crisis and the growth of an anti-Western attitude in Russia, the civilizational approach was perceived by certain textbook authors as a useful tool to combat Eurocentrism.[31]

Meanwhile, in practical terms most of the textbook authors merely reproduce Semennikova's schema. In fact, the civilizational approach, which is advertised by its partisans as a humanitarian one placing great value on individuals,[32] proves to be a new attempt to legitimate ethnic nationalism with scholarly arguments. Indeed, in the textbooks in question a civilization is defined as "a human entity sharing the basic spiritual values, persistency of sociopolitical organization, culture, economy as well as a psychological feeling of belonging"; and a civilization type is identified with "a type of a development of distinct peoples, ethnoi."[33] This definition is very close to that of "ethnos," popular among Soviet ethnographers, which was rooted ultimately in Stalin's definition of nation. This point makes clear why the admirers of the civilizational approach so strongly emphasize a national (ethnic) identity as a "defensive factor aimed at ethnic survival."[34] Some authors argue that national (ethnic) identity – that is, a "realization of a unity of people who belong to the given people, nation" – is a distinct characteristic of Russia as a civilization.[35] Presented in these terms, the civilizational approach provides any people (ethnic group) with an opportunity to identify themselves with a distinct civilization, and sows the seeds for intense, albeit fruitless, debates on who is suitable for civilization status and who is not.[36]

Civilizational approach and racism

The advocates of the civilizational approach treat Russia (with or without reservations) as an authentic, distinct civilization situated between those of the Western and Eastern types. Yet they associate Russian history mainly with a history of the Slavic Russian people, although they do recognize a merging of the Slavs with other ethnic groups.[37] Sometimes Russia is represented as a special type of civilization "closely linked with a distinct ethnic group and its state";[38] or students learn that "our direct ancestors were the Eastern Slavs."[39] Other independent states – the Kazan Khanate, Georgia, the Bukhara Emirate, and the like – that developed side by side with Russia and were integrated into the Russian Empire or the USSR only much later are neglected for nationalist reasons. The non-Russian ethnic groups are ignored or downplayed as well.

Certain authors have already noted that an emphasis on a sharp contrast between West and East, and the "Orientalization" of the latter, serves to justify colonialism, to legitimate neo-colonialism, and to stir up racist attitudes.[40] Anthropologists of immigrants' origins emphasize that a concept of a unified and well-bounded culture or civilization is able to erect an insurmountable boundary between West and East, which is similar to that of race. According to Edward Said, the East is often viewed in the West as something uniform and unchangeable, and the media cultivate this ahistorical image.[41] The same metaphysical, even mythical, image is sometimes attached to Western civilization as well.[42]

Unfortunately, there are attitudes in Europe today, sometimes articulated by major politicians, that represent it as a distinct, uniform civilization and attempt to isolate it from the "barbaric world." The late American political scientist Samuel Huntington, who also predicted a "clash of civilizations" in the near future, has advanced the civilizational approach.[43] Some American politicians and journalists greatly appreciated this idea after the disastrous attacks of 11 September 2001 on the World Trade Center in New York and the Pentagon building in Washington, DC. Muslim fundamentalists in Afghanistan and other countries of the Middle East have adopted the same approach.

It is evident that an image of the world divided into radically different separate civilizations, to the extent that they are unable to understand each other, provides a substantial basis for racial attitudes. These attitudes encourage suspicion and hostility toward newcomers from those regions considered "alien." In particular, this ideology makes up the basis for the "International Islamic Front for Jihad against Jews and Crusaders," founded by Osama bin Laden in 1998, which American journalists have referred to as the "terrorism international."[44] In bin Laden's view the human world consists of separate, local civilizations. He believes that Israel constitutes a part of Palestine, and that the latter is a part of the Arabian peninsula, which should belong to Muslims alone, as it is where their sacred sites are located.[45] His organization al Qaeda issued a manifesto on 23 February 1998 accusing the United States of illegal occupation of the Arabian peninsula. This manifesto called on all Muslims to kill any American or ally of the Americans. "The ruling to kill the Americans and their allies – civilians and military – is an individual duty for every Muslim who can do it in any country in which it is possible to."[46]

In fact, this "clash of civilizations" is an artificial outcome of crude, less sophisticated politics and propaganda accompanying processes of globalization. In particular, an indiscriminate identification of all Muslims with terrorists, suspicions toward Muslims, and persecutions of all those who wear the hijab in the street or at school stir up anger among Muslims against the West. At the same time, the anti-Arab attitudes manifested in the United States immediately after the tragic events of 11 September led not only to the growth of suspicions but also to attacks on Americans of Arabic origin.[47]

In response, the Japanese newspaper *The Japan Times* wrote: "How much harder it is, but also how much inflammatory, to eschew this kind of broad-brush approach and zero in on the responsible groups, and those who aid and abet them, without implicating entire religions, cultures, peoples or 'civilizations.'"[48] Indeed, it goes without saying that not all Arabs are terrorists and not all Muslims are fundamentalists. Moreover, even many radical Muslim organizations refrain from building up global networks and instead aim at targets in their own countries.[49] Therefore, politicians must avoid careless rhetoric that might stir up unwelcome feelings. For example, President Bush made this mistake in a speech on 16 September 2001 when he called for a "crusade" against terrorism. In Muslim countries these words recalled the medieval crusades against Islam and were perceived as a challenge,[50] and Bush had to clarify his stance to Arab-Americans.[51] Thus, at critical times when people are highly emotional and nervous, careless words are able to mobilize people along a "civilizational" line and to cause an effect that might be very similar to racial strife. This irrational "civilizational" view of a situation is provoked by an essentialist organic treatment of culture as a well-bounded ahistorical formation.[52] The approach in question is by no mean an intellectual one only; nowadays it usually articulates a political project aimed at the establishment of some "pure" ethnic state where the idea of "cultural belonging" has to replace a former "racial purity."[53] Specialists view this development as a manifestation of the "New Racism."[54] Needless to say, it is this very message that is carried by the civilizational approach.

The "Russian issue" today

The discussion so far fits perfectly with the warnings of contemporary scholars that "within contemporary societies there is a strong trend towards the creation of new essentialisms on the basis of religion, ethnicity or race."[55] Yet a fascination with racism and anti-Semitism in post-Soviet Russia has a non-trivial explanation. In Western countries such attitudes have resulted in part from a weakening and decline of the working class in post-industrial societies. By contrast, in contemporary Russia one is dealing with a less developed social class structure, which almost disappeared in communist times and began to form anew as a result of liberalization and the shift to a market economy. In addition, the Russian nation has never been fully formed. Making up the dominant majority, the Russians have never felt themselves to be a highly integrated ethnic group, and their ethnic identity was less developed.[56] Hence, there are efforts by radical politicians to direct public anger against ethnic "others" in order to consolidate ethnic Russians as a nation. Indeed, it is well proven by history that "racist thinkers sought to use ideas about race and nation to make sense of the changes and uncertainties brought about by socioeconomic change, and to provide a basis for political mobilization and action."[57] An image of an enemy proves very effective in helping achieve these ends.

It is in this environment that the civilizational approach essentializes Russia as a uniform and highly persistent, if not eternal, cultural region that is naturally fated to serve as the foundation for an integrated political body. To be sure, this project recognizes a variety of cultures that constitute the basis of Eurasia. Yet by contrast to the original Eurasianism, it fails to discuss cultural pluralism in contemporary Russia, let alone its future. The only lesson one can learn from the textbooks I have mentioned is that the Russian future is associated with a uniform Eurasian culture based on ethnic Russian values. Nothing is said of any coexistence or mutually beneficial contacts between ethnic cultures. The issues of multiculturalism and of cultural hybridity are not discussed. What is of concern to the majority of the textbook authors is the authenticity of "Russian civilization" and its deserved place in the system of world civilizations. All their efforts are devoted to solving a twofold problem. On the one hand, they are seeking to prove the superiority of the Russian civilization over those in Asia (in this way the European roots of Eurasia suppress its Asian aspect), but on the other hand they would like to isolate it from the Euro-American world in order to avoid dissolution and to retain Eurasian cultural authenticity (it is at this point that they emphasize its Asian aspect). It is evident that the civilizational approach inherited much from the geopolitical doctrine of the nineteenth and early twentieth centuries. Hence, there is a tireless aspiration to demonstrate a cultural superiority over Third World countries. At the same time the civilizational approach might be related to the project of the "European fortress" popular today.

To understand "the Russian issue" one has to consider that in their own minds the Russians were and still are an imperial people. This means that they were numerically dominant in a large multicultural empire and since the time of the Mongol yoke have never experienced any foreign rule. True, they have experienced heavy social and economic oppression, but were less sensitive toward ethnic oppression and could hardly understand the special cultural demands of non-Russian peoples. They learned to be "the elder brother" and at the same time to serve the state and to obey the strong ruler. At the same time, being oppressed by the state, they were dreaming of unrestricted freedom ("*volia*"). As a dominant majority they demonstrated an inclusive identity and welcomed those who wanted to assimilate into their entity.

Therefore, by the time of *perestroika*, many of them were advocates of so-called pan-human democratic values without properly understanding their true nature. Yet they supported the republican movements for sovereignty on these grounds. Thus, the anti-communist movements of the late 1980s, like the anti-monarchical movements of 1917, were directed against the highly centralized power, which profited from internal colonialism and appropriation of valuable resources from the periphery. In this respect, all these movements were similar to contemporary regionalism in certain Western countries. Yet the leaders of the nationalist movements in the non-Russian republics had their own views on development. Their main goal was the achievement of ethnic liberation rather than a democracy per se. It is here that their interests differed drastically from those of ethnic Russians. Thus, ethno-national values and goals proved to be more sensitive and more reasonable for the great bulk of people than more abstract, general democratic ideas.

After the disintegration of the Soviet Union in late 1991, ethno-nationalist values gained a victory. They celebrated their triumph not only in the newly established states but to a certain extent within the Russian Federation as well. As a result, more than 17 percent of ethnic Russians, 25.3 million out of 145.2 million, unexpectedly found themselves outside the Russian Federation and had to adapt themselves to a new social and national environment. They were affected by an identity crisis as well, because a great many of them had been loyal mainly to the USSR rather than to the Russian Federation, let alone non-Russian republics. In general they faced several new crucial problems that put them in a difficult situation.

First, until recently ethnic Russians were the only ones who felt themselves comfortable in any part of the former USSR, not least because of the Russian language, which served as a lingua franca throughout the country, and also because they were protected by the Soviet state. Under these conditions it is no accident that the Russians of the "near abroad" were not able to relate themselves to any specific area and considered the whole of Eurasia as a natural homeland.[58] However, after 1989 the titular languages were declared the official national ones in all the non-Russian republics. Thus, the position of a great many Russians there became less safe since they were not competent speakers of any language other than Russian. Hence, they felt a restriction of mobility, and linguistic insecurity.

Second, Russians began to lose political power in the republics where the ethnic composition of the bureaucracy changed rapidly, and all the main positions were taken by the local, non-Russian elites. Although Russians still dominated in the industrial sectors of some southern republics, they had already been eliminated from the management domain in the Baltic region in the 1980s. Thus, in some regions Russians have lost any access to power at all. In others a non-balance of power has emerged, with the indigenous elites running the political domain and Russians the economic one. Political discrimination against Russians became a hot issue, especially in the Baltic States of Estonia and Latvia, where most Russians were excluded from any sort of voting and denied local citizenship.[59] Hence, they felt targeted and politically insecure.

Third, originally many Russians moved to the non-Russian republics for better jobs, better living conditions, and prestigious positions. Many of them enjoyed privileges, as they were much better trained than the local inhabitants. More often than not, the Russians were employed by the large, all-Soviet industrial enterprises, especially the military-industrial complex, where they enjoyed high wages. However, most enterprises of this sort collapsed in the 1990s for economic and political reasons, and many Russians were threatened with or suffered from unemployment. Sophisticated welfare systems were non-existent in the post-Soviet world. Hence, there was economic insecurity.

Fourth, in contrast to local inhabitants who also suffered economic losses, the Russians were mostly urbanized people. They could not expect any help from the countryside, where, in contrast to the natives, they had no relatives. Also, their lack of competence in the local languages and a hostile environment in general made it difficult for them to find new jobs. Hence, they suffered restricted access to vital resources and a sharp decline in their standard of living, which caused social insecurity.

Fifth, the Russians faced serious cultural problems after the republican language laws were issued in 1989. These statutes provided titular languages with official status, for example giving them a dominant position in the administration, education, and mass media of the republics.[60] Actually, the problem is more complicated and is not restricted to the linguistic issue. For instance, in terms of social structure Russians are highly atomized in comparison to natives in many Muslim republics, who maintain their clan or local community organizations, helping them to withstand hardship and effectively protecting them from criminals. Indeed, in the former USSR Russians were not well integrated into local societies, especially in Central Asia and Georgia, and many of them were willing to leave for the Russian Federation.[61] Hence, there was a problem of alienation and cultural insecurity.

Sixth, the Russians were threatened with local interethnic clashes and civil wars, especially in some of the southern republics: Tajikistan, Azerbaijan, Georgia, and, later on, in Chechnya. This made their life highly unsafe.[62] Hence, there was a feeling of physical insecurity.

Finally, one has to acknowledge an additional psychological factor in that an important part of the Russian myth was the notion of their "elder brother" position. Accordingly, the Russians were considered the civilizers, the bearers of a higher culture who were obliged to share their material and intellectual resources generously with all the non-Russians, who were treated as relatively backward. The Soviet authorities consciously and intensively perpetuated this myth, especially after the 1940s. Moreover, Russians were treated as a messianic people who had to lead all of humanity to a new, just civilization. The idea had political implications in addition to intellectual ones because a faction within the Soviet authorities dreamed of territorial expansion.[63]

It is worth noting that a struggle for unification of the so-called divided peoples, such as the Ukrainians and Belorussians, under the Soviet umbrella was continuously stressed in Soviet rhetoric as an excuse for expansionism. The Russians grew up with this idea, which they perceived as unequivocal justice. What happened in fall 1991 was that the other peoples, who had been unified with Russian help earlier, established their own independent states. In contrast, the Russians suffered heavy losses, in that new national borders divided them. Needless to say, Russians in "the nearest abroad" took their new position as an abominable injustice, and accused the Russian Federation's authorities of treason. What also came as a shock, even an insult, to the Russians is that their image in the newly established states changed drastically from that of "elder brother" to that of "ethnic minority," or even "non-welcome occupants." Hence, an identity crisis broke out among Russians in the post-Soviet environment.

Why do contemporary hardship and turmoil feed ethno-nationalist and racist attitudes? As British scholars teach us, "race and ethnicity are best conceived as political resources that are used by both dominant and subordinate groups for the purposes of legitimizing and furthering their own social identities and social interests."[64] While discussing contemporary regionalism, Lothar Baier describes the logic of its advocates in the following terms. They want to prove that

> the fact that one region produces more and is more developed than another is not the result of certain investment decisions or matters having to do with the infrastructure or education, but [is] attributed to unchangeable historical and cultural characteristics. The inhabitants are entitled to their wealth because their ancestors in some distant past acquired cultural or religious merit whereby they produced architects, popes and feudal lords.[65]

Therefore, culture and early history, which legitimate contemporary political projects, are intensively referred to by the leaders and ideologists of radical ethnopolitical and regionalist movements.[66] Russia is by no means unique in that respect.

Racism and state policy

It is worth noting that by distinguishing its citizens or all the residents of the country in general according to race or ethnicity and by granting them different rights or privileges, a state itself sows the seeds of ethnic or racial tensions and conflicts. In the United States, race has long been recorded on birth certificates, and for a few decades race was recorded in all official documents, based on the so-called differentiation of all American citizens into five pseudo-racial categories.[67] This was introduced for a good end: to implement affirmative action policies.[68] Yet in the late 1990s American anthropologists were alarmed that this classification encouraged a racial approach to social reality and cultivated prejudices toward both mixed marriages and children from such families.[69]

The Soviet passport system, which recorded ethnicity in its fifth line and made it unchangeable, used to freeze ethnic identity to the extent that, contrary to its dynamic nature, ethnicity was viewed an eternal category. This was encouraged institutionally because ethnicity made up the basis of a political establishment in the Soviet Union, for example the ethnically based republics. The Soviet theory of ethnos served to confirm this policy by academic means. While emphasizing a role for endogamy in ethnic stabilization, this theory contained an implicit notion of ethnos as a biological organism. True as it was, official Soviet ethnography refused to recognize this fact because, as a thoughtful critic noted, "racialism and ahistoricity were consistently rejected in Soviet views."[70] Yet it is worth recalling that one of the important sources for the theory in question was an earlier concept developed by Sergei M. Shirokogorov in the 1920s. Shirokogorov identified ethnos as a "biological category" and emphasized the role of endogamy.[71] Gumilev, who was marginal in the Soviet academic establishment but became highly popular in the post-Soviet era, picked up this racial concept. Although the official Soviet theory of ethnos made all possible efforts to distance itself from Gumilev's approach, it evidently suffered from primordialism, and primordialism inevitably leads to a biologization of ethnicity.[72] Some specialists have good reason to remark that "Soviet ethnos theory was shaped by, and has contributed towards ethnonationalist ideologies."[73]

Thus, the Soviet discourse of nation and ethnos makes it clear how the Soviet people were indoctrinated with essentialist views of a highly integrated "culture" which automatically excluded those who did not fit in ("cosmopolitans," "bourgeois nationalists," "fops," bearers of "reactionary" traditions, "foreigners," and the like). In this context it was not difficult to extend the idea of evil to the bearers of other cultures and the holders of other ethnic identities. At the same time, whereas the Soviet theory of ethnos was discussed only within rather narrow circles of professionals in the Soviet period, it was appreciated by many politicians, officials, educationalists, and journalists in post-Soviet Russia. Many of them believed, following Gumilev, that ethnicity was the major driving factor of human evolution, and in search of arguments referred to ethnological knowledge picked up from Soviet scholarship.

A favorable environment for the arrival of racism emerged in post-Soviet Russia as a result of two important events: first, the collapse of the Soviet Union; and second, mass migrations, which affected the development of virtually all the regions. Some of the regions were losing population, but others had to host many unexpected newcomers. A fall in the Russian population was publicly discussed and emphasized by many politicians and journalists. As a result, migrant-phobia began to infect Russia in the 1990s. It reached its climax in the early 2000s, when both internal migrants and immigrants were treated as mostly negative agents violating the established order and threatening the native way of life. They were consistently accused of flooding the labor market and being responsible for the growth of unemployment among ethnic Russians, the artificial lowering of wages, tax avoidance and violation of tax rules in general, the appropriation of desirable apartments and the intention of establishing "ethnic residential quarters," illegal claims for welfare and pensions, as well as criminal behavior (fraud, drug dealing, robbery, murder, and terrorism). There were also rumors of exotic diseases being brought by migrants. Certain politicians and journalists argued that immigrants extracted huge amounts of money from Russia. Some of them went so far as to claim that immigrants had "stolen" billions of dollars from the country. One of the most common accusations was that the newcomers were unwilling to integrate and instead wanted to impose their own culture upon the natives. Nowadays, all those accusations are very characteristic in Europe as well and make up the basis for cultural racism.[74]

The early 2000s were marked by quite ambivalent tendencies. On the one hand, after the hardship of the 1990s living standards were improving, and people's views of the future became more positive. On the other hand, new challenges came onto the scene: with the consolidation of state power, democracy was shrinking; people were frightened by criminality and terrorism; and they were also alarmed at the negative demographic trend, which was simply taken as a "degradation of the Russian nation." Simultaneously, the structure of migration changed drastically: the flow of repatriates relaxed, and instead the number of labor migrants was growing rapidly. People were informed of these trends by the national media, whose reports were colored by both sensationalism and catastrophism. Public opinion responded with increased migrant-phobia.

Since then, some Russian intellectuals, including certain sociologists, have been telling the general public of the "southern peoples' demographic expansion" and a "violation of the ethnic balance," as though mass migration threatens to spoil "our ethno-demographic portrait." They also scare their audience with talk of some "critical threshold," as though its violation would inevitably cause ethnic strife. They argue that the newcomers' way of life is inconsistent with that of the Russian people. And in this respect they talk of "cultural incompatibility." This discourse exploits such expressions as "migration flood," "army of barbarians," "closed bands," "aggressive potential," "aggression from the alien South," and sometimes even "aggression against the white man." It is from those "conquerors" that the "native people" need rescuing.

This rhetoric has proved very popular and is used effectively by high officials and well-known politicians, journalists, and ordinary people. The officials threaten the general public with a large number of illegal immigrants in the country. Therefore, many politicians and intellectuals demand that strict control over migration should be implemented to prevent Moscow from becoming a "city of ethnic residential quarters." Certain nationalists argue that some ethnic and confessional groups constitute a social danger. As a result, they suggest that the principle of "the collective responsibility of ethnic communities" should be introduced into the Russian legislation.

While evaluating all those calls and reasoning, one has to consider that migration policy in Russia until very recently was based mainly on various prohibitions and did not imply any positive activity aimed at effective integration of the newcomers. This policy is fed by xenophobic myths concerning the criminality and evil of migrants in general. At the same time it is discrimination practiced by both officials and the police that usually forces migrants to break the law.[75]

In this environment the central ideas of the racist discourse are, first, the opposition "indigenous/non-indigenous" or "native/non-native," and second, "cultural incompatibility." All these arguments evidently contradict any notions of civil rights and a civic nation. Instead, a social hierarchy is being re-established which is based on people's links with a highly essentialized "ethnic culture." By this logic it is inclusion into a "cultural matrix" rather than just citizenship that provides one with full membership of society. Those unfit should be excluded. They are fated to be "second-class people" and, accordingly, their civil rights ought to be restricted. A dynamic of xenophobia in Russia demonstrates that at the turn of the 2000s an argument about "poor living standards" was losing its potency and instead a tendency to blame migrants or ethnic minorities was growing. Indeed, "living standards" have improved over the past few years. More sensitive is competition on the part of "aliens."

It is my view that there are two major reasons for contemporary racism in Russia – one economic and the other political. The economic factor concerns the highly deformed economic structure, which is based mainly on oil and gas extraction rather than material production. In this environment, people view natural resources as their "national property," the very basis of their well-being, and do not want to share it with any "aliens."[76] The political factor is a by-product of the restricted democracy. As people are unable to address directly the authorities who are responsible for their grievances, they redirect their anger against "aliens" as though the latter are depriving them of political and cultural resources. Those attitudes seek justification in the biologization of ethnicity, which forms a bridge between, on the one hand, the Soviet theory of ethnos and Gumilev's theory of ethnogenesis, and, on the other hand, ethnocentric versions of culture studies that are fashionable in Russia nowadays.

Thus, cultural racialism in Russia is by no means an entirely new phenomenon. It is based both on the previous Soviet policy of identity and on an anthropological theory developed by Soviet academics. It was also encouraged by a growing ethnocentrism that accompanied the dissolution of the Soviet Union. It is sad that primordialism still maintains its strong position in Russian scholarship. Nowadays it is manifested not only in the theory of ethnos but also in the civilizational approach, and is appreciated not only in academic circles but also in the classroom. Yet, as I have demonstrated, this is by no means only a Russian problem. Instead, it is a new challenge to all humanity.

Notes

1 Research for this article was supported in part by a grant from the Bureau of Educational and Cultural Affairs of the US Department of State administered by the Kennan Institute for Advanced Russian Studies of the Woodrow Wilson International Center for Scholars, with funds provided by the Bureau of Educational and Cultural Affairs of the US Department of State through the Galina Starovoitova Fellowship Program. None of these organizations is responsible for the views expressed.

2 P.-A. Taguieff, *Sur la Nouvelle droite. Jalons d'une analyse critique*, Paris: Descartes, 1994.

3 S. Body-Gendrot, "'Now You See, Now You Don't': Comments on Paul Gilroy's Article," *Ethnic and Racial Studies*, 21, 1998, 853.

4 A. de Benoist and Ch. Champetier, "The French New Right in the Year of 2000," *Telos*, 115, spring 1999, 135.

5 I. Semennikova, *Rossiia v mirovom soobschchestve tsivilizatsii*, Moscow: Interprax, 1994.

6 For a critical analysis of the civilizational approach, see V. A. Shnirelman, *The Myth of the Khazars and Intellectual Antisemitism in Russia, 1970s–1990s*, Jerusalem: Vidal Sassoon International Center for the Study of Antisemitism, Hebrew University, 2002; same author, "O novom i starom rasizme v sovremennoi Rossii," *Vestnik Instituta Kennana v Rossii*, 1, 2002, 76–83; "Mezhdu evraziotsentrizmom i etnotsentrizmom: o novom istoricheskom obrazovanii v Rossii," *Vestnik Instituta Kennana v Rossii*, 4, 2003, 32–42; "'Stolknovenie tsivilizatsii' i preduprezhdenie konfliktov," *Vestnik Instituta Kennana v Rossii*, 7, 2005, 22–29.

7 B. V. Lichman (ed.), *Istoriia Rossii: vtoraia polovina XIX–XX vv. Kurs lektsii*, Ekaterinburg: Ural'skii gosudarstvennyi tekhnicheskii universitet, 1995, pp. 11–12; Yu. V. Tot *et al.*, *Istoriia Rossii IX–XX vekov. Posobie po otechestvennoi istorii dlia starsheklassnikov, abiturientov i studentov*, St. Petersburg: Neva, 1996, p. 38; A. T. Stepanishchev *et al.*, *Istoriia Rossii. Uchebnoe posobie dlia kursantov Voennogo Universiteta*, Moscow: Voennyi Universitet, 1997, p. 14; D. F. Aiatskov *et al.*, *Istoriia Rossii: problemy tsivilizatsionnogo razvitiia. Uchebnoe posobie*, Saratov: SGSEU, 1999, pp. 16–17.

8 For a discussion, see V. A. Shnirelman, "Evraziitsy i evrei," *Vestnik evreiskogo universiteta v Moskve*, 11, 1996, 4–45; same author, "Lev Gumilev: ot 'passionarnogo napriazheniia' do 'nesovmestimosti kul'tur,'" *Etnograficheskoe obozrenie*, 3,

2003, 8–21; with S. A. Panarin, "Lev Nikolaevich Gumilev: osnovatel' etnologii?" *Vestnik Evrazii*, 3, 2000, 5–37; same authors, "Lev Gumilev: His Pretensions as Founder of Ethnology and His Eurasian Theories," *Inner Asia*, 3, 2001, 1–18; M. Laruelle, "Lev Nikolaevic Gumilev (1912–1992). Biologisme et eurasisme dans la pensée russe," *Revue des Études Slaves*, 1–2, 2000, 163–189.

9 L. N. Gumilev, *Etnogenez i biosfera zemli*, Leningrad: Izdatel'stvo Leningradskogo Universiteta, 1989, p. 90 and pp. 133–135; same author, *Drevniia Rus i Velikaia Step'*, Moscow: Mysl, 1989, pp. 241, 254, 326.

10 Gumilev, *Etnogenez i biosfera zemli*, pp. 252–253, 272.

11 Gumilev, *Drevniia Rus i Velikaia Step'*, p. 455.

12 Gumilev, *Etnogenez i biosfera zemli*, pp. 406–409.

13 Ibid., p. 413.

14 Ibid., p. 409.

15 Ibid., pp. 302, 455; Gumilev, *Drevniia Rus i Velikaia Step'*, pp. 254–245. For a history of this evidently anti-Semitic rhetoric, see A. Bein, "'Der jüdische Parasit.' Bemerkungen zur Semantik der Judenfrage," *Vierteljahrshefte für Zeitgeschichte*, 13, 1965, 121–149.

16 O. Platonov, *Russkaia tsivilizatsiia*, Moscow: Kul'turno-proizvodstvennyi tsentr "Rus'," 1992; E. S. Troitsky (ed.), *Russkaia tsivilizatsiia i sobornost'*, Moscow: AKIRN, 1994; N. E. Troitskaia, *Russkaia tsivilizatsiia mezhdu Vostokom, Zapadom i Yugom*, Moscow: AKIRN, 1995. For a discussion of the "civilization project" in Russia, see V. A. Shnirelman, "SMI, 'etnicheskaia prestupnost' i migrantofobia," in A. Verkhovsky (ed.), *Iazyk vrazhdy protiv obshchestva*, Moskow: SOVA, 2007.

17 S. Zemlianoi, "Ne navredi. K diskussiiam o zakonoproektakh Gosudarstvennoi Dumy po 'russkomu voprosu,'" *Nezavisimaia gazeta*, 8 September 2001, 7.

18 E. S. Troitsky, "Natsional'nyi interes skvoz' prizmu istoriosofii," in E. S. Troitsky *et al.* (eds.), *Natsional'nye interesy russkogo naroda i demograficheskaia situatsiia v Rossii*, Moscow: Shtrikhkon, 1997, pp. 13–14, 84–86.

19 Ibid., pp. 40–42.

20 Ibid., pp. 81–82.

21 Ibid., p. 74.

22 Ibid., pp. 17, 75.

23 S. Fomin, "Byt' li sobstvennomu domu?" *Moskva*, 7–8, 1992, 98–106.

24 A. M. Sudavsky, "Russkie i russkaia rasa," *Russkaia mysl'*, 3, 12, 1993, 54–60; same author, *Rus' – narod, zemlia, derzhava*, Moscow: Obshchestvennaia pol'za, 1993, pp. 5–17; S. Fomin, "Russkii vopros i budushchee Rossii," *Moskva*, 6, 1996, 113–123; F. N. Razorenov, "Istoriko-psikhologicheskie, obshchinnye osnovy russkikh natsional'nykh interesov," in Ye. S. Troitsky *et al.* (eds.), *Natsional'nye interesy russkogo naroda i demograficheskaia situatsiia v Rossii*, Moscow: Strikhkon, 1997.

25 V. A. Shnirelman and G. A. Komarova, "Majority as a Minority: The Russian Ethnonationalism and Its Ideology in the 1970–1990s," in H.-R. Wicker (ed.), *Rethinking Nationalism and Ethnicity: The Struggle for Meaning and Order in Europe*, Oxford: Berg, 1997, pp. 211–224; V. A. Shnirelman, *Intellektual'nye labirinty. Ocherki ideologii v sovremennoi Rossii*, Moscow: Academia, 2004; same author, "Russian Response: Archaeology, Russian Nationalism and Arctic Homeland," in P. L. Kohl, M. Kozelsky, and N. Ben-Yahuda (eds.), *Selective Remembrance: Archaeology in the Construction, Commemoration, and Consecration of National Pasts*, Chicago: University of Chicago Press, 2007, pp. 31–70.

26 "Kontseptsiia istoricheskogo obrazovaniia v obshcheobrazovatel'nykh uchrezhdeniiakh Rossiiskoi Federatsii (proekt)," *Prepodavanie istorii v shkole*, 4, 2000, 2–8.

27 "Obsuzhdenie kontseptsii istoricheskogo obrazovaniia v obshcheobrazovatel'nykh uchrezhdeniiakh Rossiiskoi Federatsii," *Prepodavanie istorii v shkole*, 4, 2000, 41–43.

28 "Obrazovatel'nyi standart osnovnogo obshchego obrazovaniia po istorii," in *Federal'nyi komponent gosudarstvennogo standarta obshchego obrazovaniia*, Moscow: Ministerstvo

obrazovaniia Rossiiskoi Federatsii, 2004; V. A. Shnirelman, "Rossiiskaia shkola i natsional'naia ideia," *Neprikosnovennyi zapas*, 6, 2006, 238–246.

29 V. A. Shnirelman, "Tsivilizatsionnyi podkhod, uchebniki istorii i 'novyi rasizm,'" in V. Voronkov, O. Karpenko, and A. Osipov (eds.), *Rasizm v iazyke sotsial'nykh nauk*, St. Petersburg: Aleteia, 2002; same author, *Intellektual'nye labirinty*, pp. 324–333.

30 N. Elias, *The Civilizing Process*, vol. 1, *The History of Manners*, New York: Pantheon, 1982, pp. 1–34.

31 I. N. Ionov, *Rossiiskaia tsivilizatsiia IX – nachalo XX vv. Uchebnik po istorii dlia 10–11 klassov*, Moscow: Prosveshchenie, 1995, pp. 67ff., 84, 89; V. I. Bystrenko, *Istoriia Rossii X–XIX vv. Kurs lektsii*, Novosibirsk: NGAEiU, 1996; A. A. Radugin, *Istoriia Rossii (Rossiia v mirovoi tsivilizatsii). Uchebnoe posobie*, Moscow: Tsentr, 1997, pp. 19–20, 50–51; A. T. Stepanishchev *et al.*, *Istoriia Rossii*, 1997, p. 23; M. V. Ruban, *Istoriia Rossii i mirovye tsivilizatsii*, Moscow: Rossiiskoe pedagogicheskoe agentstvo, 1997; A. Yu. Polunov, "Istoriia Rossii: tsivilizatsionnyi podkhod," *Prepodavanie istorii v shkole*, 2, 1998, 40–49; Aiatskov *et al.*, *Istoriia Rossii*, p. 24.

32 Stepanishchev *et al.*, *Istoriia Rossii*, pp. 4ff.; Aiatskov *et al.*, *Istoriia Rossii*, p. 18.

33 Aiatskov *et al.*, *Istoriia Rossii*, p. 18. See also Tot *et al.*, *Istoriia Rossii IX–XX vekov*, p. 7.

34 Radugin, *Istoriia Rossii*, pp. 20, also see Ionov, *Rossiiskaia tsivilizatsiia*, p. 67ff.

35 Aiatskov *et al.*, *Istoriia Rossii*, p. 24.

36 This reminds us of the similar late-Soviet debates on the national status of various ethnic groups. See V. Tishkov, *Ethnicity, Nationalism and Conflict in and after the Soviet Union*, London: Sage, 1997, p. 230.

37 Radugin, *Istoriia Rossii*, pp. 50–52, 56–57, 73ff.; M. V. Ruban, *Istoriia Rossii i mirovye tsivilizatsii*, Moscow: Rossiiskoe pedagogicheskoe agentstvo, 1997, pp. 13, 15.

38 Ruban, *Istoriia Rossii i mirovye tsivilizatsii*, p. 6.

39 Bystrenko, *Istoriia Rossii X–XIX vv.*, p. 5; T. V. Chernikova, *Istoriia Rossii IX–XVI veka. 6oi klass. Uchebnik dlia obshcheobrazovatel'nykh uchebnykh zavedenii*, Moscow: Drofa, 2000, p. 5; A. V. Kamkin, *Istoki. Sem' chudes Rossii. Uchebnoe posobie dlia 5 klassa*, Moscow: Tekhnologicheskaia shkola biznesa, 2001, p. 113; V. S. Porokhnia (ed.), *Rossiia v mirovoi istorii*, Moscow: Logos, 2003, p. 28. To be sure, this reminds us of the famous phrase of the French colonial educationalists: "Our ancestors were the Gauls."

40 A. Phoenix, "Dealing with Difference: the Recursive and the New," *Ethnic and Racial Studies*, 21, 1998, 868–869.

41 E. W. Said, *Orientalism*, New York: Pantheon Books, 1978, p. 98. See also L. Abu-Lughod, "Writing Against Culture," in R. G. Fox (ed.), *Recapturing Anthropology: Working in the Present*, Santa Fe, NM: School of American Research Press, 1991, pp. 143–144; A. Appadurai, *Modernity at Large: Cultural Dimensions of Globalization*, Minneapolis: University of Minnesota Press, 1996, p. 12.

42 R. Ferguson, *Representing 'Race': Ideology, Identity and the Media*, London: Arnold, 1998, pp. 72–73.

43 S. P. Huntington, *The Clash of Civilizations and the Remaking of World Order*, New York: Simon & Schuster, 1996.

44 P. Watson, T. Marshall, and B. Drogin, "How Osama bin Laden Created the First 'Terrorism International,'" *The Japan Times*, 21 September 2001, 17.

45 Ibid.

46 Y. Suthichai, "Seminal 'Clash of Civilizations' Revisited," *Daily Yomiuri*, 21 September 2001, 9.

47 J. Sheler, "Of Faith, Fear, and Fanatics," *Daily Yomiuri*, 21 September 2001, 13(A).

48 *The Japan Times*, 20 September 2001, 6.

49 S. Sangwon, "Radical Muslims Not Necessarily a Fraternity," *The Japan Times*, 21 September 2001, 19.

50 For a verdict of the Afghan clerics, see "Extracts from Verdict by Afghan Clerics," *Daily Yomiuri*, 21 September 2001, 6.

51 "Code Name Found Offensive; Change Likely," *The Japan Times*, 22 September 2001, 7.
52 L. Abu-Lughod, "Writing Against Culture," p. 146.
53 S. Hall, "Culture, Community, Nation," *Cultural Studies*, 7, 1993, 356–357.
54 C. Shore, "Ethnicity, Xenophobia and the Boundaries of Europe," in T. Allen and J. Eade (eds.), *Divided Europeans: Understanding Ethnicities in Conflict*, The Hague: Kluwer Law International, 1999, pp. 45–49.
55 J. Solomos and L. Back, *Racism and Society*, London: Macmillan, 1996, p. 145.
56 E. A. Rees, "Stalin and Russian Nationalism," in G. Hosking and R. Service (eds.), *Russian Nationalism: Past and Present*, London: Macmillan, 1998.
57 Solomos and Back, *Racism and Society*, pp. 100, 210–211.
58 D. D. Laitin, *Identity in Formation: The Russian-Speaking Populations in the Near Abroad*, Ithaca, NY: Cornell University Press, 1998, pp. 69, 308.
59 Ibid., pp. 94–96.
60 Ibid., pp. 87–88.
61 D. S. Carlisle, "Uzbekistan and the Uzbeks," *Problems of Communism*, 40, 5, 1991, 38.
62 Laitin, *Identity in Formation*, p. 86.
63 F. Chuev, "Iz besed s Viacheslavom Molotovym," *Politika*, 7, 1991, 55–56.
64 Solomos and Back, *Racism and Society*, p. 207.
65 L. Baier, "Farwell to Regionalism," *Telos*, 90, winter 1991–1992, 82–88.
66 V. Shnirelman, *Who Gets the Past? Competition for Ancestors among Non-Russian Intellectuals in Russia*, Washington, DC: Woodrow Wilson Center Press/Johns Hopkins University Press, 1996; same author, *The Value of the Past: Myths, Identity and Politics in Transcaucasia*, Osaka: National Museum of Ethnology, 2001; "The Myths of Descent: The Views of the Remote Past, and School Textbooks in Contemporary Russia," *Public Archaeology*, 3, 2003, 33–51; *Byt' alanami. Intellektualy i politika na Severnom Kavkaze v 20-om veke*, Moscow: NLO, 2006.
67 For persistency of this rule, see M. Omi and H. Winant, *Racial Formation in the United States: From the 1960s to the 1990s*, New York: Routledge, 1994, pp. 53–54.
68 D. Hollinger, *Postethnic America: Beyond Multiculturalism*, New York: Basic Books, 1995, pp. 23–33.
69 C. C. Mukhopadhyay and Y. T. Moses, "Reestablishing 'Race' in Anthropological Discourse," *American Anthropologist*, 99, 1997, 527.
70 T. Shanin, "Ethnicity in the Soviet Union: Analytical Perception and Political Strategy," *Comparative Studies in Society and History*, 31, 1989, 412.
71 S. M. Shirokogoroff, "La théorie de l'ethnos et sa place dans le système des sciences anthropologiques," *L'Ethnographie*, 32, 1936, 86–90. True, Shirokogorov noted that an ethnos has never been entirely formed because of highly dynamic ethnic relationships and a continuing recombination of its components.
72 L. Greenfeld, "Soviet Sociology and Sociology in the Soviet Union," *Annual Review of Sociology*, 14, 1988, 119, n. 8; F. J. Gil-White, "How Thick Is Blood? The Plot Thickens …: If Ethnic Actors Are Primordialists, What Remains of the Circumstantialist/Primordialist Controversy?" *Ethnic and Racial Studies*, 22, 1999, 802.
73 T. Allen and J. Eade, "Understanding Ethnicity," in Allen and Eade (eds.), *Divided Europeans*, p. 19.
74 M. Barker, *The New Racism: Conservatives and the Ideology of the Tribe*, Frederick, MD: Aletheia Books, 1981; E. Balibar, "Es gibt keinen Staat in Europa: Racism and Politics in Europe Today," *New Left Review*, 186, 1991, 5–19.
75 V. A. Shnirelman, "Tsivilizatsionnyi podkhod kak natsional'naia ideia," in V. A. Tishkov and V. A. Shnirelman (eds.), *Natsionalizm v mirovoi istorii*, Moscow: Nauka, 2007, pp. 82–104.
76 The Austrian anthropologist Andre Gingrich calls this attitude "economic chauvinism" (A. Gingrich, "Nation, Status and Gender in Trouble? Exploring Some Contexts and Characteristics of Neo-nationalism in Western Europe," in A. Gingrich and M. Banks (eds.), *Neo-nationalism in Europe and Beyond*, New York: Berghahn Books, 2006, pp. 37, 44).

8 Electoral choice, cultural capital, and xenophobic attitudes in Russia, 1994–2006

Anastassia Leonova

The collapse of the Soviet Union set in motion a number of fundamental sociopolitical processes that not only resulted in massive redrawing of borders within the post-Soviet space, but also led to the development of new state and government institutions. More importantly, these changes went on in an environment that shaped society's evolving perceptions about itself, its structure, and its defining elements.

The economic reforms of the 1990s, which entailed the legally questionable redistribution of resources, failed to improve living standards for the majority of the population. Moreover, they marginalized a significant part of it. As a result of a perceived failure of the "first-wave" liberal reformers, the "democratic ideas" professed by the early 1990s (e.g. representation, civil society, justice for all) were not internalized by the masses and were consequently treated with skepticism, even rejected. Lack of modernity and civic grounds for solidarity resulted in a gradual movement toward more traditionalist and archaic policies. While older generations favored Soviet models of societal organization, young Russians could hardly relate to those same ideals, which put greater emphasis on other readily available symbols of social unity and differentiation. However, it was general disappointment with the very idea of social unity that controlled social patterns by the end of the 1990s. Along with reassessment of a need for the self-organization of society, longing for a strong state appeared to permeate all segments of the Russian population. This led to a steady revival of archaisms, evident in the increasing importance of ethnic and regional identity, growing opposition, and strong resistance to social and geographic mobility, resulting in the emergence of openly racist anti-immigrant attitudes and movements.

Time-series studies of public opinion show that Russian xenophobic attitudes in the early phase were clearly differentiated along major sociodemographic and political lines; however, they blurred over time. Indeed, ultra-nationalistic attitudes that were first prevalent within marginal groups with radical agendas gradually became mainstream, growing in popularity among intellectually advanced Russians. By the early 2000s a qualitative change in mass political discourse appeared when ethnic nationalism was legitimized in public politics and official speech. The democratic politicians of the 1990s were almost completely removed from the political scene, which was now dominated by *gosudarstvenniki* (statists) and national populists.

In order to better understand the social underpinnings of such a steady diffusion of nationalistic attitudes among different segments of the Russian population, as well as their persistence over years, we analyzed the effects of xenophobic ideas on different sociodemographic groups. We found that growing support for chauvinistic ideas was consistent across all groups, albeit to various degrees. For some time, political orientation has been a relatively clear predictor of tolerance within Russian society. For instance, in the early 1990s populist and xenophobic ideas were first publicly introduced in the course of the national election campaign of the Liberal Democratic Party of Russia (LDPR). This tactic allowed the party to secure the support of marginalized youngsters from the Russian provinces and thereby claim a somewhat astonishing success in the national parliamentary elections. The late 1990s, however, was already marked by a less visible differentiation between the major political parties and a significant decline in political competition. Under these circumstances the overall decline in social mobility in Russia has led to the spread and popularization of imperial and chauvinistic ideas in political discourse and the media. Further popularization and diffusion of nationalistic ideas was paralleled by the continuing degradation of social forces that encouraged tolerance and universalism.

This chapter was conceived as a revision of an earlier work published several years ago that had focused on the relationship between nationalistic attitudes and the political orientation of the Russian population.[1] My analysis of public opinion surveys conducted over a ten-year period[2] showed that when sociodemographic factors are controlled for, there is a steady increase of intolerance against other ethnicities across groups with different political orientations. Moreover, this pattern persists among highly educated Russians, which contradicts the assumption that educated citizens are less likely to be affected by mainstream fears and prejudices and instead are more likely to exhibit cultural pluralism and tolerance. Indeed, in the 1990s educated elites were still supportive of democratic forces that, despite their occasional disagreements (for example, Yabloko and the Union of the Right Forces disputed the role of the state in the economy), advocated a much-needed departure from a Soviet-style closed political economy in favor of a Western-inspired model of competitive political and economic development.

Not only were their sympathizers a minority faction among a growing number of nationalists, but the overall electoral support for a democratic course quickly dissipated as well. Although it is beyond the scope of this chapter to pinpoint the exact reasons for such a failure, I am inclined to believe that the decrystallization of social values among electoral groups that supported democratic reforms was one of the most influential factors.

In contemporary Russia, studying society's xenophobic attitudes on the basis of electoral choice is less promising, for the latter has shrunk significantly. Indeed, the country's current political landscape is far from pluralistic. This is not only a result of the fact that only two or three major parties are allowed to compete in national elections, while electoral support for their contenders is often at levels below statistical error.[3] The sudden weakening of democratic institutions, prompted by Putin's ascendancy to power, society's inability to affect the development of elected institutions, lack of transparency and fairness in the judicial process, rampant corruption, the curtailing of independent media, overemphasis of the terrorist threat, the militarization of mass consciousness, and the return to isolationism in foreign affairs all point to increasing uncertainty among the Russian population about their future, overall vulnerability in the face of an unarticulated threat, and a search for enemies, both internal and external. Xenophobic attitudes are thriving under these conditions. Despite the fact that most of them are routine and casual expressions, the radical nationalistic groups have also become increasingly assertive in recent years. Migrants from the former Soviet republics are often the first targets of such attitudes, whereby people from the Caucasus and Central Asia, as well as Russian citizens who are of distinct ethnicity, are victimized with a most disturbing frequency.

This chapter aims to examine the dynamics of xenophobic attitudes in post-Soviet Russia as well as their distribution across the main sociodemographic cohorts. I shall also attempt to explore the relationship between chauvinistic ideas, political orientation, and sociocultural characteristics of the respondents. In the second part of the chapter I shall test an alternative hypothesis on the determinants of xenophobic attitudes by tracing their distribution and dynamics across generational cohorts and groups with different amounts of cultural capital. Placing xenophobic attitudes in a wider context of beliefs and opinions of social development and desirable directions of country development, I shall speculate on the directions that the further dynamics of ethno-exclusive sentiments will take.

Sociodemographic determinants of xenophobia

To determine the level of xenophobia in Russia I have compiled a number of questions that map societal attitudes toward various ethnic groups. These questions have been asked repeatedly over the past twelve years. The most recent dataset, from November 2006, is shown in Table 8.1. The level of intolerance toward several ethnic groups, measured on a scale from 1 to 4 and approximated by its mean value, will be used to compare and analyze the dynamics of nationalism in Russia.[4]

Judging by the intensity of negative feelings, attitudes toward other nationalities can be classified in two major ways. On one hand, Azerbaijanis, Chechens, and Gypsies inspire the most negative attitudes, significantly higher than neutral. Their average score, especially that for Chechens and Gypsies, approximates 3, which implies "irritation" and "dislike." Other ethnic groups inspire less hostile attitudes and on average receive "neutral" scores, while Germans and Japanese fare significantly better. Because of such contrasting values, I decided against using an integrated measure of total nationalism and instead focus on an analysis of the most intense nationalistic attitudes. By using the aforementioned algorithm I have developed a variable that describes the most pronounced attitudes of xenophobia, which is largely of a common and routine character. This indicator has been constructed by integrating values of nationalistic attitudes toward three major ethnicities: Chechens (2.69), Gypsies (2.63), and Azerbaijanis (2.37) (Figure 8.1).

Table 8.1 What is your general attitude towards…?[a] (percentages)

	Sympathy/ interest	*Neutrality/ indifference*	*Irritation/ dislike*	*Caution/fear*	*Mean (IX)*[b]
Gypsies	1	49	30	19	2.67
Chechens	1	55	24	19	2.61
Georgians[c]	2	69	20	9	2.36
Azerbaijani	1	72	20	6	2.32
Arabs	3	79	10	8	2.22
Americans	6	77	11	6	2.15
Jews	5	84	7	4	2.10
Estonians	3	86	8	2	2.09
Blacks	6	85	7	3	2.06
Germans	10	84	4	2	1.99
Japanese	12	81	4	2	1.97

Notes

a Monitoring no. 11, 2006, $N = 2{,}107$.

b The index of xenophobia (IX) measures attitudes toward other ethnicities that can be grouped into three intervals: tolerant ($IX \leq 2$ points), moderately xenophobic ($2 > IX > 3$), and extremely xenophobic ($IX \geq 3$).

c Relations between Russia and Georgia and Russians' attitudes toward Georgians have deteriorated in fall 2006 in the course of and following an anti-Georgian campaign. The Russian government undertook a number of measures, among which were the arresting of postal and transport communications between the two countries; import bans; discrimination against Georgian businesses; illegal detention, beating, and deportation of Georgia's citizens as well as some Russian citizens of Georgian origin; and other human rights abuses. The campaign has received wide support and coverage in state-controlled media. In light of generally high levels of xenophobia in Russia, mass publics have been quick to absorb the image of a new "enemy." Georgians, who have traditionally been perceived in a largely positive light, now found themselves among those ethnicities that inspired the most negative sentiments.

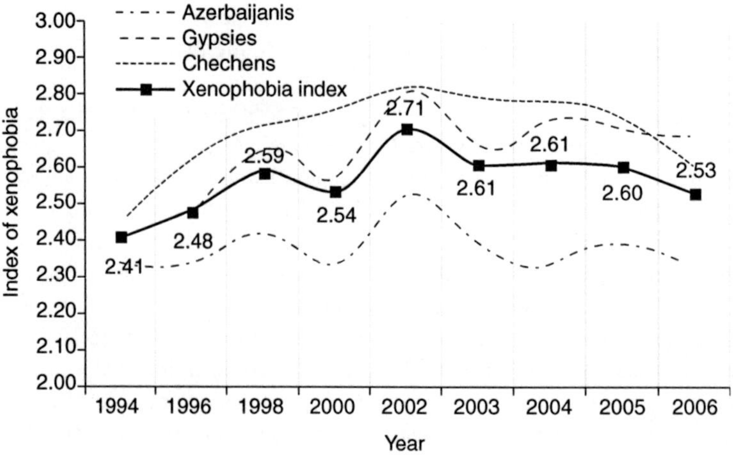

Figure 8.1 The structure and dynamics of the xenophobia index, 1994–2006.

It is worth noting that representatives of different ethnic groups are not clearly differentiated in mass consciousness, which is confirmed by a number of field studies. The choice of ethnicity toward which the irritation and dislike are directed is often determined by the situation and based on widely shared prejudices, state propaganda (which was clearly demonstrated in the course of the anti-Georgian campaign), and media reports (in particular, criminal incidents, which are often associated with non-Russians). More specifically, people tend to express caution and dislike even toward groups that they have had no direct contact with in their daily lives. Thus, it would be fair to say that the average value of the index of xenophobia reveals overall attitudes toward social environment, imagined "others," one's perceived prospects of social mobility, value deficits, etc.

Typology of xenophobia and its socioeconomic determinants

In the course of the period under study, the structure of xenophobic attitudes in Russia was changing significantly (Figure 8.2). At the very beginning, in the winter of 1994, the proportion of openly nationalistic respondents was only one-fourth of the total number of respondents. However, 2002 witnessed the highest level of xenophobic attitudes, when 40 percent of all respondents had hostile attitudes toward other ethnicities, with only one-fourth being tolerant. By the end of the study, in the fall of 2006, we noticed a certain decline in the intensity of chauvinistic attitudes, which nevertheless fails to inspire any optimism with regard to future developments. Existing long-term trends point to a continuous radicalization of xenophobic attitudes and a certain increase in the number of those who are openly intolerant toward other ethnicities. Indeed, the latter group has grown by 10 percentage points over the period of study (Figure 8.3). Changes

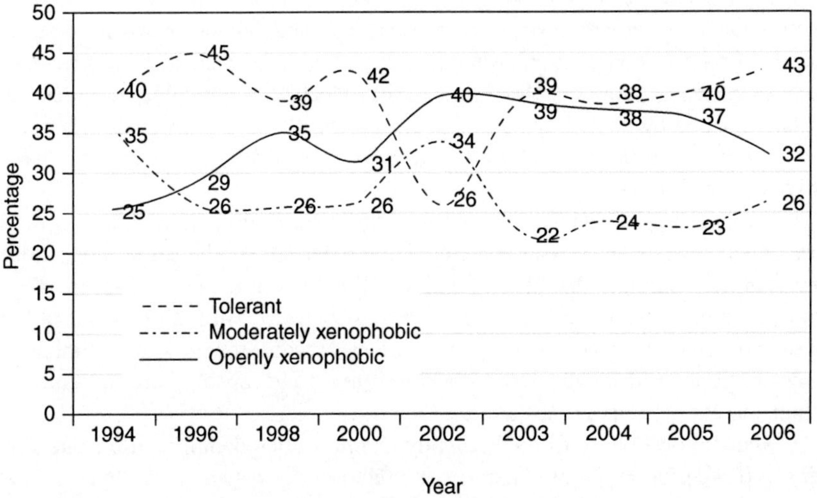

Figure 8.2 Typology of xenophobic attitudes, 1994–2006.

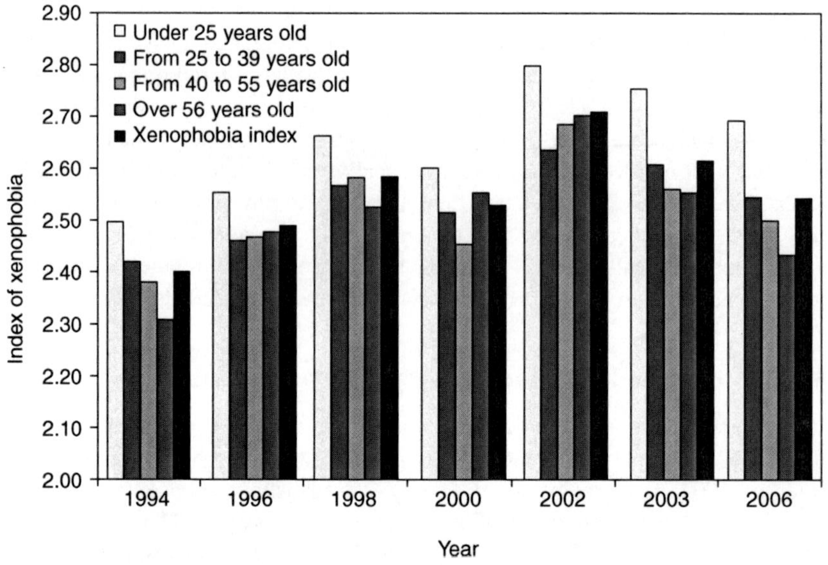

Figure 8.3 Xenophobia index and age, 1994–2006.

in the size of different groups of respondents point to an apparent variation in the intensity of nationalistic attitudes within the same social groups. This signifies the importance of situational, in addition to value-based, determinants of people's perceptions of different ethnic groups. I believe that it is possible to estimate the true nature of nationalistic attitudes (the extent to which they are rooted in societal consciousness) by looking at periods of increased tension in society (to identify the most ardent supporters of openness and universalism) as well as periods of relative conciliation (when hostility is not provoked by the underlying social conditions). This enables one to conclude that xenophobic attitudes are partially shaped by social tensions, yet tend to evolve into normative principles that continue to influence people's perceptions even after incidents that have provoked social unrest.

According to the data available, no less than a third of the population express antagonism toward those who are ethnically different. At the same time, those who routinely support the idea of universalism are in a clear minority (they make up no more than one-fourth of all those surveyed). Thus, almost half of the Russian population do not express any extreme hostility toward other ethnicities except in periods of heightened social tensions. However, they are not entirely immune to expressions of intolerance.

In what follows we shall methodically examine sociodemographic characteristics of these groups. We will explore the relationship between people's perceptions of imagined "others" and cultural-political factors. To analyze electoral preferences of the respondents I have used data from nine public opinion surveys conducted at different times within the period of post-communist parliamentarism in Russia. The surveys reveal the distribution of respondents' preferences with regard to State Duma candidates in all four electoral cycles.[5] Studying the dynamics of nationalistic attitudes across different sociodemographic groups shows that age is the single most significant predictor of the intensity of xenophobic attitudes (Figure 8.3). Indeed, the youngest among the respondents demonstrate a significantly higher than average level of chauvinism. Moreover, the intensity of such attitudes is increasing over time. Earlier records within the older age group indicate relative tolerance toward other ethnic groups. Later, however, this trend was reversed and approximates the sample average of intolerant attitudes.

I have examined changes in xenophobic attitudes in different age groups over a ten-year period by comparing survey data from 1996 and 2006 (Figure 8.4). The average value of the index of xenophobia in 1996 was 2.48, but it reached 2.53 in 2006. The balance between radicals and tolerators in the general population had deteriorated only slightly in the decade from 1996 to 2006. The proportion of the tolerators decreased from 45 percent to 43 percent, and that of radicals rose from 29 percent to 32 percent.

However, among respondents between the ages of 16 and 25 in 2006 the number of those who expressed tolerance toward other nationalities is significantly lower (by 12 percentage points), while the number of open xenophobes is higher than the sample average by 14 percentage points. In contrast, in 1996 the number of tolerant young people was only 5 percentage points lower than the sample

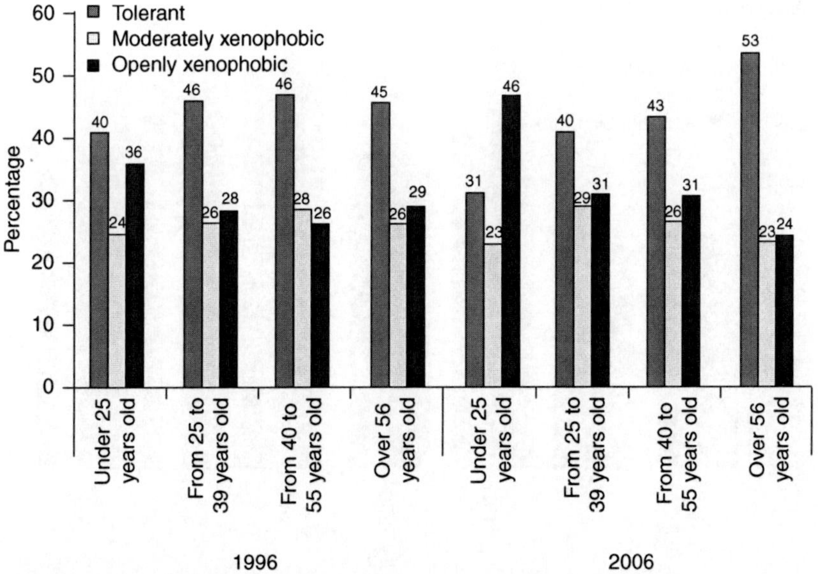

Figure 8.4 Typology of xenophobic attitudes in age groups, 1996–2006.

average, whereas the number of radicals exceeded it by 5 percentage points. The overall level of intolerance among younger generations is in itself nothing extraordinary. However, the data on Russian nationalism indicates that periodic outbursts of chauvinism tend to develop into long-lasting normative beliefs that persist after the peak of public tension has passed. As will become evident, this pattern is most prevalent among the socially active and educated who dominate the population of teenagers and young adults.

In contrast to the original assumption about the importance of education in predicting the level of nationalistic attitudes, empirical evidence suggests that even highly educated and socially advanced segments of the population are not immune to xenophobic sentiments. A comparative assessment of the dynamic of chauvinistic attitudes across groups with different levels of education shows that the groups most prone to xenophobia are the ones with secondary education and secondary special education, who were consistently ahead of other groups observed throughout the 1990s (Figure 8.5). The least educated were the least socially active in general and less prone to express nationalistic attitudes in particular. All three groups, however, exhibited a similar progressive increase in xenophobic attitudes. By the end of the twentieth century these patterns had undergone a certain amount of change. In light of an overall increase in social tensions at the beginning of 2002, college graduates demonstrated the strongest resistance to general neurosis, as the increase in ethnophobic attitudes within that group was significantly lower than that among less educated citizens. Nevertheless, deviation from the central tendency has

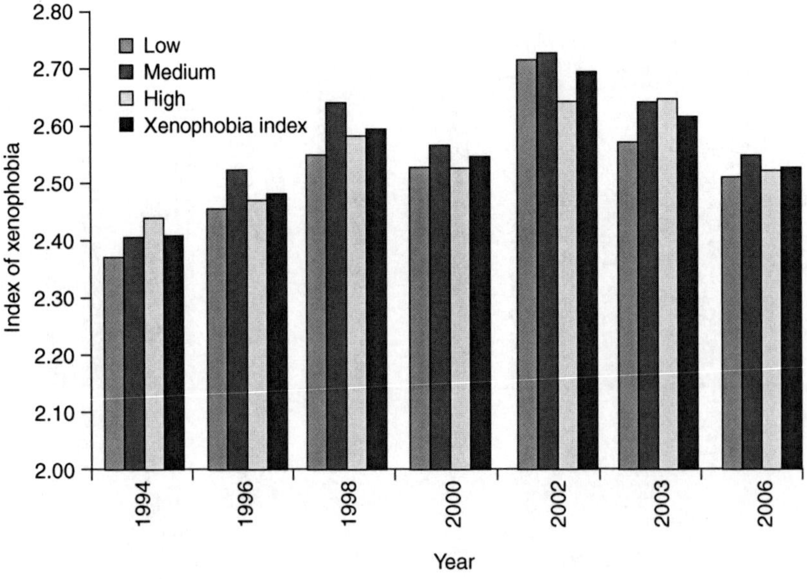

Figure 8.5 Xenophobia index and education, 1994–2006.

persisted. When social tensions have decreased, educated Russians have continued to express heightened nationalistic attitudes, catching up with those who are traditionally least tolerant.

The data presented here refute the hypothesis that the most educated segments of the population show greater support for ideas and principles of modernity. Moreover, it appears that people with greater interest in moving up the educational ladder are more likely to express intolerant attitudes toward other nationalities. Perhaps this can be explained by the fact that the most socially and economically active have perceptions about the constraints that people of other ethnicities can impose on their opportunities for advancement and thus view them as competitors. Earnings taken separately have virtually no impact on the level of xenophobic attitudes.

Contrary to the original assumption about the prevalence of nationalistic attitudes among socially disadvantaged and economically depressed segments of the population, an empirical test of the mutual relationship has not shown any significant correlation. In all income groups, xenophobic sentiments fluctuate with changes in overall social tensions. Thus, we may conclude that xenophobia is highly correlated with social activity in contemporary Russia, and that circumspection and hostility toward others have become an underlying element of everyday life and have no direct relation to any real interethnic relations and competition.

Xenophobia and electoral preferences

The issue of nationalism first infiltrated Russia's political discourse in the early 1990s, inspiring different reactions across various electoral groups. Our first public opinion survey was conducted in a dynamic environment of internal and external transformations. Accompanied by the creation of independent states, growing problems of ethnic Russians living in former republics of the Soviet Union, increasing interethnic frictions in the post-Soviet space, as well as a highly uncertain and rapidly deteriorating situation in Chechnya, Russia's first State Duma elections, held in December 1993, heralded a surprising success for political forces that made openly hostile chauvinistic and nationalistic declarations. Public opinion data, however, suggest that such extreme attitudes were typical only of a relatively small proportion of the electorate, who supported particular populist politicians.

In the first State Duma elections, voters who made electoral choices on the basis of their nationalistic preferences were categorized into two internally heterogeneous groups. Those with a more radical agenda voted for the centrist Russia's Choice or LDPR, whereas more tolerant voters cast their support for the Communist Party of the Russian Federation (CPRF) or the social democratic Yabloko. The electoral base of the first two of these groups is divided in equal shares between tolerant, and moderately and openly xenophobic voters; supporters of the CPRF and Yabloko include almost half of the "internationalists," about a third of moderates, and only a quarter of those expressing openly xenophobic sentiments.

Table 8.2 Xenophobia index for electorates of the main political parties, 1994–2006

	1994	*1996*	*1998*[a]	*2000*	*2002*[a]	*2003*[a]	*2004*	*2005*	*2006*
Agrarian Party of Russia	2.23								
Communist Party of the Russian Federation	2.31	2.54	2.56	2.53	2.66	2.60	2.65	2.61	2.44
Democratic Party of Russia	2.22								
Democratic Choice of Russia – United Democrats		2.58	2.66						
Edinstvo				2.54					
United Russia					2.72	2.67	2.64	2.53	2.55
Congress of the Russian Communities		2.58							
Liberal Democratic party of Russia; in 1999, the Zhirinovsky bloc	2.49	2.52	2.67	2.52	2.78	2.63	2.71	2.67	2.64
Our Home Russia		2.50	2.44						
Fatherland All-Russia				2.51					
Party or Russian Unity and Concordance	2.51								
Party of Workers' Self-Rule		2.66							
Russian People's Party of Workers			2.62						
Motherland						2.50	2.71	2.59	2.60
Union of the Right Forces				2.53	2.76	2.65	2.67	2.55	2.92
Choice of Russia	2.51								
Yabloko	2.27	2.49	2.58	2.52	2.67	2.72	2.44	2.69	2.50
Women of Russia	2.45		2.64		2.71				
Against all candidates	2.59	2.36	2.63	2.53	2.71	2.56	2.77	2.53	2.55
Mean XI	2.39	2.48	2.59	2.54	2.70	2.61	2.61	2.60	2.53

Note
a Projective vote.

Following the second State Duma elections, public opinion surveys showed a sudden increase in nationalistic attitudes among all voters regardless of their party identification. This surge may be explained by the first Chechen war, growing uncertainty about Russia's political future, and increasing competition between different political factions on the eve of the presidential elections. The most significant increase in nationalistic attitudes was noted among supporters of the CPRF and Yabloko, whose values almost matched those of the electorate of LDPR and the centrists.

Growing xenophobic sentiments among CPRF supporters point to a gradual shift in attitudes, primarily from moderate to open chauvinism, as a result of a decrease in the numbers of the tolerant. Within the electoral base of Yabloko, less profound transformations translated into a 5 percentage point increase in the number of the openly xenophobic at the expense of the most tolerant. The opposite trend, however, was under way among the followers of the LDPR and the centrist Our Home Russia. Despite a slight increase in the integrated index of xenophobia, the number of the extreme has fallen by 4 percentage points among supporters of LDPR and declined by 2 percentage points among followers of Our Home Russia, while the number of internationalists has grown by 3 and 9 percentage points, respectively.

Another survey, conducted a year before the third State Duma elections, indicates a continuing trend toward growing ethnophobia in Russia. This has conceivably been aided by the economic, social, and psychological trauma of the financial crisis of 17 August 1998. Supporters of the LDPR and Yabloko have shown the most striking upward move in nationalistic attitudes, while those who voted for the CPRF grew more xenophobic by a lesser degree. It is worth noting that the change in nationalistic attitudes among supporters of the LDPR and Yabloko has been most noticeable at both extremes, leading to a simultaneous increase in the number of both internationalists (by 2 and 3 percentage points, respectively) and the least tolerant (by 15 and 5 percentage points, respectively). By contrast, supporters of the CPRF have become more tolerant as a whole, with a 4 percentage point decline in the number of extreme chauvinists. In a similar fashion, those who voted for Our Home Russia saw the number of their most intolerant decrease by 7 percentage points.

This noticeable decline in overall rates of xenophobia in Russia has most likely resulted from a gradual withering away of psychological trauma arising from the 1998 financial crisis, political stabilization following Yeltsin's resignation, and renewed hope for a better future under Putin (despite the second Chechen war). One year following the third State Duma elections, supporters of the LDPR underwent the most noticeable decrease in xenophobic attitudes. The number of those openly hostile toward other ethnicities has gone down by 16 percentage points, swaying the balance in favor of the moderately nationalistic and internationalists (an 11 and a 5 percentage point increase, respectively).

Yabloko supporters have experienced a similar trend whereby the number of self-proclaimed ethnophobes has decreased by 7 percentage points. On the other hand, the number of internationalists has equally decreased (by 2 percentage points), which has resulted in an overall enlargement of the pool of the undecided. The electoral bases of the CPRF and Edinstvo have become less tolerant (by 3 and 5 percentage points, respectively).

In 2002, Russians witnessed record high levels of nationalism and xenophobia. The pattern was consistent across all groups regardless of their political identification, though with varying intensity. LDPR supporters displayed the highest degree of intolerance, and the LDPR's group average approached extreme values (2.78). In all four groups – United Russia, the LDPR, Yabloko, and the CPRF – there was a noticeable decline in tolerance: by 20, 19, 18, and 13 percentage points, respectively. At the same time, the number of those with moderately and openly xenophobic attitudes has increased.

It appears that the most influential factor contributing to the rise of nationalism in 2002 could only be the attacks of 11 September 2001 on New York, which triggered a renewed focus on national security and articulation of the terrorist threat. In contrast, the situation in Chechnya has failed to produce any noticeable impact on mass consciousness over the study period. In 2003 the nationalistic surge of 2002 subsided, but has not yet reached the low levels of the relatively uneventful year 2000. The electoral bases of United Russia, the CPRF, and the LDPR have become more polarized. Moderates have changed their position, adding to the ranks of internationalists (by 11–13 percentage points) and open xenophobes (by 2–4 percentage points).

This rather mild increase in openly hostile attitudes among supporters of United Russia, the CPRF, and the LDPR was in contrast to a defining shift in attitudes among Yabloko voters. The latter group saw a striking 24 percentage point increase in the number of those who were openly xenophobic, mostly at the expense of the moderately nationalistic. Thus, the index of xenophobia for this particular group has gone up, though less significantly if compared with the previous survey. The upward move has nevertheless become especially visible in light of a relative decrease in xenophobic attitudes among supporters of other political parties.

High indices of intolerance may be viewed as counterintuitive and unreliable for electorates of moderate centrist parties (like VR in 1994).[6] However, I would argue that the explanation of this phenomenon may be found in the heterogeneous nature of the structure of the electorates of the centrist forces, and in their respective motives for supporting their party. Not to be omitted from the analysis is the general political and social situation of the period, in which loss of group identity, anomie, and a fundamental change in all spheres of life were most characteristic.

Under turbulent reconfiguration of the whole political field, the propensity to support the center not only signifies consent for a moderate (with respect to all

Table 8.3 Index of cultural capital (ICC), 2003

ICC	*Cases*	*Percentage*	*Cumulative percentage*
0	1,020	51	51
1	462	23	74
2	318	16	90
3	140	7	97
4	47	2	99
5	17	1	100
Total	2,004	100	

extremes) course, but also anxiety about the lack of stability. An important motive for support of the center is a search for the "least of all evils" under extreme worsening of the economic situation, as well as a crisis in the foundations of citizens' political and cultural identity. Nor should one forget the possibility of multiple-meaning interpretation of the idea "Russia for the Russians," which may have been understood by some as a positive program to solve the problem of Russians in the former republics of the USSR.

Later, as we will see, xenophobic attitudes tended to be distributed more and more evenly across electoral groups. However, they we exposed in sentiments of the groups least confident about their future and seeking to lean upon any symbol of unity – be it state authority, or ethnical and cultural origins. This hypothesis is intermediately supported by the high intolerance of those who voted "against everything" (2.59 versus a mean of 2.39 in 1994). The preceding analysis of nationalistic sentiments among different sociodemographic and electoral groups points to the overall spread of xenophobia across all segments of the population, albeit to different degrees. Moreover, the empirical evidence has effectively challenged one of the assumptions about high levels of tolerance and openness among highly educated and socially advanced groups.

Sociocultural determinants of xenophobia

Because the rise of xenophobic attitudes greatly affects groups of advanced sociocultural status (mostly young and highly educated people), I believe that

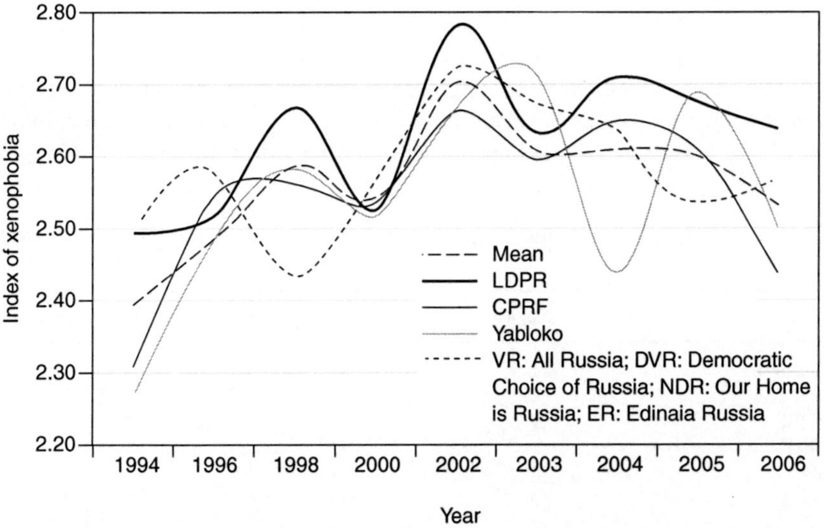

Figure 8.6 Dynamics of xenophobic attitudes in the electorates of the main political forces, 1994–2006.[7]

the trend reflects more than just occasional outbursts of xenophobia caused by periodic increases in social tensions. Instead, one is led to conclude that it signifies a more fundamental transformation on the normative level. It is particularly interesting to study the group who are of advanced sociocultural status, for its members are culturally literate and have the greatest ability to receive and reflect on the most significant social ideas. If accepted, those ideas are likely to determine the normative outlook of Russian society at large in the years to come. This fundamental normative transformation cannot be easily accessed and should be studied by applying the sequential time-series method.

Lacking such data, I have nevertheless attempted to determine differentiating factors with regard to xenophobic attitudes that cannot be uncovered through standard sociodemographic analysis. Thus, I adopted a cultural-generational approach. In other words, I set out to examine the ways in which ideas of social and ethnic intolerance spread across different cultural environments. To this end, I have used the index of cultural capital (ICC)[8] to measure the cultural potential of different social environments.

Respondents were grouped into four age categories: teenagers (born after 1979), young adults (born between 1969 and 1978), the middle-aged (born between 1950 and 1968), and the elderly (born before 1949).

The ICC values demonstrate considerable variation across different segments of the population. Half of the population (51 percent) do not share any of the aforementioned features; less than one-fourth (23 percent) identify with only one trait; one-seventh (16 percent) identify with two; and only one-tenth (10 percent) may qualify as culturally advanced. To correct for a rare occurrence of groups with high ICC values, I decided to distinguish between cultural "core" (3 points and higher), "semi-periphery" (1–2 points), and "periphery" (0 points) by combining the top three and middle two sub-groups.

Respondents classified according to the cultural variable display distinct sociodemographic characteristics. The majority (more than half) of the cultural "core" live in Moscow, St. Petersburg, or other big cities, whereas two-thirds of

Table 8.4 Distribution of cultural capital among the electorates of the parties, 2003 (percentages)

	Core	*Semi-periphery*	*Periphery*
Yabloko	21	41	38
ER	7	36	56
LDPR	7	38	56
CPRF	4	33	63
SPS	26	48	26
Others	19	36	45
Against all	11	36	53
Would not participate	9	44	47
Difficult to say	11	41	48

those in the cultural "periphery" reside in small towns and villages. Being culturally advanced is highly correlated with material well-being. Half of the "core" can be described as having substantial earnings, whereas only 10 percent of those in the cultural "periphery" can claim similar status, and one-fourth are of moderate means.

The three groups differentiated by cultural criteria also have distinct political preferences (Table 8.5). Members of the cultural "core" are slightly more likely than average to vote for a democratic party (Yabloko or the Union of Right Forces) and less likely to support the CPRF or United Russia. This group also has a more diverse range of political viewpoints and is more likely to support small political parties. The "periphery" on the other hand would be more likely to vote for the Communists or United Russia. Despite such significant differences, the level of political activism within each group remains at continuously low levels. Roughly half of all potential voters, regardless of their political orientation, are rather apathetic toward government and politics.

Two democratic parties, the URF and Yabloko, attract the greatest proportion of educated supporters (26 and 21 percent, respectively), though the sizes of their electoral bases are rather modest. In contrast, electoral choice in favor of United Russia and the LDPR and CPRF is dominated by the cultural "periphery" (56 percent and 63 percent, respectively) (Table 8.4). Young voters tend to

Table 8.5 Electoral preferences and cultural clusters (percent)

	Core	*Semi-periphery*	*Periphery*	*Mean*
Yabloko	5	3	2	3
ER	11	13	16	14
LDPR	4	5	6	6
CPRF	5	11	17	13
SPS	6	3	1	3
Others	14	7	6	7
Against all candidates	8	7	8	8
Would not participate	16	19	16	17
Difficult to say	32	31	28	30

Table 8.6 Cultural capital of the generational classes

	Before 1950; elderly		*1951–1969; mature*		*1970–1979; adult*		*After 1979; young*	
	N	*%*	*N*	*%*	*N*	*%*	*N*	*%*
Core	31	5	68	11	51	12	54	14
Semi-periphery	158	26	241	39	176	43	205	54
Periphery	412	69	302	49	186	45	121	32

support parties with a high index of cultural capital such as the URF (46 percent) as well as those, like the LDPR (59 percent), that rely substantially on support from the "periphery."

Sociodemographic characteristics of different social environments that have distinct levels of cultural capital play an important role in projecting their social functions. In terms of a generational profile, the "core" and "semi-periphery" are quite similar: almost half of them consist of young people born after 1968; one-third were born between 1950 and 1968; and only 15–20 percent were born before 1950. Within the cultural "periphery," more than one-third fell into the elderly category, while adults and youngsters each accounted for 30 percent of survey respondents.

In all cultural cohorts we find a significant correlation between age and education, geography, income level, and party identification. Distribution of the cultural factor within different age groups points to the upward dynamic, which is typical for all Eastern European societies in transition to postmodernism. Whereas only one in twenty of those born before 1950 are representative of the cultural "core," only one-third of the group born after 1978 can be classified as belonging to the "periphery," while one in seven are members of the cultural "core." This gap is likely to widen even further given that a substantial proportion of the youngest generation have yet to complete their education, which, when completed is likely to confer higher cultural status.

Inter- and intra-generational value differentiation

As the Soviet Union collapsed, Russians faced the formidable challenge of overcoming the conditions of international isolation under which more than 60 percent of the current population were born and socialized. For the Soviets, the idea of "uniqueness" was paramount to ensuring internal stability. The breaking down of this barrier has had a different effect on distinct generational and cultural groups. The surge in public enthusiasm fueled by the expectations of a rapid improvement in living standards quickly turned into disappointment and a return to isolationist sentiments (Figure 8.7). Overall, virtually half of Russia's current population believe that foreign influences should be resisted, whereas only one-fourth view integration with the rest of the world in a more positive light. The fact that a relatively large number of people have not yet arrived at any definitive position in this regard (26 percent) points to the transitory character of such attitudes and beliefs. Just as I had expected, 40 percent of those who supported greater openness belong to the younger generation, yet only 12 percent of the elderly share this sentiment. The educated are more likely to oppose an isolationist policy (39 percent) than the cultural "periphery" (18 percent). Interestingly, even among the highly educated, the number of pro-Westerners is on a par with those who support isolationism (36 percent). Thus, not only do respondents' attitudes toward rapprochement with the West vary across different cultural and generational groups, but they also serve as a significant differentiating factor within each of them. For instance, the data show that pro-Westerners hold only a slight lead over isolationists in three of the

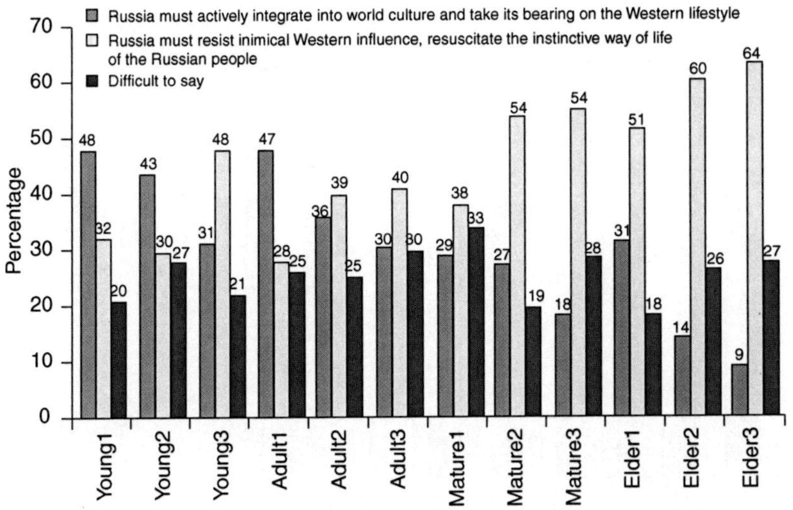

Figure 8.7 Attitudes toward dissemination of Western lifestyles in Russia.[9]

twelve cultural and generational groups (Figure 8.7). Moreover, traditionalists attract supporters even among the youngest Russians: 48 to 31 percent in the teenagers 3 group; 39 to 36 percent in the young adults 2 group; and 40 to 30 percent in the young adults 3 group. Pro-Western middle-aged and elderly people belonging to the cultural "core" each account only for one-third of the respondents.

One should not discount a definite possibility that either side could attract more supporters from the group of undecided, who make up no less than 20 percent of every cultural and generational group. Yet it would be premature to conclude that this opportunity is likely to be exploited by supporters of integration with the West, given the overall trend in the opposite direction.

Russian uniqueness figures prominently into the debate about the need for greater integration with the West. This view is shared among 57 percent of all respondents. Moreover, this proportion is subject to only slight variations (no greater than 15 percentage points) in different cultural and generational groups. Educated middle-aged respondents (33 percent) seem to be the least supportive of this argument.

This finding can be interpreted in different ways depending on the combination of cultural and generational factors. Only the poorly educated elderly believe that Russia is destined to continue on its unique developmental path (61–66 percent). This view is also popular among 25- to 35-year-olds in the cultural "periphery." Whereas 76 percent and 82 percent of the educated elderly and teenagers are rather optimistic about Russia's prospects of integrating into the international community, educated middle-aged Russians are less enthusiastic in this regard (65 percent).

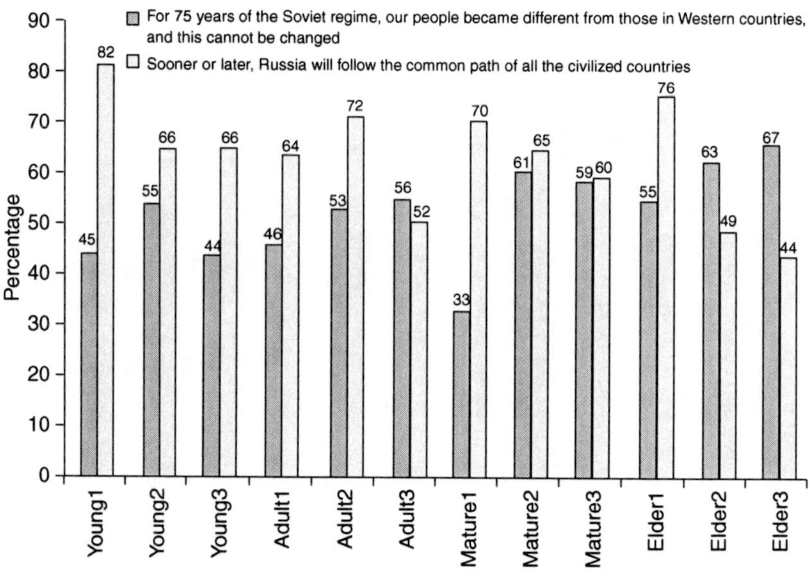

Figure 8.8 Evaluation of perspectives on integration with the West.

These results overall indicate a cautious attitude toward foreign influences, together with a certain fatalism about Russia's future trajectory, whether that will be integration with the West or isolation. The idea of uniqueness is more prevalent among older segments of the population, although youngsters in the cultural "periphery" are definitely not immune to this perspective.

Most Russians are cognizant of the problematic nature of the current situation, feeling ambivalence and frustration toward Russia's external antagonists, including those who are seen as their agents inside the country. Any attempt at consolidation of society is likely to be hampered by the absence of shared views and understandings of the past and the future, as well as a limited sense of unifying experiences. Under these circumstances, the only viable basis for social mobilization is ethnicity, which is the most diffuse, archaic, and inscriptive element.

Uncertainty about the future puts emphasis on the existence of a threat (whether external or internal), which is often and more easily articulated in terms of ethnic differences. Not surprisingly, the chauvinistic slogan "Russia for the Russians" appeals to the majority of the population, though differences are noticeable. Almost person one in five agrees with it completely, and one person in every three is sympathetic to the idea but is more likely to support it in a less aggressive form. Another third of the population, lacking a definitive normative outlook to support or react against this position, do not take part in this debate. Only one-sixth of people are categorically against the proclamation.

This pattern is consistent across all generational groups, though it does reveal slight changes when the cultural variable is controlled for. Indeed, within the cultural “core” there is a small change in attitudes from openly chauvinistic to more veiled and rather moderate (a 5–6 percentage point decrease), although the total number of chauvinists persists when compared to the sample average (53 percent). Moreover, this group has fewer undecided respondents (14 percent), while internationalists account for a healthy 33 percent.

The ordering principle of the aforementioned attitudes appears to remain constant across all cultural and generational groups. The most stable, tolerant attitudes are found among a small group of educated elderly people (48 percent), although even within this group the number of chauvinists is only marginally less than half of all the respondents and amounts to an equally representative segment. In each generational cluster, though fewer in number than chauvinists, educated Russians display greater tolerance toward other ethnicities (32:55 within the group of middle-aged 1, 34:36 within the group of young adults 1, and 27:58 within the teenagers 1 group).

Equating justice with an acknowledgment of the superiority of Russians over other nationalities, respondents support practical measures such as conferring certain employment privileges on ethnic Russians, limiting the rights of non-Russians (even Russia’s citizens) to move within Russia, controlling the entrance of migrants, and facilitating deportation procedures. The generational determinant does not appear to have any significant bearing on this attitude. Despite a certain negative correlation between such attitudes and the level of education when age difference is controlled for, the overall distribution and prevalence of approval with regard to such a policy remain unchanged.

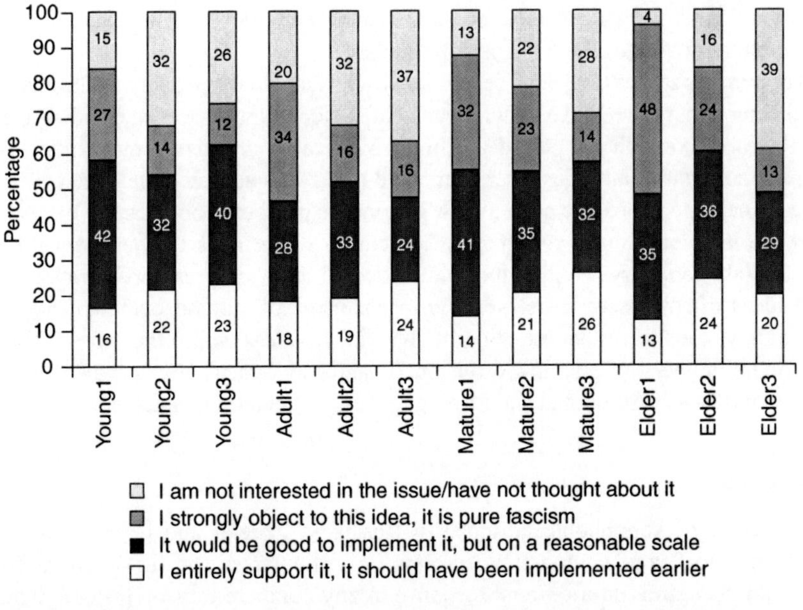

Figure 8.9 What is your attitude towards the idea of “Russia for the Russians”?

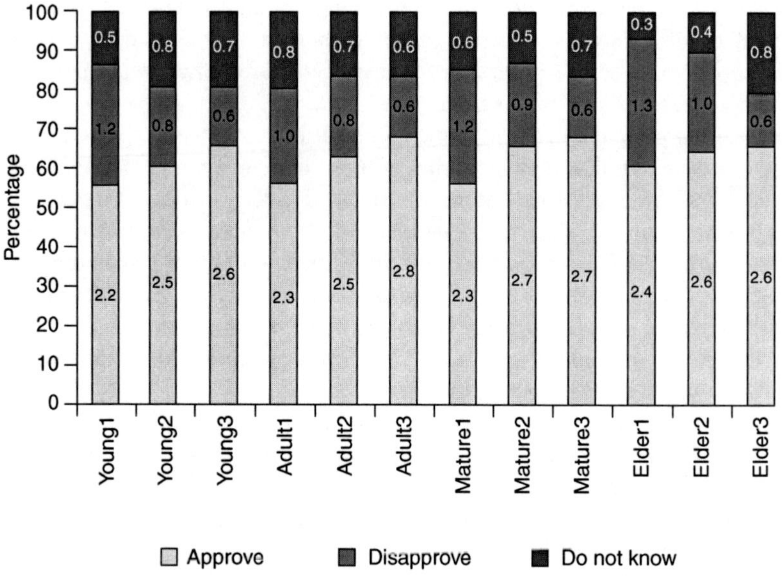

Figure 8.10 Attitudes toward discrimination against non-Russian ethnicities in Russia.[10]

Overall, such policy appeals to two-thirds of the population, which is greater than the number of open or hesitant supporters of the slogan "Russia for the Russians." This shows that most of the undecided are closer to the chauvinistic position than to that of the few cosmopolitans.

To summarize, cultural and generational analyses confirmed my preliminary conclusion about the relative insignificance of sociocultural factors in deciding the distribution of xenophobic attitudes. Although educated citizens are more likely to express modernistic attitudes when compared to the less educated, they are nevertheless unable to propagate such a view beyond their group's boundaries. Instead, most channels of cultural communication reinforce principles that are typical of the cultural "periphery." Within the cultural "core" the widespread proliferation of such ideas often offsets "core"-specific mechanisms of cultural communication, which only leads to further adoption of chauvinistic ideas within the "core." This pattern highlights the ongoing diffusion of anti-modernism and archaism in a society that lacks institutional and ideological foundations for its integration.

Conclusions

My analysis of xenophobic attitudes in Russia in general and across distinct social, political, and demographic groups in particular shows that such sentiments do not represent a rational response to any concrete threats. Instead, they most likely reflect certain societal tensions caused by continued uncertainty about the country's future, and frustrations against the imagined "other." This mechanism is helping to consolidate a society that was traumatized and disillusioned by the reforms of the early 1990s reforms and lacks other uniting forces. Thus, ethnic differentiation becomes the only readily available and the most powerful centripetal force within Russian society.

Its unifying character is evident in the extent to which the proliferation of xenophobic attitudes follows a similar dynamic within different segments of the population: from the least privileged to the elderly, to the poorly educated, and, finally, to a significantly better-off group. At some point they all embrace similar ideas and attitudes, whether to a lesser or a greater extent. The intra-group dynamic tells us a great deal about their members' reactions to the changes, and the process of their internalization.

I am particularly interested in studying the aforementioned processes that take place within the culturally advanced and highly educated group that is traditionally seen as supporting the ideas of universalism, openness, and tolerance. By definition, this group is better equipped to internalize various social tensions and disturbances and is poised to act in a rather rational way that distinguishes it from other groups in Russian society. The evidence, however, suggests that this group has failed to lead the way in promoting the ideas of universalism and tolerance amid growing sentiments of uncertainty and confusion about Russia's future. Thus, the country's "intelligentsia" appear to have been reluctantly "trying on" the mainstream attitudes of nationalism and xenophobia, which signals a crisis in its group identification. Having acquiesced to the rest of society, the group is increasingly questioning its legitimacy and future prospects.

In the early stages of economic reforms, most of the Russian "intelligentsia" had been co-opted by democratic forces. Whether accidental or not, the subsequent decrease in public support for reformist ideas coincided with the rise of xenophobic attitudes which were spreading into the ranks of Russia's "intelligentsia," who used to support and advocate openness and universalism.

The assessment put forward in this chapter reveals the dominant influence of principles and ideas espoused by the inert, conservative, and least educated segments of the population (political parties in State Duma rely on support among people with the lowest index of cultural capital, whereas representatives of the cultural "core" electorate fail to pass a 5 percent threshold). The French proverb "Le mort saisit le vif" (The dead holds the living in his grasp), made famous in Russia after being cited by Karl Marx, is still valid to describe the sociopolitical situation in contemporary Russia. Despite a significant increase in the number of educated young people, there seems no reason to expect a sudden surge in popularity of the ideas of openness and universalism. My pessimism is based on the absence of institutional foundations that would support such diffusion in contrast to the enduring efficacy of particular group mechanisms of cultural transmission that propagate just the opposite. A significant presence of traditional values and beliefs among younger generations suggests a continuing re-emergence and reproduction of archaic principles and ideas unless there is a development of horizontal mechanisms of transmission of modernistic influences.

Notes

1 A. Leonova, "Nastroeniia ksenofobii i elektoral'nye predpochteniia v Rossii v 1994–2003 godakh," *Vestnik obshchestvennogo mneniia*, 4 (72), 2004, 83–91, www.levada.ru/vestnik72.html (accessed 11 June 2008).
2 Analyis is based on data from "Monitoring" surveys conducted by the Levada Center (known as VTsIOM before fall 2003). "Monitoring" is an omnibus-type survey ensuring the most reliable data. It is conducted every two months on a sample of the urban and rural population of Russia. Two thousand one hundred respondents aged 16-plus are interviewed on a representative nationwide sample and 300 persons are interviewed on an additional Moscow sample (overall, 430 interviews are conducted in Moscow). For more on the methodology of the polls, see www.levada.ru/eng/monitoring.html (accessed 11 June 2008).
3 Statistical significance was accepted at the $p < 0.03$ level.
4 Attitudes toward diverse ethnic groups were uncovered by analyzing respondents' answers to a series of typical questions: "What is your general attitude toward (Jews, Estonians, Azerbaijanis, Americans, Chechens, Gypsies, Arabs, Germans, Japanese, Africans)?" with respondents being provided with a list of answers such as: 1 – with sympathy/interest; 2 – neutral/indifferent; 3 – with irritation/dislike; 4 – with caution/fear.
5 In our study we drew on "Monitoring" public opinion surveys conducted by VTsIOM and the Levada Center: no. 1, 1994 ($N = 2{,}005$), no. 7, 1996 ($N = 2{,}404$), no. 11, 1998 ($N = 2{,}409$), no. 11, 2000 ($N = 2{,}404$), no. 5, 2002 ($N = 2107$), no. 11, 2003 ($N = 2112$), and nos. 11, 2004, 2005, 2006.
6 I would like to thank an anonymous reviewer for pointing out the necessity of making this explanation, and for other valuable remarks on the text.
7 Data on the electorate for all parties except for United Russia and (CPRF are not representative due to the small size of the relevant groups in the sample, whose significance is often below statistical error.
8 The ICC is a multidimensional variable that has been operationalized through five indicators that measured (1) college degree, (2) determination to obtain at least a bachelor's degree, (3) and (4) the level of parents' education, and (5) a family collection of more than 500 books. The maximum value of the ICC is 5 points. Regression analysis showed that academic aspirations, which are shaped by one's social environment, exert the strongest influence on an individual's ICC. It is worth noting that one's academic aspirations are equally informed by both parents' level of education whereas one's acquired level of education is largely determined by that of the mother. Among other contributing influences, one's level of education appears to play a second important role in shaping the ICC. One's parents' level of education and the size of the family collection of books are also important, albeit to a lesser degree. Regrettably, space considerations prevent me from offering a detailed and elaborated discussion of the mathematical aspects of this method.
9 The number indicates the cultural status of the subgroup: 1 – core, 2 – semi-periphery, 3 – periphery.
10 When constructing the index of approval/disapproval a point was added for answers ("agree" or "rather agree"/"rather disagree" and "disagree") to all of the four questions. The answers of those who were uncertain were operationalized in a similar way.

9 Fear has wide eyes

Why do Russians see some migrant minorities as more numerous than others?

Mikhail A. Alexseev

When anti-migrant hostility and aggressive behavior arise, they are typically expressed as a need to defend the host society from being "swamped," "invaded," "penetrated," or "overwhelmed."[1] Similarly, most theoretical explanations in political science and sociology of attitudes toward immigration have implicitly centered on the assumption that these attitudes are a linear function of the scale of migration of any given ethnic out-group.[2] Yet migration into most states is multiethnic, and the scale of migration by group is frequently hard to estimate.[3] Moreover, as diverse migrant groups spread out within states, they arrive in different numbers in localities (provinces, regions, states, counties, etc.) that differ from one another on significant demographic, political, socioeconomic, and cultural dimensions. These differences in turn are likely to affect impressions about the scale of migration. Which ethnic groups are most likely to engender public perceptions of being swamped or overcrowded in which regions?

This may sound like a simple question but it is not. This is because *both* variation in ethnicity *and* regional context need to be taken into account simultaneously. For example, it may appear that ethnicity matters most if one examines attitudes and behavior in the European Union or the United States toward Arab migrants following 9/11. Hostility toward this migrant group palpably increased in relation to other groups across national and provincial or state boundaries. On the other hand, it may appear that regional context matters most if one considers that attitudes toward Arabs or toward most other migrant groups in any state have varied significantly by region or province at any given time. These parallel accounts suggest not only that one or the other factor may be significant, but also that neither or both of them may be. That both ethnicity and regional context matter at some level is perhaps the most intuitively plausible starting point. And yet even this premise needs to be critically re-examined. What if attitudes to migrants are predominantly shaped by individual life circumstances and/or the media regardless of migrants' ethnicity, actual migration scale, and regional context? Individual-level factors may also offer systematic explanations of anti-migrant alarmism even when the same factors seemingly do not work when aggregated by region. For example, while individual income and education levels vary across individuals in a host society, they also typically vary, on average, by province. Would the attitude toward immigration of a poorer individual in a relatively rich region differ significantly from the attitude of a poorer individual in a relatively poor region, etc.?

This study examines these questions using an opinion survey on immigration attitudes and ethnic relations in the Russian Federation (September–November 2005, $N = 4{,}740$) that I designed and directed.[4] Specifically, I ask whether perceptions of migration scale differ more according to the ethnicity of migrants or by province of Russia. The analysis controls for ethnic composition change in Russia's provinces from 1989 to 2002 and uses descriptive statistics as well as correlation and one-way ANOVA tests to examine a combination of these factors in a way that allows one to control for regional clustering effects in survey samples.

Design, data, and methods

Descriptive analysis – to be discussed in detail later – quickly established that assessments by Russians of the scale of migration varied widely both by ethnic group and by region. Descriptive results, however, were nowhere near conclusive as to whether this variation had systematic patterns. To identify whether any such patterns are present in the survey results, I designed a series of quasi-experimental tests with the survey and census data. They assess three simple hypotheses, which have profound theoretical implications.

> *H1: Perceived migration scale by ethnic group in any given region varies systematically with actual changes in ethnic composition in these regions (as measured by census data)*

While one may be tempted to critique this hypothesis by doubting the accuracy of the Russian census data, such criticism is naïve and unsustainable on three counts: (1) while the data for any specific locality may not be 100 percent accurate, the census data adequately capture *regional variation* in ethnic composition change across Russia, with the exception of Chechnya and Dagestan; (2) census data deviations from actual patterns of regional variation are statistically insignificant in this particular research design; and (3) interviews with the Russian State Committee for Statistics officials by myself and my colleagues found that the census-takers comprehensively covered the populations of most of Russia's provinces and that no systematic errors that might significantly skew the data for the ethnic groups and the regions featured in the 2005 Russia immigration attitudes survey have been identified.[5]

> *H2: Ethnicity of migrants is the principal predictor of variation in perceived migration scale.*

> *H3: Social context of the receiving region (province) is the principal predictor of variation in perceived migration scale.*

The quasi-experimental tests have been set up in such a way that H1 would be supported if the mean estimates of migration scale by survey respondents varied in the same way as the actual scale of migration (reflected in the change in ethnic composition recorded by the census) – regardless of which ethnic group size was estimated in which region. H2 would be supported if the variance of estimated migration scale differed systematically only by ethnic group regardless of the province and regardless of the actual changes in ethnic composition by ethnic group and by province. And H3 would be supported if the variance of perceived migration scale by survey respondents differed systematically only across the provinces where the survey was taken, regardless of the ethnicity of the migrant groups whose size was evaluated or actual changes in ethnic composition by group and by province.

The 2005 Russian immigration attitudes survey was designed specifically to evaluate these hypotheses. It offers an ideal setting for analyzing individual perceptions of the scale of migration for different ethnic groups in different provinces of the Russian Federation. The regional stratification of the survey sample enables one to control for important variations in the regional context where migrants arrive: (1) location along Russia's external borders (Krasnodar Krai, Volgograd Oblast', Orenburg Oblast', and Primorskii Krai) or inland (Moscow Oblast', Moscow City, the Tatarstan Republic); (2) neighboring migrant-sending states, namely the former Soviet republics (the "near abroad," post-1991 interstate borders) or other states (the "far abroad," pre-1991 interstate borders); (3) neighboring migrant-sending states having smaller or larger populations than Russia; (4) location along disputed borders; (5) location along borders in proximity to violent conflict or to politically unstable areas; (6) ethnic composition of the border territories of the neighboring migrant-sending states; (7) differences among "macro-regions" within Russia (central Russia, the north Caucasus, the Volga region, the Urals, the Far East); (8) administrative status of the province (republic, *krai* containing a republic within its territory, *krai* not containing a republic within its territory, *oblast'*, metropolis as a constituent unit of the federation); (9) levels of socioeconomic development and internationalization; (10) ethnic composition and its change from 1989 to 2002. In addition, a sub-sample representative of the Russian Federation as a whole enables one to examine how and to what extent estimates of the scale of migration within provinces relate to average estimates across Russia.

Complementing regional stratification of survey samples, the selection of ethnic groups among migrants whose size respondents were asked to estimate makes it possible to examine the impact of intergroup differences – specifically regarding (1) the percentage of these ethnic groups in the provinces where the survey took place; (2) changes of these percentages from 1989 to 2002; (3) relatively "old" and "new" migrant groups (e.g. the Tatars versus the Chinese); (4) the presence or absence of compact settlements or enclaves of each group in the provinces; (5) the association of each group with different types of threats to Russia's security (such as the strong and widespread association of the Chechens with the threat of terrorism and of the Chinese with territorial claims, as against the absence of this type of association regarding the Armenians and the Tatars). In each survey sub-sample, respondents were asked their views about five different migrant ethnic groups:

Subsample	*Ethnic groups*
Russia:	Chechens, Armenians, Chinese, Uzbeks, Russians[6]
Moscow City:	Chechens, Armenians, Azerbaijanis, Chinese, Kazakhs
Moscow Oblast':	Chechens, Armenians, Azerbaijanis, Chinese, Kazakhs
Volgograd Oblast':	Chechens, Chinese, Kazakhs, Uzbeks, Russians
Orenburg Oblast':	Chechens, Chinese, Kazakhs, Uzbeks, Russians
Krasnodar Krai:	Chechens, Armenians, Azerbaijanis, Meskhetian Turks, Tatars
Tatarstan Republic:	Chechens, Armenians, Azerbaijanis, Uzbeks, Russians
Primorskii Krai:	Chechens, Chinese, Tatars, Koreans, Vietnamese

In this manner, the combination of interregional and interethnic stratifications in the survey sampling and in the questionnaire enables one to systematically evaluate both (1) how different respondents in the same region estimated the migration trends for different ethnic groups, and (2) how respondents in different regions estimated the migration trends for the same ethnic group. And using the 1989 and 2002 census one can also examine how differences in the perceived scale of migration by group and by region relate to actual ethnic composition trends for the same groups in the same regions. All in all, this design yields 40 region–group dyads (e.g. Tatarstan – Armenians; Primorskii Krai – Tatars, etc.) for which I also have modal estimates of migration scale by survey respondents. In this study I analyze the data for 32 region–group dyads. Five dyads were excluded owing to the difficulty of aggregating the survey and the census data for these specific groups. Three dyads covering Russians from the former Soviet republics were excluded owing to the absence of census data about this group of migrants.

Perceived migration scale was measured using two survey questions asked specifically about five ethnic groups in each sub-sample: (1) "What percentage of your *krai*/*oblast'*/republic/city population are migrants of the following ethnic groups?" and (2) "If Russia's migration policy remains unchanged, what percentage of your *krai*/*oblast'*/republic/city will be migrants of the following ethnic groups in about 10 years' time?"[7]

Data analysis and the results

I Aggregate (mean) responses by region and ethnic group

To analyze perceived migration scale by region and ethnic group, I put together a dataset that includes the indicators of the principal variables (Table 9.1). The dependent variable (the phenomenon under investigation) has two measures, each being the mean score of responses to the two above-cited survey questions about the scale of migration by ethnic group. This gives us average values of the perceived scale of migration for each region–group dyad in the survey. The hypothetical demographic correlates of these measures (H1) are the size and the percentage of the same migrant ethnic groups in the same regions in 1989 and 2002, as well as their percentage-point change from 1989 to 2002. An examination of Table 9.1 reveals certain patterns in the distribution of these measures that are worth examining in detail.

Exaggeration of the scale of migration: the dominant perceptual logic

Average assessments of the scale of migration by the Russian survey respondents were never lower than actual (census) assessments for any ethnic (migrant) group in any of the regions. Exaggeration of the scale of migration was systematic. On average, for all groups in all regions, respondents exaggerated the scale of migration by 192 times. Valuations of the scale of migration also revealed significant uncertainty about migration size among the general Russian public. The standard deviation was on average 2.5 times higher than the mean estimates. Even assuming that in the Russian census the size of migrant minorities was underestimated (principally because of difficulties in accounting for illegal migrant populations), it is still implausible that the undercounts would have a statistically significant impact on the magnitude of exaggeration of the scale of migration.[8]

Systematic and non-systematic aspects of exaggeration

On average, most exaggerated was the extent of migration of two ethnic groups: the Chechens (by approximately 120 times) and the Chinese (by approximately 885 times). The picture for all region–group dyads, however, is much more complex and unsystematic than this finding may suggest. Thus, respondents on average exaggerated the percentage of Uzbeks in their regions by 53 times even though according to the census the percentage of Uzbeks was approximately the same as that of the Chechens in the survey regions. Respondents on average exaggerated the percentage of Kazakhs by 35 times and the percentage of Azerbaijanis by 32 times. Yet according to the census data, the Kazakhs comprised on average approximately 1.7 percent of the population in the survey regions, and the Azerbaijanis only 0.16 percent.

In addition, the mean estimates of migration scale of all ethnic groups differed significantly across two clusters of regions. The first includes Moscow Oblast', Volgograd Oblast', Orenburg Oblast', and Primorskii Krai. In these regions, respondents exaggerated the scale of migration for any given ethnic group by no less than 100 times, and approximately 300 times on average for all groups (316, 225, 588, and 115 times for each of the four regions, respectively). The second cluster includes Moscow City, Krasnodar Krai, and the Tatarstan Republic, where the percentage of migrants was exaggerated on average 41, 48, and 76 times, respectively – significantly less than in the first cluster. This watershed between groups of regions is in many ways paradoxical. It runs contrary to each of the three principal hypotheses of this study and cannot be explained by any combination of actual migration scale, ethnicity, or regional differences.

Table 9.1 Sizes of select ethnic groups in the provinces of the Russian Federation where the 2005 migration and ethnic relationship survey was held, and respondents' estimates of those sizes

Region–group dyad	*Group population in a province, 1989*	*Group population in a province, 2002*	*Group population in a province, 1989 (%)*	*Group population in a province, 2002 (%)*	*Group population in a province, change 1989 to 2002 (%)*	*Group population in a province (%) estimated by 2005 survey respondents*	*Standard deviation, 2005 valuation*	*Group population in a province (%) estimated by 2015 survey respondents*	*Standard deviation, 2015 valuation*	*Exaggeration rate of group population in a province (x times)*
MOW-AZR	20,727	95,563	0.234	0.920	361.1	13.3	11	19	13	14.5
MOW-ARM	43,989	124,425	0.496	1.198	182.9	11	7.4	15.9	9.8	9.2
MOW-KAZ	8,225	7,997	0.093	0.077	–2.8	**4.7**	**4.9**	6.9	6.2	61.0
MOW-CHE	2,101	14,465	0.024	0.139	588.5	9.8	7	15.8	1.2	70.3
MOW-CHI	372	12,801	0.004	0.123	3,341.1	6.5	6	10.5	8.8	52.7
MOS-AZR	5,974	14,651	0.090	0.221	145.2	13.3	9.7	18.6	14.3	60.1
MOS-ARM	9,245	39,660	0.139	0.599	329.0	10.5	9	15.3	10.6	17.5
MOS-KAZ	3,145	2,493	0.047	0.038	–20.7	**2.8**	**3.8**	5.8	6.6	74.3
MOS-CHE	664	1,941	0.010	0.029	192.3	5.3	3.6	9	9	180.7
MOS-CHI	42	180	0.001	0.003	328.6	**3.4**	**5.2**	6.8	6.9	1,250.2
KRR-AZR	11,363	11,944	0.225	0.233	5.1	8.2	7.6	13	13	35.2
KRR-ARM	182,217	274,566	3.606	5.357	50.7	23	14.7	33.5	21.4	4.3
KRR-TAT	17,213	25,589	0.341	0.499	48.7	**7**	**7.1**	9.6	10.3	14.0
KRR-CHE	1,801	2,864	0.036	0.056	59.0	8.4	7.9	13.3	12	150.3
KRR-TRK	2,135	13,496	0.042	0.263	532.1	**10.2**	**11**	14.5	18.3	38.7
VOG-KAZ	41,505	45,301	1.601	1.678	9.1	**7.5**	**8.4**	12.6	12.5	4.5
VOG-UZB	2,851	3,012	0.110	0.112	5.6	**8.2**	**8.6**	11.2	10.8	73.5
VOG-CHE	11,140	12,256	0.430	0.454	10.0	13.7	11.1	21.4	16.1	30.2
VOG-CHI	33	255	0.001	0.009	672.7	**7.5**	**8.4**	12.2	11.8	793.9

ORE-KAZ	111,477	125,568	5.136	5.761	12.6	11.7	10.3	15.7	12.1	2.0
ORE-UZB	1,746	3,275	0.080	0.150	87.6	**6.7**	**7.6**	9.8	9.8	44.6
ORE-CHE	1,159	1,996	0.053	0.092	72.2	5.8	6	9.7	11.2	63.3
ORE-CHI	27	33	0.001	0.002	22.2	**3.4**	**6.6**	6.1	8.3	2,245.6
TTN-AZR	3,915	9,987	0.108	0.264	155.1	5.6	5.3	8.6	8.1	21.2
TTN-ARM	1,815	5,922	0.050	0.157	226.3	5.2	5.6	7.2	7.2	33.2
TTN-UZB	2,692	4,852	0.074	0.128	80.2	5.3	5.2	7.8	7.4	41.3
TTN-CHE	272	706	0.007	0.019	159.6	**3.9**	**5.1**	5.9	7.5	208.8
PK-KOR	8,454	17,899	0.375	0.864	111.7	5.8	5.1	9.9	6.2	6.7
PK-TAT	20,211	14,549	0.896	0.702	–28.0	**2.8**	**3.1**	4.9	3.8	4.0
PK-CHE	459	649	0.020	0.031	41.4	4.3	4.3	8.1	6.8	137.2
PK-CHI	159	3840	0.007	0.185	2,315.1	16.2	8.9	29	15.8	87.4
PK-VTM	0	213	0.000	0.010	21,300.0	**3.5**	**4.1**	6.6	6	340.3
Mean	16,160.3	27,904.6	0.4	0.6	981.1	8.0	7.2	12.3	10.4	192.8
Std. dev.	37,087.6	55,939.2	1.10	1.35	3,772.0	4.5	2.7	6.6	3.9	451.8

The role of uncertainty and threat assessment

At the same time, these findings do not contradict the logic of the "defended neighborhood" theory developed in the sociological and ethnographic studies of anti-immigrant hostility in the United States.[9] Its causal argument is derived from the psychology of perceived threats to lifestyle and identity of the native populations. It is argued that this threat perception is more acute in initially more homogeneous neighborhoods that are beginning to experience an influx of migrants. In those circumstances, exaggeration of the scale of migration is an integral part of dealing with perceived and largely speculative threats that are plausibly associated with migration of specific groups. From this standpoint it is notable that all four survey regions in the first cluster (high exaggeration levels) are relatively more ethnically homogeneous than the three in the second. They are also located next to states or territories that one would plausibly perceive as being the likely sources of immigration. For Orenburg it is Kazakhstan and China; for Volgograd it is Kazakhstan and the republics and states of the Caucasus; for Primorskii it is China; and for Moscow Oblast' it is Moscow City. Finally, all four regions in this cluster also experienced lower rates of immigration than regions in the second cluster with approximately the same ethnic compositions (Krasnodar Krai and Moscow City).

Importantly, at its microfoundations the "defended neighborhood" logic is the logic of threat under uncertainty. One measure of uncertainty about migration size is the dispersion of individual valuations captured by standard deviation from the mean. The region–group dyads in this respect can be subdivided into two clusters. In the first cluster the mean of estimated migration scale is larger than one standard deviation. In the second cluster the mean is smaller than one standard deviation. As Table 9.1 shows, in twelve of the thirty-two region–group dyads the uncertainty levels are high because standard deviations are higher than mean estimates of migration scale. One discernible pattern was that greater uncertainty characterized the estimated size of three Asian ethnic groups (Uzbeks, Kazakhs, and Chinese) in the three survey regions where migration scale estimates were exaggerated the most (Moscow, Volgograd, and Orenburg). These findings suggest that migration from Asia in the longer run is a more likely source of anti-immigrant sentiments and interethnic tensions in Russia than migration of ethnic groups from the Causasus. As far as the Caucasus ethnics are concerned, high levels of uncertainty about the scale of their migration was registered only for one group (the Chechens) and only one survey region (Tatarstan). These preliminary findings contradict initial intuitive assumptions and hypotheses and call for more detailed investigation.

The psychology of numbers

The data in Table 9.1 also show that the perception of numbers has its own distinctive logic. This logic applies across different ethnic groups and survey regions. Thus, the variance of estimates of the scale of migration averaged for all migrant groups across provinces is relatively small (standard deviation = 4.5 for the mean = 8). At the same time, the dispersion of the actual size of these groups recorded in the 2002 Russian census is relatively large (standard deviation = 1.4 for the mean = 0.6). This indicates that ethnic groups that made up the majority of migrants comprised on average approximately 0.6 percent of the population of the survey regions, whereas the average respondent in the survey believed that these same groups comprised on average 8 percent of their regions' population. Yet at the same time the variance of actual group size was twice the mean, but the variance of estimated group size was half the value of the mean. In other words, the variance of the survey data was four times smaller than the variance of the census data.

The distinct perceptual logic of numbers reveals itself especially vividly when one compares respondents' estimates of the size of various ethnic groups at the time of the survey (2005) (see Table 9.1) and ten years into the future. As if by tacit agreement, respondents said on average that the proportion of the migrant groups in their regions would increase from 1.5 to 1.8 times – regardless of the region where the survey was held or which ethnic group size was estimated. The largest standard deviation for any of the region–group dyads was less than one-fifth of the mean estimate. Put differently, the variance of average estimates of ethnic group size in 2015 decreased twofold by comparison with the variance of the estimates of ethnic group size in 2005.

These results rule out the probability that estimates of ten-year ethnic composition trends in the provinces have been influenced non-randomly by such seemingly important factors as intergroup differences; the history of intergroup relations between the native and migrant populations; economic conditions in the regions and income differentials among respondents; differences in gender, age, and education levels; migration policy; political discourses in the regions; regional differences in media effects – or, for that matter, any other imaginable political, socioeconomic, cultural, and historical differences among the provinces or ethnic groups. Can one explain why estimates of ethnic composition converge when projected into the future by something else about the social context? If so, then the systematic explanation of this perceptual convergence must be sought in such aspects of socialization or political and media discourses or any other factor as exerted a uniform influence on public opinion both in the Soviet and in the post-Soviet period. This author cannot possibly surmise what kind of social factor this can be. It would be wise to seek at least a partial explanation of this phenomenon in the universal attributes of human psychology.

Another place where one would be wise to look for a plausible explanation has to do with the fact that respondents in the survey were asked not simply to assess trends of ethnic composition, but specifically about ethnic groups *from among migrants*. Therefore, one would expect respondents' assessments to embody, among other things, the perceptual logic of migration as a social process. The survey results indicate that precisely this logic is the likely explanation of the remarkable similarity of views about the future ethnic composition of Russia's provinces. And this aspect of the puzzle deserves further investigation.

Estimated scale of migration scale: interethnic versus interregional differentials

Descriptive results of the survey suggest certain ideas about the role of interethnic versus interregional differences in the formation of perceived migration scale. At the very least, these results show that when respondents evaluated the scale of migration for 2005 (at the time of the survey) – on the basis of which they later made projections into the future that turned out to be so remarkably uniform – the psychology of numerical estimates was not the only plausible and significant factor. Table 9.2 provides the relevant evidence. It is set up as a quasi-experimental test juxtaposing the variation of the actual and estimated sizes of different ethnic groups in the same provinces versus those of the same ethnic groups in different provinces. The averaged minimum and maximum values were computed using the data in Table 9.1 for region–group dyads.

The far right column shows that the dispersal of the actual (census-based) size of different ethnic groups in the same provinces was 7.5 times higher than the dispersal of the actual size of the same ethnic groups across different provinces (that is, the difference between the average minimum and maximum values for the former is 4 and for the latter it is 30). But this difference disappears when we compare the same average values for ethnic group size as they were estimated by respondents. The average maximum estimates exceed the average minimum estimates twofold regardless of whether they pertain to different ethnic groups in the same province or to the same ethnic group across different provinces. In sum, individual valuations practically wipe out actual regional differences in ethnic composition. This suggests that interregional differences are not as robust as interethnic differences when respondents estimate migration scale.[10] The principal paradox, however, is that significant variation in actual ethnic composition across provinces was reduced to approximately the same uniform level in the minds of individual respondents.

Additional correlation–regression analysis of the data in Table 9.1 revealed no statistically significant associations between the size (and proportions) of ethnic groups in the census and the size of the same ethnic groups in the same provinces as it was perceived, on average, by survey respondents. At first

Table 9.2 Variance of the mean estimates of migration scale by the respondents of the 2005 Russian Federation migration and ethnic attitudes survey (as a percentage of each province's population) compared with the 2002 census data for ten non-Slavic migrant groups in seven provinces of the Russian Federation

Respondents' estimates, 2005	*Census data, 2002*					
	Min.	*Max.*	*Max./Min.*	*Min.*	*Max.*	*Max./Min.*
Same regions, different ethnic groups	5	11	**2**	0.14	0.56	**4**
Same ethnic groups, different regions	7	12	**2**	0.06	1.89	**30**

glance, Pearson correlation coefficients formally show a statistically significant relationship between actual and perceived ethnic composition across survey regions ($R = 0.581$, $p < 0.001$). However, the analysis of scatter plots for the same data showed that this was due to the strong correlation between just two pairs of outliers (the census and survey estimates of the proportion of Armenians in Krasnodar and the Kazakhs in Orenburg). After the data for these outliers had been excluded, the correlation coefficient was no longer statistically significant (that is, the probability that any correspondence between the actual and the perceived ethnic composition was due to chance alone was more than 5 percent). Figure 9.1 illustrates this relationship well.

II Individual-level data

No matter how scrupulously one analyzes the data aggregated by province, it is important to keep in mind that relationships between estimates aggregated by region do not necessarily reflect relationships between individual estimates. Besides, the number of cases in Table 9.1 ($N = 32$) above is small by statistical standards, even though it is sufficient to enable preliminary analyses to be run. In consideration of these limitations, I explored the same questions using the

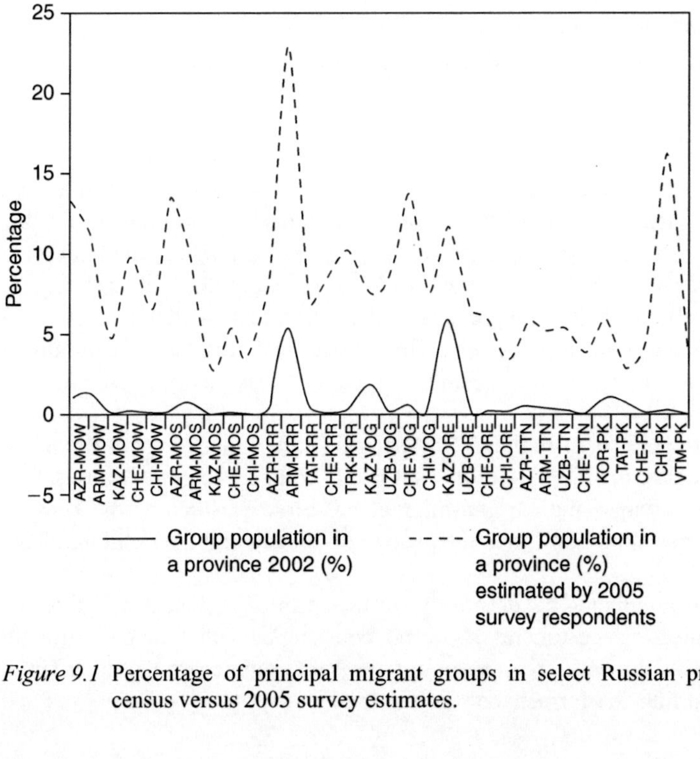

Figure 9.1 Percentage of principal migrant groups in select Russian provinces: 2002 census versus 2005 survey estimates.

complete dataset of the 2005 immigration and ethnic attitudes survey. This gives us hundreds of cases with which to test the associations between our principal quantities of interest.[11] For this purpose, I also computed new variables and entered them in the survey database: (1) the percentage of each of the five ethnic (migrant) groups (Chechens, Armenians, Azerbaijanis, Chinese, and Uzbeks) in each province based on the 2002 census data; (2) the "estimated level" of the census data, computed as a respondent's estimate of the percentage of each of these ethnic groups in a province divided by the percentage of the same group for that province in the 2002 census. I further refer to the second variable as the "exaggeration rate" of the census data, because its value was above 1.0 for the overwhelming majority of the survey respondents (for 93.3 percent of respondents for Chechens, 94 percent for Armenians, 97.3 percent for Azerbaijanis, 84 percent for Chinese, and 80.6 percent for Kazakhs). The means for this variable calculated for each ethnic group also indicate unequivocally that the size of the five major migrant groups was systematically exaggerated by survey respondents. For Chechens the exaggeration rate was 111 (with a standard deviation of 155), for Armenians it was 16 (23), for Azerbaijanis it was 30 (33), for Chinese it was 647 (1,729), and for Kazakhs it was 26 (55). Whether averaged across the thirty-two region–group dyads or across hundreds of individual responses in the survey, the results show that exaggeration rates are the highest for the Chechens and the Chinese. These are the two ethnic groups from among migrants who are most of all associated with national security challenges and threats to Russia. The Chechens are predominantly associated with the threat of terrorism, the Chinese with the threat of terrorism and also territorial claims on, and illegal settlement of, territories that respondents feel are historically Russian.

Analysis of variance

One of the problems in comparing the statistical results of the survey data from separate regional samples is how to estimate whether any differences are due predominantly to interregional differences (regional clustering) regardless of individual views or to interpersonal differences regardless of the region. Methodologically, this challenge replicates the conceptual challenge of the principal research question in this study. This challenge is resolved, in important ways, by using a statistical procedure called one-way analysis of variance (one-way ANOVA).[12]

To assess the effects of regional clustering I set up a quasi-experimental test with two variables: (1) migration size estimate ("exaggeration rate") for each of the five ethnic groups; and (2) anti-migrant hostility measured as the level of support for deportation of all migrants, legal and illegal, and their children from Russia.

Partly corresponding to the descriptive results, Table 9.3 indicates that, on the whole, migration size estimates show no consistency either across different ethnic groups in the same regions or for the same ethnic groups in different regions. Regarding the former, only in one pair of provinces – Volgograd and

Table 9.3 Differences across provinces of the estimated migration scale for selected ethnic groups based on one-way ANOVA of the 2005 Russian Federation migration and ethnic attitudes survey

Survey province	*N respondents*	*Mean values of migration size estimates (homogeneous subsets[a] in each column)*			
			Chechens		
Volgograd Oblast’	474	30.4			
Orenburg Oblast’	429	65.0	65.0		
Moscow City	328		70.3		
Krasnodar Krai/Adygea	372			140.4	
Primorskii Krai	484			143.8	
Moscow Oblast’	231			177.2	177.2
Tatarstan Republic	412				192.2
Significance of relationship within subsets		0.105	1	0.063	0.92
	Uses harmonic mean sample size = 369				
			Armenians		
Krasnodar Krai/Adygea	468	4.3			
Moscow City	338		9.2		
Moscow Oblast’	265			17.5	
Tatarstan Republic	444				32.2
	Uses harmonic mean sample size = 360				
			Azerbaijanis		
Moscow City	341	14.4			
Tatarstan Republic	445		21.5		
Krasnodar Krai/Adygea	363			35.6	
Moscow Oblast’	277				60.3
	Uses harmonic mean sample size = 347				
			Chinese		
Moscow City	332	53.1			
Primorskii Krai	623	87.4			
Volgograd Oblast’	414		827.3		
Moscow Oblast’	212			1262.6	
Orenburg Oblast’	383				1713.8
Significance of relationship within subsets		0.999	1	1	1
	Uses harmonic mean sample size = 349				
			Kazakhs		
Volgograd Oblast	469	2.0			
Orenburg Oblast	454	5.8			
Moscow City	316		59.1		
Moscow Oblast	224			69.4	
Significance of relationship with subsets		0.78	1	1	
	Uses harmonic mean sample size = 334				

Note

a Based on $\alpha < 0.05$.

Orenburg Oblast' – did the average estimated sizes of different migrant groups form a homogeneous subset including more than one group (the Chechens and the Kazakhs). Other homogeneous subsets (Moscow City–Orenburg Oblast, Krasnodar Krai–Primorskii Krai–Moscow Oblast', Moscow Oblast'–Tatarstan, and Moscow City–Primorskii Krai) covered the estimated size of one and the same ethnic group.

On the whole, estimates of each ethnic group size also fail to cluster systematically across provinces. This is clearly evident by examining Table 9.3, in which the provinces listed on the left are ranked by the estimated size of each ethnic group in ascending order (that is, the more the size of any given group is exaggerated in a province, the lower that province is on the list). The estimated migration size is grouped in columns. Each cluster of numbers in a column is a homogeneous subset – meaning that differences between values within each column are statistically less significant than differences between the values across columns. This is done for each ethnic group and the table is subdivided into corresponding sections.

When the rankings of regions across these sections are compared, we find only a partial pattern of estimated migration scale, and only in two provinces. Regardless of the ethnicity of migrants, the highest exaggeration rates are observed in Moscow Oblast' and the lowest (although less clearly) in Moscow City.

Whereas there are no consistent differences for all regions, this unanticipated contrast between Moscow Oblast' and Moscow City is again consistent with the logic of the "defended neighborhood" theory. Moscow City is the strongest migration magnet in Russia. However, in Moscow City the rapid initial influx of migrants happened in the early and mid-1990s, and the city has been learning to live with it for more than a decade. The "defended neighborhood" theory posits that as the percentage of migrants in the population increases after the initial shocks, the host society will start working out adaptive measures. Cohabitation and cooperative habits are likely to emerge and gradually dampen social tensions and anti-migrant hostility.

At the same time, with respect to sources of migration, Moscow Oblast' may be considered a border province. It borders the City of Moscow – the area with the largest concentration of migrants in the Russian Federation. Moreover, unlike the provinces located along Russia's external borders, Moscow Oblast' cannot count on border guards, armed forces, police, or other agencies that the state employs to protect its interstate borders. A resident of Moscow Oblast', therefore, would have even more grounds to be concerned about migration than a resident of a border region. To such a resident, the border with the migrant-sending area would appear not only more porous but also less plausibly defensible. Concerns would most likely be exacerbated by lack of hope.

But even that explanation cannot be regarded as conclusive, as evidenced by Table 9.4. While the average estimates of migration size in Moscow City and Moscow Oblast' differ, respondents in both samples showed approximately the same level of support for radical anti-immigrant policies, such as the deportation of all migrants, legal and illegal, and their children. In other words, this statistical test established no direct correspondence between perceived scale of migration and anti-migrant hostility. As shown in Table 9.4, the provinces where the survey was held fall into two homogeneous subsets. The first subset includes provinces with relatively lower levels of hostility – Orenburg Oblast', Tatarstan, and Volgograd Oblast'. In these provinces the average level of support for wholesale deportation of migrants ranged from 2.6 to 2.8 on a scale of 1 (completely disagree) to 5 (completely agree).[13] The second subset (based on the differences between significance levels for subsets in the third and the first columns in the table) includes Primorskii Krai, Krasnodar/Adygea, Moscow City, and Moscow Oblast'.

Conclusion: some non-trivial, counterintuitive findings

Although, as one would have expected, most respondents across Russia exaggerated the scale of migration, and by a lot, the nature and the patterns of exaggeration based on the ethnicity of migrants and on the host province offer some good paradoxes.

On the one hand, residence in any given province, the ethnicity of migrants, or the actual (census-based) patterns of ethnic composition do not systematically explain variation in the perceived migration for various ethnic groups across the survey provinces. More than that, it is hard to imagine how any combination of the above factors might explain these patterns.

On the other hand, one discerns a systematic pattern that is not predicated on these factors – at least directly: (1) the perceived migration scale was systematically higher in all survey provinces for two ethnic groups, the Chechens and the Chinese; (2) respondents were in general more uncertain about the scale of migration of Asians (Chinese, Kazakhs, and Uzbeks) than of the Caucasus

Table 9.4 Differences across provinces concerning support for the wholesale deportation of migrants from Russia based on one-way ANOVA of the 2005 Russian Federation migration and ethnic attitudes survey

Survey province	*N respondents*	*Mean values of migration size estimates (homogeneous subsets[a] in each column)*			
Orenburg Oblast'	613	2.6			
Tatarstan Republic	596	2.6	2.6		
Volgograd Oblast'	609		2.8	2.8	
Primorskii Krai	627			3.0	3.0
Moscow Oblast'	355			3.0	3.0
Krasnodar Krai/Adygea	587				3.0
Moscow City	376				3.2
Significance of relationship within subsets		1.00	0.23	0.06	0.09
	Uses harmonic mean sample size = 510				

Note
a Based on $\alpha < 0.05$.

ethnics (Chechens, Armenians, and Azerbaijanis); (c) the perceived percentage of all migrant groups across all survey provinces was expected to increase over ten years at approximately the same rate (by 1.5 to 1.8 times); and (d) the scale of migration was consistently more exaggerated for most ethnic groups in Moscow Oblast' than in Moscow City – even though the actual scale of migration between population censuses was higher in the latter.

All these partial and somewhat counterintuitive patterns, however, are consistent with two explanations. The first is what may be termed the "psychology of numbers" or the "numbers game." The second is the "defended neighborhood"/ security dilemma logic that highlights the proclivity for preventive self-defense in the face of threats – particularly new threats and in the context of uncertainty about the state's capacity to deal with the emergent challenges. And it is plausible that at the level of the Russian provinces the "defended neighborhood" logic plays out as the "defended nationhood" logic, as national security concerns are perceived through the prism of provincial issues. In the division of labor between the two, the "numbers game" logic explains why the relationship between the actual and the perceived scale of migration is curvilinear. This is because the respondents tended to round off their estimates of the percentage of migrants in the local population to the closest prominent number (1, 3, 5, 10, and so on), whereas the actual proportion of migrants was, as a rule, less than 1 percent. This suggests that "newness" is an important factor when individuals attempt to quantify the scale of migration of any ethnic group. Exaggeration of the scale is more likely to be higher with respect to newer groups. The same logic would explain why the perceived exaggeration rates decline over time for any group. It would also explain the uniformity with which respondents in all provinces assessed the ten-year migration trends for all ethnic groups.

These systematic patterns indicate that at some level the impact of migration on ethnic composition of states and provinces within states does have a systematic impact on anti-migrant and interethnic hostility. They also call for a more sophisticated analysis in the future of how ethnic groups become linked to national security concerns and why such concerns may be higher in some subnational units than in others. And when these issues – in a broader context of research on the relationship between identity and security – are studied, it is also important to control for the discrete "number game" logic, or the psychology of numbers.

Notes

1 D. L. Horowitz, *Ethnic Groups in Conflict*, Berkeley: University of California Press, 1985; M. A. Alexseev, *Immigration Phobia and the Security Dilemma: Russia, Europe, and the United States*, Cambridge: Cambridge University Press, 2006; M. S. Teitelbaum and J. Winter, *A Question of Numbers: High Migration, Low Fertility, and the Politics of National Identity*, New York: Hill & Wang, 1998; R. Koopmans and P. Statham (eds.), *Challenging Immigration and Ethnic Relations Politics: Comparative European Perspectives*, New York: Oxford University Press, 2000; C. Codagnone, "New

Migration and Migration Politics in Post-Soviet Russia," Ethnobarometer Programme Working Paper 2, 1998, CSS/CEMES.

2 For a detailed review, see J. E. Oliver and J. Wong, "Intergroup Prejudice in Multiethnic Settings," *American Journal of Political Science*, 47, 4, 2003, 567–582 at pp. 567–568. Also cf. D. L. Palmer, "Canadian Attitudes and Perceptions Regarding Immigration: Relations with Regional Per Capita Immigration and Other Contextual Factors," *Executive Summary, Strategic Research and Review, Citizenship and Immigration Canada* (August 1999), http://www.cic.gc.ca; L. Quillian, "Prejudice as a Response to Perceived Group Threat: Population Composition and Anti-immigrant and Racial Prejudice in Europe," *American Sociological Review*, 60, 1995, 590; J. Citrin, D. P. Green, C. Muste, and C. Wong, "Public Opinion toward Immigration Reform: The Role of Economic Motivations," *Journal of Politics*, 59, 3, 1997, 858–881.

3 C. Jean Kim, "The Racial Triangulation of Asian Americans," *Politics and Society*, 27, 1, 1999, 105–158; S. Oboler, *Ethnic Labels, Latino Lives*, Minneapolis: University of Minnesota Press, 1995; F. L. Jones, "Diversities of National Identity in a Multicultural Society: The Australian Case," *National Identities*, 2, 2, 2000, 175–186.

4 This study was made possible by a grant for research and writing by the Program on Global Security and Sustainability of the John D. and Catherine T. MacArthur Foundation and a research grant by the National Science Foundation (SES-0452557). All the findings and conclusions are those of the author, and they do not necessarily represent any views of the MacArthur Foundation or the National Science Foundation. The survey was carried out throughout the Russian Federation in the fall of 2005 by the Levada Analytical Center (formerly the All-Russian Center for the Study of Public Opinion) and, in Primorskii Krai, by the Public Opinion Research Laboratory of the Institute of History, Archaeology, and Ethnography of the Peoples of the Far East (IHAE) at the Far Eastern Branch of the Russian Academy of Sciences. The total number of respondents in the Levada Center survey was 4,080, drawn from a multi-stage probability sample of the adult population of the Russian Federation ($N = 680$), Moscow City ($N = 400$), Moscow Oblast' ($N = 400$), Krasnodar Krai (including the Republic of Adygea) ($N = 650$), Volgograd Oblast' ($N = 650$), Orenburg Oblast' ($N = 650$), and the Republic of Tatarstan ($N = 650$). The IHAE survey used a stratified regional probability sampling procedure to select 660 respondents, including a multi-stage stratified random selection of 402 respondents who participated in the author's 2000 Primorskii Krai survey, also conducted by the IHAE (M. Alexseev and C. R. Hofstetter, "Russia, China, and the Immigration Security Dilemma," *Political Science Quarterly*, 121, 2006, 1–32).

5 Notably, Y. Herrera, *Imagined Economies*, New York: Cambridge University Press, 2005, and Herrera's personal communications with this author.

6 Specified as Russians from the "near abroad" (former Soviet republics).

7 If the respondent specifid a fraction of the population (e.g. "one-third"), the interviewers converted it into percentage points.

8 Data used in this study do not include areas of the Russian Federation where distortions of ethnic composition may have been widespread and systematic and could have produced significant deviations from the actual numbers (which is most likely in Chechnya, Ingushetia, Dagestan, and Bashkortostan) exceeding the scale of average systemic errors or distortions in the Russian census.

9 D. P. Green, D. Z. Strolovitch, and J. S. Wong, "Defended Neighborhoods, Integration, and Racially Motivated Crime," *American Journal of Sociology*, 104, 2, 1998, 372–403; J. Rieder, *Canarsie: The Jews and Italians of Brooklyn against Liberalism*, Cambridge, MA: Harvard University Press, 1985; G. D. Suttles, *The Social Construction of Communities*, Chicago: University of Chicago Press, 1972.

10 This does not necessarily mean that the regional context is not as important as the ethnicity of migrants. But such a conclusion is consistent with the results in Table 9.2.

11 Formally, a case is one response (coded as a number) to one of the survey questions by one respondent. For questions allowing several response options, a response to each option is considered a case.

12 Since the number of respondents varied across province samples for different survey questions, I used the Scheffe method to control for the variation in the number of cases. This is achieved by estimating an average number of respondents across survey items in each sample and across samples (harmonic mean sample size).

13 In other words, even in the most "tolerant" provinces the public was on average more inclined to support the wholesale deportation of migrants.

Part IV

Construction of an official patriotism

In search of a new ideology?

10 From Belgrade to Kiev

Hard-line nationalism and Russia's foreign policy

Andrei P. Tsygankov

Throughout the post-Soviet era a number of scholars and politicians predicted the rise of hard-line nationalism in Russia, which would then be reflected in radical changes in the country's domestic and foreign policies. Despite multiple political crises in Russia, those predictions are yet to come true. Changes in leadership have not led to a fundamental revision of Russia's national identity and interests, and various hard-line opposition groups – from Gennadi Ziuganov's Communist Party to Dmitri Rogozin's Rodina – have remained marginalized in the national discourse.

This chapter concentrates on attempts by hard-line nationalist (HLN) opposition to influence Russia's foreign policy, and it asks why HLN has failed to change the official course. The HLNs, or those who advocated restoration of an empire and international alliances against Western nations, have been active participants in foreign policy discussions and indeed have been successful in introducing and circulating a number of concepts, such as "geopolitics," "Eurasia," and "Atlanticism," within elite circles. Yet the practical impact of the hard-liners has been rather modest. This could be explained by the combined effect of three forces that have undermined the appeal of the HLNs: Russia's leadership, the general public, and policies of Western governments. The former two have found the hard-line initiatives to be financially costly and politically confrontational, and the latter remained engaged with Moscow, thereby restraining aggressive nationalist reaction inside Russia.

The chapter selects three foreign policy crises – Yugoslavia/Kosovo in 1999, 11 September 2001, and the Orange Revolution in Ukraine in 2004 – to investigate the manifestation and causes of the HLN's failure to challenge the official foreign policy course. These cases are sufficiently diverse, and range from Russia's material strength, to the interests of the ruling coalition in power, to the nature of the interaction between Russia and the West. Obviously, three cases are not sufficient to allow wide-ranging causal generalizations to be formulated, but they are suggestive as to the proposed explanation and further investigation of the issue. The chapter first sets out a theoretical framework for understanding relationships between the HLN and foreign policy in Russia. It then explores the three selected cases in greater detail and concludes by summarizing the argument and some of its implications.

HLN and foreign policy making in Russia

National identity, coalition building, and foreign policy

What is the mechanism through which nations develop their foreign policies? The key variable this chapter emphasizes is national interpretation of the world challenges and its formulation into a dominant ideology. Adopted by the state, such ideology eventually becomes specified as a concept of the national interest and guides policymakers in their practical decisions. Before it happens, however, a society goes through a process of having various contesting ideologies. At this stage, various ideologies compete to achieve hegemonic status or the ability to shape public discourse. These ideologies hold different images regarding the nation's identity, the nature of the external world, and appropriate policy responses. Promoted by various politico-economic coalitions in both public and private spaces, ideological contestation is especially intense until one of the available ideologies becomes predominant. Activities of political entrepreneurs, appropriate material and ideational resources, institutional arrangements, and historical practices can considerably facilitate this process of persuading the general public and elites. When this persuasion part of the process is complete, the state appropriates the dominant national ideology as a guide to policy making.[1] Although many other factors and influences may interfere with the decision-making process, other things being equal one can expect a reasonable degree of policy consistency based on an adopted image of national identity.

The Soviet collapse of 1991 presented Russia's new liberal leadership with an opportunity to fashion a pro-Western foreign policy course. President Boris Yeltsin and his foreign minister Andrei Kozyrev pursued policies of strategic partnership and integration with the West and its institutions. Externally, they were inspired by the Western promises of support, and they expected to "join" the West within a few years. They saw the West's victory in the Cold War as the promise and the opportunity of the new liberal era. Domestically, the Westernizing coalition included – in addition to a liberal-minded leadership – intellectuals, human rights activists, and new pro-capitalist elites, particularly those with export interests in the West. The new identity coalition pursued a revolutionary agenda of transforming the old Soviet institutions into those of a pro-Western nation-state. It seemed as if a new liberal identity was finally to be established in Russia.

Yet the new post-Soviet identity became deeply contested, and the liberal momentum did not last. Soon the pro-Western policies met with formidable opposition and were replaced with the promotion of state identity and interests. The new statists acknowledged the necessity of building a market economy and democratic institutions, but saw these as subject to the main objective of strengthening the state. The new statist coalition included military industrialists, the army, and the security services – those who only saw marginal benefits in adopting the "Western" model. Led by presidential advisor Sergei Stankevich and then the chief of foreign intelligence, Yevgeni Primakov, the new statists insisted that the national interest had not changed to any major extent and still had to do with defending Russia's great power status. Over time, this reasoning proved able to win the support of both elites and the masses, and the state had to adopt the statist concept of national identity. Appointed foreign minister, Primakov argued for more restrained relations with the West and for a more "balanced" and "diverse" foreign policy. Primakov believed that Russia's new liberal values did not do away with the need to maintain the status of a distinct Eurasianist great power, and he proposed that Russia develop a strategic alliance with China and India.

The arrival of Vladimir Putin as the new president signaled yet another change in policies and a renewed interest in engaging with the West. Although Putin insisted that Russia's priority was to preserve great power status, his strategy for achieving this objective differed considerably from that of Primakov. Instead of continuing the policy of balancing against the West, Putin explicitly sided with Europe and the United States and insisted that Russia was a country of European and Western, rather than Asian, identity.

Therefore, Westernizers lost their battle, but not to ideologies of the hard-line orientation. The HLN advocated a full-fledged imperial restoration and Soviet-like security alliances (see later for elaboration of this point); instead, relatively moderate statists came to dominate in the national discourse and shape the country's international policies. The statists were able to defeat alternative ideologies because of the historic power of the statist identity and several domestic and external developments that played out in such a way as to strengthen the new discourse. Domestically, the statists benefited politically from the failure of Westernist radical economic reform. Externally, newly emerging instabilities and conflicts in the former Soviet republics and inside the country (Chechnya) in the early to mid-1990s made it extremely difficult for Westernizers to sustain their policies of disengagement from the periphery. Importantly, the West – Russia's significant Other – greatly strengthened the statist discourse by making a decision to expand NATO eastward and excluding Russia from the process. This strengthened the sense that Russia was not being accepted by the West as one of its own, and Westernizers lost public support in their bid to reduce the power of the statists.

On the other hand, the HLN ideas did not come across as particularly attractive to the elites or larger society. The mainstream political class typically viewed these ideas as too dangerous and extravagant to be implemented. Society, too, had little faith in the imperialist policies. HLNs therefore remained relatively marginalized in the Russian discourse.

HLN and its foreign policy beliefs

A broad group that united communists and supporters of a more ethnically homogeneous Russia, or the so-called alliance of "Red" and "White" nationalists, the HLNs differed from both Westernizers and statists in their core beliefs. In particular, the HLN groups consistently advocated restoration of a West-independent empire achieved through the forming of international alliances against Western nations. Neither Westernizers nor statists were committed to a similar zero-sum vision. The former supported integration into Western politico-economic institutions, and the latter were planning limited cooperation with Western nations for the sake of rebuilding Russia's economy and material capabilities.

The end of the USSR did not change the HLNs, who still refused to part with the core principles of the Soviet society. One group, the national communists, merged some old communist ideas with those of nationalism and was particularly influenced by Joseph Stalin's doctrine of "socialism in one country," which acknowledged the need for Russia to focus on developing military and economic capabilities within the Soviet boundaries. The most active promoter of this group's ideas was Gennadi Ziuganov, leader of the Communist Party of the Russian Federation.[2] Another HLN group referred to itself as Eurasianist and viewed the world in terms of a geopolitical struggle between land-based and sea-based powers. Unlike the national communists, who portrayed themselves as adherents to conservative beliefs such as religion and social stability, the Eurasianists argued that conservatism was not enough and advocated the notion of a "conservative revolution" and geopolitical expansion.[3] While the national communists had no ambitions beyond restoring the Soviet Union, the Eurasianists wanted to build a larger geopolitical axis of allies – such as Germany, Iran, and Japan – in order to resist American influences. They attracted some support from hard-line military and nationalist political movements such as Vladimir Zhirinovsky's Liberal Democratic Party. Other, less influential hard-line groups insisted on Russia's imperial restoration based on principles of Orthodoxy and Slavic unity.[4]

The HLN groups attacked the official course of foreign policy as serving the interests of the West at the expense of Russia. To them, Russia's national interest was, almost by definition, anti-Western. They had no regard for a market economy or political democracy and viewed Russia's institutions as diametrically opposed to those of the West. The West's liberalism, they argued, was nothing more than US-based unipolarity in the making. Russia's adequate response should include rebuilding its military capabilities, reforming the economy in the Chinese gradual state-oriented fashion, and preserving control over Eurasia or the post-Soviet world. In the words of the conservative periodical *Molodaia gvardiia*, "The historical task before Russia and other nations of the world is not to allow the twenty-first century to become the American century."[5]

Table 10.1 Foreign policy images of Russia's elites

	Westernizers	*Statists*	*Hard-line nationalists*
Foreign policy objectives	Integration with the West	Sovereignty; great power status	Empire; cultural independence
Foreign policy methods	Alliances with the West	Flexible alliances	Alliances against the West

When the statists defeated the Westernizers, the HLN groups welcomed the new course and the second foreign minister Yevgeni Primakov's concept of a multipolar world. Yet they challenged Primakov to go further in resisting Western influences and to adopt a more radical notion of multipolarity. The new minister planned to pursue a moderate course and consolidate Russia's position by cooperating with the West where possible, and by avoiding confrontation where such cooperation was not an option. Aware of the scarcity of available resources, he saw a multipolar world as a desirable objective, rather than a fact of life. To the HLNs, on the other hand, the notion of great power status implied restoration of the Soviet Union, and multipolarity meant isolation from and competition with the West.[6] To them, Russia was a unique civilization that must be isolated from the West in order for it to survive and preserve its uniqueness. For example, Ziuganov never reconciled himself to the dissolution of the Soviet empire, insisting that the Soviet Union was a "natural" geopolitical form of "historic" Russia, whereas the current political boundaries of the country are "artificial" and imposed by the West through covert actions. To "return" to world politics and build a genuinely multipolar world, Russia must achieve politico-economic autarky (*samodostatochnost'*) and enter a strategic alliance with China.[7] What statists saw as Russia's special geographical and ethnic features, the HLNs developed into the principal line of cultural confrontation with the West.

Failures of the HLN: three illustrations

Throughout the post-Soviet era the HLN groups sought to challenge the existing foreign policy course. This section considers in greater details how nationalist opposition attempted to influence Moscow's handling of three foreign policy crises: Yugoslavia/Kosovo in 1999, the attacks of 11 September 2001 in the United States, and the Orange Revolution in Ukraine in 2004. In each of these cases, hard-liners had their distinct foreign policy preferences, which differed sharply from those of other political groups. In the Kosovo case, nationalists wanted Russia to provide military assistance to Serbia, rather than limit its role to negotiations. In the post-9/11 context their preference was for building a strong alliance with China and the Shanghai Cooperation Organization (SCO; its member states are Russia, China, Kazakhstan, Kyrgyzstan, Tajikistan, and Uzbekistan) at the expense of relationships with the United States. Finally, in the case of the Orange Revolution in Ukraine the HLN groups favored severing all official contacts and supporting separatist trends inside Ukraine, with the idea of making its leadership comply with Russia's demands.

Three factors are helpful in understanding why the HLN groups proved unable to challenge either Westernist or statist official foreign policies. First, the general public was preoccupied with issues of economy and domestic security, and unwilling to support any foreign policy adventures at the expense of domestic reconstruction. Second, and related, the generally pragmatic Russian leadership was well aware of the country's limited resources and need to cooperate with Western nations. Finally, the West itself, despite a number of steps

Table 10.2 Foreign policy expectations of Russia's elites: specific issues

	Westernizers	*Statists*	*Hard-line nationalists*
Yugoslavia intervention	Negotiations on behalf of the West	Negotiations on Russia's terms	Military assistance for Yugoslavia
9/11	Partnership with the West	Pragmatic cooperation with the West	Alliance with China and the Shanghai Cooperation Organization; no cooperation with the United States
Orange Revolution	Support	No support; cooperation by necessity; marketization	No support; no cooperation; economic sanctions; support for separatism

perceived by Russians as containing their influence, generally abstained from hard-line actions toward Russia. Over time, this helped to keep the HLN groups at bay and limited their potential appeal in Russia.

Yugoslavia/Kosovo, 1999

As soon as NATO launched its air strike on Yugoslavia, Kosovo became the central issue of Russian foreign policy. Despite a number of important disagreements between Russia and the West about ways of handling Balkan affairs, the decision to intervene militarily came as a shock to Russia's mainstream foreign policy community. This is illustrated by Prime Minister Yevgeni Primakov's decision to cancel the upcoming negotiations with the United States and the IMF in Washington on 24 March 1999. Although his airplane was already approaching the United States, he ordered it to return home. Russia's official policy toward the resolution of the conflict in Yugoslavia was to insist that the war be stopped as soon as possible and that a settlement with Yugoslavia be reached by political, not military, means. Yeltsin's government was ready to contribute to the peace negotiations by serving as a mediator between NATO and Yugoslavia. It empowered Yevgeni Primakov and, later, Viktor Chernomyrdin to serve as Russia's envoys in the search for a peaceful settlement of the conflict.

The HLN position was strikingly different. In their view, the efforts of the West in Yugoslavia had nothing to do with human rights and a "humanitarian catastrophe" but were merely a rhetorical device for covering up the intention to establish a US-led global dictatorship. Ziuganov argued that NATO's aggression against Yugoslavia was not accidental and that "Serbia down on its knees [had to] signify the final triumph of the Pax Americana, the American model of a unipolar world."[8] He went on to identify four major goals of the West in the Balkans: dismemberment of Yugoslavia into several independent states along ethnic and religious lines; suppression of Serbian attempts to reintegrate

Yugoslavia; establishment of a pro-NATO and pro-American regime in Yugoslavia; and imposition of liberal, pro-American values on the Yugoslav people. The Pax Americana, as portrayed by the HLN groups, has severe consequences for Russia, namely the end of sovereignty as an international institution, and therefore of Russia as a sovereign state. Under such conditions, Russia was presented as having no choice but to get involved on the Serbian side. According to this line of reasoning, Serbia is viewed as a Western pillar of a great Eurasian continent traditionally controlled by Russia. By attacking Serbia, the West had therefore in effect attacked Russia. Russia's involvement, this school acknowledged, might have meant the beginning of World War III, but Russia was not the one to start it; Russia had simply exhausted all other options in its attempt to survive in this increasingly Western-dominated world.[9]

The so-called Munich analogy served as a foundation for arguing the HLN case for Russia's military involvement in the conflict. Various nationalist writers drew a historical parallel with the beginning of World War II in 1939. At that time, it was argued, Western European countries made a deal with Hitler and gave up Czechoslovakia, only to open the way to an invasion of Poland. And when Hitler did invade Poland, the Allies chose to appease him by declining to offer any real assistance to the Polish government, hoping that this would stop the aggressor. The Munich analogy has been brought up in the Western press and by Western politicians as well, implying the need to punish Milošević's hegemonic ambitions.[10] According to Russia's hard-liners, however, NATO's actions equated with those of Hitler, not those of Serbia. In their view, NATO's intervention in Yugoslavia was comparable with Hitler's invasion of Poland, which implied that the "small victorious war on the Balkans" was highly likely to develop into a worldwide war, as did the 1939 attack on Poland. The lesson here, they argue, is that for Russia the only way to stop a world war (and the eventual invasion of Russia itself) would be to demonstrate strength and the readiness to go to war with an aggressor, rather than to appease him.

With such an attitude, it is not surprising that the HLNs came out strongly in favor of establishing a union between Russia and Yugoslavia[11] and against Chernomyrdin's efforts to mediate in the crisis. To them, Chernomyrdin was not merely someone who had been "deceived" by the West; he was a "traitor" who was purposely selling out Russia to the West.[12] Whereas more moderate observers emphasized a need not to demonize or punish members of NATO, but rather to help them to correct the "Yugoslavia mistake,"[13] the hard-liners insisted that NATO should be punished as the "aggressor." They proposed reparations to the "victims of the aggression," indicting NATO as an international criminal, posing the question of outlawing and disbanding NATO at the United Nations, and condemning NATO's ideology of Atlanticism as the serving the purpose of aggression.

None of the HLN demands materialized. In practice, despite repeated failures to negotiate a ceasefire by Primakov and Chernomyrdin, Moscow seemed determined to carry on with its mediation efforts and insisted that staying closely involved, rather than isolating itself from resolution of the conflict, was the most appropriate policy. Russia continued its peace-making efforts even when, in late May, the international court issued an indictment against Milošević and *de facto* refused to negotiate with an "international criminal," thereby delivering what was domestically perceived as a major blow to Chernomyrdin's peace efforts. At the time, the widespread perception in Russia was that the West was getting ready to send ground troops to Yugoslavia. Chernomyrdin issued a warning that Russia might stop its mediating efforts should NATO do so.[14] The allies, however, stopped short of sending troops. The Russian peace efforts continued, and in early June, under pressure from Chernomyrdin, Serbia finally accepted the Kosovo plan. The war was over.

Despite the HLN pressures, Moscow managed the crisis successfully and on its own terms. One reason was that it had the necessary public support for negotiations as the appropriate strategy. The public simply had no stomach for foreign policy adventurism. Despite the 90 percent opposition to NATO's bombing of Belgrade and the overwhelming sense of threat resulting from the alliance's actions,[15] Russia had a firm sense that its domestic priorities of economic and social recovery were too important to ignore. Russia's pragmatic leadership generally reflected those public feelings. Yeltsin had no plans to throw his support on Serbia's side. Using the West's interest in Russia's involvement, he dispatched Primakov to formulate tough conditions for ending the war, which included guarantees that Yugoslavia's sovereignty would be preserved, broad autonomy for Kosovo, and the United Nations assuming leadership in the postwar settlement. The fact that it was the statist-minded Primakov, and not a Westernizer, who was empowered to mediate in the conflict also contributed to ameliorating the HLN-promoted sentiments of national betrayal.

The Western role in Russia's successful management of the conflict and bringing it to an end was hardly a significant one. If anything, the Western intervention in Yugoslavia and unwillingness to accept a number of Russia's negotiating positions made it more difficult for Russia's leadership to resist the HLN pressures. Ultimately, the peace was reached more on Western than Russia's terms. Out of fear of further political escalation in tensions between Russia and the West, Yeltsin dismissed Primakov as the key negotiator and replaced him with the former prime minister Viktor Chernomyrdin, who was much too pro-Western and inexperienced in foreign affairs to negotiate the peace that Primakov had in mind. In early June, under Chernomyrdin's pressure, Serbia finally accepted the conditions for peace, but Russia's initial conditions had not been honored. As one Russian observer described the outcomes of the war, "Russia took part in Yugoslavia's acceptance of the same NATO conditions that it had previously called unacceptable."[16] By the time of Yeltsin's dismissal of Primakov, it was already too late for HLN opposition to do anything about it.

11 September 2001

Immediately after the attacks of 11 September in the United States, President Putin offered the United States broad support for anti-terrorist operations in

Afghanistan. The measures included intelligence sharing, opening Russian airspace to relief missions, taking part in search-and-rescue operations, rallying Central Asian countries to the American cause, and arming anti-Taliban forces inside Afghanistan.[17] At the same time, Putin emphasized the significance of the United Nations in defeating terrorism worldwide, maintaining that he would not commit Russian troops to operations inside Afghanistan because the Russian Constitution proscribed such operations and the United Nations had yet to authorize them.[18] Despite the risks involved,[19] Putin became far more active in promoting Russia's relationships with the United States and Europe, and more passive on the Eastern or Asian orientation. His support for the concept of multipolarity became more muted; instead, the emphasis was on pragmatism and self-concentration in foreign policy.

The HLN groups sought to issue a strong challenge to what they saw as a new pro-American liberal course. Consistently with their critique of Western actions in Yugoslavia, they insisted that the West's role in the world was primarily destructive, and that was why the tragedy of 11 September took place. Even though the United States was attacked, the broader responsibility for the terrorist attacks lay with the West and forces of a transnational economic and military nature, rather than with the Third World.[20] The 9/11 attacks were therefore indicative of nothing less than part of an epic struggle for liberation from the unipolar and unicultural ambitions of the Western civilizations, a world in which Russia had a duty to side overtly with anti-Western and especially anti-American forces. Much like President George W. Bush, the HLNs viewed the post-11 September world in terms of a struggle between "good" and "evil," except that they found themselves on the other side of the barricade. Alexander Panarin summarized the views of the HLN school:

> We are at war. This war cannot disappear and will be repeated tomorrow, because the spiritual situation of the time remains the same. The new language of the West is a language of war.... Therefore, by providing military bases for attacks on Afghanistan, Russia in fact attacked its own cultural identity and its own people, who had no desire to be "democratized" otherwise, without an American intervention.[21]

To win in this struggle, the HLN recommended building a broad coalition of anti-American cultures and civilizations. Among these cultures and civilizations, some saw an alliance between Russia and Muslim countries as having the strongest potential to successfully resist Western modernity and hegemonic policies. Others added to the alliance China and even, potentially, Germany.

The domestic context for the HLN arguments seemed somewhat favorable. The country's most traumatic post-communist experience and the failure of Gorbachev's and the early Yeltsin's attempts to develop a strategic partnership with the West made the Russian political class, military, media, and general public skeptical toward the new efforts at rapprochement. At least three major issues drew public attention. First, many politicians and military officers pointed to the unilateral US decision to develop a national missile defense system and abandon the ABM treaty, which they continued to view as a cornerstone of strategic stability. Second, there was still the issue of NATO's expansion, often perceived as an essentially anti-Russian process. In addition, there was a concern over US and NATO troops' presence in the Central Asian states, which are in immediate geographic proximity to Russia. Because all these issues were in the spotlight of attention, few factions in the Russian Duma initially supported Putin's decision to side with the United States after 9/11. Russia's Muslim leaders reacted critically to the American military campaigns in Afghanistan and Iraq. Of special importance were a series of published "open letters" signed by retired generals, including one of Yeltsin's former defense ministers, accusing Putin of "selling out" the country and "betraying" the nation's vital interests.[22]

The HLN opposition, however, did not succeed in imposing on Putin an essentially anti-Western foreign policy. The president sought to engage Western nations in project of common significance, such as cooperation in energy and counter-terrorism, and to frame Russia's interests as consistent with strategic commitments to Western values, such as international law, personal freedoms, and a market economy. Putin's Russia wanted to be a normal great power – that is, one recognized by the outside world. Despite the existence of important disagreements with Western nations, the new leadership managed to capitalize on increasing world oil prices and to considerably improve relations with the United States and Europe. Russia also worked hard to strengthen its ties in the East and developed a number of ambitious projects with China, India, Iran, and other nations outside the West. However, against the HLN hopes, European and Western priorities remained most powerfully represented in Russia's foreign policy.

The three factors suggested above help us to understand the failure of HLN groups to challenge Russia's post-9/11 course. First, the general public was hardly supportive of issuing an explicit challenge to the West. After the terrorist attacks on the United States, Russians, in fact, felt a strong sympathy toward Americans, partly because Russians too had experienced a number of terrorist attacks. In general, as most polls indicate, the mood was largely against foreign policy grandeur and in favor of Putin's pragmatism and focus on economic modernization.

This leads us to the second crucial factor: Putin's foreign policy vision, which was consistent with the public perception. Putin picked up where Primakov left off and remained focused on the objective of preserving great power status. Yet the new leader abandoned the old strategy for achieving the objective. A multipolar world and post-Soviet integration – key tenets of Primakov's thinking – were replaced with more pragmatic means of asserting Russia's interests in global politics. For Putin, the most important national interest was Russia's modernization and economic growth, not balancing American influences in the world. Such a perspective implied that Russia had to use its resources economically and not overstretch itself in world political affairs. Balancing, therefore, needed to yield to pragmatism. That, too, corresponded with public views, which included support for the preservation of Russia as a strong power. For instance, in November 2001 – immediately after the terrorist attacks on the United States and at a time when Russians felt a strong sympathy toward Americans – only 30 percent agreed with the statement that cooperation with the West was the main condition of Russia's economic prosperity. At the same time, 61 percent supported the idea that it was necessary first to develop the economy and only then to improve ties with the West.[23]

Finally, Putin's popularity and ability to isolate the HLN groups became possible as a result of changes that had taken place on the international arena and the West's growing support for Russia's actions. One critical development had to do with the relative recovery of the Russian economy after the August 1998 financial crisis and new opportunities that the recovery was promising for the country. In addition, it was not only a case of Russians feeling a greater sympathy for Americans because of the terrorist attacks on the United States; America and the West developed a greater appreciation for Russia's struggle with terrorism in Chechnya. The 9/11 attacks created a very different social and political atmosphere inside the country. President George W. Bush proclaimed terrorism to be "pure evil" directed at freedom-loving people throughout the world and argued the necessity of launching a strategy of pre-emption. In Russia these developments provided Putin with a formidable opportunity to bolster his domestic and international posture and to vindicate his conception of foreign policy. Russia's new president wasted no time in taking advantage of 11 September to reshape Russia's relations with the United States and redefine the threats to Russia as deriving from global terrorism.

The Orange Revolution, 2004

In November 2004, under pressure from both the Ukrainian opposition and the West, the results of rigged presidential elections in Ukraine were nullified. In the course of the so-called Orange Revolution, Kremlin's favored candidate, Viktor Yanukovich, was subsequently defeated, and Russia lost his sought-after political influence.

The HLNs believed that Russia had considerable leverage over Ukraine and that, in order for Moscow to rebuild its political and economic dominance in the region, such leverage had to be exercised aggressively. Since the hard-liners perceived Russia to be destined to oppose the West's influences across the globe, they saw few things as off-limits when it came to restoring Russia's power. The HLN groups insisted, in particular, on applying power in a coercive manner against politically "disloyal" states such as Georgia, Ukraine, and Moldova. Applying economic sanctions, supplying arms to secessionist territories, recognizing their claims to independence, granting citizenship to those supporting the idea of reunification with Russia, and cracking down on labor migrants from the ex-republics are some of the tools recommended by the group to the Kremlin for keeping American influences at bay.[24] Some supporters of this view, such as Stanislav Belkovsky, proposed revising the

Russian Constitution and transforming Russia from a "nation-state" into a "nation-civilization."[25]

In line with their policy vision, the HLNs recommended that Putin apply economic sanctions or support separatism in Ukraine after the Orange revolution. After the nullification of Yanukovich's victory in the first presidential election, the eastern regions of Ukraine, particularly Donetsk, Luhansk, and Crimea, vowed to pursue greater autonomy from Kiev, and Russia's nationalist State Duma members and the mayor of Moscow, Yuri Luzhkov, visited eastern Ukraine to express their support for Yanukovich and for regional autonomy. Such autonomy claims could be manipulated to become a factor in Russian–Ukrainian high politics. Soon after the arrival of Yushchenko to power, Russia's hard-line nationalists recommended backing all political movements aimed at decentralization and federalization in Ukraine, pressuring Kiev into making Russian a second state language, and providing greater support to the Ukrainian Orthodox Church, which is canonically subordinate to the Moscow patriarchate.[26]

However, the Kremlin did not follow the advice of the hard-liners in handling the crisis and developing relationships with new Ukrainian leadership. Moscow sought an asymmetrical response. Immediately before the anticipated victory of Viktor Yushchenko, Putin issued a statement welcoming any winner in Ukraine's rerun of its presidential election and asserted that Russia had no objections to Ukraine's joining the European Union. Rather than coercing and applying pressure, the Kremlin planned to co-opt Yushchenko by mobilizing Russia's soft power and the two nations' economic, cultural, and institutional interdependence.[27] At no point has Russia tried to support separatist trends in eastern Ukraine. Sanctions, too, were excluded from the Kremlin's arsenal. The Russia–Ukraine gas dispute can hardly qualify as an example of sanctions on Russia's part. Rather, it was a dispute about correcting a heavily distorted price structure, with Moscow working to reduce the amount of subsidies to the Ukrainian economy and Kiev, understandably, resisting the effort. The results of negotiations satisfied both sides, which also suggests that Russia had no intention of "punishing Orange Ukraine," let alone destroying its economy.

In his further response to the challenge of new democratic revolutions in the former Soviet world, Putin put forward the doctrine of "continuing the civilizational role of the Russian nation in Eurasia."[28] Without ever mentioning the word "Ukraine" in his entire speech, delivered to the Federation Council in March 2005, Putin called for the promotion of freedom in the region: "Russia, traditionally linked with the former Soviet republics, and now newly independent states, by history, the Russian language, and a great culture, cannot stay out of the common striving for freedom."[29] According to the president, what Russia seeks is not the post-Soviet states' territory or natural resources, but human dignity and a high quality of life for its citizens, whom Russia regards as its own cultural compatriots.[30]

What helps to account for Putin's cautious, non-confrontational response as a way of responding to the HLN pressures is a combination of the domestic public attitude, the president's personal convictions, and the West's relatively muted, non-antagonizing behavior after the Orange Revolution. Although the general public in Russia overwhelmingly supported Yanukovich,[31] the thought of breaking economic and cultural ties with Ukraine by applying political pressures was not the dominant mood. Ukraine occupies a very special place in the hearts of many Russians, who continue to believe that brothers will find a common language without resorting to coercion and blackmail.

Putin's pragmatism was particularly important in resolving the crisis. His preferences for a winner in the Ukrainian elections were similar to those of the HLN groups, which helped to defuse their public appeal. Putin supported a candidate whom he perceived as pro-Russian, and he called on Western leaders not to "meddle" in the Ukrainian elections. He attributed the crisis to the West's heavy involvement in the elections and he was eager to continue to protect Russia's interests in Ukraine, having to do with the presence of the Russian fleet in Crimea, conditions for ethnic Russians, and conditions for Russian business. This type of connection with the nationalist public remained an important part of Putin's statist foreign policy.

Yet it was mainly his pragmatic attitude and high public ratings that helped him to ignore the HLN's advice in pushing through his vision for dealing with Ukraine. His support for Yanukovich never amounted to an effort to build a new empire or to incorporate Ukraine into Russia. The Kremlin did not seek to incorporate Ukraine, just as previously it had not sought to incorporate Armenia, Azerbaijan, or Belarus, countries that had held similarly flawed elections. Although the Russian president badly miscalculated Yanukovich's chances of winning, and although he provided strong support for the latter's election,[32] Putin was never willing to sacrifice his relations with the West over the crisis in Ukraine, and he did not let his readiness to stand for Russia's strategic interests to be turned into confrontation. The fact that Western officials abstained from publicly accusing Moscow of "imperialism," let alone taking practical steps to contain Russia, also assisted Putin in preserving his generally cautious approach to Ukraine.

Conclusion

In all three cases the HLN groups failed to change the official course because of a critical role played by Russia's leadership. In the case of NATO's intervention in Yugoslavia, Yeltsin's initial choice of the statist-minded and West-critical Primakov as Russia's official mediator between Belgrade and the West helped to diffuse the appeal of the hard-line opposition. After 9/11 the leadership's role was different, namely to engage the United States in projects of common significance such as fighting terrorism and developing energy cooperation. Here, at least initially, Putin was successful in framing his support for the United States as consistent with Russia's own national priorities. Finally, the statist-minded Putin was cautious and non-confrontational in responding to the defeat of his favored candidate in Ukraine, and he disappointed the HLNs by not severing contacts with Kiev's new leadership and not encouraging separatist trends inside Ukraine. Although Yeltsin's and Putin's visions of national identity differed, both leaders demonstrated sufficient prudence and exercised restraint in their policies.

Two additional factors – public support and the role of the West – played different yet important roles in assisting Russia's leadership in its at times difficult job of restraining the HLNs. While the domestic public was generally behind the leadership's unwillingness to get involved in any policy excesses, much less excesses of an anti-Western nature, the West's role was a more complicated one. In general, Western leaders demonstrated their commitment to engaging, rather than isolating, Russia and attempted to assist Moscow in its difficult transition from the communist system. Yet such engagement has been modest. The majority of the political class in Western nations continued to mistrust Russia well after the Soviet disintegration and showed interest mainly in reducing nuclear threats coming from the region.

This helps us understand why the West never introduced anything remotely similar to the Marshall Plan after World War II, and instead decided to expand NATO to Russia's borders and act as if Moscow was no longer so important to consult on vital issues of world politics. Western nations' decision to intervene in Yugoslavia was especially damaging to the credibility of Russia's leadership at home because it provided HLNs with the ammunition they sought against the "hegemonic" West. During the Orange Revolution, Western nations sought to prevent Russia from meddling in Ukrainian domestic politics, yet their own role in supporting Viktor Yushchenko through State Department statements about the "unacceptability" of the election results, and the involvement of various non-governmental organizations, could hardly be described as one of neutral observation. However, Western leaders abstained from harsh rhetoric toward Russia, and they sought to re-engage Moscow in resolving the crisis in Ukraine. The West's role was most helpful in the post-9/11 context, when the United States began to treat Russia as an important member of an international anti-terrorist coalition.

The last point reinforces the wisdom that the West ought to devise a strategy of more consistent and robust engagement with the Kremlin if its key objective is to deprive the HLN groups of any opportunity to control Russia's policy agenda. The West remains a key reference point for Russia, and any attempts by it to ignore Russia, or perceptions of Moscow's actions as threatening, are likely to lead to a more defiant, not a more cooperative, Russia. Despite the efforts of the pragmatic leadership in Moscow, such attempts could lead Russia off track politically by enhancing the position of authoritarian nationalist forces and providing "proof" that the West really is interested in stripping Russia of its international status, rather than strengthening its currently weak democratic institutions. Against the best intentions, lack of engagement strengthens anti-Western nationalism and pushes Russia further away from the Western nations.

Notes

1 I build here on my previous work. See especially A. Tsygankov, *Russia's Foreign Policy: Change and Continuity in National Identity*, Lanham, MD: Rowman & Littlefield, 2006.
2 See especially G. Ziuganov, *Drama vlasti*, Moscow: Paleya, 1993; same author, *Rossiia i sovremennyi mir*, Moscow: Obozrevatel', 1995; *Geografiia pobedy*, Moscow: unknown publisher, 1998.
3 A. Dugin, *Konservativnaia revoliutsiia*, Moscow: Arktogeia, 1994; same author, *Osnovy geopolitiki*, Moscow: Arktogeia, 1997.
4 For important classifications of Russia's nationalism, see P. J. Duncan, *Russian Messianism: Third Rome, Holy Revolution, Communism and After*, London: Routledge, 2000; A. S. Tuminez, *Russian Nationalism since 1856: Ideology and the Making of Foreign Policy*, Lanham, MD: Rowman & Littlefield, 2000.
5 N. Fon Kreitor, "Stoletiye novogo mira?" *Molodaia gvardiia*, 6, 1998. See also N. Narochnitskaia, "Natsional'nyi interes Rossii," *Mezhdunarodnaia zhizn'*, 3–4, 1992; A. Khatsankov, "Gorchakov – koshmar Kozyreva," *Den'*, 8–14 August 1992; E. Pozdniakov, "Geopoliticheskii kollaps i Rossiia," *Mezhdunarodnaia zhizn'*, 8–9, 1992.
6 For instance, Ministry of Defense officials such as General Leonid Ivashov dreamed for quite some time of restoring Russia's superpower status ("Rossiia mozhet snova stat' sverkhderzhavoi," *Nezavisimaia gazeta*, 7 March 1995).
7 Zyuganov, *Geografiia pobedy*.
8 This section relies heavily on my "Final Trimph of the Pax Americana? Western Intervention in Yugoslavia and Russia's Debate on the Post-Cold War Order," *Communist and Post-communist Studies*, 33, 3, 2001, 135–156.
9 In fact, many national communists and expansionists would argue that the West has already launched such a war, and in this war, new information (rather than military) technologies are being used against Russia in order to demoralize and eliminate it as an independent civilization (see, for example, S. Sultanov, "Tretiaia mirovaia voina," *Zavtra*, February 1996).
10 In the West the Yugoslav president and the Serbs were implicitly identified with Hitler and the Nazi-period Germans.
11 Some communist-minded deputies of the Russian Duma – Gennadi Seleznev, Nikolai Rizhkov, Sergei Baburin, and others – went to Belgrade and signed an agreement with Miloševic supporting the establishment of a common union.
12 In early June, after Chernomyrdin's efforts had resulted in the peace agreement, the communist-minded politicians and State Duma deputies Gennadi Ziuganov, Nikolai Ryzhkov, and Nikolai Kharitonov issued a public statement in which they condemned Chernomyrdin for what they perceived as a unilateral acceptance of NATO's conditions. They also demanded the investigation of Chernomyrdin's "treacherous" activities.
13 Sovet po Vneshnei i Oboronnoi politike, "Statement on Yugoslavia," *Nezavisimaia gazeta*, 12 March 1999.
14 *Nezavisimaia gazeta*, 28 May 1999.
15 O. Antonenko, "Russia, NATO and European Security after Kosovo," *Survival*, 41, 4, 1999/2000, 143.
16 A. Pushkov, "Sindrom Chernomyrdina," *Nezavisimaia gazeta*, 11 June 1999.
17 V. V. Putin, "Zaiavlenie Prezidenta Rossiiskoi Federatsii," 24 September 2001.
18 M. Wines, "Putin Offers Support to U.S. for Its Antiterrorist Efforts," *New York Times*, 25 September 2001.
19 Domestically, only 15 percent of the membership of the Russian Duma supported Putin's move, and it was equally controversial in the army ("Putin Policy Shift Is Bold but Risky," *Financial Times Survey*, 15 April 2002).

20 See, for example, A. Panarin, "Ontologiia terrora," in *Geopolitika terrora*, Moscow: Arktogeia, 2002, p. 46; A. Prokhanov, "Ameriku potseloval angel smerti," *Zavtra*, 18 September 2001; A. Dugin, "Terakty 11 sentiabria: ekonomicheskii smysl," in *Geopolitika terrora*.
21 Panarin, "Ontologiia terrora," pp. 48–49.
22 K. Vanden Heuvel and S. F. Cohen, "Endangering US Security," *Nation*, 15 April 2002.
23 V. A. Kolossov and N. A. Borodullina, "Rossiia i Zapad: mnenie rossiian," *Russia in Global Affairs*, 1, 2003.
24 See, for example, S. Belkovsky, "Posle imperii," *Komsomol'skaia pravda*, 18 May 2004; I. Torbakov, "Moscow Analysts Mull Proper Strategy toward Post-revolutionary Ukraine," *Eurasia Daily Monitor*, 11 February 2005.
25 "Kremlin Said to Be Working on New Constitution," *RFE/RL Newsline*, 9 February 2005.
26 Torbakov, "Moscow Analysts Mull Proper Strategy toward Post-revolutionary Ukraine."
27 Russian–Ukranian interdependence has been well documented. See, for instance, P. J. D'Anieri, *Economic Interdependence in Ukrainian–Russian Relations*, Albany: State University of New York Press, 1999; A. P. Tsygankov, *Pathways after Empire: National Identity and Foreign Economic Policy in the Post-Soviet World*, Lanham, MD: Rowman & Littlefield, 2001; M. A. Molchanov, *Political Culture and National Identity in Russian–Ukrainian Relations*, Austin: Texas University Press, 2002.
28 V. V. Putin, "Address to the Federation Council," March 2005, www.kremlin.ru.
29 Ibid.
30 In this same speech, Putin also called for the granting of Russian citizenship to legal aliens from the former Soviet Union. The newly appointed head of the Kremlin's special department for Interregional and Cultural Relations with Foreign Countries, Modest Kolerov, elaborated on the last point in his interview (see M. Kolerov, "Vse byvshie grazhdane SSSR – nashi sootechestvenniki," *Politicheskii klass*, 10, 2005).
31 Levada-Tsentr, "Ukrainskie sobytiia glazami rossiian," 16 December 2004, www.levada.ru/press/2004121601.html.
32 Europe and the United States, in their turn, did not limit themselves to political statements about the "unacceptability" of the election's results – a step in itself unprecedented in light of their previous much calmer reaction to considerably less fair elections in Central Asia and the Caucasus. Through activities of various NGOs the West also provided considerable financial assistance for Yushchenko's campaign.

11 A religion for the nation or a nation for the religion?

Putin's *third way* for Russia

Beth Admiraal

Vladimir Putin, plucked from the security services by Boris Yeltsin to become Prime Minister Putin in 1999, acting president upon Yeltsin's resignation on 31 December 1999 and duly elected president in March 2000, had little time to market himself. Undoubtedly, Putin felt considerable pressure to prove to Russia that he respected his patron, Yeltsin, but would not be his protégé. Putin went to work. With the Duma emasculated by low party identification, Putin tightened federal control over the regions through changes to the electoral law governing the election of governors and through the institution of supra-regional structures. These changes gave the center – and so Putin – more oversight of regional political processes. With the blessing of the IMF, Putin reformed many economic structures to encourage greater accountability of corporations, businesses, and individuals. This also served to enhance the legitimacy of Russian businesses in the international market. Backed by the judicial system, he confronted members of the oligarchy who appeared to threaten his power. Yeltsin never attempted such brazen challenges to the elite; Putin preferred an elite that would be firmly under his control. And in moves that provoked the ire of the United States and Europe alike, Putin seemingly snickered at the idea of an independent media, preferring to exercise significant control over industry and its output. Although Putin's terms as president ended in 2008, he transitioned – seamlessly, it appears – to the position of Russian prime minister.

Putin's unyielding efforts to centralize power have led many scholars to suggest that he represents a third way in Russia. The labels applied to this third way are plentiful: the popular ones include competitive authoritarianism, managed democracy, illiberal democracy, and electoral democracy.[1] Richard Sakwa, in a 2004 book sketching Putin's presidency, fleshes out the direction and meaning of the third way in Russia, arguing that it is built on a revival of centrism that he dubs "radical centrism."[2] In this version of centrism the autonomy of the state in the socioeconomic and bureaucratic arenas trumps other concerns. This autonomy gives the state sufficient opportunity to maneuver the difficult task of bringing order that is based on legitimate authority and not authoritarian stability, while keeping democratic tendencies toward chaos in check. Sakwa finds Russian journalist Victor Sheinis's portrayal of this centrism in Russia to be instructive: The basis of Putin's middle way is opportunistic merging of neo-conservative economics with statist politics from the left.[3] Ultimately, the state seeks to manipulate democracy to achieve its desired ends.

Yet coming from the same mold of a Soviet-born, Russian-inspired, democratically versed politician and eager to rally Yeltsin's few remaining benefactors, Putin had a strong incentive to suggest that there is continuity between Yeltsin's administration and his own. This became apparent early on in matters of religious freedom and Church–state relations, where Putin adopted his predecessor's rhetoric and agenda. According to most accounts, Putin has essentially aligned himself with Yeltsin's program for administering religious organizations and for interpreting religious freedom: the national church of Russia, the Russian Orthodox Church (ROC), dominates the scene; yet homage is still paid to religious freedom. On the basis of a number of interviews with the foremost observers and promoters of religious freedom, Edwin Bacon notes: "To many who follow religion and politics in Russia, the policy adopted by Vladimir Putin ... is not markedly different from that adopted by Boris Yeltsin from the summer of 1997 onwards."[4] At first blush, this is an uncontroversial statement. Putin, like Yeltsin, is congenial with the hierarchy of the ROC, especially during high-profile photo sessions. Putin, like Yeltsin, invokes and promotes the basic principles of the 1997 Law on Freedom of Conscience and Religious Associations; looking the other way when court rulings undermine or eliminate the activity of foreign religious organizations.

If there is continuity to be found from Yeltsin's religious agenda to Putin's religious agenda, more backpedaling might be necessary to understand where the Russian government stands today on religious matters. Did Yeltsin and Putin inherit anything from the communist regimes that preceded them? Zoe Knox, author of *Russian Society and the Orthodox Church*, noted in a 2006 lecture series *Christianity and Colonialism* that there are remarkable similarities between the religious policy of the Soviet Union and the religious policy that began under Yeltsin and continues through today. She points to three essential areas of continuity: a Soviet and post-Soviet habit of passing legislation that offers religious freedom while in practice clamping down on that freedom; privileging of the Russian Orthodox Church prior to and subsequent to 1991; and continued discrimination against unfavored faiths.[5] The Russian nation has always incorporated the Russian Orthodox faith at its epicenter; Russian politicians (and Soviet politicians before them) have always sought to capture the nation for their political programs. The Russian state and the ROC have jousted for centuries in a battle over which side should lead the nation. The state, with its swords made of metal, has generally had an edge over the Church, with its swords made of prayers. Nevertheless, neither can agree on what would constitute a win and so, still today, the state and the Church continue to play the game. This does suggest a great deal of continuity between Putin, Yeltsin, and the preceding Soviet regime.

Yet I will argue in this chapter that to speak only of continuity does not capture the underlying mood of Putin's religious program. The *third way* forged by Putin – opportunistic manipulation of democracy – may also have some relevance when one looks at his religious policy during his two terms in office as president. Bacon hints at a break in continuity when he points to the "securitization" of religious policy under Putin. The securitization of policy is a conceptual framework for understanding Putin's efforts to move normal politics into the realm of security. As Bacon states, "The Putin regime seeks first of all a manageable state," a trend that Yeltsin began late in his career but is moving at a greater pace under Putin,[6] and this is achieved by identifying an existential threat that in turn justifies policy changes outside the formal political processes.[7] When the state is threatened, who will scruple to abide by standard procedure? During the early years of Putin's tenure, Bacon comments, two policy shifts marked the continued securitization of religion: the Constitutional Court's decision concerning the Salvation Army, and the Law on Extremism, which amended Article 14 of the 1997 law on religion. The first shift effectively solidified the current balance of religious groups and the second extended the list of violations for which a religious group could be prosecuted, giving the state the potential for more control over the structure of religious groups. To this list one might add Putin's first foreign policy foray, the National Security Concept, signed in January 2000, in which he claimed, "Threats to the national security and interests of the Russian federation ... are created by the economic, demographic, and cultural-religious expansion of neighboring states into Russian territory." The preservation of national security calls for "counteracting the negative influence of foreign religious organizations and missions" and "resistance to economic, demographic, and cultural and religious expansion on the part of other states onto the territory of Russia."[8] Whereas Yeltsin hesitated to undermine religious freedom, Putin initially showed strong signs that he feared foreign religious groups would threaten Russian identity. The securitization of religion applies to Putin's first and second terms, I will argue later in the chapter.

Let me submit that Putin's religious program while in office deviated from Yeltsin's program in a related and equally disquieting way. In this chapter I will elaborate and expand on the hypothesis that Putin's religious policy shows significant deviation from Yeltsin's religious program and I will argue that it goes beyond securitizing religion. In Putin's first term and at key points in his second, Putin has used Orthodoxy as a platform for unifying the Russian *state* – as opposed to the nation – and for solidifying the Russian state's position in the near abroad. This inclination is often delicately conveyed and is not the dominant message of Putin and his administration; yet Putin's willingness to use Orthodoxy for this purpose is a decided shift from Yeltsin. In fact, it suggests that Putin's natural predecessors might be Joseph Stalin in the World War II era for his decision to embrace Orthodoxy to ensure popular support for the state's wartime efforts, or Tsar Peter the Great for his frequent use of the ROC in empire building even while criticizing its backwardness. Putin's religious agenda, however, still nods toward the twin pillars of the democratic ideal for religious life: separation of church and State, and religious freedom. Putin's *third way* in religious matters is a recognition that individuals deserve the freedom to choose their own religious beliefs and that the ROC ought to carve out its own path. However, these freedoms come at a cost: the state effectively punishes individuals and the Church for deviating from the norms of nationhood, norms that are dictated by the state. In this *third way* the state declares to the individual: you may be a Roman Catholic in Russia, but be warned that the Russian state will defend and favor the Russian Orthodox Church (so perhaps you might think about being a less obvious Catholic and find more favor?). Or the state declares to its neighbors: your Orthodox history and culture place you squarely on "our" side (so perhaps you should consider yourselves allies?).

Furthermore, I conclude that Putin's desire to protect and unify Russia, while also promoting the dominance of Russia in the near abroad, has had a profound effect on his administration even though it has been an inconsistent policy on Putin's part. The bureaucrats who work for Putin interpret religious policy in accordance with *his* views. Thus, even while Putin has emphasized the multiconfessional status of Russia and distanced himself from the Russian Orthodox hierarchy in his second term, the effects of his earlier message still resound in Russia. In sum, Putin's *third way* in religious matters has no ideological basis. Proclaiming both religious freedom and a multiconfessional state while simultaneously offering the ROC the role of religion of the state – with the job of unifying Russia and promoting the state's interests abroad – quickly degenerates into a chaotic mishmash of policy at the regional and local levels.

Unpacking Orthodoxy's claim on Russia

I contend that the unifying and imperialist religious program of Putin and his administration is easily missed because of a conceptual mistake that finds its way into common parlance, daily papers, and academic studies. There is a tendency to lump together two different notions of "Russianness": (1) a Russian is Russian Orthodox; and (2) a Russian Orthodox is Russian. For example, an article in *Religion, State and Society* by Julia Sudo, which examines Russian nationalist Orthodox theology, includes this statement: "Because 'Russian is Orthodox, and Orthodox is Russian,' Catholics, Baptists, Buddhists and other *inovertsy* ... may be attacked [by Russian nationalists] as well."[9] The initial statement on "Russian" and "Orthodox" is given an explanation by Sudo that implies that Russians are Orthodox (and therefore foreign religious groups do not belong in Russia). The second element in the clause – Orthodox is Russian – is *not* given a separate interpretation but is taken to mean the same as the first element. However, a closer examination of the second part of the phrase "Orthodox is Russian" leads to a different view of Russianness: membership in the religion is prior to membership in the nation, so that those who are Russian Orthodox are automatically given the status of "Russian."

In the former proposition (Proposition A), *Orthodoxy* is necessary to *Russian*. A Russian must be Orthodox in order to be truly Russian in the ethnic sense. This idea of Orthodoxy is no doubt behind the 1997 Law on Freedom of Conscience and Religious Associations (see below) and countless attempts, both under this law but also in other contexts, to inhibit the work of foreign religious groups. The securitization attempts that Bacon notes are part and parcel of this notion of Orthodoxy. To claim that a Russian must be Orthodox protects Russia from the loss of an integral part of its identity.

In the latter proposition (Proposition B), however, being Orthodox is treated as a sufficient condition for the Russian nation. All one needs is to be Orthodox and one can be considered Russian. An Orthodox adherent is – regardless of other characteristics – truly Russian. Whereas for Proposition A there is a test one must pass to be a good Russian – one must commit to the ROC – in Proposition B there is a conferral of identity that passes to someone who commits to Orthodoxy – a Russian identity – or, from another viewpoint, a loss of a non-Russian identity associated with becoming a member of the ROC.

The claim that a true ethnic Russian must be Russian Orthodox has been a recurrent topic of discussion in the literature on Orthodoxy and religious life in Russia for centuries. The connection between religion and nation is clearly at the heart of the Russian Orthodox Church hierarchy's efforts to maintain a strong connection with Russian identity. Furthermore, the Yeltsin and Putin administrations have spoken and acted on this claim on numerous occasions. A few examples should suffice.

In 1997, as Yeltsin felt his support in the Duma and among the public slipping, he signed into law a bill that implicitly argues that Russians belong in the Russian Orthodox Church. The 1997 Law on Freedom of Conscience and Religious Associations operates as a tool to demoralize non-traditional religions, many of which were actively evangelizing to ethnic Russians.[10] The discrimination against non-traditional religions is built into a registration system that divides religious associations into two categories: organizations and groups. Organizations are entitled to a full plate of religious freedoms, but to become organizations they must prove they have existed in Russia for fifteen years (no easy task to date one's existence to the Brezhnev era![11]) and prove their affiliation with a centralized organization (again, not an easy assignment for many new, independent religious associations). Those who failed to pass these tests were relegated to "group" status, meaning that their religious activities were restricted, particularly in public.[12] In the 1997 law the Duma and Yeltsin acted to protect the ROC's status as the religious protector of the Russian identity by voting in favor of the law.[13]

The handling of Church property following the dissolution of the Soviet Union has also indicated a strong commitment to the role of the Russian Orthodox Church as guardian of the nation. The ROC has been the clear winner in the return of Church property following nearly complete state control over property in the Soviet era. Forum 18 News Service, an organization that documents religious freedom violations in Russia and elsewhere in the post-Soviet bloc, notes that the ROC has also maintained a distinct advantage in holding services of worship free of charge in historical places of worship. Even after a land legislation bill was signed in 2004, which would have required the ROC to pay for usage of these services, the hierarchy of the ROC registered a complaint with the authorities that led to a 2005 supplementary bill, signed by Putin, nullifying the requirement that the ROC pay rental fees.[14]

Finally, the initiatives of numerous departments in the federal administrative structure indicate a strong desire on the part of federal bureaucrats and significant pressure by the ROC to increase the visibility of the ROC in schools, the military, and in the provision of social services (to name a few). The Education Ministry has been attempting to introduce lessons on Russian Orthodoxy into the public school system, although ultimately a proposal for a federal provision did not pass muster with Putin. In fact, in late 2002 the Minister of Education, Vladimir Filippov, sent a report with a recommended syllabus for teaching Russian Orthodox lessons to all schools. Although this move was not sanctioned by Putin, it was not condemned either, and many localities have acted on this implicit authorization.

Then the minister for nationalities, Vladimir Zorin, released a draft in 2002 of the proposed Law on Extremism in which the designation "extremism" included "propaganda of the superiority of a religion over another."

The draft suggested that "extremist" organizations include Protestant denominations and even the Roman Catholic Church. The final version, passed in July 2002, though less virulent than Zorin's suggestions, punishes individuals or groups who incite racial, ethnic, or religious hatred. In other provisions, the law prohibits propaganda against citizens for their religious affiliation and "propaganda of exclusivity ... of citizens according to their relation to religion."[15] A subsequent set of amendments, passed by the Lower House of the Duma in September 2006, adds to the list of offenses that are deemed extremist, including a candidate or party who engages in "seditious libel" by slandering someone holding public office. Forum 18 has documented cases in which this law has been used against Russia's traditional and non-traditional religious groups, some of them for maintaining the superiority of their faith over other religions, others for evangelizing in regions where the ROC dominates the local political system.[16] At many levels of government – federal, regional and local – we can find overwhelming evidence that religious and political leaders believe that the Russian people belong in the ROC.

But consider that, by all accounts, to be Orthodox in Russia means simply to be *nothing other than* Orthodox. John Dunlop notes in a 1995 chapter that "the Orthodox Church today consists largely of an 'unchurched' flock, people well-disposed toward their national religion and respectful of it, but who have little understanding of Orthodoxy's teachings and customs."[17] Thus, it is assumed, unless shown otherwise, that a Russian is Orthodox by virtue of being nothing besides Orthodox. The empirical evidence strongly supports this claim. A 1999 survey by Kimmon Kaariainen and Dmitry Furman, funded by the Finland Academy of Sciences survey, found that self-identified Orthodox believers ranged from 7 percent who attend church at least once a month up to 45 percent who never attend church services.[18] In the same year, B. Dubin published some of the results from the Russian Center for Public Opinion Research (VTsIOM), which showed that 13.8 percent of those who identified themselves as Orthodox attended services at least monthly, while 36.8 percent from this category never attended church services.[19] In a study completed in 2002 by Vladimir Karpov, the numbers remained surprisingly low. Karpov notes, "With 7% attending at least once a month, Russians are among the least frequent churchgoers in Europe. Given Orthodoxy's strong emphasis on church participation, this is especially striking."[20]

Thus, the phrase "a true Russian must be Russian Orthodox" can, as a practical matter, mean something closer to "a true Russian must be nothing besides Russian Orthodox." The hierarchy in the Moscow patriarchate, the main branch of the ROC, appears to use this logic in denouncing the evangelistic efforts of a wide range of religious groups, including Protestants, Roman Catholics, and Baptists: insofar as these groups are seeking converts among ethnic Russians, including those without religious beliefs of any kind, the Moscow patriarchate believes that they are poaching from the ROC.

There is a second claim about religion and nation in Russia that also works its way into the discourse and practice of religious and political leaders. I believe that this proposition must be separated from Proposition A; it follows a different logic and the motives behind these propositions can be markedly different. In fact, I argue that insofar as Putin and his administration are willing to use Proposition B as a basis for their discourse and actions, we can argue that Putin has forged a *third way* in the area of religion and nation. This *third way* allows Putin to contain forces that are working against unity in Russia and justify Russian domination in and around the Russian state while, at the same time, preserving some semblance of the democratic ideal of religious freedom. It smacks of a managed religion.

The upper echelons of the Russian Orthodox Church have good reason, in terms of political power, to support the claim that "Orthodox is Russian." After all, this justifies their control over the Ukrainian and Belarusian churches, both of which are part of the canonical structure of the Moscow patriarchate. At the 1993 All-World Russian Assembly a group of nationalists opened up Church membership to non-ethnically Russian members, but it did so by declaring any alien baptized into the Russian Orthodox Church *ipso facto* a Russian.[21] At this same conference it was determined that the term "Russian" would include Ukrainians and Belarusians, who are brother and sister Slavs.

For the Putin administration the motive for promoting this claim is less obvious. However, we can attribute two possible objectives. First, when this notion is supported by the Russian administration, it may well be acting with imperialist hopes. In its imperialist version, closely identifying "Orthodoxy" and "Russian" can justify control over the regions around Russia, particularly Ukraine and Belarus, but also non-Russian Orthodox states such as Serbia, and states in which Russian Orthodoxy is a visible presence, such as Estonia. By virtue of their Orthodox status, they become natural adoptees of the Russian state. As long as Russia is viewed as the mother hen, it can use Orthodoxy to its advantage.

Another possible motive of the Putin administration is unification within the Russian state. In this version the notion that "to be Orthodox is to be Russian" is advanced by significantly undermining or denying the religious belief and devotion of those outside of the Russian Orthodox Church. Those individuals may not become members or believers in Orthodoxy, but such membership or belief does not appear to be necessary for one to call oneself Russian Orthodox. Simply by citizens being insulated from other belief systems, they can be more easily adopted into the Russian nation. Alternatively, referring to Orthodoxy in a territorial sense (that is, Russian Orthodoxy as vital to the Russian *state*) means that minority groups are denied their beliefs, and unity is founded on the notion of Orthodoxy. In both cases the costs of professing a religion other than Orthodoxy are higher and so discouraged. Nominal Orthodoxy is tolerated, but commitment to other religious groups is not: you pay for it by being denied full membership in the Russian nation. In unity, strength; therefore make disunity cost!

Dmitri Glinsky-Vassiliev wrote in a policy memo in 2001 that while

> making Russian ethnicity the basis for state-building was politically and often personally unacceptable for members of the new ruling class, using Christian Orthodoxy for these purposes was seen as perfectly appropriate (since its profession could be as ritualistic and divorced from daily practice and way of life as Marxist-Leninist rhetoric was before it).[22]

One of the troubling aspects of ethnic nationalism is its exclusionary tendencies. An ethnic idea of "nation" and its true membership entails that some do not belong. Guarding national unity will exclude. However, some might argue that religious unity is less exclusionary so long as the religion providing unity does not require much. It is much less expensive for Putin to argue that Orthodoxy is the state's organizing principle than to declare that Russian ethnicity is the central element of the state. Even so, religious unity does exclude; members of other religious groups are treated at best as second-class citizens.

In sum, Proposition B means either conferring nation status on all members of the Orthodox Church or undercutting the beliefs and practices of the non-Orthodox to make them more easily fit within the nation. Non-Russians in the ethnic sense are given nation status simply because they are "close enough" to Orthodoxy either by being non-religious or by keeping their religion a private matter.

Putin's *third way*: looking at the evidence

Putin's efforts to use the Russian Orthodox Church for his broader political agenda of achieving unity and gaining a platform in the near abroad can be observed in a series of statements and visits during his first years in office. While these statements did not necessarily translate into religious policy, their potential for setting a religious tone that favors Orthodoxy as glue for the state is evident.

An early attempt to define Orthodoxy's unifying role for the Russian state came during Putin's first Christmas season as acting president. Putin issued Christmas greetings at an Orthodox service on the Orthodox Christmas on 7 January 2000. His address incorporated two different notions of the Russian nation: in the opening, Putin proclaimed that "Orthodoxy has traditionally played a special role in Russian history" but later noted that "[Orthodoxy is] an unbending spiritual core of the entire people and state."[23] His latter comment is remarkably controversial, even if we acknowledge the tendency of speakers to use poetic language that resonates with the audience: labeling the entire Russian territory as Orthodox territory, at the core of what it means to be Russian, undermines not only foreign[24] but also minority religious groups. The latter statement, with its strong language, was taken to be the crux of Putin's holiday message to the Orthodox community and was roundly criticized by human rights organizations. If the state in all its elements is Russian Orthodox, a unified nation follows; the state is defined by its Orthodoxy.

The following week marked the tenth anniversary of Patriarch Aleksii's enthronement, celebrated with a variety of personal and public events. Putin sent a message to Aleksii, routed through the press, congratulating him for leading the Church through a "difficult and confusing period." Putin took the occasion to promote the ROC's role in Russia: "The Russian Orthodox Church plays an enormous role in the spiritual unification of the Russian land after many years of life without faith, moral degradation and atheism."[25] His use of the Russian *rossiiskii* – denoting the territory of Russia – instead of *russkii* – referring to the Russian nation – is significant: the Church is marked as a unifying force for those on Russian territory. The ROC is conceptualized as the church of the state and not only the church of the nation. In January 2004, Putin stated during a visit to an orphanage in the monastery of St. Savva of Mt. Storozha, "Of course, in our country the church is separated from the state..... But in the people's souls everything is together."[26] Such remarks indicate a willingness on the part of Putin and his administration to use Russian Orthodoxy for the purposes of state building.

Yet unifying the state using Russian Orthodoxy is not Putin's only goal for the ROC. Putin has also shown a penchant for using Orthodoxy as a basis for dominance in the near abroad. The examples come largely from his first term in office. In March 2000, Putin met with Aleksii and the catholicos of Armenia. In a public statement at this meeting, Putin acknowledged the importance of the spiritual development of society on the basis of the eternal values of Christianity, which, he claimed, would lead to the moral health of the peoples living on the territory of both the Russian and the Armenian states.[27] Although Putin uses the broader term "Christianity" to incorporate Armenian religious identity in his proclamation, his audience of Orthodox hierarchs registered a more restricted understanding of "Christianity" for Russia.

This same use of Orthodoxy for imperialist purposes was emphasized at a World War II memorial service in early May 2000. The leaders of Russia, Ukraine, and Belarus met at a key World War II battleground in Prokhorovka, a village in western Russia near the Ukrainian border, to underline their shared heritage, launching celebrations marking fifty-five years of peace. Putin, Ukraine's Leonid Kuchma, and Belarus's Alexander Lukashenko paid tribute to Soviet troops mowed down by the Germans. With much of the former Soviet Union gearing up to mark Victory Day on 9 May, the three leaders unveiled a modest memorial in a field near the center of the world's biggest tank battle, generally known as the Battle of Kursk. Patriarch Aleksii conducted a memorial service underscoring the unity of the Slavic peoples: "In the years of severe trial, we were not divided into Russians, Ukrainians and Belarussians – we defended one country, one motherland. Although we now live in different states, we have one faith, one history, one culture." The presidents echoed the patriarch on the theme of unity, with Putin concluding: "We are one family. We vanquished when we stood together. We have common historic roots, a common fate, history, culture."[28] The memorial blessing of a church leader is stock fare for many countries, likely to perturb only devout separationists, but the inference drawn from this cohort of three leaders and one patriarchate is subtler and more momentous.

In November 2000, Vojislav Koštunica, the newly elected president of the Federal Republic of Yugoslavia, made an official visit to Russia, an initiation into the international political scene. The visit incorporated a substantial religious component to showcase the good relations between the two states. Koštunica, accompanied by the Serbian patriarch Pavle and two metropolitans from the Serbian Orthodox hierarchy, met with Patriarch Aleksii to express their thanks for the support of the ROC for the Koštunica government as it ousted the former Serbian president, Slobodan Miloševic. Putin portrayed the religious substance of his talks with Koštunica as "an essential element of the affirmation of the special relations between our states … that needs no explanation; it can only be welcomed."[29] The liberal media still felt compelled to offer an explanation, and not a particularly positive one. Editors of the popular daily *Nezavisimaia Gazeta* decried the overlapping political and religious elements in the meeting;[30] thus, the highly religious component to a political meeting of two heads of state did, in the end, find Putin on the defensive for construing Orthodoxy as integral to the state. In these remarks and others, Putin's discourse underscores the claim that Russian Orthodoxy can lead the way in building a stronghold for Russia throughout the region.

In 2003, Putin ventured into a dispute between the ROC and the Russian Orthodox Church Outside of Russia (ROCOR) that has been ongoing since 1920 when Tikhon, the patriarch of the ROC, ordered that all Orthodox believers under the authority of the Moscow patriarchate find a new home to escape Soviet domination. Over the course of the next eighty-plus years the ROCOR found new reasons for separating from the ROC's Moscow patriarchate: it was disenchanted with the ROC for its capitulation to the Soviet authorities and it strongly disagreed with the ROC's engagement in the ecumenical movement (such as the World Council of Churches). A thaw in relations began in the 1980s but did not seem to be heading toward unification. In 2003, Putin held a meeting with the hierarchs of the ROCOR to begin a process of reconciliation; he clearly attaches great importance to the unification of these churches. The ROCOR has parishes all over the world (including within Russia) and represents an opportunity for Russia to extend its influence beyond its borders. Putin accomplished his goal in 2007 with the official reunification – largely symbolic, since they remain autonomous from each other on most matters – of the ROC and the ROCOR.

While on a working trip to Greece in 2005, Putin took the opportunity to travel to the holy Mount Athos, a secluded set of monasteries that caters to Orthodox communities from around the world. According to some press reports and the

Moscow patriarchate's press releases, Putin took the opportunity to underscore the spiritual connection between Russia and Greece. Putin purportedly remarked that

> Russia is a state with a rather large Orthodox population, as the historical seeds of Christianity entered Russia from Byzantium and Greece. Thus, the relationship between Russia and Greece, which have a long and rich history, provides the necessary prerequisites for growth in a spirit of complete trust.

Later in the visit Putin stated that "the strength of Russia is spirituality before everything else ... the revival of Faith is one of the foundations of Russia's present revival."[31] This religious language is not altogether foreign to those who study American politics, where presidents often use Christian imagery or terminology in their speeches. However, the motivation appears quite different: Putin uses the ROC to court allies; Bush uses Christianity (particularly evangelical Protestant language) to court votes. For Putin the ROC provides an opportunity for expanding Russia's influence abroad.

Putin's *third way* for religion and nation takes a more peculiar route in his interactions with traditional religions in Russia apart from the ROC, namely Islam, Judaism, and Buddhism. These three religions are considered traditional to Russia, yet they do not attract the same status as the ROC. While Putin cannot be accused of discriminating overtly against these religions, their adherents are subject to Putin's efforts to unite the Russian state on the basis of Orthodoxy. Again, some examples offer a sketch of Putin's efforts to unify through Russian Orthodoxy.

Parliamentary elections were held in December 1999. Much of the debate centered on economic and foreign policy matters, leaving cultural and ethnic issues largely aside in the wider media. For the most part, the election centered on the strategies of the two most popular parties and their prospects for winning the most seats. Although religious issues played virtually no role in the campaigning, Putin did support the creation of an Islamic party, Refah, which won about a dozen seats in the State Duma (five of them through Refah itself, which was in the umbrella of the Unity party, and five to seven other deputies who called themselves supporters). His support for a party warrants attention, given his (and Yeltsin's) general distaste for party politics. The Islamic party is significant for its relatively vacuous religious convictions, which distinguish it sharply from the various radical forms of Islam in society. Putin's support for this party can easily be seen as support for an Islamic party that might easily be assimilated into the Russian nation. This benignly religious group could be construed as Russian – if not through being Orthodox, at least through being only weakly Islamic. Though not Orthodox, it is not much of a threat to Orthodoxy.

Zoe Knox remarked in the conference on *Christianity and Colonialism* that Putin prefers to deal with a "single representative" within a religious association and that this has led to persistent rivalries within the Islamic community. Knox attributes Putin's preference to his centralizing impulses.[32] One might also note that Putin's favoritism can lead religious denominations in a direction that makes them blend into the Russian state and nation more easily. There is evidence that

Putin is intruding into the affairs of the Jewish community: Lawrence Uzzell writes that Putin has anointed Berl Lazar as the "sole, legitimate leader of [Jews in] Russia"[33] after Putin spoke favorably about the position of a second chief rabbi for Russia. One can conclude that Putin continues to toy with the notion of greater cultural homogenization.

The Russian Buddhist community has not played an active role in lobbying the Putin administration for favors, with the exception of the pressure it exerted to allow the Dalai Lama to visit. His previous visit was in 1994, but in 2004 he was given permission to make another visit; however, the Buddhist community was given very little advance notice and the Putin administration largely ignored the visit, significantly undermining its significance for the Russian state.

Sakwa claims that Putin is pushing a pragmatic patriotism that is supra-ethnic and statist as one of the key elements to his nation-building plan.[34] As part of this plan, it is critical that Putin finds values that can bring together diverse ethnic groups and give them a sense of belonging. Russian Orthodoxy works well, particularly if Russian Orthodoxy requires much less than actual religious belief or participation in religious activities. On several occasions Putin has proposed the formation of a Russian national idea, a proposal that was developed by the State Duma and released in September 2006 to the public for discussion. The proposal has been met with hostility from the Muslim community in Russia, which claims that it tries to find unity in a multicultural society by promoting the role of ethnic Russians. This may leave the Putin administration with little choice but to continue its unifying efforts using Russian Orthodoxy as a centerpiece and demoralizing other traditional religious groups. Proposition B, *Russian Orthodox therefore Russian*, can be rather clumsily restated as *Nominal Russian Orthodoxy as the state religion therefore all within the state and many outside the state can be considered Russian or Russian-oriented.*

Putin's religious policy during his tenure has been less consistent than these examples may imply. One could point to numerous occasions on which he painstakingly conveyed his support for full religious freedom and distanced himself from the ROC. His administration has overseen the establishment of military chaplains from traditional religions; it has not forced religious instruction in the school system; and Putin himself met with the late Pope John Paul II in Rome in 2003. Statements made by Putin also reflect consideration for religious freedom and even, at times, a distancing from the ROC. At a 2003 appearance in Sarov for the one-hundredth anniversary of the canonization of St. Serafim of Sarov, Putin appeared to stun the patriarchate with his emphatically ecumenical language. His short message included such lines as "we value highly the contribution of all confessions of our country" and the "harmony among the peoples of multinational Russia." In this way we see Putin wandering through many different understandings of the nation and religion for the Russian state and society: on one hand, he maintains a commitment to the liberal democratic notion of religious freedom; on the other hand, his frequent promotion of Russian Orthodoxy as a harbinger of the Russian national idea and as a crucial element for unity in the state underscore his quest for a managed and manageable state.

Some implications for Putin's *third way*

It is easy to conclude that Putin's gestures at an Orthodox state or a greater Orthodox region are, if not meaningless, then sufficiently atypical and thus not warranting great concern. However, I would argue that there is more to consider. Some of the attacks against foreign religious personnel and groups, and the undermining of the separation between the Russian state and the Russian Orthodox Church by members of Putin's inner administration, nomenklatura, and the judicial system, may be connected to Putin's willingness to use language that suggests either "a Russian is Russian Orthodox" or "a Russian Orthodox is Russian."

The undermining of religious freedom has come in many different forms. In 2002, many Roman Catholic clergy were thrown out of Russia with no legal right of return. The Salvation Army and Jehovah's Witnesses are just two groups that face increasingly difficult times in obtaining the necessary registration to exist as legal religious entities. Jehovah's Witnesses were outlawed in Moscow. Russian officials, some of them with close connections to Putin, have made bold statements denouncing non-Orthodox religious organizations. In the past few years the Eurasian Department of the International Religious Freedom Association, a non-governmental organization that promotes religious freedom globally, has noted increasing intolerance against Protestants on the part of local administrations and individual representatives of the Russian Orthodox Church in a number of provinces of the Central District of Russia. The Muslim community has also been subject to questionable searches, arbitrary arrests, and difficulty finding places to worship at the local and regional levels, according to Forum 18 and the United States Committee on International Religious Freedom.

The sporadic nature of these crackdowns on religious freedom – across time and space – suggests that there is no institutionalized effort to undermine religious freedom but that the signals of the Putin administration to those on the ground are conflicting and confusing. At a minimum, Putin's willingness to use language suggesting the importance of Orthodoxy internally and externally signals a level of toleration for the promotion of Orthodoxy as a unifier of the state and a carrier of the Russian flag abroad. For Putin, Russian is Orthodox and Orthodox is Russia, depending on his audience. The first proposition provides cover from external domination; the second proposition coaxes unity and, when necessary, motivates imperialism. Religion, it turns out, can be managed as well as democracy in the *third way*.

Notes

1 See S. Levitsky and Lucan A. Way, "The Rise of Competitive Authoritarianism," *Journal of Democracy*, 12, 2, April 2002, 51–65; F. Zakaria, "The Rise of Illiberal Democracy," *Foreign Affairs*, 76, November–December 1997, 22–41; L. Diamond, *Developing Democracy: Toward Consolidation*, Baltimore: Johns Hopkins University Press, 1999.

2 R. Sakwa, *Putin: Russia's Choice*, London: Routledge, 2004, p. 79.

3 V. Sheinis, "Posle bitvy: itogi parlamentskikh vyborov i novaia Gosudarstvennaia Duma," *Nezavisimaia gazeta*, 29 December 1999, 8. Quoted in Sakwa, *Putin*, p. 80.

4 E. Bacon, "Putin's Religious Policy," paper presented at the American Association for the Advancement of Slavic Studies, November 2002, Pittsburgh, PA, 1. Used with permission from the author.

5 Z. Knox, "Continuity in Church–State Relations in Russia: The Soviet and Post-Soviet Eras," lecture given at Arizona State University, 21 March 2006. Used with permission from the author.

6 Bacon, "Putin's Religious Policy," 9.

7 Ibid., 7.

8 See J.M. Godzimirski, "Russian National Security Concepts 1997 and 2000: A Comparative Analysis," *European Security*, 9, 4, Winter 2000, 73–91.

9 J. Sudo, "Russian Nationalist Orthodox Theology: A New Trend in the Political Life of Russia," *Religion, State and Society*, 6, 1, 2005, 78.

10 Other non-Russian Orthodox religions that are traditional in Russia, including Buddhism, Judaism, and Islam, were largely unaffected by this law. Of course, this was the intent of the signatories, as these traditional religions posed no real conversion threat to ethnic Russians.

11 During Brezhnev's tenure, religious groups (including the Russian Orthodox Church) continued to suffer repression, a practice introduced by Lenin and fully adopted by Stalin. Religious groups were forced to disband or go underground, leaving the latter with little to no documentation of their existence during the Brezhnev era.

12 For more detail about the 1997 law, see Rossiiskaia Federatsiia Federal'nyi zakon, "O sovobode sovesti i o religioznykh ob"edineniiakh," *Rossiiskaia gazeta*, 1 October 1997, 2–3.

13 For an in-depth discussion on the intentions behind the MPs' designing of the law, see Z. Knox, "Postsoviet Challenges to the Moscow Patriarchate, 1991–2001," *Religion, State and Society*, 32, 2, June 2004, 87–113.

14 G. Fagan, Moscow Correspondent, "Russia: Religious Freedom Survey," Forum 18 News Service, 14 February 2005.

15 Ibid.

16 Fagan points out a number of cases in which Muslims, Baptists, Pentecostals, and Old Believers have been harassed under the guise of the 2002 extremism law. In many of the cases the charges of extremism are clearly overstated, with local authorities judging activity such as rallies at local stadiums to be extremist activity.

17 J. Dunlop, "Orthodoxy and National Identity in Russia," in V. Bonnell (ed.), *Identities in Transition: Eastern Europe and Russia after the Collapse of Communism*, Berkeley: University of California Press/University of California International and Area Studies Digital Collection, 93, 1996, p. 121.

18 K. Kaariainen and D. Furman (eds.), *Starye tserkvi, novye veruiushchie. Religiia v massovom soznanii postsovetskoi Rossii*, Moscow and St. Petersburg: Letnii Sad, 2000, p. 38.

19 B. Dubin, "Religioznaia vera v Rossii 90-kh godov," *Russian Public Opinion Monitor* (Moscow: Russian Center for Public Opinion Research), 1, 39, 1999, 31–39.

20 V. Karpov, "Orthodoxy, Religious Ethnocentrism and Intolerance in Russia," paper presented at the ASN annual meeting, New York, 16 April 2005. Used with permission from the author.

21 N. Babasian, "Russkaia Pravoslavnaia Tserkov' budet otstaivat' traditsionnye tsennosti v otkrytoi zapadu Rossii, zaiavliaet Mitropolit Smolenskii i Kaliningradskii Kirill," *Nezavisimaia gazeta*, 5 June 1993. Also see *Krasnoiarskaia gazeta*, 11 June 1993, 2–3.

22 D. Glinsky-Vassiliev, "Islam in Russian Society and Politics: Survival and Expansion," *PONARS Policy Memo*, 198, May 2001, 2.

23 Interfax, "Putin nadeetsia chto Pravoslavie ukrepit Rossiiu," Moscow, 7 January 2000.

24 The use of "foreign" in this sentence indicates those religious groups that did not have a presence in Russia prior to 1991.

25 Reuters, "Putin Lauds Church Role as Patriarch Marks 10 Years," *Reuters*, online posting, Johnson's Russia List (no. 4359), 9 June 2000, 40.
26 Portal-Credo.Ru, 7 January 2004.
27 ITAR-TASS, "Vladimir Putin neofitsial'no vstretilsiia s Patriarkhom Alexeem II i Catolicos Gargein II," 1 March 2000.
28 Reuters, "Russia, Ukraine, Belarus Leaders Recall WWII Unity," 3 May 2000.
29 A. Krymin and G. Engelgardt, "Novyi president Yugoslavii podderzhivaet traditsiiu otnoshenii mezhdu russkim i serbskim narodami," *Nezavisimaia gazeta*, 1 November 2000, 2.
30 Ibid.
31 J. D. Huneycutt, "Putin Visits the Holy Mountain," *Orthodoxie*, 10 September 2005.
32 Z. Knox, "Continuity in Church–State Relations in Russia."
33 L. Uzzell, "Eroding Religious Freedom," *Moscow Times*, 24 January 2003.
34 Sakwa, *Putin*, p. 163.

12 Making the public patriotic

Militarism and anti-militarism in Russia

Valerie Sperling[1]

Dulce et decorum est pro patria mori.

Horace[2]

By the end of the 1990s, Russia's government could recite a litany of woes. Probably topping the list was a collapsing economy in which GDP had shrunk by 50 percent since 1991, unhappy laborers and pensioners experienced extensive wage delays, crime was rising, and unemployment appeared to have become an intractable problem. The collapse of the Soviet Union a decade earlier placed the nation's superpower status solidly in the past. The state had lost control over the rebellious region of Chechnya; Russian troops had been withdrawn from the area in 1996 in defeat after what many perceived as a needlessly bloody affair botched by the military, only to return in 1999 for the second round of a brutal conflict. In a nationwide public opinion poll in early 2002 asking what "in the modern life of our country" gave rise to feelings of pride, half of the respondents to this open-ended question provided either no answer or responses deemed "not pertinent" (*net otveta, otvet ne na temu*), and an additional 20 percent stated that there was "nothing to be proud of," making that the most popular answer.[3] Patriotic pride had been eaten away by shame. As the new millennium began, the Russian government launched a campaign to reinvigorate its citizens' sense of patriotism – a campaign firmly anchored to the Russian military.[4]

From the perspective of Vladimir Putin's government, the reasons to rely on a militarized patriotism were straightforward. Russia's army, with its devastatingly bad reputation, faced widespread draft resistance and hoped that such a campaign would enlist more soldiers into its ranks. Military reforms planned for 2008, reducing the term of service from two years to one, required a larger pool of willing draftees (as would future plans to move toward an all- or mostly volunteer army).[5] The government had addressed this issue concretely, cutting the number of deferments available to draft-age men, but hoped also to reduce draft evasion significantly as a means of increasing the number of conscripts overall.[6] Patriotism was thus imagined to be a necessary recruitment device, a motivator for army service.

Patriotism could be used to bolster such willingness to serve, but on what could a renewed sense of patriotism be based in Russia? The Russian state confronted a circular problem. Without greater patriotic consciousness, citizens would continue to avoid obligatory army service to the extent of their abilities. And until citizens thought better of the army, their sense of patriotism would suffer. Hoping to disrupt the logic of this dilemma, in 2001 Russia's government put forward the first of two five-year plans to foster patriotic education.[7] These plans promoted a patriotism based on military achievements – specifically, the victory of Soviet forces in World War II, a conflict known in the Soviet Union and Russia alike as the Great Patriotic War.

This chapter explores the Russian state's policy-based attempts to foster a militarized patriotism and the social soil in which those efforts succeed or fail to take root. I investigate public opinion about the Russian (and Soviet) armed forces, the war in Chechnya, army service, and patriotism itself. In Russia, patriotic feelings are both dependent to some extent on citizens' view of the army and instrumental as a means of shaping public opinion about the army and armed service. In this light, I explore the history and present of militarized patriotic education, driven by patriotic education policy as well as by grassroots initiatives.

While few activist groups have organized resistance to militarized patriotism, such as by opposing the war in Chechnya, calling for an end to the draft, and generally criticizing conditions in Russia's armed forces, this resistance undermines state attempts to highlight the military as the focal point of patriotism. State anxiety about that resistance was visible in the Putin administration's moves against non-governmental human rights organizations, especially those seen as supporting Chechen human rights, and also in the formation of youth organizations supported by the Kremlin. The chapter thus also examines such resistance and the state's response. It concludes by considering several questions: How well are the Russian patriotic education programs working? What are the political risks involved in linking patriotism so closely to militarism? And what alternative foundations for patriotism, such as extolling Russia's long history of dissidents' resistance to tyranny, may have been missed?

The Russian military and the "dismal" 1990s

By all accounts the Russian army underwent a crisis period in the wake of the Soviet Union's collapse in 1991.[8] An enormous decline in the number of military personnel took place over the 1990s, from roughly 5 million Soviet soldiers in 1988 to 3,400,000 in post-Soviet Russia in 1992, and only 1,159,000 in 1998 (a 65 percent reduction in military personnel during the post-Soviet period alone).[9] At the end of the 1990s the military was in sad financial shape as well; as of 1998 the military had received 40 billion rubles less than the sum that had been budgeted for it, and there were significant wage arrears owed to military personnel.[10]

Military-patriotic education declined during the 1990s, reflecting a general sense of pessimism about Russia's military enterprise and the loss of empire. The 1990s began with exclusively negative images on this front, starting with the

Soviet army's recent withdrawal from the stalemated war in Afghanistan after nine years of deadly conflict.[11] The collapse of the Soviet empire in Eastern Europe and then, in 1991, of the Soviet superpower itself constituted stunning changes for which much of the population was not prepared. The mid-1990s brought the bloody struggle over Chechnya, ending with Russian troops' withdrawal and an unsettled conflict. Russian military action took place against a background of economic decline and the army's own inadequacy; its soldiers went hungry, some were sold into virtual slavery by their officers, and troops were sent unprepared into battle.[12] The armed forces' "dismal decade" ended with the sinking of the submarine *Kursk* in 2000. By the start of the 2000s, Russia's population, with its "wounded" national pride, readily embraced a leader who would renew citizens' belief in the state and army alike.

Militarized patriotism had not been absent under the Yeltsin administration, although it was less visible than it would become once Putin's regime took hold. In 1998, Yeltsin's choice to sponsor a week-long celebration of the 9 May victory over the Nazis, with a focus on both the veterans of World War II and the current officers of the Russian army, was seen as "distinctive" and also politically "pragmatic," given the impending elections of 1999. It was also in 1998 that the Russian State Military Historical-Cultural Center (Rosvoentsentr), a federal government agency, collaborated with the Russian Union of Journalists to hold a "nationwide contest" for a winning piece of journalistic work on a military-patriotic theme.[13]

Such state-sponsored efforts to promote patriotism were sparse in the 1990s. During the Yeltsin era, extreme nationalists and adherents of the Soviet Communist Party (revamped as the Communist Party of the Russian Federation) had acquired the moniker of "the national patriotic forces." To speak about patriotism at that time was largely a marker of alliance with the Communists and right-wing nationalists who had appropriated patriotism as a concept.[14] The Putin government thus set out to reclaim patriotism from the Communists and nationalists. Ideologically, this was accomplished by a shift away from the pro-Western orientation of the Yeltsin years toward a firm stance of Russian "independence," codified some years later as "sovereign democracy" by the Kremlin ideologue Vladislav Surkov.[15]

Putin's ideological shift was largely welcomed, and in the years following his election to the presidency in March 2000, Putin enjoyed enormous national trust. As measured by public opinion polls, negative attitudes toward him have been at less than 5 percent consistently since 2000, and in polls asking for whom citizens would vote if elections were to be held "next Sunday," Putin consistently surpassed all other candidates, receiving an average of 48 percent of the vote between 2000 and 2003, an average of 49 percent in 2004–2005, and reaching a peak of 52 percent in mid-October 2006.[16] In June 2006, polls showed that 58 percent of the population trusted Putin outright and only 16 percent expressed "distrust," while 23 percent said they felt both "trust" and "distrust" at different times.[17] Building on this new direction that had led him to power, Putin's reign brought a concerted effort to renew patriotic sentiment among Russia's diverse citizenry. The regime chose to tightly link its patriotism-promoting efforts to the Russian armed forces, specifically to the mid-twentieth-century defeat of the Nazis by the Soviet Union.

World War II thus became the centerpiece of patriotic education in the 2000s.[18] There were three reasons for this. First, the Great Patriotic War was the clearest instance of an effort that had mobilized the Soviet Union's multinational population to defend a state toward which some proportion of citizens had mixed feelings at best. As such, the war could serve as a model for reinventing post-Soviet Russia's national idea as a multinational one – a necessity, given the rebellious north Caucasus. Second, as I have argued elsewhere, the Soviet forces' victory stood out as a potential source of patriotic pride amid the otherwise tarnished and repressive history of the Soviet polity.[19] Third, of course, was the aforementioned desire to use militarized patriotism as a recruitment tool.

A critical effort, then, was made to link the Russian military of the present with the historical "achievements" of its predecessor. Various symbolic efforts attempted to connect the Russian and Soviet armed forces, including the official reinstatement in 2000 of the red flag that had represented the Soviet armed forces as the banner of the Russian military.[20] This retention of the Soviet-style flag did not last; in 2003 the Duma approved a new design for the military banner, featuring the tsarist Russian double-headed eagle, four five-pointed stars (one in each corner of the flag), and the words "Fatherland, duty and honor," which echoed eighteenth-century Russian military banners.[21] Despite the central placement of the tsarist-era image, the armed forces' banner retained its red background, while the red stars, originally introduced by Trotsky as the Red Army's symbol in 1918, represented a direct link with Soviet military history.[22]

Under Putin's regime, with the adoption of the first patriotic education program in 2001, the Russian military rapidly became a focal point for patriotic education. This strategy was not without risk. After all, the Russian army's reputation in the public consciousness was disastrous, owing to the abysmal conditions prevailing within many military units, and service in Russia's army had become a dismaying and frightening prospect for the majority of Russia's youth. Primary among the army's problems was the fact that severe dysfunction within the ranks produced gross numbers of non-combat deaths, and the brutal hazing known as *dedovshchina* was widespread.[23] This latter phenomenon is worth exploring in some detail.

Dedovshchina

Dedovshchina is the violent initiation, or hazing, of new conscripts (in the first six months of their two-year term of service) by conscripts who have undergone more than six months' service; those in their last six months are "senior" conscripts who enjoy various privileges and higher status (including immunity from such treatment).[24]

Scholarly analysis of *dedovshchina* suggests that hazing grew worse over the course of the 1990s, in part because of the economic liberalization that affected the army as it did the rest of Russian society, exacerbating the abuses and adding to them the economic exploitation of newer conscripts by older soldiers.[25] Nor did hazing decline once the 1990s were over. The number of "hazing-related" crimes increased by 25 percent between 2003 and 2005, according to the chief military prosecutor in May 2005.[26] Thousands of conscripts desert their units annually, complaining of psychological and physical mistreatment; in 2002 there were roughly 6,000 such deserters.[27] According to the Russian prosecutor-general, Yuri Chaika, thousands of service members are affected by hazing each year; in August 2006, Chaika announced that 17 deaths and over 100 injuries had resulted from roughly 3,500 reported hazing incidents so far that year.[28] Hazing occurs in elite contexts as well as in average army units; a 2003 case confirmed the existence of hazing at the Nakhimov Naval Academy in St. Petersburg.[29]

Hazing in the Russian army reached a gruesome new height when, on 31 December 2005, Private Andrei Sychov was beaten so violently at the Cheliabinsk Tank School that his genitals and both of his legs had to be amputated afterward. Although outrage over the incident ran high, Sergeant Alexander Siviakov was given a short four-year sentence by the Cheliabinsk Military Court in September 2006 for "abuse of power leading to grave consequences."[30] Publicity around Sychov's case drew increasing attention to the prosecution of those immediately responsible in hazing incidents – including incidents resulting in the victim's death. In October 2006, for instance, a military court in Riazan' sentenced Captain Viacheslav Nikiforov to twelve years in prison (out of a possible twenty-five) for having kicked a soldier to death earlier that year.[31] Not surprisingly, *dedovshchina* constitutes the most significant factor leading to draft evasion.[32]

Chechnya

The military campaigns in Chechnya (1994–1996, and 1999 to the present) had also done little for the army's reputation. A national survey from autumn 2001 found overwhelming discontent with Russia's military policy in Chechnya; 94 percent of adults surveyed sought some change in that policy, whether by increasing the number of troops or by finding a more peaceful means of concluding the conflict. A full two-thirds of the population expressed "alarm at the large losses of Russian troops."[33]

The Putin administration's popularity, however, seemed unaffected, in part because the media were reined in and prevented from broadcasting images or stories about the war that would inflame anti-Putin sentiments. The second phase of the war, characterized by lawless behavior by Russian troops and "even greater disregard for civilian casualties and refugees" compared with the first phase of the war, was "accompanied by tight control over the media and an effort to downplay casualties so as to capitalize on public support, minimize protest, and promote Putin's popularity."[34] Putin's government "established the PR center, *Rosinformtsentr*, to shape stories about the war," and "punished" journalists who violated the authorities' guidelines in that regard. The administration further reduced the spectrum of discussion on the war through harassment campaigns, and by taking control of news sources (such as the television station NTV) that voiced opposition to the war. "Other news outlets, which had also borrowed money from the state but which toed the line on Chechnya, were left alone, allowing editors and publishers to draw their own conclusions."[35] In a further attempt to limit media coverage of the war in Chechnya, in August 2004 the Interior Ministry gained control over the issuing of permits to journalists hoping to visit the war-torn region.[36]

Despite thoroughgoing attempts to control reportage on the war, the ongoing conflict in Chechnya detracted from popular enthusiasm for army service. A 2001 poll by the All-Russia Center for the Study of Public Opinion (VTsIOM) found that 69 percent of Russians surveyed would "hate to have their close relatives drafted into the army"; the top two reasons provided were the high injury and fatality rates of troops sent to Chechnya (noted by 38 percent), and hazing (noted by 30 percent).[37] Indeed, from the start of the second phase of the war, public opinion evinced a steady deterioration in support for Russian military action in Chechnya. If in November 1999, 64 percent of the population approved of those actions, by August 2002 the corresponding figure was only 30 percent.[38] By December 2005 only 21 percent of the population supported continuing military operations in Chechnya, and by November 2006 a mere 18 percent considered it "necessary to continue military action in Chechnya," while 67 percent favored entering into negotiations.[39] Protests against the war in Chechnya also increased in frequency over the course of the second phase of the war; 68 rallies were held between January 2000 and the end of 2005; 45 of these took place after January 2004, roughly 1.88 per month (as compared with 1.2 per month during the first phase of the war, under Yeltsin). Cumulative attendance in the protests was higher during the second phase of the war, reaching approximately 38,000 participants, compared to roughly 23,000 during the first phase of the war. Although the protests were mostly small in size (averaging 932 people during the first phase of the war, and 564 per protest from 2000 to 2005), labeled "pocket protests" under Putin, they indicated some level of popular discontent with the Kremlin's military policy in Chechnya.[40] The unpopularity of the war in Chechnya, combined with *dedovshchina*, contributed to the state's concern about increasing conscription.

Within a year of Putin's taking office, the state had set itself the task of rebuilding patriotism, centered on the military. With the implementation of the first state patriotic education program in 2001, the Defense Ministry set out to alter the army's image in the public imagination. As the state's campaign got under way, public opinion poll data on patriotism, the army, and army service told a story that state officials most likely found quite alarming.

Public opinion and the image of Russia's army

In the wake of the 1990s the Russian army was consistently seen as riddled with significant problems. The salience of these problems, however, shifted over time. In February 1999 a national survey showed that 50 percent of respondents chose "hazing and bullying" as the most important problem of the Russian army, a number that increased to 62 percent by February 2004 (by contrast, the "poor feeding of soldiers" was noted by only 38 percent of respondents in 2004, down from 51 percent in 1999).[41] *Dedovshchina* had become a more prominent issue during that time period.

In October 2002, 78 percent of respondents in a national poll believed that hazing and bullying were widespread in the army. When asked (in an open-ended survey question) why they thought "young boys do not want to serve in the army now," respondents provided extensive evidence that the Russian army's image had suffered considerably over the past decade: 42 percent noted the "bad situation in the army," including hazing (noted by 24 percent of respondents); an additional 9 percent pointed to "fears for one's own life and health," and 16 percent pointed to fear of being sent to a "hot spot" such as Chechnya. In response to a separate question about the potentially negative effects of army service on an individual, 14 percent of those surveyed pointed to health-related debilitation, particularly from hazing (one representative response was that "*dedovshchina* makes the boys invalids").[42]

More people fear *dedovshchina* than service in a "hot spot." In January 2005, when asked whether they would like their "son, brother, husband, or other close relative to serve in the army now? If not, why not?" 33 percent of respondents said they would not want that person to serve, because of the "possibility of death or injury in a conflict such as the one in Chechnya," a number outweighed only by the 36 percent of respondents who pointed to "*dedovshchina*," "non-statutory relations" (the euphemism employed by military officials to describe *dedovshchina*), and "violence within the army."[43] This result is interesting, given that a total of 12,000 members of the Russian armed forces (including 8,000 Defense Ministry troops) had been killed in Chechnya by September 2003, including those who died in the first phase of the war, from 1994 to 1996.[44] On the other hand, Russia's defense minister had announced in January 2005 that "young draftees no longer serve in Chechnya and will never be sent there again," and by May 2006 all Defense Ministry conscripts had indeed been withdrawn from Chechnya.[45] Contract servicemen had taken their place, along with Interior Ministry troops (who themselves were slated to be replaced by contract servicemen by the start of 2007), so army conscripts were unlikely to be sent to Chechnya.[46] *Dedovshchina* may in fact have presented a greater risk.

Not unexpectedly, more than half of the respondents polled on a question since February 1998 about whether they thought positive, negative, or neutral attitudes toward the army "predominated" in "contemporary [Russian] society" believed that societal attitudes toward the army were largely negative. In February 1998 that number was 56 percent.[47] In February 2003, more than half the population (52 percent) thought that a negative attitude toward the army "prevail[ed] in Russian society," and among 18- to 35-year-olds the figure was 56 percent.[48] In 2004 the percentage of people suggesting that contemporary Russian society held a negative attitude toward the army decreased to less than 50 percent for the first time since the survey question was asked in 1998 – reaching a "low" of 49 percent. Although a majority no longer believed that negative attitudes toward the army predominated, those who perceived a negative attitude far outweighed those who believed that positive attitudes toward the army prevailed (only 28 percent, up from 21 percent in 1998).[49] Attitudes toward the army remained strongly negative but were improving, perhaps reflecting three years of state efforts under the 2001–2005 patriotic education program.

Attitudes toward the Defense Ministry itself were similarly negative. In August 2002, 49 percent of respondents in a national survey felt that "the Defense Ministry today performs its duties poorly," in large part evidenced by "the endless war in Chechnya" (noted by 13 percent of respondents) and by the frequency of army desertion and hazing (noted by 6 percent).[50] In January 2007 the Putin administration finally responded to these negative impressions, creating a "Public Council for the Defense Ministry," aimed at improving the public "image of the armed forces." The council itself features clerics and cultural luminaries, and is led by the well-known film director and actor Nikita Mikhalkov.[51] Similarly, in February 2006 the Defense Ministry announced a joint venture with the Union of Veterans of Afghanistan, titled "Army Service Shouldn't Scare You" (*v armii sluzhit' ne strashno*). The goal of this campaign, to be conducted across the country, was to explain to future conscripts that they had "no cause to fear military service."[52]

The perceived poverty of military officers very likely constitutes another obstacle to increasing enthusiasm for service. A nationwide survey in 2002 revealed that 19 percent of respondents pictured a Russian military officer as impoverished: "I imagine a poor man"; "the state has forgotten him"; "forsaken by the state." To some extent the first few years of Putin's presidency brought a perceived upgrade in the material well-being of Russian military personnel. Focus group participants in Voronezh in 2002 pointed to improvements in that area: "Two or three years ago, things were much worse in the army than they are today. More care from the state. New arms are being bought"; "[The Defense Ministry] maintains the army alright, various exercises take place. Recently I watched a TV report about the Lipetsk Flight School. They say they have fuel again, so they can fly."[53] A concerted effort to show military successes and general improvements may be responsible for such (albeit rare) positive perceptions.[54]

Public opinion and draft evasion

Given the off-putting image of Russian army service in the years since the USSR's collapse, and the significant contraction in the size of Russia's armed forces, it is not surprising that the military service rate has declined. According to the Defense Ministry, as of 2004 roughly 10 percent of young men were engaged in military service, as versus 27 percent a decade earlier. Draft evasion by means of corruption (paying various sums for medical or other deferments) contributed to this decline and to an increase in the relative number of conscripts from families of limited means.[55]

Widespread knowledge of the hazards involved in combat and non-combat army service apparently produces strong popular support for draft evaders. A national survey in January 2003 found that 41 percent of respondents would sympathize (or be likely to sympathize) with men who avoided the draft "without good reason."[56] A similar survey in October 2002 found 54 percent of respondents ready to sympathize with draft dodgers, and 53 percent sympathetic to the plight of deserters from Russia's armed forces.[57]

Public opinion and patriotism

In initiating the patriotic education programs, Putin's administration had hoped to increase the number of Russian youth willing to serve in the military, and to achieve this goal by inculcating a patriotic sentiment that had been diminished during the 1990s. Russian experts polled in August 2000 likewise saw the Yeltsin era as a time of declining patriotism; 54 percent believed that "the sense of patriotism among Russians has markedly weakened over the past ten years," while only 37 percent thought there had been little change in that area.[58]

Patriotic identification within Russia's population varied by age, a fact of which the patriotic education program planners were well aware. In December 2006, while 57 percent of Russian citizens surveyed called themselves "patriots," 30 percent did not. This "patriotism gap" was more distinct among those aged 18–35, of whom 53 percent considered themselves patriots as against 65 percent of those aged 55 and older, and the non-patriots among 18- to 35-year-olds registered at 34 percent versus a national average of 30 percent.[59] Moreover, the level of perceived patriotism among Russian citizens had changed little over the previous five years. Asked "what part of the Russian population would you consider patriotic?" the answers of respondents in November 2001 and in December 2006 were almost identical: about 18 percent thought a majority of the population were patriotic; about 20 percent thought half the population consisted of patriots; 42 percent thought that only a minority of their co-citizens were patriotic; and about 7 percent thought there were no patriots in Russia.[60] Over the course of the first patriotic education program nothing appeared to have been altered in people's views of each other's patriotism.[61]

But what *was* patriotism? In December 2006 the Public Opinion Foundation (FOM) asked 1,500 Russian respondents about the essence of patriotism by providing them with a set of criteria. Respondents agreed overwhelmingly (76 percent) that "a person who does not care about the natural environment cannot be called a patriot," and that patriots must know the history of their country (70 percent).[62] Sixty-nine percent agreed that "a patriot would not dodge military service," but the number was lower among 18- to 35-year-olds, only 62 percent of whom felt this way.[63] Even among the younger respondents, though, draft evasion was seen as unpatriotic by a majority – independent of whether respondents identified themselves as being patriotic or not.[64] For roughly two-thirds of the population, then, patriotism involved a certain level of willingness to serve in the military – a response that might be expected to delight the state patriotic education program planners.

The relationship between patriotism and military service, however, was indirect at best. Indeed, Russian patriotic sentiment toward the state – and service to the state – was complex in the aftermath of the 1990s. Asked whether they sided with the view that "a patriot should love his fatherland, his state and his government" or whether they thought "a patriot should love only his fatherland and is not obliged to love his state," a majority of those aged 18–35 (54 percent) no doubt disappointed state officials in 2000 with their support for the latter position. Among the total population, 50 percent sided with the second position as well; polling analysts saw this as evidence that "the state is an alien (at best), if not a hostile force" for half the population surveyed. Focus-group participants backed the survey results: "The state for me is a monster fighting against the people"; "The state doesn't fulfill its functions"; "They are stealing from us."[65] In the same poll, 3 percent of respondents asked to define patriotism said, "there is no patriotism," and raised similar sentiments: "if your country cares about you, if the country needs you, then you are ready to give your life for the Motherland, but now, patriotic feelings have disappeared; people are not needed by the Motherland, and, therefore, it is foolish to die for it."[66] As one "expert" polled at that time remarked, "A patriot should love his Fatherland, while the power structure exists to love its citizens. A patriot is not obliged to love the authorities."[67]

Focus groups held in November 2001 indicated that patriotism was seen largely as a reciprocal venture: the state and the citizen should be mutually responsible to each other. A "breach" in that relationship on the state's part was deadly to patriotism. One participant remarked:

> The state doesn't care about the ordinary people, the rogues robbed the people, and the state left everyone to his fate. The Chubaises and Mamuts use it in their own interests. But now they want patriotism, so that everybody will forgive and support them. When nothing was left to steal, they remembered patriotism.

Asked if they regarded themselves as patriots, some participants similarly pointed to the reciprocity problem: "As recently as 10 years ago, I would have said 'yes,' but now I don't know. Because over these years there was no mutuality between me and the state."[68]

Similar issues discussed by focus groups in early 2004 gave rise to further evidence that patriotic feelings depend on the state's behavior above all else. As one polling analyst put it, "a patriotic upbringing is understood [by the population] not as a complex of educational measures, but as a creation of certain conditions where people would start to experience patriotic feelings." Along these lines, one focus group participant in Samara noted, "I understand patriotism as love for the Motherland. But love is a mutual feeling." The participant's next phrase, "It's important for me that my Motherland …," was completed midstream by another participant: "… loves me, too." A third participant agreed: "Yes, patriotism will appear when the state loves you back."[69]

The impact of this reciprocity belief on young men's willingness to serve in the army was summed up by one focus group respondent in Moscow in 2004: "When I was drafted into the army, I felt very positive about it. I wouldn't join the army now, and would do everything I could to dodge it. Why should I defend someone's wealth and throw my body into a machine? What for?"[70]

Such data revealed a clear need, from the government's perspective, for a patriotic education plan centering on the armed forces. The state under Putin set out, then, to remake the image of the Russian military machine. These efforts were codified in two federally sponsored patriotic education programs, the first of which ran from 2001 to 2005, with a second designed to continue the work between 2006 and 2010. In devising these programs, the planners would draw extensively on the Soviet experience of military-patriotic education.

The State Patriotic Education Program

Military-patriotic education in the Soviet Union

Militarized patriotism has long roots in Soviet history. In the 1930s, Stalin's government mounted an enormous propaganda campaign focused on the need to prepare for a future war with capitalist states – a war that seemed inevitable. According to historian Anna Krylova, the Soviet population underwent at that time a thoroughgoing series of military-patriotic education initiatives aimed at "Soviet youth" in particular – those born after 1910, and thus too young to have participated directly in either the Bolshevik Revolution or the civil war that followed it from 1918 to 1921. The Soviet youth organization, the Komsomol, "repeatedly presented the future conflict as youth's great historical test, equivalent to the one their parents had already passed in preceding battles." During the 1930s, Krylova explains, "the task of bringing up young Communists increasingly became tantamount to the task [of] raising 'fighters.' "[71]

The government's perceived need to have a youth population eager and ready to defend the state was pervasive. In 1927 a new state-supported organization was formed in order to further promote the military readiness of the population to defend the country. This was OSOAVIAKHIM, the Society for Promotion of Defense, Aviation, and Chemical Development, which provided Soviet youth with "a vast and growing network of shooting galleries, flying clubs, parachute-stands and airfields where youth could add practical military skills to their designated war duties."[72] Together, the Komsomol and OSOAVIAKHIM raised the military skill levels of hundreds of thousands of Soviet youth and increased their readiness for service to the state.[73]

Military-patriotic education, so intensive in the period leading up to World War II, was revived in the 1970s for the younger generation, which had no direct experience of the war itself. Journalist Zaira Abdullaeva recalls that in the context of "relative stability" in the mid-1970s the state sought to "consolidate society [and] ensure [that] future generations would be devoted – or at least loyal – citizens," and found a means to do so in patriotic education, specifically about World War II. Her own generation's education, as a result, was "very militarized."[74] Introduced in 1967, basic military training (known as *nachal'naia voennaia podgotovka*, NVP) in schools became ubiquitous; students assembled and disassembled Kalashnikovs, and used Makarov pistols in target practice "at the school shooting range."[75] Abdullaeva's textbook (probably used nationwide) exhorted male students to serve in the military: "no one, apart from cowards and despicable outcasts, refuses to serve in the Soviet Army."[76]

One element of military-patriotic education that emerged in the 1970s was a nationwide war game called *zarnitsa*.[77] *Zarnitsa* took place during the school year but was also widespread at summer "Pioneer" camps.[78] While the format differed from school to school, and the game itself was not ubiquitous, *zarnitsa* as a concept remains familiar across the generation educated in the 1970s and 1980s. A cross between a competitive game like Capture the Flag and a military-patriotic training exercise, *zarnitsa* entailed organizing students into teams which, in some cases, would face off in battle lines and "engage" their enemy (ripping the insignia off each other's uniforms as a symbol of defeat), and in others involved "crowds of 15-year olds being bused to a forest … where we would run around shouting 'Hurrah,' while scouring the area for the military flags of the imaginary enemy."[79]

Various experiences of military-patriotic education were recalled by a handful of Russian citizens schooled in the Soviet orbit in the 1970s and 1980s in locations as diverse as Tomsk, Krasnodar, Moscow, and a Soviet-run school in Algeria.[80] These experiences ranged from "zero" exposure to military-patriotic education ("no meetings with war veterans") at an "elite school" in Moscow, to a full-fledged *zarnitsa* competition in a forest on the outskirts of Moscow, where elementary school students competed in the very trenches used by the defenders of Moscow in 1941.[81] One man from Krasnodar remembered his own military-patriotic education as consisting of only a meager parade in early elementary school, but vividly recalled reading newspaper accounts of *zarnitsa*, which described how some youthful participants crouched in sturdy concrete-reinforced trenches as tanks roared overhead, and lobbed mock anti-tank grenades after them. A woman in Tomsk recalled a military-sporting competition (with more emphasis on sports than on military training) where she and her fellow students spent two days learning to use a compass and to set up tents, and learning other outdoor skills transferable to a military environment. She also recalled a yearly event where each class conducted military drills, marched in formation, and chose a "marching song" to sing. Her high school choir sang a widely known *zarnitsa* song as well, although her school did not participate in the war games themselves. The song's chorus proclaims: "*Zarnitsa*, *zarnitsa*, our favorite game / *Zarnitsa*, *zarnitsa*, our military game," and one stanza illustrates clearly the military-preparatory aspect of the event:

> "So what that it's just a mock enemy.
> So what that our rifles are plywood.
> We've still got real bravery and steadfastness
> And the strength of Soviet soldiers."[82]

Such competitions and outdoor training exercises were recalled with fondness by these respondents. Other forms of military-patriotic education seemed more mundane. These took the form of obligatory meetings with World War II veterans, and viewing war movies and photography displays. One woman recalling her elementary school experience in Moscow described poster-sized photographs of scenes from World War II; these filled one hallway of her elementary school (and thus "unfortunately lost their impact" after repeated exposure). Her school also featured an "elaborate and moving museum" dedicated to the war, and in the ninth grade her class took a memorable day-long field trip (*pokhod*) tracing the route taken by a Russian partisan guerrilla, Zoia Kosmodemianskaia, who had been executed by the Nazis.[83]

A similarly militarized patriotism – including the focus on World War II – would form the hub around which the Putin regime's patriotic education plans revolved.

The State Patriotic Education Program, 2001–2005: the first five-year plan

The first patriotic education program (the State Program "Patriotic Education of Russia's Citizens, 2001–2005") constituted a multifaceted approach to raising the level of patriotic consciousness, particularly among youth. The program bemoaned the deterioration in Russian society's patriotic consciousness, the rise of an unhealthy "nationalism," and the "loss of the true meaning and understanding of internationalism." Accompanying these negative phenomena, the program noted, were other problems, such as "egoism, individualism, cynicism ... a disrespectful attitude toward the state and societal institutions," and an ongoing "tendency toward the declining prestige of military and state service."[84]

As a corrective, the program proposed a wide variety of approaches necessitating a "unified state policy [and] state system of patriotic education." The program asserted the need to create regional councils and centers to coordinate patriotic education initiatives, to educate "cadres" specializing in patriotic education, to hold conferences, seminars, and round-tables on patriotic education, as well as bringing together patriotic associations at a nationwide congress. In order to foster the proper willingness to engage in service to the state, the program's authors planned for a series of military-patriotic events and activities including the creation of museum exhibits and "organizing the activity of patriotic, military-patriotic, military-historical, cultural-historical, military-technical, and military-sporting clubs and associations," as well as celebrating significant military dates, and supporting "recovery" operations (*poiskovye meropriiatiia*) whereby battlefields were searched for the remains of Soviet citizens who died in World War II. Veterans' groups, it was hoped, could be called upon to work closely with youth as a means of "preserving and continuing [the state's] glorious military and labor traditions." The program also sought to coordinate the activities of groups holding events memorializing Russia's military glory.[85]

The patriotic education program envisioned mass media support for its campaign, including television programming that would "objectively" convey historical and current events, and thereby counter the "falsifications" of the history of the fatherland, and would also bring in well-known state and societal personages, educators, and veterans to discuss the issue of patriotic education on a regular basis. The program planned for the creation of films, theatrical productions, and written publications (including textbooks) highlighting patriotic themes designed to appeal to the population in all its diversity. Finally, it called for the establishment of various contests and prizes for patriotically themed work in the creative arts.[86]

As is explained in its founding document, the program was expected to generate several outcomes by which its effectiveness would be judged. On the socio-ideological front it was anticipated that five years of patriotic education would help unify Russia's multiethnic society and lower the "degree of ideological opposition"; on the economic front the program was to contribute to economic stability; and in the realm of defensive capabilities (*oboronosposobnost'*) it was expected to result in "young people's aspiration (*stremlenie*) to serve in the Armed Forces, citizens' readiness to defend the Fatherland, and the preservation and development of [the country's] glorious military and labor traditions." Russia's future as a strong state was thus explicitly tied to the "patriotic consciousness" of its citizens and their willingness to manifest that consciousness in military service.[87] In the words of a journalist at the newspaper *Segodnia*, the patriotic education program would, "in the conception of [its authors] … cause youth to accept the right values, reject the wrong, and enter draft age with a feeling of profound pleasure in heading off to active military service."[88]

Although the program's relatively low level of financing (roughly 177 million rubles) denoted a less than top-priority status, the program's planned activities were widespread and anticipated extensive collaboration with existing federal government agencies, as well as non-governmental groups (youth groups, veterans' associations, religious organizations, and "creative unions") that could be marshaled for further patriotic educational efforts.[89]

Put into effect in February 2001, the patriotic education program was a multi-Ministry effort pulling together the Defense Ministry, the Education and Science Ministry, the Ministries of Culture and Media, and the intelligence agencies: the Federal Security Service (FSB) and the Foreign Intelligence Service, under the coordinating role of the Russian State Military Historical-Cultural Center (Rosvoentsentr), a federal government agency.[90] Founded in 1997, Rosvoentsentr was charged with developing and carrying out programs and plans of a military-historical, memorial, and cultural-educational character. Its main tasks were to organize measures related to the military-patriotic education of youth, improving the defensive capacity of the country, providing support for military memorial events, and publishing materials in the mass media that would reveal the heroic history and military traditions of the Russian army and navy.[91] The roots of the state program may be traced in part to Vice-Admiral Yuri Kviatkovskii, who, as the head of Rosvoentsentr in 1998, began urging the adoption of a program on patriotic education.[92]

As part of the Patriotic Education Program of 2001–2005, a new government institution was created: the Russian Center for the Civic and Patriotic Education of Children and Youth, or Rospatriottsentr for short. Rospatriottsentr was entrusted with creating a system to coordinate the activities of the various subdivisions of the Ministry of Education and other institutions engaging in civic and patriotic youth education, and, specifically, to coordinate the activities of the regional centers on patriotic education stipulated by the 2001–2005 program.[93]

Rospatriottsentr would also coordinate the various associations conducting battlefield "recovery" operations across Russia, a cornerstone of the patriotic education program. According to the Ministry of Education, as of 2002 these "military-patriotic youth and children's organizations" working to perpetuate the memory of the defenders of the fatherland counted over 12,000 participants taking part in recovery expeditions – not including the "enormous number of students and organizations working to preserve the memory of those who died in the Great Patriotic War, carrying out research to establish the fate of those who perished." In that year such work was carried out in twenty-six regions that were battlegrounds during World War II, and in twenty-seven other regions "in the rear." The yearly excursions and other efforts to establish the identities and bury the remains of the dead in an honorable fashion constitute a "teachable moment," according to the document on Rospatriottsentr's responsibilities:

> Most of the participants in recovery work are youth between the ages of 14 and 30. Having gone through "recovery school," the youth see the history of our country through new eyes, and come to truly be proud of the heroism and bravery of our soldiers.

The desired spillover effect – whereby the pre-draft-age male participants might view their upcoming army service with a less jaundiced eye – is obvious. Rospatriottsentr also manages a wide variety of contests on themes associated with the victory in the Great Patriotic War, and organizes youth meetings with "veterans of the Great Patriotic War, of the Chechen wars, and of local conflicts; as well as meetings with various types of soldiers."[94]

In carrying out its duties, Rospatriottsentr collaborates with various military-related associations, including the "Victory" committee, the military-memorial center of the Russian Federation's Armed Forces, Rosvoentsentr, the Russian Veterans' Committee, the international association "Military Memorials," the Intergovernmental Coordinating Center on preserving the memory of the defenders of the fatherland, and the Foundation for Heroes of the Soviet Union and the Russian Federation.[95] Indeed, although Rospatriottsentr is based within the Federal Education Agency (itself a sub-agency within Russia's Ministry of Education and Science), all of its collaborators listed in the document describing Rospatriottsentr's official duties are tied to the military in one way or another.

The events carried out under the patriotic education program ranged from lighthearted contests to produce patriotically themed material, such as a Russia-wide song competition held in the town of Belgorod and titled "I Love You, Russia!" to the explicitly military-patriotic activities that dominated the program.[96] The "Plan of Patriotically Themed Events" published on the Rospatriottsentr website, for instance, listed forty events set to take place across Russia in 2005 (in Moscow, North Ossetia, Primorskii Krai, Tatarstan, and Tambov, among other locations; some were designated as Russia-wide events, to occur in multiple places at once).[97] More than half of these (twenty-one) were focused explicitly on World War II, involving search and recovery clubs, celebrations of the sixtieth anniversary of Victory Day, "*Vakhta Pamiati*" projects memorializing those lost in the war, the "Hero Cities" where substantial battles were fought, and meetings between veterans and youth. Another seven activities had a military-patriotic theme generally speaking (such as military-sporting events and camps, meetings of military-patriotic clubs, and the like).[98] As planned, the program had also sponsored the production of movies and television shows "that cast the military, police and intelligence agencies in a positive light." According to the *Moscow Times*, the 2004 television season featured several new series in this vein, including "National Security Agent," "Liquidator," and "The Motherland Is Waiting." The program also funded military-sporting games for young people, "celebrations of military victories, and the production of patriotic souvenirs."[99]

On 30 September 2005, at the close of the 2001–2005 patriotic education program, the Federal Education Agency (Rospatriottsentr's home base) sent out a request to the directors of youth policy and education policy agencies across Russia's regional subdivisions, asking them to fill out a form reporting on their patriotic-educational activities from 2001 to 2005.[100] The form itself is a grid with the years 2001–2005 across the top, and a list of evaluation criteria down the left side. These include

> the number of events of a patriotic nature; the number of extant patriotic associations, clubs, and centers; the number of children and youths who are members of these patriotic associations, clubs, and centers; the number of children and youth (in thousands) participating in these patriotic events; and the volume of financial resources earmarked for carrying out patriotic events.

Below, the form asks for information on the presence (or perhaps absence) of an interdepartmental (coordinating) council (or center) on issues of patriotic education among youth, asking specifically for the title, founding date, and level of the council or center (e.g. regional, municipal, etc.), reflecting the fact that such institutions were supposed to be established under the rubric of the 2001–2005 program. It also requested information regarding the presence of a local governmental institution handling issues of civic and patriotic youth education, such as the institution's full name, the date on which it was founded, and the full name of its director and his or her contact information (address, telephone, and email address). In short, the agency sought information about the extent to which the desired patriotic-education bureaucracy had been formed, and, with respect to the conduct of patriotic events, appeared – like many bureaucracies – more interested in quantity than quality.[101]

The State Patriotic Education Program, 2006–2010: the second five-year plan

The Putin administration evidently regarded the first patriotic education program as at least a limited success. Pressure to introduce a second stage of the program came primarily from top-level officials in Russia's "power ministries": the defense and security agencies. Viktor Ozerov, chair of the Federation Council's Committee on Defense and Security, reported that

> several lawmakers from his committee as well as the defense ministry's top brass and a number of Russian military-connected NGOs officially appealed to President Vladimir Putin, asking for his personal support in pushing the program through the governmental bureaucracy. The Kremlin leader appeared to favor the concept, and the document was finally adopted.[102]

A continuation of the 2001–2005 program, the State Program on the Patriotic Education of Russian Federation Citizens, 2006–2010 continues to draw a link between fostering a militarized patriotism and Russian youth's readiness to enter army service.

As the second patriotic education program got under way, Putin made explicit the connection between patriotic education and military service in his annual address to Russia's Federal Assembly in May 2006. There, Putin noted that one means of combating the deterioration of the draft pool was patriotic education:

> A huge number of young men of conscript age today suffer from chronic diseases and have problems with drinking, smoking and sometimes drugs as well. I think that in our schools we need not just to educate our young people but also see to their physical and patriotic development. We need to restore the system of pre-conscription military training and help develop military sports. The government should adopt the appropriate programme in this area.[103]

Putin has also linked (albeit indirectly) the issue of fertility rates and population decline in Russia with the need for a more robust male population of conscript age in the future. In that same annual address, he stressed the demographic issues facing Russia, promoting a plan to increase birthrates by offering various incentives. The tie to military service was highlighted when Putin introduced the topic of fertility. "And now for the most important matter," Putin stated. "What is most important for our country?" A male voice from the audience interrupted him, calling out, "Love (*liubov'*)!" It was Sergei Ivanov, Russia's defense minister.

"Correct (*pravil'no*)!" answered Putin. "The Defense Ministry knows what is most important. Indeed, what I want to talk about is love, women, children. I want to talk about the family, about the most acute problem facing our country today – the demographic problem."[104] Responding to these remarks, Andrei Illarionov, a former aid to the president, believed Putin's distress over demographic trends was motivated by his desire for a larger draft pool. "It seems that the Defense Ministry is the only institution that understands why it is necessary to solve the demographic problem in Russia," Illarionov stated after the address.[105]

Like the first program, the 2006–2010 plan was to be organized by Rosvoentsentr and implemented with the assistance of the various ministries that had played roles in carrying out its predecessor. In its preamble the new program noted that under the previous (2001–2005) patriotic education program, "the fundamental tasks of patriotic education ... have been solved," since the "main goal" of that program had been to establish "a system of patriotic education." This system, according to the new program, was now in place, since regional interdepartmental coordinating councils and centers for patriotic education had been formed and were operating in the majority of Russia's regions, and the "preparation of specialists on patriotic education" had been "organized."[106] Work carried out under the rubric of the first program had also "achieved some change in tone" among the mass media on the subject of patriotic education. And between 2002 and 2004 nearly 115 million rubles had been spent on addressing "urgent issues of patriotic education."[107]

Still, the text of the new program argued, there were gaps in the system, requiring the continuation and expansion of the patriotic education program. Some regions lacked coordinating councils on patriotic education (despite plans to create them under the 2001–2005 program); educational and cultural institutions at all levels lacked materials; and specialists in patriotic education were as yet insufficiently prepared. In short, the program announced, "Patriotism has not yet fully become the unifying basis for society."[108]

Although the program aimed to raise the patriotic consciousness of all age groups, its "priority" was to reach the young generation of "children and youth." The varied means proposed by the program to achieve its goals therefore included "raising the quality of patriotic education in schools, turning them into centers of patriotic education" for the young generation, and getting more organizations and individuals on board with the patriotic education process. Among the tasks inherent in "perfecting" the patriotic education process were several of those appearing in the initial program, such as encouraging the remembrance of soldiers "who perished defending the Fatherland"; ordering patriotically themed productions in the area of culture, the arts, and the mass media; financial and other types of support for the expansion of patriotic themes in television programming, newspapers, and literature; and granting journalists, writers, and filmmakers access to archival materials in order to create materials for patriotic education.[109] The program would organize "festivals, competitions, seminars, [and] exhibitions" on patriotic themes, and also mentioned military-patriotic summer camps and military sports.[110] Russia's state symbols (such as the flag, the coat of arms, and the anthem) were also to become more widely seen and discussed in schools and elsewhere.

The program's "effectiveness" would be measured "by citizens' aspiration and degree of readiness to fulfill their civil and patriotic duties, in all their various forms," which itself would be evaluated in "reports" written by the various agencies participating in the program, and also by means of "regular sociological polls" of the population.[111] Such duties were understood as encompassing

> citizens' responsibility for the fate of their county, prioritizing societal and governmental principles over personal or private interests, loyalty to one's Fatherland, and readiness to fulfill one's constitutional obligations, such as defending the interests of one's Motherland, and, of course, service in the Armed Forces for young citizens subject to the draft."[112]

The funding to carry out the 2006–2010 program was slated to almost triple that set aside for the 2001–2005 program, to nearly 500 million rubles (roughly $17 million, up from the $6.4 million allocated for the first plan), including 378 million from the federal budget, with the remainder to be provided by various cultural and scientific organizations participating in patriotic education, as well as corporate and individual sponsors.[113] To some extent the program appears to be an unabashed attempt to purchase patriotism in popular culture.

A sixty-three-page appendix to the program, listing 189 separate projects, events, activities, proposed laws, new medals and awards, and so forth, provides some idea of how this level of increased patriotic consciousness is intended to be achieved. Of the many measures (*meropriiatiia*) listed there, more than half exhibit an overtly militarized component. Patriotic education, according to the steps specified in the document, is closely associated with familiarity with the past achievements of Russia's armed forces and respect for the military more generally. One column of the appendix lists the "expected result" of each measure. Testimony to the fact that at least one explicit intention of the patriotic education program is to decrease the number of youth attempting to evade service in the armed forces is the presence of numerous measures in this "results" column *explicitly* intended to "develop respect" for Russia's armed forces, to "raise the prestige" of military service, and to "instill in young people a readiness for the armed defense of the Motherland" (or in some cases, Fatherland) and "for service in the Russian army." This latter constitutes the expected result of a planned military-patriotic event (to be held yearly between 2006 and 2010) called "We believe in you, Soldier!" (*My verim v tebia, Soldat!*).[114] Along with this, a yearly holiday, Conscripts' Day, is to be introduced, to "develop a feeling of civic duty among conscripts," as well as a planned yearly event in which conscripts will take their military oath in museums and at monuments "dedicated to military glory" and with the participation of "parents, veterans, and youth not yet of draft age."[115]

The connection between patriotism and military activity is explicit in the 2006–2010 program. Victories by Russia's armed forces are stressed particularly, though not exclusively. The appendix includes fifteen measures devoted to the sixty-five-year anniversary of the victory in the Great Patriotic War, as well as several events dedicated to other victories, such as the seventy-year anniversary of the defeat of Japanese forces in 1938 at Lake Hassan, and the 300-year anniversary of Russian victory at the Battle of Poltava in 1709. While World War II is the focus of many of the planned events in the program, it is not the only historical military sacrifice to which attention is paid in the document. One event was planned for 2009 to commemorate the twenty-year anniversary of Soviet troops' withdrawal from Afghanistan, an event intended to "inculcate a feeling of respect for participants in those events."[116] Another, planned for 2010, would mark the feat (*podvig*) of the airborne troops of the 6th Company, 104th Guards Parachute Regiment of the Pskov-based 76th Airborne Troop Division, eighty-four of whom had perished ten years earlier in Chechnya (leaving only six survivors). This commemorative event was designed to "immortalize the memory of those airborne troops (*desantniki*) who perished in the Chechen Republic."[117]

The program does not rely exclusively on the military as a source of patriotism, but in general the measures planned under the 2006–2010 patriotic education program show a pervasive association with the Russian armed forces.[118] Political scientist Douglas Blum finds that the "single most striking and important feature of the Patriotic Education Program is the extent to which it extols the military and militaristic virtues," and cites Putin's May 2006 comments on the importance of military service for Russia's future as illustrative:

> We must explain to the entire generation of young people that the question of whether or not to serve in the army should not even come up for a young person to begin with. We must all realize that without the army there would be no country. Nobody should have the slightest doubt on this score. No army, no Russia."[119]

Putin's remarks neatly sum up one of the driving forces behind the continuing program of patriotic education.

Patriotic education in Russia and the Great Patriotic War

Nearly sixty years after it ground to a bloody halt, World War II or, as Russians call it, the Great Patriotic War continues to be a hub around which patriotic pride and identification center.[120] Ninety-eight percent of Russia's population surveyed in 2003 recognized 9 May as Victory Day (*den' pobedy*), and 83 percent of them saw it as an "important holiday" for a variety of reasons. Victory Day represented, first and foremost, the defeat of "fascist Germany." Yet the survey revealed that this victory was fast becoming a matter of "knowledge" rather than "memory," and, as such, its salience was in decline among the youth of Russia. While 92 percent of respondents over age 50 saw Victory Day as important, and 84 percent of those aged 36–50 agreed, only 70 percent of those aged 18–35 felt it was an important holiday for them, and 22 percent said it was not.[121] This in part explains the prevalence of patriotic education programming on the Soviet army's victory in World War II: it serves as a means to maintain the centrality of that achievement in the pantheon of Russian patriotism.

The years of *glasnost'*, with their revelations about Stalinism, including the devastating purges of Soviet Red Army commanders on the eve of World War II, the totalitarian commonalities between the fascist and the Soviet communist systems, and the treatment of Soviet POWs imprisoned as spies on false charges upon their return, complicated the Soviet victory in World War II as a point of patriotic pride.[122] I. Klimov, an analyst at the Public Opinion Foundation, however, notes that "this new ambiguity" did not affect the greater significance of the Soviet victory in the national imagination. As one participant in a focus group discussion put it in 2003, although her own family members had not fought in the war, she believed the victory to be one of "Good over Evil ... And it is another occasion for all Russians to remember that actually we are a great people and we should esteem ourselves in accordance with our victories." Still, Klimov argued, "Integration of newly disclosed and often negative information on the war into the system of the nation's consciousness is a topical task we are facing today."[123]

Evidence from a 2005 survey of 2,000 Russian citizens aged 16–29 suggests that Stalin is still closely and positively associated in the popular imagination with the Soviet victory in World War II. More than half of the respondents in this age group (56 percent) believed Stalin had done "more good than bad," and "[o]nly 28 percent felt that Stalin did not deserve credit for the Soviet victory in World War II." An astonishing 19 percent of respondents said they "would definitely or probably vote" for Stalin, were he alive and running for office today – a nearly 6-point increase from 2003.[124]

Focus-group discussions in December 2004 shed light on these survey results. Participants volunteered a commonly held belief that Stalin had presided over "repressions and famine" but "it was with him that we won World War II."[125] The authors of this study about Stalin's ongoing popularity suggest that such views reflect a woefully inadequate education about the Stalin era, pointing out that Stalin and Stalinism receive little coverage in high school history courses. In 2003 a history text "hailed for its thorough and meticulous discussion of Stalin's repressions and his role in World War II" was removed from the public school curriculum with Putin's approval.[126]

Indeed, under Putin, Russian state officials did not shy away from highlighting Stalin's leadership role in World War II. In March 2005 the city administration of Volgograd (previously Stalingrad), the site of a decisive battle against German forces, sanctioned the erection of a monument to Stalin featuring the former dictator seated with Roosevelt and Churchill, thereby commemorating Stalin's leadership in World War II.[127] Similarly, in July 2004 Putin ordered that "Stalingrad" replace "Volgograd" on Moscow's Monument to the Unknown Soldier, a decision made in advance of the sixtieth anniversary celebrations of Victory Day, "and taking into account the significance of the Battle of Stalingrad, the turning point of the war, giving due respect to the heroism of the defenders of Stalingrad, and with the goal of preserving the history of the Russian state."[128]

Surveys exploring the Russian citizenry's feelings of pride and shame shed light on the regime's choice to feature military victories in its patriotic education programs, particularly the victory in World War II. According to poll data, national shame consistently outweighed pride within the Russian population, and between February 2002 and December 2006 the ratio of Russian citizens' feelings of pride and shame remained roughly constant. Answering the question "Would you say you are proud or ashamed of the nation?" 26 percent expressed pride in 2002 and 2006, and 39 percent and 38 percent expressed shame in 2002 and 2006 respectively.[129]

The sources of this shame were both historical and contemporary. According to a 2002 survey, historical sources of shame included Stalin's regime (18 percent of responses), the war in Afghanistan (6 percent), and other "events of Soviet history" (a total of 31 percent of responses), as well as "events after 1991" (10 percent of responses) including the war in Chechnya (3 percent). Both Soviet and post-Soviet history appeared tainted to a significant portion of respondents. Asked about sources of shame in their contemporary life, a plurality of respondents indicated "economic crisis" (35 percent), but an additional 10 percent noted "events in Chechnya," and 2 percent pointed to "breakdown of the army."[130]

By contrast, when citizens responded to an open-ended question in 2002 asking, "what in the historical past of our country makes you feel pride?" the number one answer provided was "victory in the Second World War" (41 percent). Other respondents (3 percent) pointed to Russian military victories before 1917, and another 3 percent indicated that "strong armed forces" were a source of pride for them, bringing the total percentage of militarized responses to 47 percent.[131] This strong feeling of militarized patriotism, already shared by a significant plurality of the population, provides a focal point around which to construct a patriotic education program.

Pride in military achievement, however, did not rank highly when citizens were asked about contemporary sources of pride. In 2006, of the 72 percent of respondents who expressed some feeling of national pride, including the 7 percent who had said it was "hard to answer" whether or not they felt pride), 21 percent pointed to athletic accomplishments as the basis for their pride. Second place, at 18 percent, was occupied by "hard to answer/no answer," and only in third place, tying for a mere 4 percent, were Russia's "economic growth" and "the Russian army and the growth of Russia's defense capacity." Two percent noted "the victory in the Great Patriotic War," testifying to its resonance even as a "contemporary" foundation for national pride.[132]

These survey results clearly imply that past military victories are far more popular as a locus of pride than are the contemporary Russian armed forces. The patriotic education planners apparently believed that in order to strengthen public support for the latter, the former should be used as extensively as possible, and that the link between the Soviet forces who won the victory in 1945 and today's Russian military should be made explicit. An imagined continuity between the victorious Soviet army in the Great Patriotic War and the contemporary Russian army is therefore one of the goals that the patriotic education programs seek to achieve. These programs therefore highlight not only the Russian military more generally, but particularly the globally recognized victory against fascism and the ways in which that victory can be parlayed into support for service in Russia's armed forces today.

In keeping with the patriotic education programs, a revival of militarized patriotism – often, but not always, focusing on World War II – has been visible in various forms in Russian schools, popular culture, and state-sponsored public events. Representative examples of this trend are discussed in the following sections.

Military-patriotic education and training, 2000–2006

While children entering school in the 1990s found a less militarized environment than that of earlier decades, as the obligatory "basic military training" (NVP) dropped out of the curriculum, and as *glasnost'* caused significant confusion in history curricula, by the start of the twenty-first century some resurgence in military-patriotic education was in evidence.

Daily forms of military-patriotic training appear to have been reintroduced, although not as thoroughly or consistently as was the case under Soviet rule. On 31 December 1999, as acting president, Putin signed a decree reintroducing military training programs into schools (including instruction for male students on the assembly and disassembly of Kalashnikov assault rifles).[133] This attempt to revitalize the Soviet tradition of basic military training (NVP) failed. In September 2005 an advisor to the Ministry of Education reported that NVP had not been reintroduced in fact, or at least not widely enough to have merited much attention.[134] Perhaps to rectify this gap, in July 2005 the Federation Council passed a bill "amending previous laws so that schools must make rudimentary military training a mandatory subject for students."[135] Nor was this bill broadly implemented.

Variations on NVP persist, however. Although lessons in assembling and disassembling weaponry were not in evidence, one teacher at a Moscow middle school asserted that NVP "hadn't gone anywhere," but rather was now part of a course on "life safety skills" (*okhrana bezopasnosti zhiznedeiatel'nosti*, OBZh). At the associated high school, the textbook for the OBZh class included a section on what boys should do in order to be prepared to go into the army.[136] In this light it is worth noting that the state patriotic education program of 2001–2005 stipulated "the development of textbooks" that would foster patriotic values among youth, "to prepare [that generation] for military service and dignified service to the Fatherland."[137] According to Igor Innokentievich Melnichenko, the director of the Federal Education Agency's Department on Youth Affairs and Children's Education and Social Welfare (and the informal head of Rospatriottsentr), although OBZh is not part of the fundamental course of study, it "is recommended and taught in many schools" across the country, and includes first aid and other skills useful in the event of natural or technological disasters, as well as basic military skills. Such classes were typically taught by men: military reservists, gym coaches, and shop teachers.[138]

As might be expected given the stress on World War II in the patriotic education program documents, Russian public schools carry out patriotic educational events related to the war.[139] Whether this is the result of suggestions from Rospatriottsentr (through the Federal Education Agency and Ministry for Education and Science) or of initiatives by teachers themselves is difficult to say. The form of some of these events, however, recalls previous efforts at military-patriotic schooling in the Soviet era.

The extent to which schools take part in militarized patriotic education varies. At one "upscale" Moscow elementary school in 2005, students commemorated the sixtieth anniversary of the Soviet victory in World War II in only a "small" way, inviting a single veteran in to talk with the children, and holding a commemorative concert. Such meetings between students and World War II veterans had been explicitly encouraged by the first patriotic education program.

Other schools construct more creative events stressing the oral history and memory of World War II. In 2006 a highly competitive public middle school in Moscow staged a game similar to *zarnitsa* to commemorate the sixty-fifth anniversary of the Battle of Moscow.[140] In this competition, called "Bring the Dispatch to Headquarters" (*dostav paket v shtab*), nine teams (made up of ten to fifteen students from each of the school's nine classes) competed in an extensive Great Patriotic War-themed role play.[141] Teams included students playing nurses, war reporters, commanders, war historians, wire-communications specialists, and so on. The teams competed, fulfilling tasks at a series of "command posts." The tasks included singing war songs and reciting war poetry (scored for presentation), bandaging each other (scored for timing), answering questions about the war (such as the main battles, commanders, and the locations of factories evacuated eastward from the western areas of the country), and running outside to lob mock grenades at a wooden tank. In addition to receiving scores, teams collected one word at each command post, and at the end of the competition used these to decipher a coded message.

Such elaborate staging of events related to the war, while clearly encouraged by the patriotic education programs, depends to some extent on the enthusiasm and level of interest on the part of teachers. At this particular school, students prepared posters about their families' history during the war, and a history teacher (the originator of the "Bring the Dispatch to Headquarters" competition) created a temporary exhibit of war memorabilia brought in by students and teachers. She also constructed a detailed diorama of a battle site outside Moscow, taking a group of older students to that area and digging out helmets and shells from the soil. Such activities – as well as exhibiting impressive pedagogy – point to an ongoing tradition of patriotic education, perhaps interrupted by the 1990s but now openly encouraged by the Russian government, through the patriotic education programs.

Militarized patriotism in popular culture

Coincident with Putin's ascension to the Russian presidency began a revival of military-patriotic-themed popular culture, ranging from animated films and toys aimed at children, to full-length movies, television serials and documentaries. Some of these emphasize Russia's history of "hard and brilliantly won" battles. In fall 2006, for example, there appeared a wide variety of commemorative programming on the Battle of Moscow. These efforts included public banners, posters, and multiple television documentaries. One such program was a daily television spot lasting only five minutes, which described each day of the battle (on the date it occurred, sixty-five years later).[142] Such programming is fully in line with the measures commemorating the war that are listed in the 2006–2010 patriotic education program. Patriotically themed books for elementary school children are also widely available now, by contrast with the 1990s. One such volume, *Moia rodina – Rossiia* (My Country – Russia), includes portraits of famous Russians, the Russian anthem, and the state seal and flag, a direct echo of the 2006–2010 program's directive to publish materials spurring the recognition and proper usage of Russia's state symbols. Books about "pioneer heroes" (Soviet children who blew up Nazi tanks and performed other military feats during World War II), popular in the 1970s and 1980s, were "among the first to be republished" as the Putin era began.[143]

One new Russian television series intended perhaps to improve the image of military service and of military officers in particular is *Kadetstvo*, a "dramedy" about life in the Suvorovskoe uchilishche, a prominent military academy. *Kadetstvo*'s first season was broadcast in September–October 2006 (twenty-six episodes were shown, and a total of forty episodes were planned). The slogan for the series is a saying originating with Alexander Suvorov (1729–1800), a Russian general famous for never having lost a battle: "If you train hard, the battle will be easy" (*nelegko v uchenii – legko v boiu!*).[144] A popular TV sit-com, *Soldaty* (Soldiers), also features the army.[145]

Popular entertainment regarding the military is not uniformly positive and lighthearted, however. One example is the film *9-aia rota* (9th Company), directed by Fiodor Bondarchuk and broadcast after a large advertising campaign on Russia's state-owned TV Channel 1. The film was also shown in theaters; in October 2005, *9-aia rota* reportedly became the highest-grossing film in post-Soviet Russia.[146] Based on the experience of the Soviet army's 9th company during the 1980s war in Afghanistan, the film portrays the soldiers' pointless effort to defend hill 3234, a position that is finally overrun. When the remaining soldiers are rescued via helicopter at the close of the film, they discover that they were supposed to have retreated a week earlier. As a reassessment movie, similar to some of the films that circulated in the United States in the wake of the Vietnam War, *9-aia rota* attempted to rescue military service as such from the political corruption and inept leadership that surrounded it: the soldiers in the trenches were heroic, but trapped and betrayed by their commanders and the political leadership. Military service thus was valorized in the film. Under Putin's regime the prosecutions in some high-profile hazing cases, as well as Putin's own image as incorruptible, aimed to reassure the population that military service was no longer service to an inept, broken state bereft of ideological commitment, as the Soviet Union may have seemed to be in its last decade.

Militarized patriotism and the mass media

Russia's Media Ministry quickly acceded to the ethos pervading the first patriotic education program, announcing in early 2002 that it was spending $16 million on over 200 "'military-patriotic' media projects involving 27 mass media outlets in 19 Russian regions." According to Deputy Media Minister Mikhail Seslavinsky, the goal was to rouse media "interest in military-patriotic education." Seslavinsky admitted that the Ministry's efforts had not yet produced results; he could not point to "radical change in public opinion toward the military," and explained that his Ministry was collaborating with the Defense Ministry on developing "additional programs to encourage 'military-patriotic publications.'"[147]

One well-funded media effort coinciding with the first patriotic education program was the launch of a military-patriotic television station, Zvezda (Star), in April 2005, just in time for the sixtieth anniversary of the Nazis' defeat in World War II in early May. Zvezda reportedly sported a $7 million budget (clearly exceeding the $6.4 million earmarked for the Patriotic Education Program of 2001–2005).[148] Planning to air documentaries, war movies from the Soviet era, children's cartoons, and musical events, as well as news, the station's "ideology," according to its general manager, Sergei Savushkin, was straightforward: "In order to defend, one has to love."[149]

Zvezda, despite Savushkin's assertions that it was a "commercial project with no government involvment," was evidently closely tied to the Defense Ministry: its "equipment, transmitters, and license belong to the Defense Ministry's Central Television and Radio Studio."[150] The license (ostensibly won by the Defense Ministry through a competitive process), according to Savushkin, "allots military topics 10 per cent of broadcast time and 90 per cent of broadcasting is exclusively a civilian project" aimed at a wide audience.[151]

Although national broadcasting by Zvezda ostensibly began (via satellite) on 22 April 2005,[152] the station's signal was not widely received; as of late 2006, several Muscovites questioned about the station reported that it was "invisible," and had concluded that its broadcasting license had fallen through.[153] A notice posted by a technology company, Vidau Systems, in January 2006, however, confirmed Zvezda's "large order" of virtual studio technology from a French company, to be used once Zvezda had moved from a temporary studio it had occupied since February 2005 into "new facilities in Moscow in May 2006." According to the seller, Zvezda planned to "expand its broadcast transmission to ten channels, both terrestrial and satellite," covering the entirety of Russia's territory.[154]

By early 2007 the efforts of the patriotic education programs had created an incentive for the large-scale media to take up more patriotic programming. Igor' Innokent'evich Mel'nichenko, the informal overseer of Rospatriottsentr, thought that a "positive role" in this regard had been played by several competitions held by the Media Ministry for the "best and most systematic coverage" of patriotic-educational themes. Such contests, even if they did not create a dramatic change in the focus of the media, had "served, at least, to attract the journalistic establishment toward work in this area." Mel'nichenko also pointed to the programming on regional television, as well as on two national television stations, Kul'tura and the above-noted Zvezda, as providing an "exception" to the fare typically found on television, where historical programs, patriotic films, and youth programs received little airtime compared to talk shows, box-office hits, and other forms of entertainment.[155]

Militarized patriotism and public holidays

Public celebrations present another venue (beyond the educational system and the mass media) in which the government seeks to spread the militarized patriotism embraced by the patriotic education programs. The anniversaries of major battles such as the Battle of Moscow and the Battle of Stalingrad, as well as Victory Day in May 1945, are celebrated extensively in Russia, and in recent years such events have been the focus of significant attention. Festivities in central Moscow in January 2005, for instance, featured a gigantic New Year's fir tree (*elka*), along with a performance starring Russian folk-tale characters, and concluded with a speech about the victories achieved in World War II, as boxes of candy inscribed "1945–2005" were distributed.[156] Whether or not this particular event was planned under the 2001–2005 patriotic education program, the state programs certainly include support for such commemorative events and the "souvenir" paraphernalia associated with them.

A variety of military-patriotic holidays aside from those associated with World War II have been introduced in recent years. In an attempt to replace the 7 November holiday (the Soviet Union's most important holiday, marking the Bolshevik takeover in 1917), Putin's government introduced the Day of National Unity (*den' narodnogo edinstvo*), to be celebrated on 4 November. The new holiday commemorated Moscow's liberation from Polish forces in 1612, representing the end of the "Time of Troubles." This Day of National Unity was first officially observed in 2005. Both a military victory and an instance of national cohesion (not unlike the Soviet effort against the Nazis), the holiday celebrating the defeat of the Poles was chosen as an embodiment of the values expressed in the patriotic education programs.[157]

Another holiday intended to foster militarized patriotism is the celebration of the Battle of Kulikovo Field, where Moscow's Grand Prince Dmitri Donskoi won a victory over the Golden Horde in 1380. This new state holiday, sanctioned by Putin, was celebrated in 2005 starting on 18 July, when the head of the Russian Orthodox Church "opened celebrations with a liturgy," and continued through 21 September, the actual anniversary of the battle.[158] Unlike the Day of National Unity, this holiday, though intended to foster civic togetherness and a national civic identity, proved ethnically divisive, provoking protests among Russia's Tatar population.[159]

Further efforts to promote militarized patriotism were evident in November 2003, when Russia's Duma approved a "new list of military anniversaries" to be celebrated by the armed forces. The list, presented by the presidential apparatus, included the aforementioned liberation of Moscow in 1612 and the Battle of Kulikovo Field, as well as "the anniversary of the Battle on the Ice against Teutonic Knights in 1242, ... the defeat of the Swedes by Tsar Peter the Great at Poltava in 1709, and the capture by Russian forces of the Turkish fortress at Ismail in 1790, among others."[160] Measures associated with several of these appeared in the 2006–2010 patriotic education program. Putin also decreed 23 February as "Defender of the Fatherland Day" in 2002, making it a state holiday.[161] And in January 2007 the Duma began consideration of a new holiday slated for 9 December – "Heroes of the Fatherland Day" – harking back to pre-Revolutionary Russia, when 9 December was the most widely recognized date for celebrating Russia's troops.[162]

Attention to militarized patriotism continued under Putin's nominal successor, Dmitri Medvedev. On 9 May 2008, within days of his presidential inauguration, Medvedev presided over Russia's yearly celebration of Nazi Germany's defeat. For the first time since 1990 the Victory Day parade through Red Square featured a dramatic display of Russian military personnel and equipment, including T-90 tanks and Topol-M intercontinental ballistic missiles. Public opinion polls reported enthusiasm for this revival of the traditional military parade among no fewer than 70 percent of the population.[163]

Social reactions to militarized patriotism

Resistance to militarized patriotism

A few activist groups in Russia counter the state's hegemonic discourse extolling the virtues of militarized patriotism. Primary among these are the various committees of soldiers' mothers. *Dedovshchina* and the withdrawal of deferments for young men receiving post-secondary education served as the original motivations behind the formation of soldiers' mothers committees in the late 1980s.[164] Reorganized in 1999 as the Union of Committees of Soldiers' Mothers and then transformed in 2004 into a political party (the United People's Party of Soldiers' Mothers), the organization's goals center on reforming Russia's military forces and bringing an end to the draft.[165] Since its founding in 1989 the Committee of Soldiers' Mothers has challenged the state's romanticized image of military service, and, in the view of historian Julie Elkner, succeeded in "shattering" the image of universal service as a patriotic duty to a beneficent state.[166] The organization has undermined this image in various ways, from counseling young men and their families on legal methods of avoiding the draft, to holding demonstrations against the war in Chechnya, lobbying for alternatives to military service,[167] and drawing public attention to *dedovshchina* and the alarming rate of non-combat deaths in the Russian army.[168]

The Soviet state, in its time, had little success either in delegitimating the Committee of Soldiers' Mothers or in imposing a uniform concept of patriotism that required unquestioning allegiance to the state's military. Much like later polls showing support for draft dodgers, a poll conducted in early 1991 "found that 62 per cent of respondents believed that it was unfair to accuse critics of the army of 'insufficient patriotism.'"[169] The Committee of Soldiers' Mothers continues to enjoy considerable public support, particularly for its work helping young men avoid the draft. According to a national survey in January 2003, 81 percent of the Russian population aged 16 and over were familiar with the organization, and 68 percent regarded its actions in a positive light (28 percent regarded the Committee of Soldiers' Mothers neutrally, and only 5 percent took a negative view).[170]

Activists with the Committee of Soldiers' Mothers have challenged the state's linkage between militarization and patriotism. Asked in 2001 about the meaning of patriotism, several volunteers offered answers defying the Putin administration's efforts to reassert a patriotism focused on the military. Tatiana Mikhailova offered this reply: "Patriotism is love for the Motherland, as we usually say.... If someone doesn't want to fight in Chechnya, it's said they're not patriotic. But what does that have to do with patriotism? ... I just think that if a person can do something, like me, to bring others in, to teach, to establish some legal norms, to make the laws actually work, well, that's patriotic work."[171] Patriotism, in this view, is centered on rule of law and the rights of individuals that it entails, rather than on statism and service (military or otherwise) to the state.

Among Russia's small community of anti-militarist activists is also the Antimilitarist Radical Association (ARA), a self-described "liberal and libertarian" movement affiliated with the Transnational Radical Party (based in Italy). As of 1998 the ARA claimed over 200 members in forty-nine Russian cities. For several years the ARA lobbied for an alternative service law that would not place an onerous burden on those claiming conscientious objector status, as well as for ending the draft and moving to a volunteer army, and for the "demilitarization of Russian society more generally."[172] Apparently reorganized as the Russian Radicals movement (Rossiiskie Radikaly) in December 2004, the group continued its work on military issues, as well as lobbying, demonstrating, and organizing petitions on a broad range of issues including the legalization of marijuana, gay rights in Russia, the right to euthanasia, elimination of the death penalty, opposition to religious teachings within the public school system, an end to state-controlled media, and the initiation of temporary administration of Chechnya by the United Nations.[173] The movement's secretary (the main organizer) is Nikolai Khramov, who is also the secretary of the League to End the Draft (Liga za otmenu prizyva), a project created at the initiative of several members of the Radikaly; its sole purpose is to end the draft by means of preparing and conducting a national referendum on the subject.[174] The League held its founding congress in Moscow in July 2005 and works closely with organizations like the Committee of Soldiers' Mothers.[175]

The Radikaly movement's methods entail political lobbying and consciousness raising through demonstrations, and its members follow principles of non-violence in their actions.[176] Using a technique familiar to social movements in the West but unusual in Russia, the Radikaly and the League to End the Draft staged an "anti-draft die-in" at Russia's Ministry of Defense in central Moscow on 9 August 2006, explaining on their website that anti-war and anti-draft activists in the United States in the 1960s and 1970s had used such methods of "active non-violence" and that it seemed appropriate as a means of protesting against the deaths and injuries caused by *dedovshchina*.[177] The die-in was intended to commemorate the thousands of conscripts

> who have died in Soviet and Russian barracks, the hundreds of army conscripts who have already died or been crippled in this year alone, as occurred with Private Sychov, and the hundreds that will die by the end of this year, following the fall call-up.[178]

The Radikaly also gather signatures on petitions as another means of raising public consciousness. On the eve of the fall call-up in 2005, the League to End the Draft held its first public protest – with the Radikaly – collecting signatures at tables in Pushkin Square to support a referendum that would end conscription. The event announcement noted that 662 conscripts had died of non-combat causes since the start of the year, according to official Defense Ministry figures – and used the startling and appalling calculation "one death every ten hours."[179] According to the Defense Ministry, of those 662 deaths, 182 were suicides, 183 resulted from "vehicular accidents," 175 were due to other accidents, 60 resulted from "violent clashes with civilians," 14 were killed by "fellow soldiers," and 16 died as a result of improper handling of weaponry. Meanwhile, a total of 74 Defense Ministry troops had perished in Chechnya that year.[180]

By November 2006 the combined membership of the Radikaly and the League to End the Draft totaled only 91 people; the group's finances suffered accordingly.[181] As a result of this low level of direct public support for their initiatives, in January 2007 the Radikaly held a meeting of their coordinating council at which they considered whether to dissolve the movement, given its "political, organizational, and financial crisis situation," or to continue their efforts. The council decided in favor of the latter, and planned to start afresh with a membership drive. Although the movement's activities over the past year had been limited, "concentrated mainly on the internet and occasionally on the streets of Moscow," the group retains a symbolic significance within the Russian polity.[182] Still, the capacity of this relatively marginal organization to counter the massive weight of the Russian state's propaganda efforts on militarized patriotism is clearly limited.

State anxiety about resistance to militarized patriotism

The Soviet state attempted in various ways to silence the Committee of Soldiers' Mothers and to stifle public debate on the issues they raised, but the genie refused to re-enter the bottle. The contemporary Russian state continues its efforts to disable anti-militarist groups and other organizations critical of the regime in general and of the military project and related human rights abuses in

Chechnya in particular. The persecution of non-governmental organizations and journalists who tread this dangerous territory reveals a certain level of state anxiety about maintaining a hegemonic discourse and practice regarding militarism, patriotism, and the Kremlin's power.

The persecution of NGOs and journalists

In April 2006 a new law regulating non-governmental organizations (NGOs) in Russia came into effect. Numerous human rights activists and NGO leaders, including Irina Yasina, a senior officer of the Open Russia Foundation (the bank accounts of which were frozen after the arrest of its benefactor, the "oligarch" Mikhail Khodorkovsky), feared the law would be used to crack down on NGOs that worked counter to Kremlin policy, particularly human rights NGOs such as the Committee of Soldiers' Mothers or the Russian–Chechen Friendship Society.[183] Such groups, Yasina argued, had raised the hackles of the authorities, "who have no need for such organizations." Yasina attributed a "KGB mentality" to Russia's state officials, saying that the Orange Revolution in Ukraine had provoked a certain "paranoia" – and that the authorities were troubled by the "independence" of groups like the Committee of Soldiers' Mothers, Memorial, and Open Russia, despite their small size and relative weakness as a societal force.[184] Indeed, shortly after the passage of the NGO law, the Committee of Soldiers' Mothers received a notice from a Moscow court to appear in a suit brought by the Federal Registration Service (a department of Russia's Ministry of Justice) calling for the cessation of activity by the Committee.[185]

While the Committee of Soldiers' Mothers' activity was largely unimpaired (the Federal Registration Service "suspended" its case), other human rights NGOs were not so fortunate.[186] The founder of the Russian–Chechen Friendship Society, Stanislav Dmitrievsky, was convicted in a criminal trial in February 2006 of "inciting hatred or enmity" against Russians. His "crime" was to have published statements by Chechen leaders calling for peace two years earlier.[187] Dmitrievsky's group had run afoul of the Kremlin by providing humanitarian assistance to people in Chechnya, as well as monitoring human rights violations there and publicizing these in a newsletter, *Pravozashchita*.[188] In January 2007, Russia's Supreme Court confirmed the "liquidation" of Dmitrievsky's organization by a lower court.[189]

Russian NGOs that provide legal support to Chechens whose human rights were violated in the course of the military conflict have also been harassed by the Putin administration and threatened with closure. One NGO that helps Chechen civilians bring cases to the European Court of Human Rights (typically because Russian law enforcement agencies have refused to investigate properly the "disappearances" of Chechen men), the Moscow office of the Stichting Russian Justice Initiative (SRJI), founded in 2001, was refused registration in November 2006 on the basis of three technicalities in its application. In the previous six months the European Court had decided four cases of human rights abuse in Chechnya in favor of applicants represented by the SRJI.[190] The Russian government took a different approach toward the International Protection Center (IPC), one of the foremost Russian NGOs in the field of helping Russian citizens make appeals to the European Court; in July 2005 the IPC was the astonished recipient of a tax bill demanding $180,000 in back taxes for grants received from foreign sources between 2002 and 2005.[191] The IPC's cases at the European Court include an attempt to appeal Khodorkovsky's conviction, as well as cases seeking "accountability for victims of human rights violations in Chechnya."[192]

The Kremlin's apprehension about NGOs' opposition to its policies in Chechnya is revealed in restrictions that have been foisted on the press as well. Press freedom in Russia has deteriorated over the past decade. Freedom House rated the press in Russia as "partially free" in 1994 but altered its rating to "not free" in 2004.[193] In a telling statistic, Russia ranked 147th out of 168 states on the 2006 index of World Press Freedom compiled by the NGO Reporters without Borders.[194] While journalists like Dmitrievsky have been punished by the courts, the assassination of Anna Politkovskaia in 2006 – a well-known critic of the Putin administration and of the conduct of the war in Chechnya – highlighted the severity of the constraints on independent journalism in Russia. Between 2000 and 2006, thirteen journalists in Russia perished in such "contract-style" killings, and none of the murders was solved.[195]

The Putin administration has made efforts to maintain a hegemonic discourse about the Russian armed forces in Chechnya and in general, betraying some anxiety about grassroots resistance to the idealized image that the state is attempting to maintain. As we have seen, this unease is revealed in the repression of some of the groups challenging militarized patriotism and military practices in Chechnya. It is also visible, however, in the Kremlin's sponsorship of "patriotic" youth organizations that embrace the regime's militarized-patriotic agenda.

NASHI

NASHI (Ours) is the most visible of these pro-patriotic, pro-Putin youth organizations. Founded in 2005, NASHI sponsors a variety of events and programs intended to foster patriotic sentiments among Russia's youth and to reinforce the political status quo in Russia and the power of Putin's party, United Russia. At a summer camp session held in July 2005, NASHI brought 3,000 Russian youths to hear lectures and seminars, as well as rock concerts, all in the name of patriotic defense of the government. Gleb Pavlovsky, a political consultant to the Putin administration, was among those who addressed the campers. "Your task is to physically resist any attempts to carry out an unconstitutional coup," he advised them.[196] Similarly, NASHI's leader and founder, Vasili Yakemenko, announced at a December 2006 press conference that NASHI would not permit an "Orange Revolution" in Russia to occur. Said Yakemenko, "If anyone tries to deceive our people the way it happened in Ukraine, when the will of the people was subverted by the will of the mob (*volei ploshchadi*), we will not allow them to do so."[197] In so saying, Yakemenko was putting quite a twist on the Ukrainian events, where hundreds of thousands publicly protested the fraudulent result of presidential runoff elections in November 2004, resulting finally in a second runoff a month later, and the defeat of the Kremlin's favored candidate. Yakemenko's claim was seconded by Vladislav Surkov, Putin's deputy chief of staff, and one of the Kremlin ideologists who "helped set up" the NASHI organization, who confidently promised in the wake of the Ukrainian events, "There will be no uprisings here."[198]

Closely connected to Putin's administration, NASHI constitutes the second attempt to form a Kremlin-supporting youth group.[199] Yakemenko is reputed to be a frequent visitor at both the Kremlin and Putin's offices, and Putin has met with NASHI "commissars" as well. NASHI's patriotic message extends symbolically to support for the war in Chechnya; the NASHI offices in Moscow sport a doormat portraying the image of a Chechen rebel.[200]

Although NASHI's website divides its activities among four rubrics – education, anti-fascism, rights protection, and social welfare – and the movement labels itself the "Democratic Anti-Fascist Youth Movement, 'NASHI,'" much of the group's activity supports the promotion of militarized patriotism. In May 2005, for instance, Russia celebrated the sixtieth anniversary of the defeat of Nazi Germany, and NASHI organized a 60,000-strong march in Moscow as part of the victory celebrations.[201] The NASHI event was called "NASHA *pobeda*" (Our victory)[202] – emphasizing continuity between the Soviet army's victory and the present-day patriotic youth movement. Several thousand veterans joined the NASHI march and "presented the young participants … with medals in the shape of a 1940s-vintage shell casing on which was engraved, 'Remember the war, protect the Motherland!'"[203] The symbolic association between the Soviet army's victory and this exhortation to defend the nation is in keeping with the patriotic education program's ethos of motivating Russia's youth to serve in the army. At NASHI's two-week long summer camp in July 2005, another overt link to the Great Patriotic War took the form of an eternal flame commemorating the war dead, watched over perpetually by two NASHI "commissars."[204]

Support for the Russian military ranks high among the movement's priorities. In April 2006 at NASHI's second annual convention, 700 NASHI members from across the country heard "several speakers [stress] the importance of 'supporting the army,'" and a spokesperson for the organization claimed that any NASHI member "found to be dodging the draft will be reduced to the status of a supporter."[205] Among NASHI's priorities is to reclaim military service as an element of patriotic duty. As part of that campaign, NASHI members planned to serve together and to establish NASHI cells within military units, in order to monitor and reduce hazing incidents.[206]

NASHI's education department also exhibits a focus on the Great Patriotic War – especially when anniversaries of significant military events approach. In December 2006, for example, under the "education" rubric several press releases could be found about NASHI's sponsorship of lectures in high schools, technical schools, and university settings – all devoted to teaching about the Soviet victory in World War II. December 2006 marked the sixty-fifth anniversary of the Battle of Moscow, which resulted in a grueling but decisive victory for the Soviet army between December 1941 and January 1942. In Kostroma, NASHI adherents taught a lesson about the Battle of Moscow to high school students in the village of Karavaevo, "who listened with interest" as a veteran of the battle told them how he "burnt a fascist tank and was awarded a medal" – and how he spent the New Year "in the trenches, defending the Motherland."[207] Another article recounted how NASHI leaders gave two weeks of lectures about the Battle of Moscow to a total of nearly 1,400 people in Saransk.[208] And at the International Institute of Computer Technology, NASHI commissar Alisa Moiseeva met with students to tell them "about the Great Patriotic war, about the veterans' achievements for the sake of their country," and stressed that in 1941, young people had enjoyed no New Year's celebrations, since they were busy "fighting off the 'brown plague' that was swallowing many European states." The students' obligation, the commissar explained, was therefore to return that lost holiday to the veterans. By the end of the lesson, the press release reports, "all the students agreed with the commissar's assertions, and were prepared to give assistance to veterans in the near future."[209]

NASHI's main event in December 2006 featured an enormous gathering in Moscow commemorating the Battle of Moscow. This event, entitled "A Holiday Returned," aimed to return the lost New Year celebration of 1941 to surviving veterans across the Russian state.[210] More than 70,000 NASHI commissars and supporters, dressed in Grandfather Frost (*Ded Moroz*) and Snow Maiden (*Snegurochka*) costumes (in red and white, echoing the colors of the NASHI emblem), gathered peaceably in central Moscow to mark the sixty-fifth anniversary of the Battle of Moscow, and from there dispersed to nearly 200 locations, where they met and celebrated with a total of 24,000 veterans.[211]

Although Yakemenko stressed that the activists traveling to the "Returned Holiday" event received no government funding (*bez ispol'zovaniia kakogo-libo administrativnogo resursa*), such events are perfectly in keeping with and encouraged by the 2006–2010 patriotic education program. Yakemenko explained the event's underlying purpose:

> The main problem … lies in the loss of historical memory.… We fear that … within 10–15 years, fascists will walk the streets of our cities. They are already there, with stylized swastikas on their shirtsleeves, hiding behind various slogans. And people have started to look at this without alarm; they even justify such people. So that this doesn't happen, the young generation – the youth 17 years old and above – need to know about what the Great Patriotic War was, who the veterans are, and at what cost we achieved victory, and who the fascists are.

The holiday event provides a "new patriotic format" in which such education can take place, according to Yakemenko. "And this means that we can solve any tasks – state tasks, patriotic tasks – attracting tens and hundreds of thousands of young people to our events. That for us is the main result."[212]

Harking back to the discourse used to describe the Soviet victory in World War II, NASHI devotes much of its energy to public campaigning against "fascist" elements in Russian society. NASHI makes much of its "anti-fascist" credentials. Its website sports multiple articles about NASHI activists' efforts to rid various cities of fascist graffiti, eliminating swastikas (and "anti-Semitic slogans") in Riazan, and fascist "tag lines" or inscriptions (*nadpisi*) in Smolensk.[213] Interestingly, in a photograph accompanying the Smolensk story, NASHI activists are shown erasing not a swastika, but rather the hammer-and-sickle symbol used by NASHI's main political enemy, the National Bolshevik Party (an extremist nationalist/leftist group with anti-Putin politics). NASHI's choice to stress its own struggle against "fascism" hardly seems coincidental, given the overwhelming popularity of the Soviet army's victory in 1945 (frequently described by respondents in public opinion polls as the victory "over fascism") and the group's desire for popular support.[214]

The NASHI website is not completely militarized. Under the rubric of "rights protection" a short article appears in which a lawyer working with NASHI advises a young man that he is legally entitled to appeal his local military commission's draft notice because of his family situation.[215] But other articles on the site clearly portray military service as necessary and desirable. In one, a NASHI commissar from the Riazan division of the organization is shown taking the military oath (*prisiaga*); the article comments: "We are certain that upon concluding his service, Andrei will become a true defender of the Motherland, steadfast, strong, brave, and manly."[216] In a similar vein, NASHI's website posts a letter from NASHI's Briansk commissar, Sergei Zuev, to his mother, from his military unit. The letter assures her that the unit is well provided for materially: they are fed well and properly outfitted, the officers are respected, and so forth.[217]

At the level of popular culture and grassroots organizing, NASHI reflects and embodies several of the goals of the patriotic education programs. Namely, NASHI aims to rehabilitate army service as a necessary and desirable period in a young citizen's life, to promote the memory of the Great Patriotic War, and to make overt a connection between the two. The movement is thus a mass vehicle for the militarized-patriotic education of its adherents. But what of the rest of the population? How effective have the patriotic education programs been, to date? The next subsection explores this issue, looking at public opinion on army service and on patriotic education itself.

The effects of patriotic education in Russia: is it working?

As the first patriotic education program reached the end of its five-year term, some changes in people's patriotic sentiments were in evidence. The co-chair of a Moscow-based children's organization, for instance, Valeri Gergel, pointed to children's active participation in the sixtieth anniversary celebrations of the 9 May victory over the Nazis, arguing that patriotism was on the rise among children: "Just three or four years ago we could not even imagine that our children would be proud to march in Red Square."[218] Also, in a nationwide survey on pride and shame held in 2006, a mere 3 percent of those polled responded that "there is nothing to be proud of," down from 20 percent in 2002, suggesting that the "pride gap" of the early 2000s (most likely reflecting the "dismal 1990s") was closing fast.[219]

Although it is impossible to isolate the effects of the patriotic education programs from other variables, they could be responsible at least in part for some changes in public opinion about army service. For example, the first patriotic education program may have exerted some influence within the population regarding whether army service should be required or voluntary. In October 2002, 51 percent of those surveyed felt that army service for young men should be mandatory and 44 percent believed that it should be an individual choice. Among those aged 18–35 the percentage was reversed; only 43 percent believed that service should be mandatory, while 51 percent thought choice should be involved.[220] By July 2004, however, 60 percent expressed the view that "every young man must serve in the army" and only 37 percent thought that each "young man has the right to decide on his own whether to serve or not." Little progress had been made among those most likely to be enlisted, however: 45 percent of 18- to 35-year-olds thought service should be mandatory and 53 percent thought it should be up to the individual.[221] In February 2005 the numbers were roughly the same: 58 percent of respondents felt that "every young man should serve in the army" and 38 percent believed it should be an individual's decision; among 18- to 35-year-olds, 42 percent thought service should be mandatory and 56 percent thought it ought to be a matter of individual choice.[222] While the patriotic education program may have provoked some shift in attitudes among the general population, it was not visible within the 18–35 age group, the program's foremost target audience.

Another indicator perhaps showing a small change in public opinion regarding army service is whether respondents see army service as a "school of life" or "the lost years." In November 2000, before the first patriotic education program began, 31 percent of respondents evaluated army service as amounting to "lost years"; by February 2005 that number had declined slightly to 27 percent.[223] In October 2001, however, respondents in a national survey felt strongly that "most young people are unwilling to serve in the army" (86 percent), with only 7 percent thinking that most young people were willing to do so.[224] This number remained consistent in 2004, with 87 percent of the population reporting that they did not think "most young men want to serve in the army today."[225] Three years of patriotic education initiatives had not altered public opinion on this point.

Nor do individuals voice enthusiasm for army service. National surveys asking respondents whether they (if they were male) would serve in the army if they had a choice about whether or not to do so found in October 2001 that 49 percent would not, and only 41 percent would choose to serve (a percentage considerably higher than the 15 percent who answered affirmatively a separate question about whether they themselves had served in the army). The same question asked in October 2002 again showed that 49 percent would not serve.[226] In early 2006, "willingness to serve in the Russian military [had] dropped to less than 40 percent" according to a Levada Center poll, a number quite comparable to the 41 percent in October 2001.[227] Apparently, the first round of the state's patriotic education program (2001–2005) had not made a dent in this statistic.

Perhaps spurred by this evident societal disaffection for army service, two military analysts from the Center for Military-Strategic Studies of the Russian Armed Forces General Staff wrote an article in 2005 arguing that the armed forces were suffering from inadequate patriotic preparation of "the human factor." They bemoaned the "disastrously low spiritual and moral level of the people and [the] loss of the traditionally Russian patriotic mentality and sense of duty to the Fatherland, especially among the young," and lauded the enactment of the patriotic education program (2001–2005) and other official statements on patriotic education. But such steps, they continued, had produced "no visible results." Their recommendation was to "develop a Russian national state ideology" to make clear the "meaning and purpose of the existence of the Russian state, its place and role in the development of the human civilization," to "recreate" a national system of "spiritual and moral education," and to "upgrade the military-patriotic education of the population, especially young people."[228] This latter task was undertaken by the second patriotic education program in 2006.

The patriotic education programs might have been expected to find receptive soil in Russia in the early 2000s, given the fact that in 2004, 89 percent of the population thought that the "patriotic upbringing of young people" deserved "more attention" than it was getting, and that only a fifth of the population thought that "contemporary schools foster patriotism."[229] The public also favored the reintroduction of military preparation in schools at that time – and probably identified patriotic education with military education, given the close bond between the two in the Soviet era. In November 2003, one well-respected polling firm counted 84 percent of the population as favoring the mandatory introduction of "basic military training" (NVP) in schools.[230] The Soviet system of patriotic education, "which ... used to foster heroic sentiments and had a quite clear military and ideological orientation," was apparently no longer in place. In February 2004, 62 percent of Russian citizens "favor[ed] the idea of reviving" the Soviet practices in this area (versus 22 percent), and even "young respondents" approved of it (46 percent) more than dismissing it as undesirable (34 percent).[231]

Yet few believe that patriotism can be inculcated "from above," by the state. Focus group participants in 2004 argued that state attempts to introduce patriotic education in the absence of concrete "grounds [on which] to take pride in their nation" would be ineffective. As one participant put it, "There will be patriotic lessons at school, teachers will say one thing and students will say different things. This education would do nothing but harm."[232] Such reactions do not necessarily mean that patriotic education and attempts to foster patriotism among youth would be unwelcome in all quarters.

Indeed, political scientist Douglas Blum sees a strong impetus for patriotic education as stemming from the grassroots: "the clamor for patriotism is perhaps as much bottom-up as top-down."[233] The 2006–2010 program, for instance, seeks to "co-opt" pre-existing grassroots civic organizations motivated by patriotic sentiment, such as the youth groups that scour battlefields to find and bury soldiers' remains.[234] Enthusiasm for patriotic education also comes, not surprisingly, from within the educational establishment. Blum interviewed educators and other local officials involved with youth policy in 2004 in several Russian cities, finding that the educators he spoke with saw army service as beneficial to a "healthy way of life" for (male) youth. In the eyes of educators, Blum asserted, "patriotism means service to the state." Educators perceived the military as a "means to overcome the gulf between the generations"; in their view, the military acted as "identity cement," and army service connected the Russian citizenry (the male citizenry, at any rate) across generations.[235] Blum saw educators' zeal for patriotic education as stemming largely from their desire to repair Russians' sense of national pride and shared identity:

> Teachers and librarians were pushing an agenda broader than [militarized] patriotism: Russian literature, culture, and civilization. Among their issues was World War II, defeating the Nazis, and the enormous national sacrifice it involved – that was a huge thing [in the educators' understanding of patriotic education]. Their message was, "Be proud of being Russian. Russia is a great country." They were fighting against shame – trying to recapture something. So the patriotic education program was nationally welcomed; it plugged into something much larger than just the draft. It's about trying to recapture a sense of national identity.[236]

Not everyone – even in the youthful target audience – was enthusiastic about the patriotic education programs, however. One member of the Central Council of "We" (*My*), a youth group critical of Putin, commented (upon hearing about the 2006–2010 program):

> I have nothing against patriotism, but who is going to teach me how to love my motherland? Who? The people who ruined Russia's strongest oil company and [former Yukos CEO Mikhail] Khodorkovsky? I don't want these people to teach me patriotism.[237]

Such views were echoed by the head of the Yabloko party's youth wing, who remarked: "There is no place for the state in matters like believing in God or loving one's motherland. As [nineteenth-century Russian satirist Mikhail] Saltykov-Shchedrin said, if state officials start talking about patriotism, it means they want to steal something."[238] The co-chair of a Moscow children's organization who had expressed enthusiasm about the renaissance of children's patriotism in recent years did not believe that the program's stress on "developing military sports and military patriotic camps" would be effective, since such efforts would be " 'managed by representatives of the Soviet, pre-reform army.' "[239]

There are limits to what any state can accomplish through patriotic education. A group of third-year undergraduate students in an Ethnic Studies (*etnosotsiologiia*) course in Moscow were asked to share their thoughts on patriotism in a written assignment given by their professor, Maria Zolotukhina, in November

2006.[240] They were asked what patriotism meant, in their view; whether they identified as patriots; and how or whether patriotism should be taught. Their responses reveal a mixture of attitudes that a state hoping to inculcate a militarized patriotism might both appreciate and hope to counter. Of fourteen students who completed the assignment, six identified as patriots (one weakly) and five did not; three failed to answer that part of the assignment. In defining patriotism, one student imagined "a person going into battle against the enemy of the Motherland," and saw the need for the inculcation of patriotism among her generation (and the next one). "Patriotism," as this student pointed out, "is what holds America together. It leads to solidarity among the people … even at the banal level of throwing trash into a can on the street." Her contrast between Americans' and Russians' supposed level of patriotic affiliation was both implicit and pointed.

A few students thought that patriotic education should start in childhood and suggested the organization of patriotic "circles" (clubs) as well as "propagandizing patriotism through the media," and using seminars and lectures as well as "publishing articles and books, and making movies," much as the state patriotic education programs planned to do. Another student, who did not identify as patriotic, pointed to groups like NASHI with some disdain: "These days, some youth movements and subcultures consider themselves patriots; they make a cult of themselves, an ideal, and they try to 'defend' it and 'clean up the filth.'" This student doubted that the spirit of patriotism could be taught: "We have a free society now.… This isn't Soviet times, when an order could be given and people would carry it out and believe that better times were on the way." Another student agreed: "Patriotic education isn't necessary. I think a person can become a patriot on their own. And if they don't – well, that just means that's the kind of country it is." A third concurred: "The more they try to force us to be patriots, the less patriotic we'll become."

One student pointedly drew the link between patriotism and army service:

> [T]here should be a struggle to counter both cruel hazing and poor conditions in the army; after all, in the past, people thought that a man who didn't serve in the army wasn't a man. [Now] nobody wants to serve, and that's bad. I think that the first sign of patriotism, under normal circumstances, is conscientious service in the army.

Russia's circumstances, by implication, were not normal – and until that situation was corrected, this student believed, patriotism would not be manifest.

Several students made reference to World War II in their responses about patriotism. One student who did not see herself as particularly patriotic wrote, "I think that people who call themselves patriots are proud of the past," and made a reference to 1945 as the source of that satisfaction. Another believed that the only way to develop a patriotism that would unify the population was

> one enormous tragedy – something that would affect not just one city, but the whole country (God forbid!). A banal example is the Great Patriotic

> War. To this day, patriotism is aroused within us from year to year, only around the 10th of May.

Another thought the basis of patriotic feeling in Russia was the "various holidays (9 May, 4 November)" – an interesting response, given that the student mentioned both Victory Day in World War II and the "new" 4 November holiday (the Day of National Unity) intended to replace the commemoration of the Bolshevik Revolution in 1917, which had been celebrated on 7 November. The same student, in listing things of which Russians could be proud, included the victory in World War II above all, followed by Soviet achievements in space, and then by figure skating:

> In the [Russian Federation] one can take pride in the fact that in 1945 the Russian army was victorious in the bloody war, and in so doing, saved the world from a horrible fate. One can be proud of the fact that Russia became the first world power to put a rocket in space, and that the first person to go into space was the Russian cosmonaut, Yuri Gagarin. And for a long time, Russians have stood on the podium in figure skating.

The students' responses mirror many of the ideas expressed in the patriotic education programs at the same time as they offer up resistance to patriotism as a state-sponsored sentiment. The theme of patriotism as being connected to the military, however, echoes repeatedly within the students' responses, as it does in Russian survey research more generally. Whether this is evidence of the recent influence of the patriotic education programs or of long-standing beliefs about the tie between militarism and patriotism is unclear.

Conclusion: "a lifetime of service to the state"

> Flags are bits of colored cloth that governments use first to shrink-wrap people's minds and then as ceremonial shrouds to bury the dead. When independent, thinking people (and here I do not include the corporate media) begin to rally under flags, when writers, painters, musicians, film makers suspend their judgment and blindly yoke their art to the service of the nation, it's time for all of us to sit up and worry.
>
> Arundhati Roy[241]

From reading the patriotic education program documents, one gets the sense that state officials not only sought to solve the problem of an apparently missing national idea, but were quite desperate to do so. The authors of the patriotic education programs – in addition to keeping an eye toward increasing the size of the draft pool – seem to have seized on the Russian military as a vehicle through which to renew citizens' sense of shared national identity. But in setting militarized patriotism at the center of its patriotic education efforts, the Russian state made a political choice that may well have long-lasting effects for the democratic development of the polity. As Douglas Blum points out, the patriotic education programs rely on this militarized patriotism as a means to underscore citizens' responsibilities to the state: "Precisely by emphasizing the state, including its achievements and military trappings, as well as the primacy of obligations over rights, the practice of patriotism provides a milieu in which the youth can be socialized for a lifetime of service."[242] Patriotic education, then, places the stress on statism rather than on the political value of individual rights.

In this regard, according to Stephen Hanson's keen analysis of nationalism in post-Soviet Russia, Putin's state-building strategy is in essence "post-ideological." It centers instead on the notion of *gosudarstvennost'*, which Hanson freely translates as "loyalty to the state." This loyalty, Hanson explains, "in the form of obedience to central [Kremlin] authority, seems to serve as the key indicator by which Putin divides 'patriots' from 'traitors.'" Hanson views the pro-Putin NASHI movement as "the culmination of this trend: those who stand up for Kremlin policy are 'ours,' and all others are alien (*chuzhie*)."[243]

Putin's various statements on the subject, as well as the patriotic education program documents, make clear that among the major indicators of loyalty to the state are military service and a pledge to defend the state. NASHI stresses these in its activity and PR material; recall its leader's pledge that NASHI would not permit a challenge to the incumbent regime in the form of an "Orange Revolution," were such to occur in Russia. Patriotism, mobilized in the form of youth movements, can be used by the state to limit oppositional protest. In short, among the state's objectives, then, is to employ patriotism as an ideology with which to support the status quo and the preservation of the current elite's own power. Patriotism in this view means supporting the Putin regime, in whatever form it may continue following Medvedev's ascension to the presidency.

The choice of a state-centric, militarized patriotism has ramifications for the future of political pluralism in Russia. Other foundations for a renaissance of patriotism in Russia that would potentially expand rather than restrict the political spectrum can be imagined, though they may not hold much appeal to Russia's political leadership. To judge from public opinion polls, the remains of Soviet history (outside of the victory in World War II) and its aftermath appear to offer up precious little on which to base a vigorous Russian patriotism. But what might happen if a less statist and more liberal leadership had seized on the idea of creating a new basis for patriotism, rooting it in the Russian population's tradition of resistance to oppression? Patriotic pride could then dwell easily in the fact that Russia had succeeded in emerging from its decades-long period of stultifying Communist Party domination, its citizens having put an end to dictatorial rule.[244]

A patriotic education program of this sort could promote Russian citizens' pride in the small-scale but critically important dissident movement; in the courageous gulag prisoners who protested – even during the Stalin era; in the myriad methods of daily resistance to the regime's abuses; and in the flourishing of *samizdat* literature, quietly, slowly, and bravely undermining the Soviet regime.[245] Its national heroes would include Eugenii Zamiatin, whose science fiction novel *We*, finished in 1921, makes supremely clear the danger of putting service to the state above the notion of individual rights. In the novel, Zamiatin's sometime self-doubting narrator, D-503, embraces the statist ideology of his government, the One State, in a chilling passage about the "absurdity" of individual rights:

> Even among the ancients, the most mature among them knew that the source of right is might, that right is a function of power. And so, we have the scales: on one side, a gram, on the other a ton; on one side "I," on the other "We," the One State. Is it not clear, then, that to assume that the "I" can have some "rights" in relation to the State is exactly like assuming that a gram can balance the scale against the ton? Hence the division: rights to the ton, duties to the gram. And the natural path from nonentity to greatness is to forget that you are a gram and feel yourself instead a millionth of a ton.[246]

Zamiatin's critique of statism is starkly painted; in his novel, dissidents are finally forced to submit to an operation in which the center of the brain that provides imagination is excised, leaving only dully compliant citizens who can no longer dream.

The 1990s – disappointing as they may have been in some ways – brought about the widespread activation of civil society and the media, and offered the potential for a new, democratic Russian polity to take root. This decade offered the possibility for regime reassessment and the chance to move in a more liberal and less statist direction; the possibility to embrace Russian history as a tale of hard and heroic battles against oppression; and the opportunity to celebrate the protection of individual human rights.

From Putin's – and now Medvedev's – perspective, no doubt dissidence against a repressive regime and resistance to authority are unlikely (and probably undesirable) sources of patriotic pride. Indeed, it would take a supremely confident government to endorse a patriotic education program that placed dissent against abuses of political and military power at its core. Relying on the armed forces' achievements as a fundamental source of pride may be practical, from the perspective of a state primarily concerned with the preservation of its power. But even as civic and individual rights – from voting for governors, to enjoying a free press – disintegrate in Russia, a patriotism centering on Russia's successful striving for freedom from tyranny remains a possibility, if a distant one.

Notes

1 The author thanks the following people for sharing their insights on this topic: Golfo Alexopoulos, Nadia Anderson, Vita Aronson, Douglas Blum, Georgii Derluguian, Sam Diener, Dmitri Glinski, Pamela Jordan, Alla Kassianova, Sergei Medvedev, Igor Innokent'evich Mel'nichenko, Brian Taylor, and Mariia Zolotukhina (and her family). The author also gratefully acknowledges the Francis A. Harrington Public Affairs Fund at Clark University for a grant supporting this research.

2 "It is sweet and proper to die for one's country." Horace, *Odes*, Book III, 2, line 13, in Horace, *The Complete Odes and Epodes*, trans. W. G. Shepherd, London: Penguin

Books, 1983, p. 131. Wilfred Owen powerfully critiques this notion in his best-known poem about the horrors of war. See Wilfred Owen, "Dulce et Decorum Est," www.warpoetry.co.uk/owen1.html (accessed 21 May 2008).

3 "Russia: Pride and Shame," Report/Population Poll, FOM, 14 February 2002; see also http://bd.fom.ru/report/cat/man/patriotizm/d020608 (accessed 2 April 2007). Note: All public opinion polls by the Fond Obshchestvennogo Mneniia (FOM) cited in this chapter are accessible from the website http://english.fom.ru.

4 In the Russian language these are rendered not as *russkii* but as *rossiiskii*, a more inclusive term that refers not to ethnicity but to the occupants of the territory of the Russian Federation.

5 The decree changing the term of service was signed by Putin on 12 March 2007, to take effect on 1 January 2008 (see "Putin Cuts Draft to One Year," *RFE/RL Newsline*, 13 March 2007).

6 In June 2006 the State Duma voted to eliminate nine of the twenty-five existing categories of draft deferments (see "Duma Scraps Nine Categories of Draft Deferments," *RFE/RL Newsline*, 14 June 2006). Also, in 2005 the Defense Ministry had eliminated a "loophole" exempting thousands of young men from conscription yearly when it reduced the existing 229 "military departments" at post-secondary educational institutions to only thirty; in the future, students at the thirty universities retaining military departments will become reserve officers and, in exchange for financial aid, will have to serve on active duty for several years following graduation. See "Defense Ministry Closing 'Military Faculties' to Crack Down on Draft Dodgers," *RFE/RL Newsline*, 26 July 2005, and D. R. Herspring, "Putin and Military Reform," in D. R. Herspring (ed.), *Putin's Russia: Past Imperfect, Future Uncertain*, 3rd edn., Lanham, MD: Rowman & Littlefield, 2007, p. 188.

7 These were titled "State Program: 'Patriotic Education of Citizens of the Russian Federation, 2001–2005'" (*Gosudarstvennaia programma "Patrioticheskoe vospitanie grazhdan Rossiiskoi Federatsii na 2001–2005 gody"*) and "State Program: 'Patriotic Education of Citizens of the Russian Federation, 2006–2010'" (*Gosudarstvennaia programma: "Patrioticheskoe vospitanie grazhdan Rossiiskoi Federatsii na 2006–2010 gody"*).

8 For a survey of the problems plaguing Russia's military forces in the 1990s, see Herspring, "Putin and Military Reform," pp. 174–177.

9 J. Van Bladel, "Is the All-Volunteer Force a Solution for Draft Problems?" in F. Daucé and E. Sieca-Kozlowski (eds.), Dedovshchina *in the Post-Soviet Military: Hazing of Russian Army Conscripts in a Comparative Perspective*, Stuttgart: ibidem-Verlag, 2006, p. 289.

10 "Celebrating Victory Day, Russians Honor the Veterans and the Armed Forces," WPS [What the Papers Say – a Russian independent media monitoring agency], 10, 11 May 1998, www.wps.ru/en/pp/military/1998/05/11.html (accessed 21 May 2008).

11 For some portion of the liberal-minded public in Russia, the withdrawal of Soviet troops from Afghanistan and the "end of empire" in Eastern Europe represented a welcome move toward ending the Cold War, rather than a defeat (Dmitri Glinski, personal communication, 20 February 2007).

12 "Slavery Said 'Flourishing' in Russian Army," *RFE/RL Newsline*, 26 February 2001. The selling of conscripts continued beyond the 1990s. In October 2006 a soldier voiced his intention to prosecute his commander (who had reportedly "'sold' him to an unnamed businessman as a 'slave laborer'") for human trafficking. The commander had been charged only with abuse of his position. See "Soldier to Seek Justice for Having Been 'Sold' as a Laborer," *RFE/RL Newsline*, 24 October 2006.

13 "Celebrating Victory Day, Russians Honor the Veterans and the Armed Forces."

14 Mariia Zolotukhina, author interview, 26 December 2006.

15 On Surkov, see G. L. White and A. Cullison, "Putin's Pitchman," *Wall Street Journal*, 19 December 2006, A1.

16 "Electoral Trust/Distrust Ratings," FOM, 19 December 2006, http://english.fom.ru/ratings_eng/764.html (accessed 17 January 2007); "Electoral Ratings," FOM, 12 December 2006, http://english.fom.ru/ratings_eng/765.html (accessed 17 January 2007).
17 "The Situation in Chechnya: Monitoring," Population Poll, Table, FOM, 29 June 2006.
18 On the ways in which Stalin and his successors used World War II as a focal point for patriotism and as a means of legitimizing the Soviet regime, see N. Tumarkin, *The Living and the Dead: The Rise and Fall of the Cult of World War II in Russia*, New York: Basic Books, 1994, and A. Weiner, *Making Sense of War: The Second World War and the Fate of the Bolshevik Revolution*, Princeton, NJ: Princeton University Press, 2001.
19 V. Sperling, "The Last Refuge of a Scoundrel: Patriotism, Militarism, and the Russian National Idea," *Nations and Nationalism*, 9, 2, 2003, 235–253.
20 "Upper Chamber Backs Soviet Anthem," 20 December 2000, http://archives.cnn.com/2000/WORLD/europe/12/20/russia.anthem/index.html (accessed 1 February 2007).
21 "New Banner for Military Taken Up," *RFE/RL Newsline*, 5 June 2003.
22 "... And Backs Defense Ministry's Request to Restore the Red Star," *RFE/RL Newsline*, 27 November 2002. The flag can be found at: www.mil.ru/849/12215/12346/12338/index.shtml.
23 Two thousand service members perished in non-combat "crimes and incidents" over the course of 2002. See T. P. Gerber and S. E. Mendelson, "Strong Public Support for Military Reform in Russia," PONARS Policy Memo, 228, May 2003, p. 1.
24 Van Bladel, "Is the All-Volunteer Force a Solution for Draft Problems?" p. 287.
25 F. Daucé and E. Sieca-Kozlowski, Introduction," in Daucé and Sieca-Kozlowski (eds.), Dedovshchina *in the Post-Soviet Military*, pp. 18, 21.
26 "Military Prosecutor Says Crime Rising among Senior Officers," *RFE/RL Newsline*, 25 May 2005.
27 "... As Liberals Say Hazing Claims Thousands of Soldiers Each Year," *RFE/RL Newsline*, 24 February 2003.
28 "Prosecutor Says 17 Dead This Year from Hazing," *RFE/RL Newsline*, 4 August 2006. Anna Colin Lebedev provides detailed descriptions of *dedovshchina* and various other maltreatment of conscripts from letters written to the Committee of Soldiers' Mothers. See A. Colin Lebedev, "The Test of Reality: Understanding Families' Tolerance regarding Mistreatment of Conscripts in the Russian Army," in Daucé and Sieca-Kozlowski, Dedovshchina *in the Post-Soviet Military*, pp. 47–74.
29 "Military Prosecutor Confirms Hazing at Petersburg Naval Academy," *RFE/RL Newsline*, 7 March 2003.
30 "Outrage over Sentence in Hazing Case," *RFE/RL Newsline*, 27 September 2006.
31 Nikiforov's superior officer, Colonel Mikhail Klimenko, was also fired and discharged from the military as a result. See "Commander Sacked over Soldier's Death," *RFE/RL Newsline*, 16 August 2006.
32 Daucé and Sieca-Kozlowski, "Introduction," p. 23.
33 T. P. Gerber and S. E. Mendelson, "How Russians Think about Chechnya," PONARS Policy Memo, 243, January 2002.
34 G. Lapidus, "Ethnicity and State Building," in M. R. Beissinger and C. Young (eds.), *Beyond State Crisis? Postcolonial Africa and Post-Soviet Eurasia in Comparative Perspective*, Washington, DC: Woodrow Wilson Center Press, 2002, p. 352.
35 T. P. Gerber and S. E. Mendelson, "Russian Public Opinion on Human Rights and the War in Chechnya," *Post-Soviet Affairs*, 18, 4, 2002, 298–299.
36 "Interior Ministry to Regulate Journalists' Access to Chechnya," *RFE/RL Newsline*, 2 August 2004.
37 Cited in K. Bannikov, "Regimented Communities in a Civil Society," in Daucé and Sieca-Kozlowski (eds.), Dedovshchina *in the Post-Soviet Military*, p. 44.
38 A. Petrova, "Approval for Russian Military Actions in Chechnya Is Steadily Declining," Report, FOM, 5 September 2002.

39 Levada Center, "Chechnya – Trends," www.russiavotes.org/Mood_int_tre.htm#170 (accessed 4 January 2007).
40 J. M. K. Lyall, "Pocket Protests: Rhetorical Coercion and the Micropolitics of Collective Action in Semiauthoritarian Regimes," *World Politics*, 58, April 2006, 379, 390–391.
41 A. Petrova, "Is the Army Improving?" Report, FOM, February 19, 2004. Living conditions in the army and the social status of military personnel did not disappear as troublesome issues; in February 2005, 40,000 people, including members of veterans' organizations, protested in Moscow against a range of problems, from the unpopular reforms to the social benefits system to the "decay of the armed forces and the war in Chechnya." See "Veterans and Military Protests Continue," *RFE/RL Newsline*, 24 February 2005.
42 "Army Service," Report/Population Poll, FOM, 3 October 2002.
43 Levada Center, "Armiia," www.levada.ru/army.html (accessed 4 January 2007).
44 The Interior Ministry had lost 3,850 troops and the border guards, FSB, and other agencies had lost 150 people in the course of the conflict. *Novaia gazeta*, 10–16 September 2003.
45 "No More Conscripts to Be Sent to Chechnya, Minister Says," *RFE/RL Newsline*, 4 January 2005.
46 Vladimir Putin, "Annual Address to the Federal Assembly" (transcript and video), 10 May 2006, http://kremlin.ru (accessed 11 May 2006).
47 A. Petrova, "Attitudes on the Army Are Still Negative," Report, FOM, 19 February 2004.
48 "The State of the Armed Forces," Table/Population Poll, FOM, 20 February 2003.
49 A. Petrova, "Attitudes on the Army Are Still Negative."
50 E. Shamseeva, "Military Officers: Sitting in Headquarters or Serving in Garrison," Report, FOM, 29 August 2002.
51 "Ministry Launches Public Relations Effort," *RFE/RL Newsline*, 17 January 2007.
52 M. Moshkin, "Bez vraga i oruzhiia," *Gazeta*, 30, 22 February 2006, http://gzt.ru/society/2006/02/21/214646.html (accessed 21 May 2008).
53 Shamseeva, "Military Officers: Sitting in Headquarters or Serving in Garrison."
54 After three years of stagnation, officers' salaries were raised in 2006 by 15 percent, and were planned to rise by 67 percent by the end of 2008; whether such rises will be sufficient to reverse the perception of poverty is unclear. See D. R. Herspring, "Putin and Military Reform," p. 186.
55 Lebedev, "The Test of Reality," p. 53.
56 Gerber and Mendelson, "Strong Public Support for Military Reform," 3.
57 "Army Service," Report/Population Poll, FOM, 3 October 2002.
58 "Testing of a Notion: 'Patriotism,'" Report/Expert Poll, FOM, 2 August 2000.
59 "Defining Patriotism," Table/Population Poll, FOM, 7 December 2006. By contrast, 92 percent of Americans surveyed in September 2002 agreed with the statement "I am very patriotic" either completely (54 percent) or mostly (38 percent). See J. Scott, "The Changing Face of Patriotism," *New York Times*, 6 July 2003, Section 4, 1.
60 "Defining Patriotism."
61 It is worth noting that Putin himself (in 2001) was volunteered by 19 percent of Russian respondents in answer to a request to name a contemporary public figure who could be called a patriot, but that 56 percent of the respondents could not provide a response. See "Patriotism and Patriots," Report/Population Poll, FOM, 29 November 2001.
62 "Russian Views on Patriotism," Report/Population Poll, FOM, 7 December 2006.
63 "Defining Patriotism."
64 Ibid.
65 I. Klimov and S. Klimova, "Testing of a Notion: 'Patriotism,'" Report, FOM, 2 August 2000.
66 Ibid.

67 Ibid.

68 I. Klimov, "Patriotism and Patriots," Report, FOM, 29 November 2001.

69 E. Vovk, "A Patriotic Upbringing: Words or Deeds?" Report, FOM, 5 February 2004.

70 Ibid. This idea that willing army service is contingent upon state behavior is supported by Margaret Levi's analysis of patriotism and conscription in *Consent, Dissent, and Patriotism*, Cambridge: Cambridge University Press, 1997. Levi argues that when citizens "believe government actors promote immoral policies, have ignored their interests, or have actually betrayed them," they are "unlikely to feel obliged to comply with the laws" – including the laws on conscription. Citizens' failure to conform to the state's rules "reduces the willingness of otherwise willing citizens to comply," explaining widespread draft avoidance such as that witnessed in Russia (see Levi, p. 16).

71 A. Krylova, "Stalinist Identity from the Viewpoint of Gender," *Gender and History*, 16, 3, 2004, 631.

72 Ibid., 632.

73 Interestingly, these clubs and trainings were not limited to men; women participated actively in everything from parachuting circles to sniper competitions. Ibid., 633–634.

74 Z. Abdullaeva, "The Great Patriotic War Today and Yesterday," *Moscow Times*, 25 June 2003, www.cdi.org/russia/263-11.cfm (accessed 21 May 2008).

75 Ibid. Reintroduced after the passage of the Law on Universal Military Service in 1967, which reduced the term of service for Soviet conscripts, NVP was a military skill-training program for high school students, designed to facilitate recruits' transition into the armed forces. See Van Bladel, "Is the All-Volunteer Force a Solution for Draft Problems?" p. 285. Although widespread, NVP was not taken as seriously as was ideological education, either by students or by teachers (Mariia Zolotukhina, personal communication, 7 February 2007).

76 Cited in Abdullaeva, "The Great Patriotic War Today and Yesterday."

77 The full name of the competition was *Vsesoiuznaia pionerskaia voenno-sportivnaia igra "Zarnitsa."*

78 The "Pioneers" was the communist equivalent of the Scouts organizations in the United States.

79 Mariia Zolotukhina (author interview, 22 December 2006), relaying the experience of an acquaintance in Moscow; also, Abdullaeva, "The Great Patriotic War Today and Yesterday."

80 These memories were shared with the author through email correspondence.

81 This latter took place when the respondent was in second or third grade, in the early 1980s. For the games, the school was "divided into two camps: North–South or East–West," and mock checkpoints were established at the school's entrance. She recalled forming battle lines, "but there was no battle."

82 *Pust' budet protivnik uslovnii / Fanernyi puskai avtomat / No v nas nastoiashchaia smelost' i stoikost' / I sila sovetskikh soldat.* Translation mine.

83 Mariia Zolotukhina, author interview, 22 December 2006.

84 "Gosudarstvennaia programma 'Patrioticheskoe vospitanie grazhdan Rossiiskoi Federatsii na 2001–2005 gody,'" 16 February 2001, www.ed.gov.ru/junior/new_version/gragd_patr_vospit_molod/1641/ (accessed 26 April 2006). Henceforth, "Patriotic Education Program, 2001–2005."

85 Ibid.

86 Ibid.

87 Ibid.

88 A. Makarin, "Hello, 'Zarnitsa!'" *Segodnya*, 22 February 2001, www.cdi.org/russia/johnson/5112.html (accessed 21 May 2008).

89 Patriotic Education Program, 2001–2005.

90 A. Medetsky, "The Drive to Churn Out Patriots," *Moscow Times*, 14 May 2005; see also Patriotic Education Program, 2001–2005.

91 Ustav Rosvoentsentr.

92 Makarin, "Hello, 'Zarnitsa!' "

93 "Gosudarstvennoe uchrezhdenie 'Rossiiskii tsentr grazhdanskogo i patrioticheskogo vospitaniia detei i molodezhi' (ROSPATRIOTTSENTR)," www.ed.gov.ru/junior/new_version/gragd_patr_vospit_molod/ (accessed 26 April 2006). Hereafter, "Rospatriottsentr."

94 Ibid. The mention of veterans of the Chechen wars in the rest of the Patriotic Education Program's literature is scarce, however.

95 Ibid.

96 "Polozhenie o Vserossiiskom konkurse patrioticheskoi pesni 'Ia liubliu tebia, Rossiia!' " www.edu.gov.ru/junior/new_version/gragd_patr_vospit_molod/ (accessed 26 April 2006).

97 "Plan meropriiatii patrioticheskoi napravlennosti," www.edu.gov.ru/junior/new_version/gragd_patr_vospit_molod/ (accessed 26 April 2006).

98 Ibid. *Vakhta Pamiati* (loosely translated as "Memorial Vigil") projects in Soviet days involved the compilation of logs listing the World War II dead from one's own region, field trips to war monuments and battlefields, and the like. *Vakhta Pamiati* projects seem to have become somewhat centralized under the Patriotic Education Programs. A Rospatriottsentr communication from February 2006, for example, announced the opening of the year-long Russia-wide "*Vakhta Pamiati* – 2006," memorializing the sixty-first anniversary of the victory in the Great Patriotic War. This event was slated to include an opening ceremony (to take place in Tver' Oblast'), an interregional conference on the "Recovery Movement (*poiskovoe dvizhenie*) as a Form of Patriotic Education of Youth in the RF," a "solemn ceremony for the reburial of the remains of Soviet combatants who died on the territory of Tver' *oblast'*," a meeting to discuss the conduct and organization of recovery expeditions in 2006, an "evening of recovery-themed songs" (*vecher poiskovoi pesni*), and trips to sites of military glory. This particular event was directed toward leaders and specialists in the field of patriotic education and recovery operations, rather than to the broader public (the announcement noted that each region could send a delegation of no more than two people). See "Informatsionnoe pis'mo Vakhty Pamiati – 2006," 2 February 2006, www.edu.gov.ru/junior/new_version/gragd_patr_vospit_molod/ (accessed 13 January 2007).

99 A. Medetsky, "The Drive to Churn Out Patriots."

100 "Pis'mo N. 13-11-221 ot 30.09.2005: Forma otcheta o vypolnenii regional'nykh programm po patrioticheskomu vospitaniiu," www.edu.gov/ru/junior/newversion/gragd_patr_vospit_molod/ (accessed 4 January 2007).

101 Igor Mel'nichenko, director of the Federal Education Agency's Department on Youth Affairs and Children's Education and Social Welfare, and also the informal head of Rospatriottsentr, thought that the Vakhta Pamiati events, the aforementioned patriotic song competition, a Russia-wide series of meetings between veterans and youth, called "To the Glory of the Great Victory" (referring to World War II), and an All-Russia military-sporting game called "Victory" were among the most successful events of the 2001–2005 program. Igor Mel'nichenko, written responses to interview questions, received via email 31 January 2007. Hereafter, Mel'nichenko.

102 I. Torbakov, "Rebirth of Agitprop: Russia's Spending on Patriotic Propaganda Will Triple," *Eurasia Daily Monitor*, 2, 142, 22 July 2005.

103 V. Putin, "Annual Address to the Federal Assembly," 10 May 2006, www.kremlin.ru/eng/speeches/2006/05/10/1823_type70029type82912_105566.shtml (accessed 4 January 2007).

104 V. Putin, "Annual Address to the Federal Assembly" (transcript and video), 10 May 2006, http://kremlin.ru (accessed 11 May 2006); and C. J. Chivers, "Putin Urges Plan to Reverse Slide in the Birthrate," *New York Times*, 11 May 2006, A 1, A 6.

105 Quoted in "Putin's Address Heralds Return to Soviet Times – Illarionov," Mosnews.com, 12 May 2006.
106 "Gosudarstvennaia programma: 'Patrioticheskoe vospitanie grazhdan Rossiiskoi Federatsii na 2006–2010 gody,'" 11 July 2005 (on file with author). Hereafter, Patriotic Education Program, 2006–2010. By early 2007 fifty such centers and councils existed, staffed by "specialists in the field of working with youth – teachers, leaders of patriotic NGOs, retired/reserve military officers, and others concerned about the patriotic education of youth." Regional programs on patriotic education had also been adopted in many of Russia's territorial sub-units. See Mel'nichenko.
107 Patriotic Education Program, 2006–2010.
108 Ibid.
109 Ibid.
110 C. Bigg, "Russia: Here Comes the Sun for Putin's Patriotic Youth," *RFE/RL Newsline*, 20 July 2005; O. Sobolevskaya, "Russian Society, Mass Media and Business to Train Patriots," RusNet, www.rusnet.nl/info/2005_07/06.shtml (accessed 21 May 2008).
111 Patriotic Education Program, 2006–2010.
112 Mel'nichenko. In addition to the two-year period of army service, Mel'nichenko also noted a short period of military training following university studies (*prokhozhdenie srochnoi sluzhby*) for those who attended a university with a military-training department (*voennaia kafedra*).
113 "Spending on Patriotism Will Triple," *The Moscow Times.com*, 19 July 2005, 3, www.themoscowtimes.com/stories/2005/07/19/012.html (accessed 19 July 2005). The largest sponsor financially is the Federal Education Agency, contributing 85 million rubles. Patriotic Education Program, 2006–2010, appendix 2.
114 Patriotic Education Program, 2006–2010, appendix 1.
115 Ibid.
116 Ibid.
117 Ibid. The disastrous defeat of these Russian troops was portrayed as a devastating but successful struggle against a group of roughly 1,500 Chechen fighters, killing 700 of them and temporarily stopping the progress of the rest. See C. W. Blandy, *Chechnya: Two Federal Disasters*, Camberley, UK: Conflict Studies Research Centre, 2002, p. 21.
118 In addition to military-related measures, some of the program's planned events highlighted folk culture, Cossack history, "internationalism" (a festival celebrating Turkic cultures, for instance), and Russian and Soviet achievements in space exploration. See Patriotic Education Program, 2006–2010, appendix 1.
119 Quoted in D. W. Blum, "Official Patriotism in Russia: Its Essence and Implications," PONARS Policy Memo, 420, December 2006.
120 I. Klimov, "Victory Day," Report, FOM, 5 May 2003.
121 Ibid. As further evidence that World War II is losing its significance among Russia's youth, 18 percent of people under 35, surveyed in June 2002, had no idea that 22 June was the day that Nazi Germany attacked the USSR. See A. Petrova, "June 22 Is the Day the War Began," Report, FOM, 25 June 2002.
122 I. Klimov, "Victory Day," Report, FOM, 5 May 2003; see also Abdullaeva, "The Great Patriotic War Today and Yesterday."
123 I. Klimov, "Victory Day."
124 S. E. Mendelson and T. P. Gerber, "Failing the Stalin Test," *Foreign Affairs*, 85, 1, 2006, 2.
125 Ibid.
126 Ibid.
127 "Stalin Monument to Be Erected by V-Day," *RFE/RL Newsline*, 1 April 2005.
128 "President Restores Name 'Stalingrad' to Moscow War Memorial," *RFE/RL Newsline*, 23 July 2004; the city's name was changed to Volgograd in 1961 in the context of Khrushchev's de-Stalinization campaign.

129 "Pride and Shame of the Nation," Report/Population Poll, FOM, 7 December 2006. Confidence in Putin is strongly correlated with whether a person reports feelings of pride or shame in the nation. A full 64 percent of those distrusting Putin express shame in the nation, while only 28 percent of those who trust him express such shame.

130 "Russia: Pride and Shame," Report/Population Poll, FOM, 14 February 2002.

131 Ibid.

132 "Pride and Shame of the Nation" Report/Population Poll, FOM, 7 December 2006. For purposes of comparison, in 2002 national athletic accomplishments had been mentioned by a scant 7 percent of respondents, putting that answer in second place; the answer "there is nothing to be proud of" took first place that year, with 20 percent of responses. See "Russia: Pride and Shame."

133 "Russia to Reintroduce Military Training for Schoolchildren," *RFE/RL Newsline*, 11 February 2000.

134 Svetlana Korotkova, personal email communication, 16 September 2005, on file with author.

135 "Upper Chamber Passes Controversial Election Bill …," *RFE/RL Newsline*, 14 July 2005.

136 As relayed by Mariia Zolotukhina and her 11-year-old daughter, Sasha (author interview, 22 December 2006).

137 Patriotic Education Program, 2001–2005.

138 Mel'nichenko referred to OBZh variously as "*Osnovy bezopasnosti zhiznedeiatel'nosti*" and "*Obespechenie bezopasnosti zhiznedeiatel'nosti*."

139 Many such events focus on the personal experiences of Soviet survivors, as well as the vast scale of Soviet suffering and sacrifice during the war, rather than on battlefield events and military glory (Mariia Zolotukhina, personal communication, 8 February 2007).

140 The game was described to me by Mariia Zolotukhina and her daughter, Sasha, a participant (author interview, 22 December 2006).

141 The competition was voluntary; not all the students participated.

142 Mariia Zolotukhina, author interview, 22 December 2006.

143 Ibid.

144 See www.Ctc-tv.ru/series/Kadetstvo/ (accessed 16 January 2007). As of 1998, Russia boasted 150 various "cadet educational institutions," including "corps, schools, boarding schools, and cadet classes." See "Celebrating Victory Day, Russians Honor the Veterans and the Armed Forces," WPS, no. 10, May 11, 1998.

145 N. Holdsworth, "U.S. Series Go to Russia, Are Loved," *Hollywood Reporter*, 4 January 2007, http://login.vnuemedia.com/hr/content_display/news/e3i35916161ed1086e8de658749c5da3f9 (accessed 13 January 2007).

146 "9 rota," http://imdb.com/title/tt0417397/trivia (accessed 13 January 2007).

147 "Media Ministry Decides to Support 'Military-Patriotic' Mass Media," *RFE/RL Newsline*, 21 March 2002.

148 Medetsky, "The Drive to Churn Out Patriots."

149 Quoted in S. Lee Myers, "Red Star over Russian Airwaves: Military TV Network," *New York Times*, 11 February 2005, A4; J. Bransten, "Russia: Patriotic TV Channel Nearing Launch, but Will Anyone Watch?" RFE/RL, 16 February 2005, www.rferl.org/reports/mm/2005/02/5–240205.asp (accessed 25 January 2007).

150 Bransten, "Russia: Patriotic TV Channel Nearing Launch."

151 Quoted in "… And Military's Patriotic Television Station Gathers Steam," *RFE/RL Newsline*, 14 April 2005.

152 Medetsky, "The Drive to Churn Out Patriots."

153 Mariia Zolotukhina, author interview, 26 December 2006.

154 "ZVEZDA TV, the new Russian Patriotic TV place [sic] a large order for HYBRID MC virtual set solutions," 5 January 2006, www.hybrid-mc.com/v6/Hybrid%20MC_

ZvezdaTV.pdf (accessed 28 December 2006). The order itself was for five "Easy Set virtual set solutions" made by Hybrid MC.

155 Mel'nichenko.

156 Mariia Zolotukhina, author interview, 22 December 2006.

157 One Russian website explains the defeat of the Poles as an instance "of heroism and the unity of the entire people, independent of their ancestry, their creed, or their social status." See www.prazdniki.ru/event/# (accessed 21 May 2008).

158 "Russian Orthodox Church Celebrates 14th-Century Victory over Tatars ...," *RFE/RL Newsline*, 20 July 2005.

159 "... Despite Protests by Tatar Activists," *RFE/RL Newsline*, 20 July 2005.

160 "... And Duma Approves New List of Military Celebrations," *RFE/RL Newsline*, 19 November 2003.

161 Formerly labeled Red Army Day during the Soviet era, 23 February had been called Russian Army Day between 1993 and 2002. See "Russia Celebrates Army Day ...," *RFE/RL Newsline*, 24 February 2003.

162 "Gosduma mozhet vvesti novyi prazdnik – Den' geroev Otechestva," 25 January 2007, www.nashi.su/nashi.php?n=11564 (accessed 27 January 2007).

163 "Strategic Missiles Once Again Roll through Red Square," *RFE/RL Newsline*, 9 May 2008.

164 L. McIntosh Sundstrom, "Soldiers' Rights Groups in Russia: Civil Society through Russian and Western Eyes," in A. B. Evans, Jr., L. A. Henry, and L. McIntosh Sundstrom (eds.), *Russian Civil Society: A Critical Assessment*, Armonk, NY: M. E. Sharpe, 2006, p. 180. Julie Elkner provides a history of the Soldiers' Mothers' organizing efforts regarding *dedovshchina*, in "*Dedovshchina* and the Committee of Soldiers' Mothers under Gorbachev," in Daucé and Sieca-Kozlowski (eds.), Dedovshchina *in the Post-Soviet Military*, pp. 121–143. For a discussion of the Committee of Soldiers' Mothers' activities in the 1990s, and some of their activists' views on militarized patriotism, see Sperling, "The Last Refuge of a Scoundrel," 235–253.

165 "Soldiers' Mothers' NGO Becomes a Party," *RFE/RL Newsline*, 8 November 2004.

166 Elkner, "*Dedovshchina* and the Committee of Soldiers' Mothers under Gorbachev," p. 145.

167 An alternative service law was passed by the Duma in June 2002 and entered into effect on 1 January 2004, albeit without sufficient supplementary laws and decrees to implement it. The law was widely regarded by groups lobbying for alternative service as punishing; the term for service is double that of regular army service (four years, instead of two), and those opting for alternative service would be shunted into "heavy manual labor, including working for polar expeditions or doing sanitation work at hospitals," according to the Labor Minister. See "Putin Signs Decree on Alternative Service ...," *RFE/RL Newsline*, 23 July 2003; "... As Labor Ministry Does What It Can to Make the Alternative Unappealing," *RFE/RL Newsline*, 23 July 2003; and "Duma Adopts Bill on Alternative Service," *RFE/RL Newsline*, 19 April 2002.

168 These were estimated at 3,000–5,000 per year in the 1990s, according to the Committee of Soldiers' Mothers. See L. McIntosh Sundstrom, *Funding Civil Society: Foreign Assistance and NGO Development in Russia*, Stanford, CA: Stanford University Press, 2006, p. 62. In January 2003, Defense Minister Ivanov provided much lower numbers, claiming that "two Russian soldiers are killed in Chechnya each week, and two are wounded. This is comparable to the losses suffered in other military districts where there is no combat activity." See "Minister Nixes Idea of Chechnya Withdrawal," *RFE/RL Newsline*, 6 January 2003.

169 Elkner, "*Dedovshchina* and the Committee of Soldiers' Mothers under Gorbachev," p. 173.

170 Gerber and Mendelson, "Strong Public Support for Military Reform in Russia," 5.

171 Tatiana Mikhailova, chair of the Orlovskaia Oblast' (Orel region) Committee of Soldiers' Mothers, author interview, 8 June 2001. The informal director of Rospatriottsentr agreed, in large part, with Mikhailova about the patriotic nature of the CSM. Asked to share his view of the CSM, Mel'nichenko stated that it was a "major human rights organization" the effects of which were "unquestionably positive." He added: "Despite the criticism of Russia's army, one cannot say that the work of the soldiers' mothers is 'antipatriotic.' The Union of Committees of Soldiers' Mothers of Russia tries to provide qualified assistance, within the law, to all who turn to them, and to protect their rights. And up to 50,000 people turn to them each year across Russia, which undoubtedly means that the organization is necessary."

172 Sundstrom, *Funding Civil Society*, pp. 65–66.

173 See www.radikaly.ru/ (accessed 15 January 2007).

174 www.otmenaprizyva.ru/ (accessed 3 November 2006).

175 Nikolai Khramov, email message on radikaly-news listserv, "19 Fevralia v Moskve sostoitsia pervoe zasedanie general'nogo soveta ligi za otmenu prizyva, v povestke dnia – priniatie plana deistvii ligi na 2006 god. Khramov nameren predlozhit' proekt po organizatsii osen'iu v Moskve antiprizyvnogo marsha desiati tysiach," 13 February 2006.

176 Sundstrom, *Funding Civil Society*, p. 68.

177 "V sredu 9ogo avgusta, v den' pamiati Nagasaki – anti-prizyvnoi 'die-in' radikalov u ministerstvo oborony na arbatskoi ploshchadi," 7 August 2006. www.radikaly.ru/news-3997.html (accessed 4 January 2007).

178 Ibid.

179 Russian Radicals, on the radikaly-news listserv, "662 pogibshikh v armii s nachala goda, odna smert' cherez kazhdye desiat' chasov," 30 September 2005, www.voinenet.ru/forum/showthread.php?p=32939 (accessed 4 January 2007).

180 "Defense Ministry Issues Figures on Military Deaths, Including Suicides," *RFE/RL Newsline*, 13 September 2005.

181 "Spravka ob itogakh kampanii po zapisi na 2006 god, podgotovlennaia k zasedaniiu 20 ianvaria 2007," 19 January 2007, http://radikaly.ru/news-4142.html (accessed 23 January 2007).

182 "Koordinatsionnyi komitet Dvizheniia 'Rossiiskie Radikaly': Itogovyi dokument zasedaniia 20 ianvaria 2007," 20 January 2007, http://radikaly.ru/news-4145.html (accessed 23 January 2007).

183 C. J. Chivers, "Russia Effectively Closes a Political Opponent's Rights Group," *New York Times*, 18 March 2006, A6.

184 I. Iasina, "The New NGO Law and Russian Civil Society," lecture, Harvard University, 27 April 2006. In addition to its original impetus (working to correct the historical record about political repressions and state terror in the Soviet era), Memorial monitors human rights abuses in the Caucasus. See www.memo.ru/hr/hotpoints/caucas1/index.htm (accessed 21 May 2008).

185 Valentina Melnikova, head of the Union of Committees of Soldiers' Mothers of Russia, interviewed by Ol'ga Bychkova on "Ekho Moskvy," 19 April 2006 (transcript), http://echo.msk.ru/interview/43027/index.phtml (accessed 25 April 2006). Earlier harassment of soldiers' mothers groups included a "warning" from Russia's Ministry of Justice to a soldiers' mothers' organization in St. Petersburg, labeling the group's activities as "religious," and thus inconsistent with their charter (the accusation pointed to the religious posters and icons displayed in the organization's office). See "Soldiers' Mothers under Pressure in Putin's Hometown," *RFE/RL Newsline*, 25 July 2003.

186 "Moscow Targets Foreign NGOs," *RFE/RL Newsline*, 20 April 2006.

187 Dmitrievsky was given a two-year suspended sentence, perhaps because Amnesty International had planned to list him as a prisoner of conscience should he receive a jail term. See "Stanislav Dmitrievsky Sentenced to Two-Year Suspended Term," *In*

Their Own Voices: Eurasian Human Rights Digest, 7, 30 January – 6 February 2006.

188 Human Rights First, "Russian Defender Faces Prison," 26 January 2006, www.humanrightsfirst.org/defenders/hrd_russia/alert012506_dmitrievsky.htm (accessed 4 January 2007).

189 "Supreme Court Upholds Liquidation of Chechen NGO," *RFE/RL Newsline*, 24 January 2007.

190 "Russian Government Rejects Registration of Russian Justice Initiative," 23 November 2006, www.srji.org/en/news/2006/11/23/ (accessed 7 December 2006).

191 "Russian NGO Receives Tax Bill for Foreign Grants," *RFE/RL Newsline*, 25 July 2006.

192 International Commission of Jurists, "Russian Federation: Tax Order Threatens Leading Human Rights Organization," press release, 31 July 2006, www.icj.org/IMG/PR_Russia_Protection_Centre.pdf (accessed 21 May 2008).

193 M. Steven Fish, *Democracy Derailed in Russia: The Failure of Open Politics*, New York: Cambridge University Press, 2005, pp. 74–75.

194 Reporters without Borders, "Worldwide Press Freedom Index 2006," www.rsf.org/article.php3?id_article=19384 (accessed 4 January 2007).

195 Committee to Protect Journalists, "Russia: Thirteen Murders, No Justice," www.cpj.org/Briefings/2005/russia_murders/russia_murders.html (accessed 9 November 2006).

196 J. Bush, "Patriotism and Putin Rock!" *Business Week Online*, 8 August 2005.

197 "NASHI postaraiutsia ne dopustit' v Rossii 'tsvetnoi revoliutsii,'" 21 December 2006, http://nashi.su/nashi.php?n-10525&PHPSESSID=4e3e2a69f85a8a1e7387fed57cfc7db3 (accessed 28 December 2006).

198 G. L. White and A. Cullison, "Putin's Pitchman," *Wall Street Journal*, 19 December 2006, A1. Also see "Spiegel Interview with Kremlin Boss Vladislav Surkov: The West Doesn't Have to Love Us," *Spiegel*, 20 June 2005, www.spiegel.de/international/spiegel/0,1518,361236,00.html (accessed 13 January 2007).

199 The first, less successful group was Moving Together (Idushchie vmeste), founded in 2000 by Iakemenko. See D. Robert Buchacek, "NASHA Pravda, NASHE Delo: The Mobilization of the NASHI Generation in Contemporary Russia," *Carolina Papers in Democracy and Human Rights*, 7, 2006, 4.

200 A. Cullison and J. Bandler, "How U.S. Citizens Mysteriously March for Kremlin Causes: Russian Émigrés Pay Them to Flail Chechen Rebels as TV Moscow Films It All," *Wall Street Journal*, 24 June 2006, A1.

201 Bush, "Patriotism and Putin Rock!"

202 Buchacek, "NASHA Pravda, NASHE Delo," 5.

203 Ibid., 34.

204 Ibid., 37–38.

205 "Youth Group Affirms Support for Army," *RFE/RL Newsline*, 18 April 2006.

206 Cheerfully presented instances of this campaign are described under the rubric NASHA armiia (Our army) at http://nashi.su/akcent.php?a=11 (accessed 19 January 2007).

207 "Kostroma: 'Uroki Pobedy' prodolzhaiutsia," 20 December 2006, http://nashi.su/nashi.php?n=10497 (accessed 28 December 2006).

208 "Saransk: Bolee tysiachi chelovek uznali znachimost' pobedy v bitve pod Moskvoi," 12 December 2006, http://nashi.su/nashi.php?n=10226 (accessed 28 December 2006).

209 "Voronezh: Nash komissar rasskazal studentam o podvige 65-letnei davnosti," 13 December 2006, www.nashi.su/nashi.php?n=10283 (accessed 28 December 2006).

210 The Battle of Moscow encompasses the German forces' attempt to capture the city, and the successful counterattack by Soviet forces. The struggle lasted from October 1941 to January 1942; the Soviet army's victory came at a cost of between 650,000 and 1,280,000 lives (see http://en.wikipedia.org/wiki/Battle_of_moscow).

211 "'Vozvrashchennyi prazdnik' – novyi patrioticheskii format," 21 December 2006, http://nashi.su/nashi.php?n=10536&PHPSESSID=4e3e2a69f85a8a1e7e87fed57cfc7db3 (accessed 28 December 2006).
212 Ibid.
213 "Smolensk: Storonniki vkliuchilis' v antifashistskuiu kampaniiu," 25 December 2006, www.nashi.su/nashi.php?n=10686 (accessed 28 December 2006); "Riazan': Gorod ochishchen ot svastik," 26 December 2006, www.nashi.su/nashi.php?n=10698 (accessed 28 December 2006).
214 For one example of such an open-ended survey question, see "Russia: Pride and Shame," Report/Population Poll, FOM, 14 February 2002.
215 "Kursk: NASHI sovety prizyvniku," 26 December 2006, www.nashi.su/nashi.php?n=10720 (accessed 28 December 2006).
216 "Riazan': NASHI armeitsy prinimaiut prisiagu," 6 December 2006, www.nashi.su/nashi.php?n=10713 (accessed 27 December 2006). For a brief illustrative essay on the interplay between militarization and masculinity, see C. Enloe, "Macho, Macho Military," *The Nation.com*, 7 March 2006, www.thenation.com/doc/20060320/enloe (accessed 21 May 2008).
217 "Briansk: Pis'mo mame, komissara Sergeia Zueva," 27 December 2006, www.nashi.su/nashi.php?n=10737 (accessed 28 December 2006).
218 Sobolevskaya, "Russian Society, Mass Media and Business to Train Patriots."
219 "Pride and Shame of the Nation," Report/Population Poll, FOM, 7 December 2006.
220 "Army Service," Table/Population Poll, FOM, 24 October, 2002.
221 "About Army Service," Table/Population Poll, FOM, 8 July 2004.
222 "Army Service and Draft Deferments for Students," Report/Population Poll, FOM, 10 February 2005.
223 Ibid.
224 "Army Service," Report/Population Poll, FOM, 3 October 2002.
225 "About Army Service," Table/Population Poll, FOM, 8 July 2004.
226 "Army Service," Table/Population Poll, FOM, 24 October 2002.
227 Cited in War Resisters International, "Conscientious Objection in Russia Highlighting the Right to Refuse to Kill," *Peacework*, December 2006/January 2007, 14–15.
228 Capt. 1st Rank Ye. A. Kiselyov and Col. M. V. Shimanovsky, "Spiritual and moral support for RF Armed Forces development: problems and solutions," *Military Thought: A Russian Journal of Military Theory and Strategy*, January–March 2005, www.findarticles.com/p/articles/mi_m0JAP/is_1_14/ai_n15400332 (accessed 21 May 2008).
229 Vovk, "A Patriotic Upbringing: Words or Deeds?"
230 Levada Center, "Armiia," www.levada.ru/army.html (accessed 4 January 2007).
231 Vovk, "A Patriotic Upbringing: Words or Deeds?"
232 Ibid.
233 Blum, "Official Patriotism in Russia," p. 4.
234 Ibid.
235 D. Blum, author interview, 4 October 2006.
236 Ibid.
237 Quoted in D. Babich, "The Roads Not Taken," *Russia Profile*, 10 April 2006, www.russiaprofile.org/page.php?pageid=Themes&cont=Youth+(Issue+3%2C+April+2006) (accessed 21 May 2008).
238 Quoted ibid.
239 Sobolevskaya, "Russian Society, Mass Media and Business to Train Patriots."
240 The students whose remarks on patriotism are cited here are part of a group of twenty-two third-year undergraduate students at the Institute of Social Engineering, housed in the Moscow State University of Design and Technology (MGUDT).
241 A. Roy, *War Talk*, Cambridge: South End Press, 2003, p. 47.
242 Blum, "Official Patriotism in Russia," p. 4.

243 S. E. Hanson, "Russian Nationalism in a Post-ideological Era," unpublished manuscript, University of Washington, 2006, p. 25.

244 If such a project were to function as a unifying national idea, however, it would have to strike a delicate balance within the population and avoid condemning or alienating those many citizens who supported (or whose family members supported), to varying degrees, the Soviet regime and its assorted policies. Celebrating resistance to tyranny could be effective as a unifying idea only if a means could be found to incorporate and validate the diverse set of strategies citizens used (including collaboration and mundane participation) when coping with the many forms of repression manifested in the Soviet "experiment."

245 Such an education program would not necessarily be well received by Russia's populace. Popular support for Soviet dissidents in the 1970s was highly circumscribed, and thirty years later support for civil liberties (such as freedom of speech and association) in Russia remains weak. On the gap between the views of typical Soviet citizens and dissident intellectuals, see V. Chalidze, *To Defend These Rights: Human Rights and the Soviet Union*, trans. Guy Daniels, New York: Random House, 1974. For a detailed discussion of support for civil liberties in contemporary Russia, see Gerber and Mendelson, "Russian Public Opinion on Human Rights and the War in Chechnya."

246 E. Zamiatin, *We*, trans. Mirra Ginsburg, New York: Avon Books, 1972, p. 115.

Index